MW00795792

TANUM

A Story of Bumping Lake and the
William O. Douglas Wilderness

TANUM can be purchased for educational, business or sales promotional use. For information, please visit **www.susansummitcyr.com**

FIRST EDITION HARDCOVER PUBLISHED IN 2022

Cover design by Rebecca Bush
Cover art and maps by Susan Summit Cyr
Illustrations by Catherine "Kiwi" Cyr
Photo editing by Jo Gershman

Library of Congress cataloging in publication
Data has been applied for

ISBN 978-0-578-9-8530-5

To Tom,
who showed me the forest,
and so much more

Bumping Lake and Mount Rainier. The Bumping Lake Resort was located at the end of the dam on the extreme right. The Bumping Lake Marina is the bright spot on the far lakeshore, while the Bumping Lake Campground is the light area on the near shore. (Courtesy of United States Bureau of Reclamation)

CONTENTS

CHAPTER HEADING PLATES

AUTHOR'S NOTE

I am amazed at the way a single question can change the direction of a life. In 2005, I was asked to document water use at our family's cabin in Ecology v. Acquavella, an ongoing water rights adjudication case in Yakima, Washington. The research required for my testimony drew back the curtains on a whole other world of understanding of a place that I had long visited and thought I knew. I journeyed back in time and my eyes were opened to clues of the past that were hiding in plain sight. Visits to Bumping Lake became treasure hunts and discoveries were mysteries to be solved. Where were the "beehive ovens" from Camp 22? What is hidden in the mountainside above deserted Copper City? How did Hindoo John perish? Why in the world is a novel on the bookshelf inscribed with birthday greetings from a famous United States Supreme Court Justice?

As I tromped through the tangled woods, I found more anomalies which led to additional questions. The journey to find answers has been an adventure of discoveries, not of the type that would make headlines, but those that when patched together told of the lives of hardy people who lived and died here, who labored so hard to make something of their lives in this remote mountain wilderness. Their stories mirror on a small scale the story of the exploration and exploitation of the West.

In the process, I have also come to know the rhythms and the secrets of this ancient forest. I have encountered trees so vast they make their own topography and blot out the sky. I discovered the closeted glades where elk bed down and old snags that bears tear apart for grubs. I have witnessed giant salmon return to the same nest of pebbles in the river where they were born four years earlier before they traveled the world. I have traced the underground mycelium pathways of mushrooms by their perennial fruiting bodies above. With time, I have come to recognize the ebb and flow of time and the vast interconnected webs of tenacious life that are the underpinnings of the place where the history happened.

But the past is decaying, and the forest is changing. The sticks and stones marking lives are being reclaimed by the forest as inexorably as

fallen trees become soil for the next generation of monarchs. I am compelled to tease the stories out of the jumbled remnants before they are completely erased.

Digging into the history of this spectacular place, populated by
a fair share of quirky characters, has held my interest for almost twenty
years of research. During that time, as I have been mentored by generous
historians, archaeologists, and academics, I have been reminded frequently
of the importance of primary sources. These are the words that are "from
the horse's mouth" so to speak. Books, letters, maps, photographs, and interviews of those who took part are all primary sources. Secondary sources
are those recorded by bystanders, historians, and some reporters describing
events as they understood them to have occurred.

The sources that I relied on most heavily are all primary: *We Never
Got Away* by Jack Nelson, *The History of Goose Prairie and the Ira Ford
Family* by Robert I. Ford, and several of William O. Douglas' books (*Of
Men and Mountains, My Wilderness: The Pacific West,* and *Go East Young
Man.*) Uncounted hours of enjoyable interviews with Goose Prairie native
Betty Jean Gallant Ford and careful examination of old photographs, maps,
and letters rounded out my primary sources. I scoured Gretta Gossett's
Beyond the Bend for information too. While it is a secondary account, it
relies on interviews Gossett conducted with the first European settlers of
the area and is, for the most part, quite accurate.

I tried to resolve the inevitable discrepancies and contradictions
that arose with even more research. But since so little has been written
about the area and survives, sometimes reconciliation seemed impossible.
That is when the words "around" and "approximately" and "reportedly"
came in handy.

It is not possible to complete a project of this magnitude alone.
Many brilliant people have helped me along the way. I acknowledge them
in a long list at the back of the book.

And though I have spent an inordinate amount of time verifying
facts, figures, and stories, inevitably there will be mistakes as well as inadvertent bias in the text. Those errors are mine. Please forgive me for them—
and feel free to suggest corrections via the book's website.

Lastly, I hope you might take the trouble to read the notes at the end of the book which are interspersed with the literary citations. I could not resist adding these side stories of local interest. To make accessing them simpler, I suggest you read with *two* bookmarks; one to mark your place in the endnotes.

I am in love with the wild land of the Bumping Lake Valley and the surrounding William O. Douglas Wilderness, for what it holds and what it promises. Thank you for your interest in this magnificent area which has, against all odds, survived relatively intact well into the twenty-first century.

Long live the Bumping River Valley and everything in it!

Susan Summit Cyr
May 30, 2021

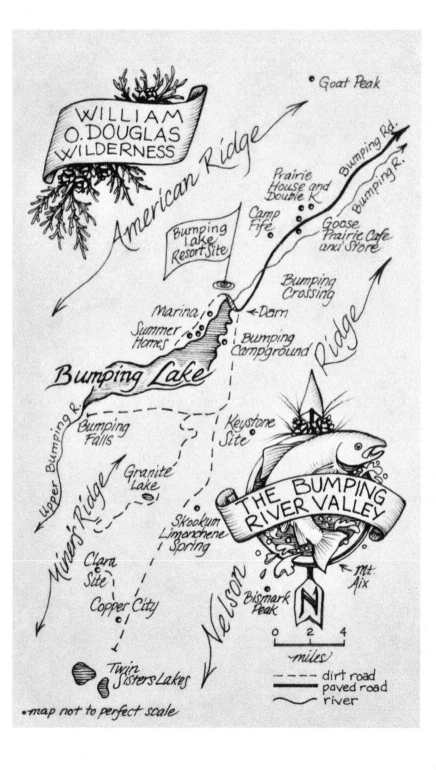

WILLIAM O. DOUGLAS WILDERNESS

• Goat Peak

American Ridge

Bumping Rd.

Bumping R.

Prairie House and Double K

Camp Fife

Goose Prairie Cafe and Store

Bumping Lake Resort Site

Bumping Crossing

Marina

← Dam

Summer Homes

Bumping Campground

Ridge

Bumping Lake

Upper Bumping R.

Bumping Falls

Keystone Site

THE BUMPING RIVER VALLEY

Granite Lake

Miner's Ridge

Skookum Limonchene Spring

Clara Site

← Mt. Aix

Copper City

Nelson

Bismark Peak

N

0   2   4
miles

Twin Sisters Lakes

- - - dirt road
——— paved road
⌇⌇⌇ river

• map not to perfect scale

PREFACE

I'd like to tell you a story about a place I have come to know. I think it is an interesting story, but I also think that wild mushrooms and salamanders are interesting—and petroglyphs—so you will need to judge for yourself.

In the center of this place is a lake with a most curious name: Bumping. Its waters collect at the base of an inconspicuous fold among the countless crumpled ridges of the Cascade Mountains of Washington. Over time, things happened there. A dam was built. A man and his wife moved to the mountains to watch over it. They lived in a house on its scalloped shores. Their home is the same building that my family and I now head to on weekends to escape a satisfying but over-full life in the city. It is where I lie down at night with my husband and recall that the man Jack slept within these same walls every night with his wife Kitty, continuing to love her as their bodies aged and withered.

They remained as long as they could, safe behind stout logs while winter winds howled and snow piled up past the windows. They stayed through their last summer together, the sweet lake air dancing up to them and pausing just long enough to caress a cheek, to lift thinning white hair before sighing away upslope.

Once Kitty had gone, the wind's warmth and soft touch were gone. The mountains, the cabin, the lake seemed empty. And soon, Jack would be gone as well. But the home that they built together, out of trees from the forest and stones from the ground, still stood, to become the heart of a new family who came to love it as much as they did.

Chapter One

WINTER

"Every part of this soil is sacred…every hillside, every valley, every plain and grove has been made hallowed by some sad or happy event in days long vanished. Even the rocks which seem to be dumb and sad as they swelter in the sun…thrill with memories of stirring events, connected with the lives of my people…At night when the streets of your cities and villages are silent and you think them deserted, they will throng with the returning hosts that once filled them and still love this beautiful land. The white man will never be alone."
—Chief Seattle, 1854

"Nature never did deceive a heart that loved her, for a true lover becomes a student of his mistress's character enough to not demand impossibility…"
—Theodore Winthrop, *The Canoe and The Saddle*, 1862

The third time Jack Nelson slipped off a slick boulder and into an icy pool in the river's bottom, he must have wondered if Mother Nature had finally deserted him. It would have been a fleeting thought, and barely registered in his consciousness. He was by nature an optimistic man and until now Mother Nature had been his faithful companion. She had tramped through countless miles of forest with him, shared long valley vistas, and revealed to him her intimate forest secrets. The fourth time he slipped, he climbed up the side of the riverbed, soaked and shivering, and perhaps took a moment to wonder if he might die that day.

The day had started out so simply. It had been snowing hard at daybreak when he had looked out onto the snow-covered path, but Jack had traveled up and down this mountain road many times in heavy weather. He had started out the day before, from the snug cabin at the lake that he shared with his wife Kitty, not long after he picked up the telephone receiver and learned that the line was dead.

This phone line was their only connection to the outside world and was especially vital during the long winter months when they were snowbound and alone at the lake. The telephone system was also central to Jack's job as caretaker of the Bumping Lake Dam since he was expected to call the Reclamation Service headquarters daily to transmit weather conditions and water levels. It was his responsibility to maintain twenty-two miles of #9 uninsulated wire which was strung from tree to tall tree down the long, twisting road to Yakima, fifty-two miles away. Silence on the telephone always meant a trip out was in order. In winter, the journey would have to be made on skis.

Jack found the break in the line late in the afternoon on the first day, seventeen miles from the lake. A heavy branch, overloaded with snow, had snapped the single wire. In short order, Jack climbed the tree, re-threaded the big ceramic insulator, and spliced the wire. But now it was late, and he was far from home. Jack retraced his route and traveled six miles back up to the halfway cabin that he and Kitty had built to serve as a way station on longer journeys out of the Valley.

The little building was well stocked with firewood, dry goods, and even a telephone, so Jack was not uncomfortable as he settled in to spend the night. He would have called Kitty to let her know he would not be home. The fact that it had started to snow again probably did not bother him—until the next morning.

So much snow had fallen silently overnight that Jack, striding out at first light, with his wide skis strapped tight and backpack buckled, immediately bogged down. Yesterday's trail was obliterated, and he was obliged to break a new one, now heading uphill. To make matters worse, the wind was picking up, raising the prospect of a heavy storm blowing in.

Jack struggled through the deep snow, making pitiful progress. After two hours, he gave up, reluctantly turned around and returned to the shelter of the halfway house, stacking his skis at the door. It was still snowing.

🌲 🌲 🌲

Jack had first traveled into this little river valley tucked high in the Cascade Mountains of central Washington years before, in the spring of 1910 on a weekend camping trip with a friend from Yakima. Having heard of the incredible fishing in the Bumping River, he was looking forward to dropping in a line and exploring new country. Even though he was working indoors in a Yakima pharmacy, Jack was fit and full of adventure. When he became aware of mountain territory accessible via a new road cut through the virgin forest barely a year before, he planned a weekend trip.

Serviced by a wagon stage, this road rolled out of Yakima and up the Naches River Valley winding west towards Mount Rainier. As the elevation increased, the terrain got wilder and rougher. Grassy hills evolved into rock-studded precipices which pressed in upon the narrow river valley. The dirt wagon road crossed and re-crossed the rushing Naches River by rough log bridges, and hugged banks which widened sometimes into pleasant meadows of waving bunch grass. Tall, heavy-limbed ponderosas started to appear, which mingled with the rock ramparts and soon grew dense enough to obscure the rock formations altogether.

The stage typically made its first stop of the day to change horses at the Lindsey Ranch near the head of Nile Creek—one of the last homesteads before it plunged into the raw wilderness. This home marked the previous end of the old road and the beginning of the new and the change must have been immediately evident to the passengers on the stage.

So rough was the new road and so primitive the stage, that the more experienced passengers carried with them between one and three quarts of whiskey to help soften the ride. The stage, pulled by six horses, was no more than a wooden supply wagon with a box attached for the driver and, for the up to eighteen passengers, planks nailed crosswise on which to sit. There was no roof to keep out the weather and no walls or even handrails to grasp as the stage made its way over the dusty, uneven ground.

Only six feet wide, the road for the most part followed the old prospectors' trails, which had traced ancient Yakama natives' paths, which in turn roughly followed the river. It wound around especially large trees and where there was room, dropped low, skirting the steepest rocky outcroppings. Where the ridges extended into the river, the stage road was routed up and over them. On the steepest grades, passengers were ordered out of the wagon and were required to walk so that the horses could climb the summit. Low, swampy sections of the road were surfaced with corduroy: logs laid next to one another across the width of the path to make, if not a smooth surface, at least a passable one. Novice travelers soon learned that most of the route was either steep, muddy, rocky, twisted, dusty, or rutted.

By the time the stage turned south at the junction of the Bumping and American Rivers, thirty-five miles out, the horses and travelers would have been exhausted and looking forward to their second and final stop. Horses were unharnessed and stabled and the passengers ventured into a crude mess tent to eat.

Despite the dreadful conditions, Jack was enthralled by what he saw from the stage. "Some of the blood of my Scottish forbearers came to the surface at my first look at the towering trees and I seemed to feel at home," he would later write. The further he ascended into the mountains, the taller the trees became and the closer they pressed in until the road became no more than a twisting path through the primeval forest. Vast stands of old growth trees grew, flourished, and died, their great bulks covered in thick moss and decaying back into the duff to nourish the next generation of their seedlings. The tangled forest, which opened occasionally to bright meadows and the splashing river, beckoned to Jack.

Jack and his friend returned whenever possible throughout that summer of discovery to the rough country which both soothed and excited his soul. By the end the season, he was so captivated by the little river valley that he vowed to return the following summer to work as a laborer with the crew that was building a dam at the lake's mouth—as much to escape the confines of his job in Yakima as a pharmacist as to remain in the wilderness that had captured his heart

Now, these many years later, that same wilderness threatened to overwhelm him. Based on his second day's progress, Jack figured it would take him a week to travel the eleven miles home. Not willing to work his way back so laboriously, he came up with a wild idea. As gate tender at the Dam, he knew that the flow of the Bumping River was controlled by operating the water gates at the dam. He reasoned that he could walk up an empty riverbed far faster than he could break trail in the deep, heavy snow on the road. So, he picked up the telephone receiver and dialed the lake. He instructed Kitty to go to the middle of the dam and close the gates to stop the flow of the Bumping River.

Early the next morning, he swung his small pack onto his back but left his skies at the door. He set off again, sliding down into the now empty riverbed. At first the going was relatively easy, his heavy boots splashing only occasionally into small puddles in between the cobbles. Soon though, where the river narrowed, the rocks were larger and the pools wider and deeper, too. Furthermore, everything was coated with a rime of ice. It became impossible to skirt the accumulated slush and snow. Time and time again, Jack slipped off the rocks into ice covered pools or had to wade through them to proceed. As bad as the situation was, he was at least making progress towards the lake. But Jack was soaked from the waist down. The temperature was falling, and it was still snowing.

As her husband struggled in the riverbed, Kitty Nelson found herself skiing across the dam in the deepening gloom of a late winter afternoon.

The blizzard probably did not concern her, so used to the vagrancies of weather and confident of her abilities had she become in her time living at the lake. Others noted that fear was not in her makeup and it likely wasn't with her on this day either. Kitty, despite being prone to wearing skirts and stylishly fitted blouses even in the wilderness, was strong and tough when it came to physical challenges, often reaching distant destinations before her husband. So, despite the conditions, she surely did not hesitate to head out into the gale on skis to reach Jack.

Once across the dam, she turned left on the Bumping River Road, peering through the blowing snow in vain for any sign of her partner. She hadn't heard from him since early morning when he called to say good morning and goodbye. He had promised to turn back if the river route proved impossible and she could only assume that he was still on the river, fighting his way through the storm. She unstrapped Jack's skis from her back and, as they had discussed that morning, carefully set them where Jack could find them. Still not seeing him, she decided to continue a bit further down the road.

At Bumping Crossing, more than two miles from home, she took shelter under the bridge to wait and might have willed his form to appear against the backdrop of the shadowy trees.

Jack wrestled with the riverbed all afternoon, suppressing the exhaustion that threatened to take over his body and the fear that threatened to overwhelm his confidence. He might have distracted his mind by recounting the memories of his past and dreaming of the future that he still hoped for, together with Kitty in these mountains. He could have reminisced about all the visitors to their lodge who had become friends, the sound of years of laughter echoing off the hills. And he probably found comfort recalling his favorite trees and birds that were companions to him as well.

But he had spent enough time in the wilderness by now to fully appreciate the danger of his present predicament. As much as he was tempted to stop and rest—if only for a moment—his anxious mind understood that if he stopped moving, he might not start again. So he pushed on, ever forward to the salvation of home.

Kitty reluctantly took one last look downstream, slowly turned and started back up the road. Her strong arms would have swung rhythmically along with her gliding skis. Back at their lakeshore home, she likely propped her skis against the outside wall, opened and quickly closed the heavy door, to keep out the furious night.

When he finally discerned the shadowy bulk of the bridge ahead, Jack's pace would have quickened. He dragged himself out of the riverbed and struggled to the shelter of the bridge. Kitty was not there, but her footprints sheltered by the bridge overhead, were. Jack might have felt the warm comfort of her earlier presence there. With Kitty's trail to follow, Jack made more rapid progress and pushed on now in the dark, still against the wind, and still uphill. What long miles those last two must have been. Finally, the road veered to the right, and he reached the dam and located the stashed skis.

As he started across the dam, he saw a small, swinging light in the distance advancing towards him. When the two figures met in the middle of the dam, in the midst of that icy valley full of whipping wind and swirling snow, they fell into each other's embrace and wept from their hearts, without shame.

Chapter Two

INTO THE WOODS

"The trail took us speedily into a forest-temple. Long years of labor by artists the most unconscious of their skill had been given to modelling these columnar firs. Unlike the pillars of human architecture, chipped and chiseled in bustling, dusty quarries, and hoisted to their site by sweat of brow and creak of pulley, these rose to fairest proportions by the life that was in them and blossomed into foliated capitals three hundred feet overhead."
—Theodore Winthrop, *The Canoe and the Saddle*, 1862

"Climb the mountains and get their good tiding. Nature's peace will flow into you as sunshine flows into trees. The winds will blow their own freshness into you and the storms their energy while cares will drop off like autumn leaves."
—John Muir, 1901

"We went up to the mountains on our honeymoon, and we are still on it."
—Jack Nelson, 1946

I first became acquainted with Jack Nelson when I was still young. I was visiting my college boyfriend from my home in sunbaked, asphalted Los Angeles. As I fell in love with my future husband Tom, I also fell for the rugged Pacific Northwest he called home. We first visited all the tourist sites in Seattle, but it was when we left the city behind and headed up into the dark green Cascade Mountains for a weekend at the family cabin that my heart beat faster.

We aimed towards towering Mount Rainier then climbed up and over Chinook Pass, winding our way past impossibly picturesque alpine lakes and meadows then plunging down into the endless emerald expanses of the Eastern slopes of the Cascades. We rolled through tiny Goose Prairie and up into the far reaches of the secluded mountain valley that cradles Bumping Lake. The landscape was nothing like I had ever seen before. A right turn and short drive over a low dam brought me for the first time to a gracious log lodge perched above a sparkling lake.

My introduction to Jack came between the covers of a small book that Tom's mother gave me to read during that first trip to Bumping Lake. She explained that the man who had built their vacation home, the one which now embraced us, had written a memoir, *We Never Got Away*, about his life in the area. As summer rain ran down the windows of the old building, I read Jack Nelson's reminiscences, finely tuned over decades of repetition and smiled at his folksy humor and wisdom. I was enchanted.

During my next summer's visit, with these stories still effervescent in my mind, I started venturing out, exploring, and discovering the few traces and remnants of the area's history that brought Jack's tales to life. Just upslope of the lodge, scattered foundation blocks marked the location of the rental cabins that had made up his and Kitty's nearly forgotten Bumping Lake Resort, originally built at the dawn of the new century. By this time, the early 1980s, only the resort's main building, the lodge, remained. This was the couple's last home and they it called Normandie.[1]

Down the driveway and across the road, I found a curiously straight demarcation through the meadow grasses in a clearing next to

the dam's spillway. That line turned out to be the remains of a pathway—
the sidewalk which ended at the front steps of Jack and Kitty's long gone
original house beside the lake; the home that they moved into as newly-
weds when they arrived in the fall of 1911 when both the dam and their
life together were new.

      Construction of the dam was officially completed on November
26, 1910 and the new lake, now a reservoir, began to fill with autumn
rains. The new dam was left in the charge of a watchman, Mr. O'Hagen,
who lived at the lake with his wife over the winter. Jack wrangled a
three-month leave from his job and returned late in the spring of 1911
as a laborer to clean the dam site. After the O'Hagens departed in July,
Jack assumed the task of measuring and reporting the water levels of
the lake and river. By late summer, his supervisor Mr. Ross encouraged
him to apply for the position of dam caretaker and Jack, having no
wish to return to civilization after his taste of mountain living, applied
for the job.

      As the dam or gate tender, he would be wholly responsible for
the supervision and operation of the dam. He would be required to live
onsite, year round. Duties included maintenance and adjustments of the
dam gates and charting daily temperatures, water flow, lake levels and
river depth readings. Those measurements, along with weather conditions and precipitation, were to be communicated daily by telephone to
the Reclamation Service's Tieton headquarters in Yakima. The needed
adjustments to the gates were then relayed back based on the water needs
downstream.

      Additionally, the tender was required to keep the spillway area clear
of any debris, look for any seepage through the dam and report any repair
or maintenance needs to the central office. As a government employee, Jack
was expected to be an exemplary citizen, clean shaven and neatly dressed
at all times, of upstanding character and disposition to serve as an example

of propriety to the public. The last requirement for application may have been a surprise to Jack. He was informed that the dam tender needed to be a married man. Jack was not.

"Give me a week and I will take care of the marital status," was his legendary reply.[2] Contingent on that precondition and pending character references, Jack got the job.

Jack was not an idle boaster or a swinging playboy. Up until he had requested leave from the Yakima drugstore to work as a laborer high in the Cascades, he had led a rather conventional life. Jack's father, Henry, had emigrated from Scotland and found work in New York in his familial trade as a stonecutter. In time, he paid passage for his fiancé, Barbara Croy, to follow him to the United States. They settled in the Washington Heights neighborhood in New York City where they were blessed with a baby boy on October 21, 1880. The couple named him John Henry Nelson. The family soon moved to Winnipeg, Canada where Jack attended school. Tall with a strong build, a shock of wavy hair and twinkling brown eyes, Jack loved the outdoors and athletics. During high school and college, he played soccer, hockey, and was goal tender for a national lacrosse team that toured the United States and Canada. He graduated with a degree in pharmacy from the University of Manitoba in Winnipeg. His decision to study pharmacology was due in part to his mother's outspoken admiration of her brother, Jack's uncle, who was a pharmacist.

A brief vacation to the Pacific Coast convinced Jack that he had to move west. Soon he was working as a pharmacist in Seattle. The wet climate there, however, exacerbated a chronic throat condition, and on the advice of a doctor he moved to the growing town of Yakima in Eastern Washington.[3]

The drier weather of his new home suited Jack. On weekends, he eagerly explored the sagebrush-covered hills that surrounded the small city, gravitating especially to the inviting green mountains that beckoned just beyond Yakima's western horizon.

Flora Belle "Kitty" Rusho Bryden also loved the outdoors but labored inside managing the dining room at the Savoy Hotel in downtown Yakima. She was a striking woman with large, heavy-lidded eyes and full lips that smiled often. Her thick, prematurely platinum hair, always piled into a bun, emphasized her dark features. Her firm jaw matched a no-nonsense, get 'er done attitude, but her hazel eyes glowed with warmth and friendliness.

Kitty was barely in her thirties but had already led a full life. She was born in Ord, Nebraska in 1878, the youngest of four girls. When she was still a small child, her family struck out west by covered wagon. Their overland journey took two long years. The family homesteaded in the Coulee country in eastern Washington State, where her father started ranching. Kitty was such a proficient student that at just fifteen years old she started teaching in small schoolhouses along the Pend Oreille River.

On October 4, 1898 when she was twenty years old, Kitty married Thomas J. Bryden, a Canadian man seventeen years her senior. Their first daughter, born in 1900, was named Jessie. A second daughter, Frances, followed in 1901. For reasons that are not clear, the couple soon separated, and their marriage ended in divorce in 1907. Kitty, with her two young daughters, moved to the town of Moxee near Yakima.[4]

In 1908, a typhoid epidemic broke out in Yakima, spurred by abysmal sanitary conditions in the rapidly growing city. Infrastructure could not keep up with the exploding population and the food supply was far from sanitary. Other problems concerned waste disposal and cross-contamination: the city was dumping raw sewage into the Yakima River. Cities all along the river valley pulled water from the Yakima for both irrigation and drinking water. Moxee is one of the first cities downriver of Yakima.[5]

In 1909, Kitty's daughter Jessie fell sick. Soon she was gravely ill with meningitis as a complication of a typhoid infection. On July 21, little blond Jessie, only nine years old, died.

A year later, Kitty met Jack in the dining room of the Savoy Hotel, a favorite destination for Reclamation Service employees. She was thirty-two years old and somewhat of a maverick of the time: a divorcee and a single mother, working in rough and rowdy Yakima to support herself and her daughter. Fortunately, her parents lived in the city and so could help look after Frances.

Flora Belle (Kitty) Rusho Bryden before her marriage to Jack Nelson. Kitty is standing in the rear with her parents Anthony and Ellen Rusho and an unidentified girl, perhaps one of her daughters, Jessie or Frances, seated in front. Photo from between 1907-1911. (Cyr family collection)

Their independent spirits and mutual love of the outdoors apparently were well matched because Jack and Kitty were already discussing marriage when Jack was offered the position of dam tender at the lake. From the lake, he wrote a long letter to Kitty explaining the requirements of the job—including his need to change marital status. He weighed the choice between the secure career path which he had expected to follow as a pharmacist in town versus a life of the unknown in the wilderness deep in the woods.

Kitty had the more difficult decision. Frances was turning ten and needed to attend school. Kitty's parents were relatively young and were already raising Kitty's two nieces. Kitty loved adventure, the outdoors, and Jack. But how could she leave her only surviving daughter? She would be more than fifty hard miles away and unable to come out for six months or more once the snow started to fall. She might as well have gone to the moon.

Finally, Kitty wrote back, suggesting they try it for a year. Jack was overjoyed, embracing the idea of living in the woods which had so enchanted him. Now the prospect was made that much sweeter by the idea of sharing his life there with the woman he loved.

Jack and Kitty were married in North Yakima on September 6th, 1911. Kitty packed up and prepared to move to the Lake. Frances would be left behind.

❧ ❧ ❧

The home that Jack brought Kitty to on a dark and rainy night in the fall of 1911, was not one a new bride might have dreamed of. Jack said later that he was grateful that she was of hearty pioneer stock, had experienced hardship and deprivation, and knew how to make do with what was on hand, or she might not have stayed. Their "government house" had been relocated there as the watchman's residence the year before from the main dam construction settlement, Camp 22.

While it claimed an enviable location at the edge of the new lake's spillway with a fine view to the south across the lake to the surrounding peaks, the one-room building had been put together quickly in a rough and simple manner befitting the transient nature of the construction camp itself. Their new home contained little more than a wood stove, a fifty gallon wooden barrel for water supply, three homemade wood chairs, a couch, and a bed consisting of a bedspring and mattress balanced on four discarded nail kegs.[6]

The sturdy dishes, also left over from Camp 22, were made of enameled metal so that they would not break if dropped. There was no refrigeration and food storage was in a log-lined root cellar dug into the rocky ground beneath the building. Light was via dim kerosene lanterns, and the wash house was outdoors. So, of course, the outhouse. The house did come with that telephone however, which would become the Nelsons' vital link to the outside world for the long winter to come.

Kitty and Jack Nelson in front of their first home at Bumping Lake that they moved into in the fall of 1911. The two young women may be Kitty's daughter Frances and a friend, or they could be employees of the Nelson's Lodge. (Franklin Press, *We Never Got Away*, 1963)

Jack and Kitty wasted no time preparing for the approaching winter, filling both the cellar and the woodshed with supplies for six months. Jack split wood day after day and stacked it neatly under cover. Kitty put in as much variety of non-perishables as possible. She stocked dry goods, canned food and cured meat including ham, corned beef, and bacon. Last to go in were the eggs, sixty dozen, stored in large crocks of a sodium silicate solution, 'water glass,' to preserve them.[7] If they were turned periodically, they would remain relatively fresh until March or April—or so they hoped.

On November 8th they said goodbye to the Reclamation engineer, Charles Crownover, who had been at the lake to see after their needs. For the next six months, until May 15th of the following year, they would have only each other for company.

John and Maude Fontaine, twenty-two miles away in the Naches River Valley, were their nearest full-time neighbors that winter and in case of a real emergency, could be called upon to relay for help. Crownover would be in phone contact with Jack and Kitty several times a week and give them news of the outside world.

The couple filled their days with chores but also explored their new world by snowshoe and ski, marveling at the daily changes in the scenery as fall froze into winter, winter swirled about them and then finally melted into spring. With the sun dropping behind American Ridge well before four o'clock in the afternoon all winter, evenings were long. The Nelsons were relatively warm and comfortable, and their food stores were proving ample, if not varied, but they very soon ran out of books to read during the long dark hours. In their concern to prepare for the necessities of survival, they had neglected to collect reading material. They soon resorted to searching the empty bunkhouses at Camp 22 for anything at all to read.

Jack and Kitty seemed to be made for mountain living. They both felt that there was no challenge that could not overcome by hard work, and they were equally willing to do it. Kitty especially seemed to have no fear of anything she might encounter in the mountains. She quickly learned to fish and soon was hunting and trapping too. Jack and Kitty's relationship from the start was a team effort in which the first thought in each of their minds was how they could best help the other and lighten their load.

They went everywhere together that first winter. When the telephone line was broken, Kitty would as often as not accompany Jack out on these excursions. Soon they were both as comfortable on their long, homemade skis as they were in their tall lace-up work boots.

On their trips in and out of the valley, the Nelsons got to know the miner Tom Fife, whose cabin in nearby Goose Prairie opened onto the road. His permanent invitation "to come in and break bread," meant they rarely passed without stopping. The bulbous pot hanging in his fireplace and a big black skillet were Tom's only mode of cooking, but he produced savory pine squirrel stew, fried cauliflower mushrooms, and baking powder biscuits which he readily shared.

Having spent so much of his life prospecting, Tom knew the area intimately. He freely shared his mountain knowledge with Jack and Kitty, teaching them all about the high country. They learned, too, that Fife was a gentle man who couldn't bring himself to hunt anything larger than a squirrel and may have been surprised to discover this rough mountain man's most prized possession was a worn copy of Robert Burns poetry which he would read and reread by the hour.[8]

The couple's first Christmas together was simple but perfectly captured the spirit of the holiday. Jack draped cedar boughs over the doors and windows. Kitty fashioned a centerpiece out of a small tree surrounded by a carpet of moss with lichen and fir cones all arranged on an enameled tray.

The holy day was crystalline, so they skied three miles down to Goose Prairie and Kitty fished the river on the way back. For dinner they shared snowshoe rabbit, coleslaw, Kitty's 'unforgettable' biscuits and mince pie for dessert. Jack's gift to his wife was a sideboard for the kitchen which he had crafted from some rough boards salvaged from the dam. He described it as lacking grace and refinement but serviceable after many hours of planing and sanding.

Kitty's gift to Jack was charitable. The couple enjoyed a nightly game of pinochle, a contest perfectly suiting Kitty's sharp mind. They habitually logged their win/loss record. For Christmas, Kitty forgave Jack the thirty-six games he was in arrears.

Kitty and Jack Nelson in 1912 near Bumping Lake. (Franklin Press, *We Never Got Away*, 1963)

By the end of that first long winter of 1911-12, Jack and Kitty's compatibility, their growing familiarity of the area and their ability to respond to the challenges of their remote existence, convinced them that they had made the right decision by moving to the lake. By then, they couldn't imagine leaving. "The rest of the world seemed far away," said Jack. "The Mountains had us in their grasp. We had embarked on a great adventure and did not realize it." [9]

At the end of summer 1988, Tom and I married, and I moved to Seattle. One of the most delightful parts of my new life in the Pacific Northwest was making regular weekend trips over the mountains to Bumping Lake. We would stay in Normandie lodge, where the warmth of the old wood walls seeped into my soul and the rugged beauty of the area wound around my heart.

The Bumping Lake area does not boast the spectacular scenery of a national park. There are no jaw-dropping sights that attract crowds of phone-toting tourists, who swarm about to capture a bit of the grandeur as a digital memory. The surroundings are subtler, on a more human scale that you can approach, get inside of and become a part of. Rivers rush, waterfalls spill, meadows glow brilliant in the sun. Everywhere animals roam, as they have since the end of the last ice age. Bumping Lake, cupped between the protecting peaks along Nelson and American Ridges with the House Mountains and majestic Mount Rainier standing sentry to the west, feels like a protected refuge, a haven to come home to, a place to be yourself in and just enjoy with no pretense, no artifice.

I eagerly explored this new country with my new husband, sometimes grinding up old gravel mining or logging roads in the car, but more often on foot on long day hikes. As the miles passed beneath my hiking boots, Tom took me up his favorite trails and led me to all the special places which he had come to know during his childhood visits. Many common plants started to become familiar, and I started learning their names, their preferred habitats, and their lifecycles, all of which made me feel more a part of the wondrous wildness.

When fall came, Tom's mother, Virginia, introduced me to the elusive treasures of the forest: the rainbow-hued mushrooms that appeared in seemingly arbitrary places from the road shoulder to the deep wood. We collected delicate pure white coral hedgehog mushrooms that hung from fallen logs and looked like multi-tiered icicle chandeliers. Fluted yellow chanterelles enlivened mossy areas and we found heavy-bodied boletus pushing up through newly fallen leaves along the old Gage House Road. Some sported velvety chocolate brown caps, others were brilliant purple. Virginia helped me sort the bitter from the sweet, delicious from the deadly. Back at the cabin, when she cooked up the delicacies we had collected in our baskets, I was introduced to a whole new culinary world.

Soon the golden fall faded into frozen grays of November, the mushrooms returned to the earth, and it was time to close Normandie for the winter. I was as reluctant as the rest of the family to pack up the last of the food, drain the pipes, hoist and lock the snow shutters, and drive away for the last time knowing we would not be back until the very distant following spring.

Jack and Kitty's second winter at the end of 1912 to the beginnings of 1913 was both easier and more difficult. Determined not to be caught bookless, they had borrowed several boxes of books from close friends and the Yakima County Library. They hoped these would last them through until spring. In addition, they subscribed to several magazines, and a newspaper. Since they would not be delivered up to the lake, the couple planned to pick them up periodically from the Fontaine's home, the last stop on the mail route. A round trip of forty-four miles down into the valley and back up to the lake on skis or snowshoes was apparently considered a fair price for access to current events and entertaining articles.

The weather, however, was ferocious that winter. The Nelsons were battered by countless storms which roared down the lake and hit their house so hard it shuddered. Worse than the storms from the southwest which brought heavy snow with them, were cold fronts from the north that swept down the Frasier River Valley in British Columbia and brought numbing temperatures that effectively curtailed most outside activities.

Both Kitty and Jack later admitted that had such weather accompanied their first winter at the lake, they might not have stayed. But by the second year they were so completely at home there that they did not for a moment consider leaving.

Despite their brutal onslaught, the aftermath of these storms was incredible. The couple was constantly amazed at the perfect beauty of the forest in the wake of nature's fury. The lake was often swept smooth with millions of minute planes of snowflakes sparkling in the low winter sun. Huge snow drifts piled into soft, sculptural sweeps all around the lakeshore, rounding the harsh edges of the new lake that still showed the scars from the recent dam and reservoir construction. The trees were the centerpiece of the winter tableau. The bare branches of the deciduous trees were outlined in brilliant white like finely crocheted doilies while the evergreen tree branches drooped under snow piled impossibly high. Each type of conifer wore its snow load differently, creating intricate patterns and weaving a magnificent tapestry of whites.

The Nelsons discovered a special grove of trees nearby that became a favorite place to visit especially after a heavy snow. Beyond the dam and nestled against the foot of Nelson Ridge was a forest of ancient trees which had escaped the ravages of fire, disease, and the axes of man.[10] Douglas fir, Western hemlock, and Engelmann spruce trees grew so massive there that they blotted out the sky—and the rest of the world. A completely different ecosystem of mosses and tender plants thrived below in the misty air. In the winter, silence was complete, and the colossal trunks soared to the heavens like columns in a cathedral.

To enter this copse was to transition into a different world and both Jack and Kitty spoke in reverent terms when referring to it. "It would seem that Nature deliberately concealed this temple-like haven of rest for the surprise and delight of all who enter its portals." [11] The pair would leave "the Sanctuary" with their faith refreshed and spirit renewed.

The couple slowly started to get to know their neighborhood; not just the towering trees but the enigmatic animals that left evidence of their passage with their prints in the snow. Elk, deer, snowshoe hares, and coyotes all passed by their home and left it to the couple to decipher their activities from their tracks. Jack said that venturing out after a storm was like reading the morning paper. The Nelsons made it clear to the few human residents of the area that their home was open to all and so the trappers and miners who passed by on their way to the high country stopped in to visit for a bit and be warmed not only by strong coffee but good company.

They went visiting too, making long journeys on snowshoes or skis to collect their mail and connect with their far away Naches Valley neighbors, the Andersons, the Fontaines, and soon the Steindorfs. Bonds formed quickly between the couples likely because of their common isolation and shared experiences so far from civilization. Jack and Kitty's homemade potato bag knapsacks were always topped off by gifts of food and literature from their friends before they heaved the heavy packs onto their backs for the long return journey.

Neighbors gather at the Anderson ranch in the upper Naches Valley. From left are a college friend of John Cryder's, John Anderson, Jack Nelson, John Cryder, Curley Steindorf, Anthony Krober, John Fontaine, Mrs. Fontaine, Mrs. Krober, Myrtle Anderson Steindorf, and Kitty Nelson. (Courtesy of Gretta Gossett Gregg)

At the end of his long life, Jack still marveled at Kitty's strength and stamina. They both were strong and fit because of all their activity, but Jack relates that invariably Kitty would arrive at the end of a twenty-three-mile long ski trip less tired than he.

Jack and Kitty's journey home after visiting was a two day affair. They would stop for the night at their halfway house, which Jack said

seemed like the "Waldorf Astoria" when they finally reached it after a full
day's trekking. Rebuilt the previous summer out of the chief engineer's office from the dam's construction camp, it was located near the junction of
the American River and the Bumping River right at the halfway mark of
their journey.

The tiny building was stocked with food stored securely inside an
animal-proof safe also salvaged from the construction camp, and the bedding was hung on a wire to keep it out of the rodents' reach. Firewood,
kindling, and shavings were always kept in good supply and a telephone
was tied into the line from the lake to the Yakima headquarters. The key to
the front door hung above it, as all were welcome to use the cabin and its
contents. Many did use it for the next twenty years or so until an all-year
resort at American River was established, making the overnight shelter un-
necessary. Mountain rules and traditions expected users to replenish stores
and clean the shelter before departing.[12]

Cascadians Pearl Snyder and Elsa Hanft in front of the "Halfway" cabin at Cedar Springs
in February 1923. The structure was built using materials from the engineer's quarters at
Camp 22, the dam construction settlement. (Courtesy of the Richardson family)

Upon their return to the lake, the couple eagerly read and re-read the large load of accumulated mail and periodicals. If there was to be a long interval between visits, Kitty would ask their neighbors down in the Valley to open and read their mail over the phone line and then they would dictate return letters for them to send.

Jack's supervisor, the Reclamation engineer Charles Crownover, became a cherished friend as well through his regular phone calls to inquire after their welfare. His calls were eagerly anticipated with news from the outside world in addition to instructions regarding water regulation and dam operations.

Inevitably, the heavy storms became less frequent and winter's grasp slowly let go of the mountains. Snowbanks thinned and water appeared everywhere. Freshets ran down every crease in the land and gathered into streams which rushed towards the lake. The lake ice puddled. But long before it melted, Jack and Kitty cut the last ice blocks from the thickest part to store in their double-walled icehouse for use in the summer. Low spots around the house became small ponds and the exposed road turned to mud. As soon as the snow receded, snow cap mushrooms and glacier lilies pushed up through the wet earth with vanilla leaf and queen's cups unfurling soon after, so the world seemed to turn green almost at once.

Soon, the couple would hear the first hoarse croak of a frog from down in the spillway which quickly became a cacophony of toads and frogs calling to prospective mates. This may have become the sound of spring for Jack and Kitty. Bears, bats, ground squirrels—long dormant— began to wake up. Migrant birds flew back, and the Nelsons happily noted each animal's reappearance.

As the snowmelt steadily rose behind the dam, Jack's duties multiplied by the day. Untold amounts of slash and cut trees had been left in the reservoir bottom when the pace of dam construction outpaced the clearing crews, and now all that wood was pushed by the wind and water into the spillway at the north end of the lake. Absent Jack's daily excursions to clear, pile, and later burn this debris, the spillway would clog, so many of his early spring days were spent keeping the vital spillway open.

In May, Jack and Kitty began to prepare the road for opening by clearing rocks and trees from the eleven miles between the lake and the junction at American River. By this time, they had not eaten any fresh vegetables for over four months and the last of the eggs had expired months before.

Finally, by mid-May, with the road at last passable, the Reclamation Service sent up engineers Crownover and Paul Taylor in a horse-driven hack to deliver fresh greens, thirty dozen eggs, and other foods. With great anticipation, the Nelsons awaited their arrival. They were still waiting when the sun slipped behind the mountain on deliverance day.

At 11:00 o'clock in the evening, long after the couple must have given up all hopes of a fresh dinner, the men arrived, exhausted and apologetic. As they had traveled up the road towards Bumping River, three miles short of its junction with American River, the tongue of the hack dropped out of the neck yoke, and the team of horses became unmanageable. Fearing that the rig was going to overturn, the men jumped out. The horses, still in their harnesses, ran off in the direction of the lake. The men caught up with them at the turnoff road at American River, walked them back to the wagon and hitched them back up. By the time the supplies reached the lake, they were nearly unrecognizable, and the eggs had all been scrambled.

The opening of the road meant a happy crush of visitors would soon be pushing their way back up to the road to Jack and Kitty's door. Certainly, the very most anticipated would be the face of Frances who each spring would be on one of the first vehicles to reach the lake over the snowy road.

Normandie was showing its age by the time Don and Virginia Cyr of Seattle bought it in the mid-1970s from the final owners of the resort, Weldon (Mac) and Dorothy McIntyre. McIntyre had been ill for the last several years and he and his wife had been unable to maintain the sixteen buildings, plus outhouses, that were the last vestiges of the Bumping Lake Resort. Chimneys tilted away from cabins, septic tanks built of stacked logs were collapsing and bare electrical wires zig-zagged from tree to tree. The death knell for the resort was a failed water test drawn from the little stream that served as the water source for the facility. With McIntyre unwilling to install a chlorination system to sanitize the water supply and unable to upgrade all the other failing structures, the Forest Service ordered the resort shut down.

The rental cabins, so pleasantly tucked about the hillside above the lake, were sold off one by one. They were jacked up and hauled across the dam and down the road to Goose Prairie where they were reincarnated as summer homes in the small community there. All that was left was the lodge Normandie and a few assorted outbuildings: a tool shed, garage, generator shed, and icehouse.

The Bumping Lake Resort, place of so many happy times shared by so many people for sixty years, was no more.

When the Cyr family took over Normandie, rocks were falling out of the foundation, paint was peeling from the eaves, window screens were missing and there was a general air of neglect that hung about the place like an unwelcome guest. Inside, the furnishings and carpets were worn out and musty, and there were so many gaps in the walls that deer mice and pack rats made themselves at home in the attic and crawlspaces. Holes on the underside of the roof meant that little brown bats were included on the resident roster and could be heard chattering away to each other from their roosts above the upstairs rooms.

Additionally, McIntyre had been a hoarder, hanging onto any object or piece of equipment that he came across. Every building and all the crawlspaces, the attic and the cellar of Normandie was crammed full of cast-offs: broken appliances, lengths of pipe, coils of old cloth-covered wire. A heavy old governor from a faraway elevator somewhere lay tipped on its side under the power shed, waiting in vain to be hooked up to the electrical system, along with every diesel generator that had ever powered the lights. Behind a small clump of trees, towers of old apple boxes filled with miscellany teetered between overflowing garbage cans and even more refuse was slowly collecting in the forest behind the buildings.

But old lodge itself was rock solid and still straight, built with care in another generation.

✸ ✦ ✹

Jack and Kitty hired local builder R. A. "Chuck" Hammond to build Normandie in 1933. At the time, they were still living in the dam tender's cottage at the edge of the spillway and this new building was to be their retirement home. Just halfway through a lifetime of living at the lake—Jack would not leave government service for another fifteen years or so—they were planning for the time when Jack would be replaced, and he and Kitty would have to move out of their government-supplied lodging. Not wanting to leave the area, they built their new home on the hill just behind the cottage, still within sight of their beloved lake.

Normandie was built from the forest and of the forest. Nearby trees were chopped down and then placed upright again, nailed onto a base plate over a foundation of mortared stones gathered from a nearby rockslide. The tall vertical logs were then chinked with heavy cording and canvas strips to keep out the cold. Large windows faced south to gather light and were fitted with pleasantly rippled glass—top quality for the time but wavy compared to modern machine-made panes.

The new building was sited above the north lakeshore, with a view looking to the south over the dam, the lake, and the surrounding mountains. A large lawn full of tiny meadow flowers in time filled in the slope between the house and driveway that curved up to access both the lodge and the rental cabins that would soon be built. Towering, dark woods framed the new buildings and American Ridge rose immediately behind them; the enormity of that mountainside cloaked entirely in green.

The Nelsons built Normandie for themselves, and it reflected their personalities and needs exactly. Sturdy and strong, practical and functional, it was built for purpose and comfort. But it was also an elegant living space, with ten-and-a-half-foot ceilings, five-foot windows, and over-sized rooms throughout.

The building would serve several roles. In addition to being the Nelson's home it would be the nerve center, office, and lobby for their resort, which had grown over the years to accommodate increasing numbers of visitors to Bumping Lake. It also needed a large kitchen and dining area to entertain guests who came to visit—not as paying customers but treasured friends accumulated through their long tenure at the lake. Extra bedrooms were included upstairs for the same purpose. A single bathroom was deemed sufficient for the lodge and its six bedrooms. A full root cellar beneath the kitchen allowed Kitty to can her bounty from the summer and store it away to bring a taste of the sun to the middle of winter.

The focus of the living room was an imposing stone fireplace crafted by local stonemason Ernesto Jimenez.[13] With an opening large enough to hold five-foot-long logs, and an arched niche above it suitable for displaying finds from the forest, the fireplace was made for storytelling: a gathering spot for fellowship after a day of toil or recreation outside. Hundreds of visitors would eventually pull a chair up to its warmth to hear Jack recount the legends of the lake and pass on polished gems of wit and wisdom gathered from the forest.[14]

Common folk from Yakima, Selah, or Toppenish were just as welcome at the lake as the elite moneyed leaders from Seattle, legislators from Washington, D.C., or international dignitaries from abroad. They all convened here, drawn to the legendary hospitality of Jack and Kitty. A pharmacist-turned-mountain man and his pioneer stock wife, self-described simple folk, became magnets to a broad slice of humanity who flocked to them. Year after year, visitors found a warm welcome and friendship at that hearth and left far richer than they had arrived.

The shabby appearance of the lodge when they took ownership in the 70s wasn't that important to the Cyr family: they were all just happy to be there and spent most of their time outside anyway. In the early years they hiked, paddled the lake in kayaks, cast about for silvers (also called kokanee or silver trout), and for thrills, jumped off the raised spillway into the cold Bumping River. After rigorous hikes, the two Cyr boys sprawled on rickety, folding lounge chairs, soaking up the summer sun and paging through paperback bestsellers. Rainy weekends in the spring and fall meant more time inside contentedly playing board games together, drawing or quietly reading. Virginia took all responsibility for the meals: menu planning, shopping, and cooking for a crowd, whether there were a few of them or a full house. Buying Normandie had been her idea, as a way to continue the family's tradition of vacationing at Bumping Lake.

The tradition had started back in the twenties when Wellie and Nathalie Cyr, newly immigrated to Yakima from Alberta, Canada, discovered Bumping Lake. The family would often head to the hills for a picnic on Sunday after church. They camped along the river, and so soon met Jack and Kitty. With a shared familial background in Canada, the Cyrs immediately bonded with the Nelsons and soon became regulars at the resort, perhaps staying in the tent cabins along the spillway. Wellie and Nathalie's four children all loved the lake. The oldest, Alyne and her boyfriend Clarence, courted along its shores, married, and kept returning as their family grew to seven and then continued with grandchildren in tow. The youngest, Donald, brought his girlfriend up for an "outdoors test" once they started dating seriously. Virginia, already an ace skier and avid mountain climber, easily passed and they were soon married.

Even before their two children were born, Don and Virginia made a regular summer pilgrimage to the Bumping Lake Resort, staying for a week in one of the rental cabins along with their German Shepard, Ladybug. Both sons Bill and Tom's very earliest memories are the evocative smells of those buildings: the pine paneling, the wood smoke from the stove and the aroma of sizzling bacon they woke up to. The boys ran around freely, making forts and rocket ships in the trees and castles in the sand beside the water. Don taught them to fish, and later they learned to waterski, towed behind friends' boats on wide wooden skis.

Lynne and Elda "Mom and Pop" Turner, Virginia Cyr's mother Marion Bernard, Virginia Cyr, and sons Tom and Bill near Normandie Lodge at the Bumping Lake Resort about 1967. (Cyr family collection)

Virginia and Don loved having a getaway for the family and they both relished the quiet seclusion that the forest setting offered, in contrast to the densely populated West Seattle neighborhood where they lived the rest of the year. However, not soon after it was conceived, Virginia's dream of cabin ownership was nearly extinguished by power plays in faraway Washington D.C.

Only three years after the dam was competed in 1910, and then perennially every few decades for the next sixty years, the Bureau of Reclamation had proposed building a replacement dam at Bumping Lake that promised solutions to a variety of problems, depending on the current circumstances.[15] In 1979, the Bureau was putting the finishing touches on an ambitious plan to deliver more water to farmers in the Yakima Valley from a new, higher dam at Bumping Lake. The lake level would rise 223 feet, inundating Normandie along with nearly 3,000 acres of surrounding forest.[16]

Flood control, better in-stream fish flows, and enhanced recreation were all projected benefits but most important, was the promise of more water. Fortunately, it was not to be. Fiscal conservatives, environmentalists, and Republicans lobbied hard against the plan and the bill to authorize funding of the project was not passed by Congress. The immediate threat to the future of the cabin had passed but the lingering memory of this near-miss meant that every time there was shortage of winter precipitation and even the possibility of drought loomed, everyone in the family got anxious that the Yakima farmers would again look to Bumping Lake to solve their water woes. The threat of a new dam was really the only shadow on an otherwise cloudless horizon of vacation lake bliss.

When Don prematurely passed away from cancer in 1984, all cabin maintenance responsibilities shifted to Tom and Bill, the bulk of which consisted of repairing and improving the water system to ensure there was electricity and clean water. The family weathered their tragic loss as best they could and continued visiting Bumping Lake every free weekend.

In those early years when we were newly married, Tom and I had so little extra money that we undertook few renovation or remodeling projects. We cleaned things up a bit, maintained the existing systems and mostly just loved the old building as it was. Visiting the lake then seemed so simple, and without purpose, agenda, or plan. We just went.

Chapter Three

CASCADE COUNTRY

*"It is well to remind ourselves sometimes that
the world is not wholly squatted over."*
—Theodore Winthrop, *The Canoe
and the Saddle,* 1862

The lake that we so happily visited is not at all well known, especially to those on the west side of the Cascade mountains. "Bumping who?"
is the common question when we disappear for the weekend. Its anonymity
is due to several factors, one being is its seclusion. Bumping Lake lies within
the Okanogan-Wenatchee National Forest and is completely surrounded by
the William O. Douglas Wilderness. This Wilderness abuts Mount Rainier
National Park to the west and the Norse Peak and Goat Rocks Wildernesses
to the north and south.

The lake is at the end of a dead-end mountain road, forty-five
miles from the nearest town of any size. It is eleven miles off State
Highway 410, a seasonal mountain pass road only open six months of
the year. The shortest drive from Seattle over this pass requires exiting the
freeway only fourteen miles from downtown, nearly one hundred miles
from the destination.

Though the drive is spectacularly beautiful once you get out of the suburbs, the route up and over Chinook Pass is not for the faint of heart or those with any fear of heights. The approach to the pass is more curves than straight. One side is a solid rockface and the other is a sheer drop thousands of feet down to the White River drainage far below. At these most precipitous places, there is no guardrail or barrier to keep a careless vehicle from careening into the abyss. At other critical sections there are short lengths of rather tenuous timbers placed on rock bases, but the logs, as old as the roadway, are rotted and falling away, and in any case could not hold back much more than a wayward bicycle.

If the weather is clear though, the lucky travelers who have survived the approach and the hairpin turns that follow, are treated to a view they will never forget: Mount Rainier, glaciered and magnificent, with glittering Lake Tipsoo perfectly placed in the foreground. It is a scene that is reproduced endlessly, printed on calendars, Starbuck's mugs, and tourist brochures.

Clear weather isn't the norm. Bumping Lake is nestled close against the ridge of the cloud-catching Cascades, only six miles east of the crest. Most of the abundant clouds that pile up against the west side of the ridge spill over its top and then drop what is left of their rain. This makes Bumping Lake a wet spot, averaging nearly four feet of precipitation a year. For anyone living in rain-drenched Western Washington where there are lovely lakes galore, there is little reason to venture so far for the same weather when there are so many options closer to home. For Yakima residents with fewer water options, Bumping Lake is a favorite mountain getaway and one that is refreshingly cool during regular midsummer hot spells in the lower valley.

Lastly, there is just not much development on or around the lake. For overnight visitors who make the long trek to the end of the road, the choice is to sleep in a tent or a trailer, or under a tree. There is one Forest Service campground on the lake and one small private campground with a marina.[1] There are no hotels, resorts, bed and breakfasts or rental cabins.

What the area does claim is an intact forest ecosystem that is relatively untouched by man. Too far initially from a sawmill and railway for logging companies to bother with, spared by luck or geography from recent catastrophic forest fires, and too lean in precious metals to support mining operations more than partially developed holes in the ground, the entire valley looks and functions much as it always has. The exception of course, is the river environment which has been cut in two by the dam, the existence of which brought our cast of characters into this story.

Because of its physiographic location, the forest ecosystem here is almost unbelievably diverse. Being so close to the dividing line between wet Western Washington and the arid Eastern part, the valley is a meeting place for plants and animals from both halves of the state. Additionally, at a moderate elevation of 3,426 feet, the lake environs are amenable to the overlapping ranges of low, middle, *and* high elevation species. Bumping Lake is at a sweet spot of habitats: east and west, high and low. The late United States Supreme Court Justice William O. Douglas, amateur botanist among other things, claimed that the area contained more conifer species than anywhere else in the country, seventeen species in all.

His big statement overreaches slightly as the Klamath-Siskiyou area of northern California and Oregon hosts an even greater variety of conifers.[2] But there is a tremendous diversity in the valley. Growing in the vicinity of Bumping Lake are the big three conifers from Western Washington: Douglas fir, western red cedar, and western hemlock. Western larch and Engelmann spruce are also common here as are three species of pine: lodgepole, western white, and ponderosa. White-bark pine grows on the high ridges that ring the lake and they cling to the sides of the peaks there. We count four true firs: grand fir, Pacific silver fir, and noble fir which grow abundantly in the Valley while subalpine fir flourish in the upper elevations. The shyest of our conifers, the Pacific yew, hides all over in the understories of the more statuesque trees. Mountain hemlock, usually restricted to subalpine regions, is perfectly at home around the lake and Alaska yellow cedar mixes freely with the red cedar especially in the wetter soils. Most commonly occurring as a shrub, the common juniper hugs the ground in rocky outcroppings in the area.

Within walking distance of the lake then, grow eighteen species, making the Bumping area among the most diverse conifer forests in the region. A remarkable thirteen species can be identified just within sight of Normandie's front porch. Seedlings sprout in every open space and grow in thick clumps stretching to the sun. Except in dry areas like the Borrow Pit where the lodgepoles rule, everywhere there exists an exuberant mix of trees, like a diverse neighborhood thriving together.

Undergirding all of these trees is a similar soup of smaller plants. Nine species of orchids exist, fifteen ferns, five different violets.[3] There is so much variety in fact, that most of the time the forest is a bewildering mélange of life, creating a multifaceted backdrop to our human activities.

This complex assembly of species may not be readily evident to the casual visitor. It takes time to tease out the differences between all of the trees, shrubs, understory plants, and ground hugging herbs. Additionally, much of what borders the road up the valley is a rather homogenous blend of plants that can tolerate the disruption of the asphalt. Effort is required to experience the exceptional diversity, which means getting away from thoroughfares and campsites.

That is of course, its own reward.

🌰 🌰 🌰

The Bumping River Valley, as wild and untamed as it was in Jack and Kitty's time, and ours as well, did not always look as it does now.

During the last Alpine glaciation, glaciers entombed much of the land in the northern part of what would become Washington State. About 15,000 years ago, the vast ice sheets started to thin.[4] As the earth warmed, the glaciers retreated back up the valleys. In the Bumping River Valley, water collected in a deeper spot, creating a small lake where new life began to flourish.[5]

Plants took root in the newly exposed soil and giant mammals lumbered over the land. Humans followed this prey and spread out on the new landscape, separating, and evolving into distinct bands whose customs reflected the resources surrounding them.

One group adapted to the lands to the east of the dividing line of mountains in the south-central part of what would ultimately be known as Washington State. Even though the tall mountain range captured much of the rainfall before it reached them and caused a great part of their land to be arid, this population thrived on edible plants, game, and abundant fish that were found in the higher reaches of their territory. Some of these indigenous people called themselves "Chimnapum" but were later referred to as "E-yakimas" and then "Yakamas." [6]

By 7,000 years ago, the Yakama peoples had established a large winter settlement near the place where a sprawling Fred Meyer store in the city of Yakima would one day be built. Their homes were earth lodges, partially excavated pits with a domed roof made of packed soil. The village probably had sweat lodges for ceremonial purposes which would have been located next to the Naches River for bathing.[7] Religious activities might have occurred a short distance to the west where ancient people painted figures and symbols on the basalt cliffs that can still be seen today. Many of the dozens of portraits there depict smiling faces.

In the spring, when the river started to rise, small groups moved out in all directions to gather plants, hunt, and fish. They followed food resources upriver and set up temporary camps as wild foods came into season, digging roots and bulbs as they swelled, picking berries as they ripened, and capturing salmon as they returned from the sea.[8]

Since a time buried in prehistory, the Yakamas followed a turbulent tributary of the Naches River up into the mountains until its headwaters slowed and collected in a curved lake nestled between two rocky ridges. It was watched over by the massive bulk of a mountain that the indigenous people called Tahoma or Tacoma, later to be christened Mount Rainier. Bumping Lake was the only lake in the lower Naches River drainage.

Near the lakeshore they set up camp and got to work. Pole and tule (a type of reed grass) mat lodges were erected. Horses were let loose to graze in the thick grass that grew in the moist meadows through which small creeks flowed on their way to the lake.[9] Cooking fires were lit.

There were likely few better places to gather in the late summer and fall to provision for the winter. The lake bottom was alive with crayfish and mussels. Fat deer and elk, migrating downslope to winter ranges were funneled by the steep sides of the Bumping River Valley to the bottomlands. Chinook salmon the size of small seals arrived in the river and masses of crimson sockeye fought their way up to the lake to spawn. As the fish paused in pools and eddies to rest, they made easy targets for the men who caught them using spears with detachable stone points. It was said that in those days, and even into the time of European explorations, the river ran red with sockeye and there sometimes seemed to be more fish than river.[10]

The salmon were dried on racks above a low fire and then pounded and mixed with salmon oil. The mixture was then packed into salmon skin bags, sealed shut and stored for up to several years of winter sustenance. These rich, succulent fish were the Yakamas' primary protein source.[11]

Huckleberries were the other most important food item to be gathered at the lake. At that time, they were everywhere. As in other resource areas, the Yakamas carefully maintained their huckleberry grounds by controlled burns that kept the forest from encroaching and the bushes flourishing in the sun.[12] The fields were vast. Glistening berries festooned the bushes which may have carpeted much of the land from Bumping Crossing in the north to the Deep Creek drainage in the south, from the east lakeshore to mountain base. By one researcher's estimate there were more than 700 acres in berries along the east lakeshore.[13]

Berries were collected in finely-woven bear grass and red cedar bark baskets and once picked were covered with green leaves to protect them. They were dried in trenches or on sloping boards in front of a smoldering fire and then processed in a number of ways for later use and for trading.[14]

At the lake camp, smoky fires would have burned almost constantly to dry all of the food. Rich aromas mingled in the still air. Children laughed, dogs barked, horses whinnied as the sun's golden rays slanted lower.

For thousands of years this seasonal spectacle was repeated until life started to change as an era began to close. Introduced Old World diseases were sweeping through native populations. The bands traveling to the lake dwindled. At some point, government officials told the Yakamas they could no longer start fires there. There were buildings going in—and a dam—and those structures couldn't be risked.[15]

In the absence of continued burning, the Lodgepole pines which so readily seeded after each fire, could finally grow unimpeded. The trees flourished in the open landscape and soon filled in the fields which had been so carefully tended. A hundred years later, the slim pines still dominate the former grounds and serve as a living legacy of those who were here before.[16]

The lake might have held special significance for the Yakamas because of the name that they bestowed upon it. Long before it received its curious English moniker of Bumping Lake, it was known to native people as *Plenam, Naneum, Tah-Tannum, Tannum* or simply *Tanum* which meant "fatherland, home, or close to the heart."

The indigenous peoples of the Northwest lived in splendid isolation until the outside world belatedly became aware of this resource-packed wonderland. In 1792, Captain George Vancouver viewed a massive volcanic peak from Puget Sound and christened it Mount Rainier. In 1805, Lewis and Clark passed to the south of it while mapping and documenting the lower Columbia River. It was not until 1841, that Europeans were recorded in the immediate area. That year, Lt. Robert E. Johnson as part of the Charles Wilkes Expedition, led an exploring party from Puget Sound east over the mountains through a pass later known as Naches. They followed a river down into the Yakima Valley.[18]

Theodore Winthrop followed a similar path in 1853 and introduced Americans to this part of the Northwest in 1862 with the publication of his best-selling book, *The Canoe and The Saddle.* The book, published posthumously, recounted his adventures over the Cascades with only three horses and a Klickitat guide. He was just twenty-five years old. Winthrop's journey started on Puget Sound, wound around the north side of Mount Rainier and over the Cascades also at Naches Pass. From there, he dropped into eastern Washington following the Little Naches River very nearly until it joined up with the Bumping River. He then continued southeast to the Columbia River, down to the Dalles and then back home to the east coast.

Other explorers and fur trappers soon ventured into the river valleys east of Mount Rainier, pushing into some of the last reaches of the western frontier looking to exploit the resources there. By the mid-to-late 1800s, thousands were crossing the plains or disembarking ships from distant ports, drawn to these mountains by the desire to find treasure, to uncover the secrets of the unknown, or merely to put their personal stamp on what to them, was a newly discovered and richly promising land.

Trappers quickly set about exploiting the abundance of animals in the area, establishing remote mountain bases from which they tended long trap lines, selling furs to Hudson's Bay Company, then at the furthest reaches and in its last years of a continent-wide trading network.[19]

Oscar Brown was one of the first trappers to venture into and settle in the Bumping River Valley. He had traveled to what would become Washington Territory as a child on the Oregon Trail and received his education in the young city of Seattle at the Territorial University, which modern students know as the University of Washington. In 1866, he homesteaded in the upper White River area and over time made his way to Bumping Lake. He established his home about two miles above the lake at the junction of the Upper Bumping River and Cougar Creek. In this remote location, he honed his skills as a trapper as he established a trap line of 120 miles in the backcountry around Bumping Lake.[20]

One section of Brown's line ran from Fish Lake to Twin Sisters to Copper City; another part went from Bumping Lake to American Ridge to Crow Creek and there was an additional spur line to Swamp and Cougar Lakes. He negotiated the entire route on foot or in snowshoes staying in stopover cabins and lean-tos that he built and stocked with food, dry wood, and bedding. He became such a skilled trapper that it is said that one spring in the early years he came out with over a thousand dollars' worth of furs.[21]

Oscar Brown dressed the part of the mountain man that he had become. He wore a cap made of flying squirrel hides complete with tails that swung as he walked, and he slept on a bed of lynx hides that were incidental catch and remained unsold because their low market value. He worked his trap line all winter and in summer, he repaired his traps and buildings and expanded his line.

During the fall, Brown replenished all of his supplies in the overnight cabins, packing in everything he needed for winter by horseback. One winter, he nearly drowned as he was skiing across Bumping Lake with a large load of furs on his back and fell through the ice. Legend has it that he broke through 300 feet of ice with his skis to reach the shore, saving both himself and his precious pack of furs. He survived the icy waters of the lake only to nearly perish during the long two-mile trek back to his cabin on the Upper Bumping River. Not normally a drinker, he credited the alcohol he consumed at his cabin with saving his life.[22]

Brown was also an adventurer. In 1891, he planted the first flag on top of Mount Rainier (the mountain was first summited twenty years earlier by Hazard Stevens and P.B. VanTrump). His ascent drew attention to the mountain, its iconic importance to the region and the need to protect the peak and its surrounding area as a preserve.[23]

When Mount Rainier Forest Reserve was established in 1897, Oscar Brown became one of the first forest rangers for the west side of the park (Henry Sedge was the first on the east side of Cascade). Just inside the Nisqually entrance gate, he built a fanciful ranger station in 1908 as his home that became a model for national park structures and is the oldest building still standing in the park.[24]

Brown left the Park for the Olympic Mountains when Rainier got "too crowded" for his taste.

Because fur trappers were most busy during the winter months when their quarry sported thick, luxurious coats, many prospected once the snow melted from the ground. One of the early dual career men was Jack Campbell who worked the area just west of the Bumping River Valley both mining and trapping for thirty years starting in the 1890s.

In the winter, Campbell ran a long trap line with cabins in the Upper American River watershed from which he pulled mostly marten but also fisher, mink, red fox, beaver, lynx, and otter. Fur prices fluctuated with world events and markets but were high at the time he started with marten worth sixty dollars per skin at one point and as high as seventy-five dollars during World War I. Wolverines were occasionally a problem when they plundered trapped animals, so Campbell devised a trap for marten that he placed and wired inside a hole drilled low in a tree trunk that was too small for wolverines to enter.

When the snow was melted, Campbell scoured the ground for clues to underground riches. He filed his first mining claim high on the east slope of the Cascades near Chinook Pass within the newly established Summit Mining District. Located on Morse Creek, he called it Silver Mountain and it was likely the richest claim in the area. At one point Campbell was reportedly offered $75,000 for it.[26]

Campbell developed another claim on the west side of the Cascades crest near Silver Creek. Present day skiers familiar with the Crystal Mountain Ski Resort may not realize that Campbell Basin and the Campbell Chairlift are named after Jack Campbell and his mining operations there.[26]

Living for six months alone in a remote mountain cabin did not seem to bother this quiet man. He told Jack that he talked plenty to himself so he never got lonesome.[27] Even though he was far removed from any sort of civilization, Campbell became well known and beloved in the area, traveling up and down Pleasant Valley in a little two-seater hack once the roads were developed. He deeply loved the grand forests and their verdant meadows and at every chance brought friends from the lower valley up to picnic in and enjoy his beautiful mountain home.

Eventually, trappers like Brown and Campbell (who claimed to stop trapping each season once they reached a set number of animals) knew the trapping era was nearing its end as populations could not withstand the relentless pressures of the trade. Even though originally there were so many animals that they were considered a nuisance, by 1913 beaver trapping was banned altogether. Fur animal populations were falling all over the Northwest.

Some trappers reluctantly turned to farming but most redoubled their efforts to find and extract minerals from the mountains. They joined the earliest prospectors who were at the time hiking up every draw and climbing over every ridge in search of tell-tale signs of ore-bearing quartz. These were the men who gave the rivers and streams their first English names as they traveled along them into the high country and by 1853 Bumping River had its present name (though there is no historical account regarding its origin).

Two widely publicized expedition reports only encouraged more would-be miners to migrate to these mountains. The first, the famous Pacific Railroad reports, chronicled Captain George B. McClellan's expedition seeking a railroad route across the Cascades in 1853, the same summer that Winthrop rode through.[28] McClellan's expedition geologist, George

Gibbs, reported (erroneously) that there was gold on all the tributaries of the Yakima River.

A report published by the Northern Pacific Railroad in 1860 mentioned gold deposits on the same rivers. Because of these and similar reports, thousands of miners clawed their way over the passes and poured into the network of river valleys from the east to search the headwaters for their own paths to riches. By 1858, newspapers reported that there were fourteen hundred miners working in the Yakima and Wenatchee watersheds.[29]

While populations of transitory men scattered widely and were in flux in the eastern part of Washington Territory, settlements on the west coast were consolidating rapidly. In 1851, the city of Seattle was founded. It grew steadily, spurred by immigrants arriving at the ports of Puget Sound and overland from the east via the Oregon Trail. Hoping to divert more of the desired newcomers into their fledgling city, Seattle promoters and newspapers started agitating for the development of a mountain route to link their city to the eastern part of the Territory. The shortest path linking Seattle to Yakima was at a little dip along the ridgeline a short distance from the growing community of Enumclaw southeast of Seattle. The trail crossed the crest of the Cascades at Naches Pass, about fifteen miles north of present-day Chinook Pass and Crystal Mountain Ski Resort.

This was a well-worn trade route used since ancient times by the native populations between the inland areas and the coast. With the introduction of the horse, travel increased significantly over the pass. Disparate indigenous groups, originally divided by the formidable barrier of rugged mountains, became closer. Bands cemented bonds of friendship through trade and marriage and created trans-mountain alliances. The first explorers and fur traders quickly recognized the Indian trail as a shorter and safer alternative to the only other known trade route to the sea which was via the notoriously difficult Columbia River passage.

Naches Pass might have been only marginally safer, however. The Longmire-Biles wagon train was the first emigrant train to traverse the Cascades, crossing at Naches Pass in 1853. Although the travelers had been assured that a wagon road over the mountains existed, they found instead only a winding footpath and a nearly impossible terrain. Theodore

Winthrop described the route as a "harsh defile at best for a trail to pursue" with "somber basalt walls" that were as "sheer and desperate as suicide."[30]

The Longmire-Biles wagon train had originated in Iowa. In Oregon, the migrants decided to take a new and largely untested route into the Puget Sound region via the Yakima Valley. Leaving the well-established Oregon Trail, the large group of thirty-six wagons and about 170 travelers moved slowly west following trail blazes. As they trudged up the Valley and into the foothills, they reportedly crossed the Naches River sixty-eight times, heading up and over ridges into the timber where the river was too deep to ford. Every tree that blocked their way had to be gone around or chopped down.

Their slow progress meant that by the time they reached the higher hills, it was late in the season. Ignoring the calendar, they pushed forward into the foreboding mountains having heard that a good road to the summit from the west side had been completed which would mean a quick descent. (This "Citizens Road" was started in 1852 when local settlers in Steilacoom raised money through subscription: a total of $128.00. The road builders did not get far before the funds ran out).

When the travelers finally gained the summit, they rested their exhausted animals for two days despite being nearly out of food and the heavy clouds threatening snow. To the west of the summit though, instead of the expected highway, they encountered sheer cliffs—and no road in sight. It was too late to turn back. The thirty-foot-high cliffs seemed unsurmountable and the thirty-three-degree grade immediately below them was equally chilling. It has been said that tragedy was averted when James Biles sacrificed several of his oxen to make rawhide ropes long enough to lower the wagons down the grade. One wagon was lost when the ropes broke. The men then attached brushy trees to the wagons and fashioned "rough locks" on the wheels to slow the wagons down the rest of the 2,000-foot descent to the Greenwater River.

As the women and children wound their way down the gentler Indian trail, they were surprised to encounter a young man, Andrew Burge, on horseback. Burge had been sent to deliver food to the west-side road builders, but they had already broken camp having given up for the season. Finding no one there, he rode up the beginnings of the new road to sightsee and soon came across the weary women who were nearly beyond hope. Burge left all of his food with them. He then wrote notes of encouragement to the group which he tacked onto trees to brighten their remaining journey into civilization. Downriver residents were alerted and sent back food and supplies for the spent wagon train, earning them the emigrants' lasting appreciation.[31]

As white populations steadily rose on both sides of the Cascades, travel over Naches Pass increased and, despite the primitive state of the "road," a few more wagon trains traveling west on the Oregon Trail managed to struggle over this branch of the route to reach Puget Sound. As cities grew, demand for consumer goods and food rose, creating a market for dry goods and meat, neither of which was being produced in the area.

Cattle were initially trailed into the area to provide meat for the early miners. Cattlemen utilized the available high-country meadows for summer forage and moved their small herds all over the Northwest, following the mineral rushes. The cattle were brought into the eastern part of the Washington Territory from California to supplement small herds that had been established by the Hudson's Bay Company in the 1820s. Stockmen immediately recognized the value of the native bunchgrass that grew thick and belly high in the Yakima and Naches Valley bottoms and fattened cattle quickly. Soon, there was two-way traffic over Naches Pass as stockmen herded their cattle to markets on Puget Sound and then returned with young stock back over the Pass to be fattened in the green valleys on the east side.

The need for forage increased again when sheep ranching was introduced which utilized high mountain meadows for summer pasturage. Some of the first sheepherders were men who trapped in the winter and turned to herding for supplemental income in the spring and summer. Many of these men were of Scottish origin, coming from old shepherding families with generations of experience raising "woolies." Sheepherders followed the snow line upslope from June to October and ranged widely in all the high country around Bumping Lake.

James Templeton from Scotland ran sheep from "...Mount Hood to Mount Baker." [32] Billy McGuffie was the "king of the sheepherders" who was resourceful and "hard as granite" but also jovial and friendly. He loved telling tall tales in front of a roaring fire, especially with fellow Scot, Jack Nelson, in counterpoint. The sheep industry would become a significant part of the culture of the mountainous Northwest by the end of the century.

The new arrivals coming into the area, for the most part transitory men, did not initially pose a threat to the Yakamas who had called this land home for so long. Trappers, in particular, were a welcome source of novel trade goods such as ornamental beads, metal tools, and weapons that had the potential to enrich and transform lives.

As the composition of the newcomers started to change however, so did the attitude of the indigenous people to them. Some of these new-comers started to build homes, put up fences, keep livestock, and birth babies and it became clear that they were planning to stay. But as long as there were not too many people using the area, the Yakamas could avoid settlers and move about as they always had, following the seasons, and gathering resources.

But each year there were fewer Yakamas moving over the land-scape. Introductions of novel viruses for which there was no immunity had raced through indigenous groups, gutting populations, and carving away rich cultures. By the mid-1800s, multiple waves of smallpox, measles, and influenza had killed up to ninety percent of some bands, leaving villages deserted and survivors reeling. The two groups of peoples were on a col-lision course with incompatible motivations: one caught up in a fever of expansionism and the other in a fight for its very survival.

In 1855, a singular event upset the uneasy status quo between the two. In May, Territorial Governor Isaac Stevens gathered representatives from most of the major native groups of the interior northwest (parts of Idaho, Oregon, and Washington) to push for a land treaty. The contract would transfer title of a vast area from native groups to the Federal govern-ment. Though none of the bands wanted to give up their land and move onto designated reservations, Stevens threatened war and three treaties were reluctantly signed. The Umatilla, Nez Perce, and Yakama Reservations were established, and all of the remaining tribal lands of this part of the country were ceded to the United States.[33]

Though Stevens promised the bands that they would have two to three years to relocate to their reservations, he immediately violated the terms of the agreement. He announced through the newspapers in Washington and Oregon that all of the Indian lands east of the Cascades (except for the reservations) were available for immediate settlement.[34]

Within weeks, prospective settlers poured into the eastern parts of Oregon and Washington Territories. The immigrants traveled up every major river valley from the Columbia, stopping and sampling promising land as they came upon it. The first arrivals got the most accessible and desirable home sites and, where they could, filed homestead claims. These land grants equaled 160 acres to single men 320 acres to married men which meant that much of the low-lying land quickly moved into private hands. Land too steep or too remote to farm was sold as timber claims for as little as $1.25 to $2.50 an acre.

When gold was discovered in northeastern Washington near Colville that same year, even more opportunists streamed into the area on their way to the gold fields. Their arrival further threatened the native peoples who feared being pushed out of their last ancestral lands and into oblivion. Prospectors crossed the new reservation boundaries, stole horses, and abused women. Sentries were posted at points of entry to reservation lands to warn away the invaders. When they were ignored, whites were killed, soldiers were sent in, and battles large and small ensued in what became known as the Yakima Indian War.[35] In 1858, after a series of defeats, the Yakamas and their allies signed peace treaties with the federal government resulting in an uneasy truce for the next twenty years. There would be a few rebellions of native peoples desperate to salvage their traditional way of life, but after the last uprising in 1878, the white man's dominance would not be threatened again.[36]

As violent hostilities subsided for good, local settlement picked up again. Newcomers found ways to make a living off the land and started to coalesce into small communities. Rural minded immigrants coming into the Yakima area headed toward the hills, leap-frogging previously claimed prairies and moving relentlessly up the river bottoms, settling on the grassy flats where the valleys widened enough for a home site.

The further they pushed upriver though, the lonelier and more perilous the living was. John Emerick was just eighteen years old when he settled in the Naches River Valley and applied for a homestead claim. With no close neighbors and few travelers passing his outpost on the edge of the wilderness, John sometimes set a box over the tracks of those who traveled by to preserve their footprints. This way, he could look at them and touch them when he was in particular need of human companionship.[37]

John Emerick established a homestead in the Nile
Valley when he was only eighteen years old and
later worked as a laborer helping to construct the
Bumping Lake dam. (Courtesy of Gretta Gossett
Gregg)

The pioneers' industriousness and grit have been well documented,
and that determination served them well here on the far reaches of the frontier. The newcomers also had to be versatile and capable as they explored,
sampled opportunity, claimed land, tried to survive, and started to build
a future.

Andrew Burge, (the young packer who chanced upon the struggling
Longmire wagon train) was a perfect example this type. Before he claimed his
land on upper Wenas Creek north of present-day Naches, he had worked as
a teamster in the army, trailed cattle from California to Oregon, and made a
home in Steilacoom where he raised hogs. In the mid-1850s he packed for
the road crew making the "emigrant road" out of Enumclaw as well as for
Lt. Slaughter during the Indian Wars. Burge is credited with the first ascent
of Mount Adams in 1854. After moving to the nearby Wenas Valley, he first
plowed his land for food crops and then built a cabin, hauling in rocks for

Andrew Burge assisted the struggling Biles-Longmire emigrant wagon train on the west side of Naches Pass when he was just a teen. He was the epitome of a successful pioneer who possessed a wide skill set. From raising hogs to packing for the Army, to constructing roads and building his own home, it seemed as if Burge could do anything. (Courtesy of the Yakima Valley Museum)

the fireplace and milling his own flooring. He and his son trailed a herd of 150 cattle east over the mountains to his new home, trained them and then led them back again in pairs to sell as logging "bulls" on the west side. In 1893, he was exploring the high country around Chinook Pass for sheep pasturage.[38]

Sarah Sedge, the prim wife of early settler Henry Sedge, became a reluctant veterinary surgeon when the family cow, after gorging on green alfalfa, bloated. To save the animal, she got out their copy of a livestock "doctor book," measured on the animal's side where to stick a long knife and inserted it, releasing the excess gas, and saving the cow. She had her daughter hold the book open for her.[39]

Small farms sprouted along each river and settlements soon crept west up the river valleys towards the timber. These were extremely primitive homesteads carved from the wild lands, lacking every comfort and convenience. Uninsulated log cabins served as shelter, while a small patch of rocky soil and a scattering of livestock provided food. Unpleasant weather and the presence of wild animals added constant stress and worry—especially for those who had come from more urban areas. However, for the most part, the new residents were tough, hard-working, and determined to stay. And those who ventured to settle in the highest reaches of the Naches River Valley would soon become friends with a man and his wife who were making their home even higher in the mountains.

When the Northern Pacific Railroad line was completed to North Yakima in 1885, it opened new markets in the east. Sheep no longer had to be trailed west over the mountains to the Puget Sound region. With expanded access to markets nationwide, sheep companies and their flocks exploded in size and number.

By the 1890s there were so many animals in the forest—260,000 sheep in the Rainier Reserve alone—that most of the permitted acreage was overgrazed, leading to significant damage and long-lasting changes to stream beds and native vegetation.[40] Each spring, flocks numbering in the thousands were driven into the mountains along broad "driveways," where the animals' cloven hooves cut the vegetation as effectively as a line of plows. Herders would move their charges upslope, following the snowline until they reached the high meadows. There, with dentition perfectly adapted for close cropping, the sheep spread out on the soft ground. By the time they moved on, the thick mélange of tender meadow herbs had been quite simply swallowed. In his 1902 report describing forest conditions in and around the Mount Rainier Forest Reserve, Fred G. Plummer wrote that the flocks had "in many places denuded the ground of every trace of vegetation." [41]

As the damage became more widespread, it became obvious there was just too much livestock on the fragile forestlands. At the turn of the century, permits were introduced for the first time in an attempt to impose some order, but as available acreage declined, conflicts began to escalate between cattle and sheep interests. Each group claimed they could not survive without access to these public lands for their stock. Although there were attempts to cooperate, tensions ran high enough that sheep and cattlemen were regularly housed on separate floors at the Stockman Hotel in Yakima.[42]

Forage was in high demand not just for sheep and cattle but for horses as well. Whether under saddle, pack or harness, horses were the underpinning of the working economy of the time, and they needed fuel. In the high country particularly, good forage grass that could keep a horse working was limited and grew almost exclusively at the head of streams and in ancient lake beds that had evolved into meadows. However, because of the Homestead Act of 1862, much of these lands had been claimed and were off limits for grazing.

Even though open meadows in the Bumping Lake area were considered among the best high summer ranges in Washington, raising stock on them was not easy even when grass was available.[43] Distances between high pastures and winter headquarters were long and margins were low. Wolves, and to a lesser extent cougar, preyed on strays and young animals. Stock and sheep herders were constantly on guard and routinely shot and killed predators, including bears, when they were encountered. Naches Valley rancher Elijah Denton killed five wolves in 1883 alone but said there were "still packs of them roaming the country."[44]

Weather could be deadly too, with two notable winters in the early years that devastated many herds. The terrible winter of 1860-61, when the Yakima River froze in the extreme cold, decimated stock in the area. Just twenty years later, severe cold and deep snows killed thousands of animals throughout the region with an especially heavy toll exacted on the larger operations that depended entirely on rangeland for their animals. This setback was the beginning of the end for the large cattle operations in the area until decades later when cattle started being confined to feed lots for fattening.

As a whole, the land that white settlers were moving into was not promising. Any soil not adjacent to a river grew sagebrush and rocks. Lieutenant Thomas W. Symons of the Corps of Engineers of the United States Army summed up his impression of the Columbia River basin in his 1879 report. "All in all, it is a desolation where even the most hopeful can find nothing in its future prospects to cheer."[45]

The first farmers in the lower Yakima Valley experimented with a wide variety of crops and methods including dry land farming. The long days of pure sunshine (because of the rain shadow effect of the Cascades), an extended growing season, and incredibly fertile volcanic soil made the area almost perfect for a multitude of crops. Early on, horticulturalists recognized that central Washington was ideal for growing apples, particularly.[46] The only ingredient lacking was sufficient rainfall. None of the introduced plants could survive without supplemental water. But if it could be applied, farmers could take advantage of the full potential of the land and their crops, it was hoped, would flourish.

Ironically, irrigation was originally introduced in the Yakima Valley both by and for the benefit of the native peoples who had begun to be relocated to reservations. In an effort to assist their settlement to a restricted location, priests at reservation missions worked with the hunter-gatherers to grow conventional (to Europeans) crops using simple water supply ditches.

The first ditch in the Valley was dug by the revered Chief Kamiakin, along with Father Pandosy and Father Chirouse, in 1852 at the St. Joseph Mission which was located on Kamiakin's summer camping grounds. The channel ran a short distance from Ahtanum Creek to a small vegetable plot that soon sprouted wheat, corn, melons, potatoes, and pumpkins. The Yakima Indian War put a quick end to the new irrigation efforts when the entire compound was burned by United States Army troops from Fort Vancouver.[47]

Early irrigation efforts by white men consisted of small channels off Ahtanum Creek that delivered water to the nascent town of Yakima in 1871. Ditch irrigation quickly spread throughout the valley and before long, all the lands adjacent to the Yakima River and its tributaries were watered by gravity-fed canals. Sagebrush and bunch grass gave way to crops which flourished in the sun and heat. After kitchen gardens, the first crops put in were forage plants like timothy hay and feed grains to sustain the animals that the settlers depended upon for work and food. It was soon discovered that hops thrived, and acreage exploded for that crop. Within a generation, the first of the hundreds and then thousands of acres of fruit trees were put in. The valley was on its way to becoming one of the most productive agricultural areas in the country.[48]

But of course, the river water was not unlimited. By the late 1880s, much of the low water flow of the streams in the Yakima Valley had been diverted onto newly planted farmlands. At the time, there was no way to store the abundant spring snowmelt and by late summer, when it was most needed, water was scarce over the entire valley. If agriculture was going to expand, there needed to be a way to deliver more water in the growing season. The only answer was storage.[49]

Walter N. Granger was successful irrigation engineer in Montana who was invited by the Northern Pacific Railroad to look over its holdings in the Yakima Valley. If water could be supplied those lands could be sold at many times over their almost worthless value as desert scrub. Granger liked what he saw and incorporated with local investors and farmers, as the Yakima Canal and Land Company in 1889. Almost immediately, the Northern Pacific Railroad was asked to join when the company recognized the need for more capital.[50]

The irrigation company's ambitious plan, backed by one million dollars in capital, was to construct six reservoirs in the surrounding mountains and build hundreds of miles of conveyance canals to deliver water to vast acreage in the Yakima Valley.[51] This was the start of what came to be called the Sunnyside Project; a complex plan which included drawing water from the Tieton River that would then be replaced downriver in the Naches by water impounded by a dam to be built at Bumping Lake.[52]

In 1892, a small group of men rode up the Naches River and from there to the distant Bumping Lake to start construction of the first reservoir in the company's plan, near the outlet of the natural lake there. Under the supervision of James Stuart, a crew of ten cut 200 larch trees on the site and dressed them flat on two sides. The lumber was to be stacked up to create a wooden barrier. Unfortunately, winter weather intervened before the dam could be constructed and the prepared logs remained piled next to the lake.

In the meantime, down in the Yakima Valley, work commenced on the Sunnyside conveyance canal. In March of 1892, an elaborate event celebrated the completion of the first forty-two miles of canal. Dignitaries from across the country attended and it was grandly proclaimed that this was the "beginning of the most important system of canals in America." [53]

Though its beginning was marked by setbacks, the Sunnyside Project soon became the largest private canal system in the Pacific Northwest. In 1904, the system was watering 32,000 acres.[54]

The Financial Panic of 1893 and the sustained national depression that followed brought an end to the enterprise when the Northern Pacific, Yakima, and Kittitas Irrigation Company collapsed and was foreclosed.[55] The neatly stacked beginnings of a dam at Bumping Lake rotted into the ground.

Because of the dearth of local money, local irrigators appealed to legislators of the new state of Washington for financial assistance for the large-scale projects that were necessary to expand agricultural production in the Valley. By the end of the century, the state had surveyed and segregated over 77,000 acres of land to be set aside for reservoirs and canals, including the Bumping Lake reservoir site. The lake was surveyed first in 1895 by the state and again in the summer of 1897 by Cyrus Babb for a twenty-five-foot-high dam.[56]

By the turn of the new century, the need for more irrigation water was undeniable but the means to deliver it were in disarray. Dozens of private irrigation companies had been formed and collapsed because of lack of capital, confusing western water laws, incompetence, and the 1890s Depression.

The entire Yakima River system had become vastly over-appropriated and in 1904 water restrictions were imposed. Instead, additional canal construction that year actually *increased* withdrawals. In 1905, there were fifty-five canal systems diverting water on the Naches and Yakima alone and the Yakima River was recorded at its lowest level ever. That summer, the Washington Irrigation Company blew up a rival's temporary dam at Lake Cle Elum.[57]

It had become clear that something had to be done to organize the mess and deliver water on the scale that it was needed.

In 1902, President Theodore Roosevelt appointed Representative Wesley Jones from Yakima and others to develop a federal irrigation policy to "reclaim desert lands." The result was the federal Reclamation Act which was swiftly passed by Congress in the same year. The new United States Reclamation Service (later the Bureau of Reclamation) was charged with planning and constructing irrigation infrastructure projects which would be funded by the sale of public lands in thirteen states. The costs of the irrigated land would be repaid by irrigators through fees for the water used.[58]

The Reclamation Act would transform the Yakima Valley and the entire arid western portion of the country. The agency quickly became the biggest dam builder in the world and ultimately dammed nearly every major river—and many minor ones—in the West. Despite the welfare aspect of the plan and its chronic under performance relative to pre-construction claims, not to mention vast ecological damage to river ecosystems, the passage of the Act and its implementation by the agency, allowed for the development of western cities and agriculture as we know them today.

The Bureau of Reclamation now operates over 600 major dams in our country providing irrigation for ten million acres which produce sixty percent of the nation's vegetables and twenty percent of its fruit and nuts.[59] Almost all the large population centers of the West expanded and still thrive with water or power provided by Bureau projects including many of the major hydroelectric power facilities. All of what the West enjoys in terms of technologically-driven economies, thriving cities, agriculture production, suburbs, swimming pools, and more is due in part or whole to Bureau of Reclamation projects.

After the 1902 Act was passed, Washington State started working in cooperation with the federal government. Before long, the state abandoned its slate of conflicting water policies and relinquished all its designated water resource lands to the federal government. Although there was fierce local opposition to the federal takeover of irrigation, eventually the remaining private water companies acquiesced, acknowledging their own limitations, and handed over or sold their companies and their land to the government.[60]

Individual water rights had to be untangled, sometimes litigated, and documented as well. Given the chaotic arrangement and number of competing claims it is surprising that the water rights were sorted out by July of 1906, but they had to be. Construction could not begin on any of the projects until all the rights were adjusted.[61]

The value of upper watershed vegetation was recognized early. By 1890, local irrigation groups were already petitioning the president to protect forests from timber cutting and excessive grazing. In response, the federal Forest Reserve Act was passed by Congress a year later allowing for the designation of Forest Reserves which would secure and protect the sources of the highly-valued water.[62] The complete control and management of water was so successful in this portion of the Cascades that Yakima County rapidly became the most intensively irrigated part of the state and by the 1940s was ranked fifth in the country in value of agricultural production.[63]

But to get to that level of agricultural production, water had to be first collected, stored, and distributed. The newly formed Reclamation Service wasted no time examining regions and irrigation projects already under construction. Those projects selected first were the ones that showed the most promise although engineers were working with few precedents and had scant data regarding stream flow, geology, and weather. What resulted was an unprecedented intervention in water engineering. In just one year, five projects—each consisting of an integrated system of dams, reservoirs, and canals—were approved. Five years later, thirty more were underway.[64]

In December 1905, one of the largest federal projects to date was approved by Congress. It would be called the Yakima Project.[65]

The Yakima Project would eventually grow to irrigate 464,000 acres. The only way to deliver the colossal amount of water to cover that land (originally designed to deliver the equivalent of forty-six inches of rain during a six month growing season starting April 15) was to capture it in the spring when the snows melted off the mountain peaks to the west. To carry out plans of this magnitude, however, the impound work would be immense. The first step was determining the most feasible locations for reservoirs. Four mountain locations were obvious from the start: the triplet lakes: Keechelus, Kachess and Cle Elum at the head of the Yakima River and further south, Bumping Lake. In the end, there would be six dams with reservoirs: Bumping Lake, Kachess Lake, Keechelus Lake, Cle Elem Lake, Rimrock Lake (McAllister Meadows site) and Clear Lake (at the head of the Tieton River). These dams would affect the entire 1,120 square miles of watershed that make up the Yakima Valley and its headwaters. Construction of the impound dam at Bumping Lake was to be the first major piece of the reservoir work to be tackled.

But first, they needed to build a road.

Chapter Four

BIG PROJECTS FOR A LITTLE VALLEY

*"Paradise is in the geologic center of the State of Washington,
the home of the big red apple, where dollars grow on trees."*
—Dr. C.H. Burbank to the National
Congress of Irrigators, 1911

*"A history of irrigation in the Yakima Valley comes
near to being a history of everything."*
—William D. Lyman, *History of
the Yakima Valley*, 1918

The road that was eventually built is the same one that delivers us to the lake now, although today's route would be unrecognizable to its earliest travelers. That primitive original road has since been straightened, widened, lowered, raised, culverted, and finally, in 1950, paved so that a road that once swallowed wagons is smooth enough today to make driving all but effortless.

The improvements have come at a cost, however. One long-time resident of Goose Prairie reminisced that she liked the old dirt road better before it was paved. "People drove more slowly," she said.[1] The price our family has paid for speed and time saved is scenery unseen and experience unrealized. How many times have we sped by Flaming Geyser, Skookum Falls, American Forks, Soda Springs? Never in our desire to culminate our journey have we stopped to sample the unique pleasures that each has to offer. And as much as I try to appreciate the view out the window, the small treats of the forest—the evening grosbeaks, the gem-studded puffballs, the calypso orchids—are obscured in a blur of green.

The road is also a sort of time machine, like a wormhole to the past that we drop into once we head out of the last suburbs of the city. As the miles spool beneath our tires and settlements thin, we roll further and further away from civilization, technology, and the present. Indeed, while much of the rest of the western part of this country has flourished, this lit-tle river valley has seen a slow decline in industry and population over the years. Where there was once a thriving vacation resort, there is now a quiet mountain cabin. Where there was connectivity by telephone and public transportation, now there is none. In Goose Prairie, a short two miles from the lake, the gas station, post office and general store all closed decades ago, followed by the closure of the only restaurant a few years back. There are no utilities, no internet availability, no cell phone coverage. Most people in the valley, whether living here full time or visiting on weekends, chop wood for heat, obtain their water from a stream or their own well, and light their homes by flickering gas lights. When we arrive at the lake, we find a place almost unchanged in the past one hundred years.

As we make the last turn onto the Bumping River Road, we drop even further back in time. Trees lean closer, the road narrows, and all of civilization seems to fall behind. As we slowly wind our way up to the lake, we pass by landmarks once well known to the old-timers but that have now slipped into obscurity. Unmarked on maps and for the most part invisible, these places we drive past stir my imagination as I ponder the particulars of events, whether traumatic, humorous, or recurring, that were signifi-cant enough for a name to persist for so long: Devil's Elbow, Moon Shine Point, Dead Horse Hill, Suicide Point, Little Slide. Further along are Salt Pudding Camp, Lantern Point, and The Pharmacy.[2]

We easily traverse Gumbo, an amusing name for a section that caused so much grief to early settlers and still does to road crews today. Not far from the highway turnoff, the moist slope above the Bumping Lake

Road continues to slip, sending sticky mud over the road every winter. These days, a dozer makes quick work of the mess, but for decades residents of the valley waged a war with hand shovels against the slippery barricade to open their road to the world for another year.

Stripped of modern conveniences, we live a life at the lake much like Jack and Kitty, not by trying to emulate them but because our circumstance and environment are so much the same. It is a simpler existence with more physical work, fewer outside diversions, a greater focus on each other, and enhanced attention to smaller pleasures like the melody of a morning bird's song or a well-crafted evening's meal. Without resources available around the corner, we make do or make things ourselves and we feel resourceful and powerful. This simplicity and self-reliance are deeply satisfying.

The road that takes us into the past took travelers a hundred years ago into the future. They were part of a push into the country's last wilderness, hoping both to explore and exploit. They were partaking in an experiment no less ambitious than to transform the landscape through irrigation and make it do what it had never done before.

This grandiose vision was first imagined, then legislated, and in due course constructed by a complex of interconnected projects that began with a small road into the mountains. As simple as the result is today: a plain, two-lane asphalt ribbon to a lake, the construction of it was anything but simple, from beginning to end.

The route surveyed for the road started near the mouth of the Tieton River in the lower Naches Valley and followed the tortuous Naches River up to the junction of the American and Bumping Rivers. From there, the route wound along the Bumping River to the little lake eleven miles further into the mountains.

On paper, the route did not look so bad, but on the ground, it was hell. The rivers that this road was to follow carve deep and narrow valleys as they careen downslope. They twist and turn in response to the terrain and where the adjacent rock does not yield, cliffs rise out of the waters on one or both sides.

Yakama Chief Owhi described his route through the terrain to Winthrop in 1853:

> "...the Nachchese River...went tearing down a terrible gorge, through this my path led, sometimes in the bed of the stream, sometimes when precipices drew too close and the gulf too profound, I must climb, and trace a perilous course along the brink far above, where I might bend over and see the water roaring a thousand feet below." [3]

Because of the contraction of the upper valley, the furthest upriver settlement in the Naches Valley was the Anderson homestead which was literally the end of the so-called road. Beyond that outpost, there was only a faint trail. Up to the Anderson's however, the road was too rough and steep to be used for freighting and would have to be rebuilt. The county and the state would jointly remake this segment.[4]

By the beginning of July 1906, the State had prepared specifics for the new road section and called for bids. One bidder, contractor C.E. Lum, declared this to be the most difficult project in the county due to the isolation of the site, the poor condition of the existing road, and the extreme grades, some up to thirty percent. Furthermore, he didn't believe the construction could be completed in the ninety days called for in the contract.[5]

His public doubts notwithstanding, Lum was awarded the contract on July 14 and started construction just two days later. His $19,000 bid was to build twenty-nine miles of new road and one bridge starting at the end of the old.[6] Lum was apparently well organized because just ten days after winning the contract he had forty men and twenty teams of horses hard at work and was advertising for more men.

The crews slowly worked their way up the valley immediately alongside the river using the crudest of equipment. "Fresno" graders[7] pulled by horses roughly scraped the roadbed while filling the low spots with rocks and dirt. Poles cut on site bridged gullies and small streams. Where there was no room for both road and river, crews blasted the points off ridges which extended to the water and then used the resulting rubble to fill wooden cribs that extended into the river. If the toe of the ridge was too large to blast, crews defaulted and went up and over the obstacle resulting in grades as much as twenty percent in some places (current highway standards in the U.S. prohibit grades over seven percent). The horses providing the power were not unlike machines of today; they were trained to adjust logs "as little as a fraction of an inch to move them in their final place" for bridges and crib work.[8] Work proceeded well all summer with Lum predicting completion in November, only a month late, seemingly with permission from the county.

Mother Nature had other plans. At the beginning of November, snow was already deep in the Cascade Mountains when the temperature began to rise ominously. A Chinook wind started to blow and falling snow turned to rain.[9] By November 13, all the rivers in the area were swelling with snowmelt compounded by rain. The Yakima Daily Republic headlines shouted that "The greatest flood in the history of Yakima Valley is now coming down from the mountains." [10]

The flood turned out to be the second worst in the Valley's history (only by inches), but it made mockery of the hard-working crews' efforts to get a road into the mountains. Miles of new or rebuilt road were completely washed away, along with piles of equipment. All of the three bridges that were under construction, vital to tying the road together, were either partially damaged or completely destroyed, their pilings and framework washed away like chopsticks. Even worse was that the Naches River itself changed course dramatically in several places—up to 250 feet—so that at least one partially built bridge was stranded mid-stream or even ended up on the wrong side of the new river channel.[11]

State officials, anxious to keep the project's momentum forward, downplayed the destruction claiming the roads could be repaired quickly but damage estimates of up to $400,000 dollars for the Valley suggested otherwise.[12] Even though transportation dollars had been scarce, somehow more state and county money was scraped together to repair and rebuild the washed-out road and bridges. Construction resumed though some bridges had to be moved and other sections were rerouted altogether.

Lum, who had earlier announced that he would stop work at the place where his funds ran out, did just that. In December, after making some flood repairs, he made it as far the deep canyon near present day Cliffdell and packed up. He was still a full twenty miles short of Bumping Lake.

The flood was a serious setback for the Reclamation Service. Knowing Lum was not going to make it to the lake, the Service had jumped into the road building business in order to get the road finished. It had seventy-five men constructing the route at the time of the flood. Upon assessing the damage, the Service pulled those crews for work on the Tieton Canal and the road sat, unfinished for nearly two years.[13]

At some point in 1907 or 1908, the Service hired local James Stuart to supervise the construction of the rest of the road. Reportedly, Stuart had trouble marshaling enough men as labor was short, even with pay in the region the highest in the country at two dollars and fifty cents for an eight-hour day. Stuart eventually assembled a pilot crew headed by Jim Dunn, who went ahead with a portable sawmill and put up log buildings along the way to house the road builders. Eleven camps, with cooking and sleeping tents, were spaced over the distance, with each camp responsible for a specific length of road. Local men were contracted to supervise each of three new bridges to be built.[14] To deal with the rock work at the Bumping River Bridge, a hard-rock miner named Ruben Root was hired, a man who would later play a major role in Bumping River Valley mining activities.

This job was grueling work to conduct by hand. Foot by foot, the crews and their horses wrestled out a narrow passageway alongside the river and up to the construction site. The Reclamation Service announced that the road was complete at the end of 1908. Chief Clerk George Mair went so far as to call it and "excellent highway," but in fact, it was barely passable even for the freighting teams. Horse crews would continue grading work on it in the coming months. The vital telephone line to the lake was completed at the same time as the road.[15]

Reclamation Service crew building the Bumping River Road in 1908. Horse teams pull Fresno graders to level the surface, but the bulk of the cut and fill work was completed by hand. Log cribbing at the river's edge helped create a minimal road width. (Courtesy of the United States Bureau of Reclamation, Columbia-Cascades Area Office)

Connected now to the outside world by a winding roller coaster of a road, little Bumping Lake was about to be changed forever.

Even before the last mile of road was scraped, construction materials had been ferried through and were stockpiling at the lake. But there was to be another delay. Even though specifics had been prepared for the new dam way back in 1906, when bids were solicited in September of that year for the construction of the dam, there was no response. Again, due to the inaccessibility of the site no company wanted to risk their financial well-being on such a distant and risky venture, and this was a $140,000 job. After another call the following year, an extension, and still no bids, the federal government was obliged in November 1908, to hire crews directly and serve as contractor to build the dam.[16]

Local homesteader John Anderson had been contracted to pack in the long pipes used for making test holes at the proposed dam site. A tall Norwegian who was completely at home on the back of a horse, Anderson was friendly with local natives and traded regularly with them for their horses. These cayuses were small, but tough. He packed for railroad survey crews, early map makers, miners and even visiting scientists (including Professor Meany of the University of Washington). He was known to be able to get almost any object anywhere once wrangling a giant boiler that he slung between six or eight horses up twisting mountain trails to the Gold Hill mines. When his horses mired in the snow, he improvised snowshoes for them made of boards and canvas.

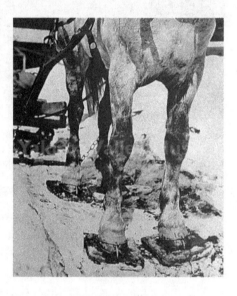

Draft horse wearing "snowshoes" during construction at Lake Keechelus in 1916. Similar equipment was utilized during the construction of the Bumping Lake Dam a few years earlier. (Courtesy of the Yakima Valley Museum)

Transporting the dam's test pipes was an ordeal because they were so long and they were hauled in early before the road was cut through. The pipes were hung on both sides of two horses tied nose to tail, but the trail was so convoluted that it was nearly impossible to make the turns. Even worse, when they came to a log across the trail—a common experience—the horses were forced to jump one and then the other over the obstacle, lurching and lunging throughout the procedure. Anderson's daughter later claimed that so difficult was the task that it amounted to near torture for the animals involved.[17]

The Reclamation Service built an office and large warehouses in the brand-new town of Naches City in 1907, and the following year a railroad spur was extended there from Yakima to deliver the vast quantities of materials that would be needed for construction of the dam.

By the beginning of 1909, all the pieces were finally in place and the pace began to pick up in preparation for what would be by far the biggest construction project in the region to date.

There was a tremendous amount of material to be moved. Dozens of small dump cars, wheelbarrows and graders, tools of all kinds, shovels and pickaxes, explosives and structural steel, iron pipes and rails, an entire sawmill, tons upon tons of hay and grain for the animals, harnesses and tack, food and cooking equipment for the crews, china and silverware for hundreds, beds and bedding, bolts of canvas for tents, thousands of tons of cement, and much more. All needed to be transported by horse drawn wagons up into the distant peaks.[18]

Local livery stable owners Frank Corey and William Dimmick had been awarded the contract for freight hauling. The men hired Jim Templeton (the old sheepherder), Walt Gallant, Floyd Preston, Edgar and Ordie Akers, and others as "teamsters" to drive the wagons.[19] Before long every available freighter in the area was employed on the project.

Thirty-five teams of horses were soon rolling in a finely synchronized schedule up and down the valley. Typically, three teams of four to six horses were sent out each morning. The number of horses needed depended on the weight of the load with the average being 5,500 pounds and the record, 7,800 pounds.[20] Teams consisted of light draft horses or draft mules, bred for strength and endurance, both of which were needed for the long haul into the mountains. The slow clop-clop of hooves must have echoed off the hills nearly continuously as the wagons rolled by.[21]

Teamsters line up in Naches to begin their three day journey to Bumping Lake, hauling material for the construction of the Bumping Lake Dam. The first wagon is driven by Floyd Preston, the second by Edgar Akers, and the third by Ordie Akers. (Courtesy of the John Thompson family)

Because the road was narrow, and the job was doubly difficult for the loaded teams moving uphill, it became customary for the outbound teams to wear strings of bells. The returning empty wagons could then have warning of their approach and pull out to give the loaded wagons the right of way. So much material was needed for the massive project that teams ran almost continuously during the winter and early spring. In general, the snow was light at the lower elevations, but the wagons were replaced with sleds as the snow deepened. When the sleds could progress no further in the snow, equipment was offloaded into tents and the vital supplies were packed up to the lake by individuals on foot.[22] Presumably, the tons and tons of bagged cement were stockpiled to wait for the road to clear in late spring.

One particularly difficult spot for the teams was at a tight turn below present-day Cliffdell that became known to the teamsters, or skinners, as Devil's Elbow.[23] When the eight horse teams hauling the massive head gates uphill to the dam site lost momentum at this bend, they almost turned back on themselves, and all manner of persuasion had to be used to keep the straining animals moving forward.

Another problem area that persisted throughout construction was a place near Cliffdell known as "Soapy Slide" by the locals. Every winter a deposit of greasy clay slipped down from a cliff above onto the road where it caused havoc to any vehicle trying to traverse. When the road was improved, it was "paved" corduroy style with crosswise logs, which helped, but it needed to be rebuilt every year. During the winter of 1909-10, despite the improvements, a horse team and wagon with a load of cement slipped and plunged into the river. One of the teamsters became entangled while trying to extricate the horses from their harnesses and drowned along with two of the horses.[24]

Progress up the new road was slow for the heavy wagons, even without obstacles, with the trip to the lake taking three days from Dimmick's livery barn in Naches. With the average daily mileage being only eighteen miles for a loaded wagon, there were two overnight stops for the forty-six uphill miles to the lake (the third day's mileage was shorter because of the steeper grade). The first rest stop was nine miles from Naches at Warm Springs, soon known as Nine Mile Flat, where the horses could be watered at a good year-round spring that did not freeze over in the winter. The teams then stayed overnight near Sam William's place at the mouth of Nile Creek where hay and water were available. Dick Darlington was hired on as the cook at this camp. During the second day's travel, all rested midday for a good meal at the Fontaine Ranch. The second overnight stop was in a "dugout" on the Bumping River just above its junction with the American River. Dubbed "Skinner's Roost" by the teamsters, it was a rude mess tent, partially dug into a hillside and attended by two highway maintenance men, Ernie and Charlie Taylor. On the third day freighter teams arrived at the construction camp, eleven miles from the last stop at American River. At camp, the animals were handed off to the "barn dog" for care.[25]

The road was so rough and the going so laborious that the skinners required extra fortification for the trip. Typically, they would bring at least a gallon of whisky and a one-pound plug of Star chewing tobacco. Common courtesy of the time called for the outbound skinner to produce the jug for the inbound when they passed on the path.[26]

The return trip took only two days, because it was downhill, and the wagons were empty. One full day was required back in Naches to over-haul equipment and reset horseshoes before the wagons were reloaded, teams harnessed, and the entire outfit started up the valley again.

Workmen were transported to Bumping Lake via the much speedier "stage." F.M. Case and R.W. Parker were awarded the government contract for passenger and express business for the 1910 season.[27] The stage ran three times a week and arrived at the lake at nine o'clock in the evening on the same day it departed. To make such quick time required eighteen horses each way: six horses pulling and changed out twice, once at the Lindsey Ranch in the Naches Valley and again at the American River station. There, the horses were stabled in tent barns to rest until they were re-harnessed on the next stage.

This operation was the same crude setup that initially delivered Jack Nelson to the area in 1910. He and other passengers were mildly out-raged that the Service charged three dollars for the trip up and two for the return, a considerable sum for such a terrible ride. With a base pay of two dollars per day, but meals costing twenty-five cents each, and a one dollar per week hospital deduction, Jack used to complain, "It took a week's work just to get even with Uncle Sam!" [28]

As the men arrived at the dam site, they disembarked into a busy camp that would become their home for the season. Camp 22 was a city in miniature with a main street that accessed a mercantile, hospital, bath house, a Young Men Christian Association (YMCA) building, two cook shacks and two mess tents, in addition to huge storage warehouses and materials tents. The engineers and more important employees enjoyed privacy in their own small, framed houses and offices while the workmen slept in large tents or framed bunkhouses. Latrines and trash pits were tucked behind buildings amongst the trees but being open-air they must have been smelly and fly-ridden during the hot summer months. A glowing newspaper report from August suggests otherwise, describing a clean and sanitary camp with screened sleeping and eating rooms for laborer and boss alike. The writer stated that he had visited many similar construction camps, and he had never seen one "where such thorough care was taken to safeguard the health of the men." [29]

A little road house operated at the end of the road too. Lee Greer and his wife offered meals to laborers, freighters, and visitors for the standard twenty-five cents. The six horses that pulled the passenger stage were put up in the same building as the diners, with the Greers caring for them until they were needed to relieve the next team trotting in.[30]

The work horses and mules were stabled down the road from the residence section of the camp in massive tent corrals. A huge log barn stored hay and another, tack and supplies. The blacksmith shop was located not near the stables, but next to the dam site itself, for quick repairs and shoe resets to minimize work delays. A sawmill, repair shop, and later, a light shop rounded out the camp.[31]

A drive across Bumping Lake Dam today gives no hint of the magnitude of the construction project undertaken so long ago. The dam is low and completely unimpressive, faced with large, jumbled rocks on the lake side and river cobbles and loose dirt on the back. The gate house in the middle of the dam is gray concrete and reminiscent of a prison tower. Seeps at the bottom of the back side collect into little streams filled with stringy green algae.

But looks can be deceiving. To construct this humble barrier, the site had to be first cleared of dense tree cover, excavated down towards bedrock and then built back up, finishing at sixty-one feet high, twenty feet wide at the crest, and 3,425 feet long. The fill material came from a site half a mile away.[32] The volume of dirt moved, 245,000 cubic yards, was astronomical. A wide spillway for overflow needed to be constructed in addition to the conduit (outlet tunnel) through the dam along with its adjacent outlet flume. A tall gate house had to be constructed around the massive gates that would control the flow of water into the conduit. Crews would mix a total of 3,000 cubic yards of concrete. Finally, 800 acres of the enlarged reservoir site had to be logged and cleared for the future lake.[33]

All of this construction was originally proposed to be done in twelve months, in the middle of a vast wilderness, forty-six miles away from the nearest railhead and sixty miles from nearest population center. It would be accomplished by man and horsepower; with picks, shovels, plows, wheelbarrows; and only two pieces of machinery to assist. To complete all of this, crews would ultimately number 250 men working in shifts with nearly a hundred horses and mules to carry out the heaviest work.[34] The logistics of feeding and housing so many humans and animals for a project of this magnitude, so far away from any kind of civilization, were stunning.[35]

After the preliminary surveying and soil testing, one of the first orders of business to prepare for construction was to erect a sawmill to supply the vast amounts of lumber that would be needed for the project. A small structure was erected near the banks of the Bumping River just upstream from where the dam was to be built. The initial timber supply could not have been simpler: the mill was completely surrounded by towering trees.

Soon, buildings large and small started to go up. Engineers, under the direction of Chief Engineer Arthur P. Davis and Supervising Engineer Charles H. Swigart, identified north and south rock quarries (actually the toes of rockslides) and roads were built to them. The rock hauled from these sites would surface the front of the dam. A dependable water supply was needed for both the camp and for use at the dam. Two water sources were developed, one for the north end of the dam and one for the south.[36]

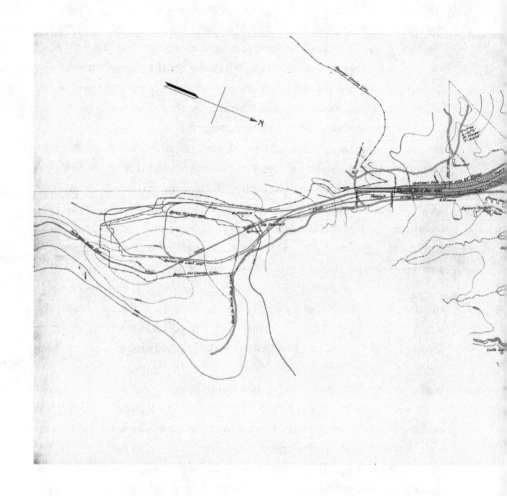

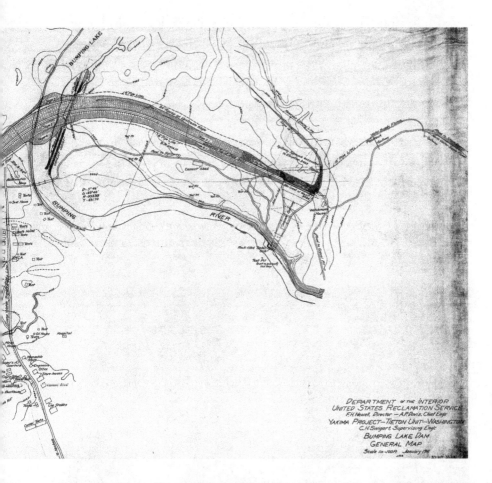

Before construction on the dam could begin, a resident camp was built and infrastructure was installed. This 1911 site plan shows all of the facilities at the Bumping Lake Dam. Included is the resident Camp 22, the Borrow Pit, and roads to offsite resources. The watchman's house where the Nelsons would live is indicated on the extreme right. (Courtesy of the United States Bureau of Reclamation, Columbia-Cascades Area Office)

To clear the site for the dam and its spillway, loggers had to first take down the huge, old growth fir, spruce, larch, and cedar trees that completely covered the area. Next, powder crews dynamited the stumps and any large rocks along with them. The rocks were moved aside to be used later. The stumps were then wrenched into piles by horse and mule teams to be burned.

The few photos which document this herculean task do not tell the whole story. First, surveyors marked the area to be cleared and fallers worked in pairs with crosscut saws to drop the trees, trimmers then trimmed them, buckers cut them into lengths and choke-setters hooked them up for the horses to drag to the sawmill. Horse teams then graded flat the tortured ground and men picked off the thickets of twisted roots. The forest was erased.

Once the virgin forest was cut, the entire dam and spillway area had to be "stripped" of stumps, roots, and boulders. Two, three, and four-horse teams work to clear the dam site on May 25, 1909. This view looking south shows Nelson Ridge in the background. (Courtesy of the United States Bureau of Reclamation, Columbia-Cascades Area Office)

At the mill, the logs were hewn into lumber not only for buildings but for the tall trestles that needed to be constructed and for thousands of short railroad ties. Once the lumber needs were met, all of the rest of trees which were taken down were burned in huge pyres.

The Reclamation Service had not been able to solicit a single bid for the millions of board feet of standing timber in the reservoir bottom.[37]

Rare photograph of the original Bumping Lake before it was enlarged by the dam. The dam site has been cleared and shows at the middle-bottom towards the right. What will become the reservoir is covered in heavy timber. Mount Rainier looms in the background. Photo taken from nearby Mount Baldy at 7,200 feet on May 30, 1909. (Courtesy of the United States Bureau of Reclamation, Columbia-Cascades Area Office)

The same clearing process was required at the area chosen to provide the fill material to raise the embankments of the dam. Engineers had identified what would be known as the "borrow pit" after careful soil testing all over the area. To find the least permeable material out of which to build the dam, the engineers took numerous soil samples which they packed into two-by-two- foot wooden boxes. Next, they timed how long it took for a measured amount of water to penetrate the soil and drain out of the bottom of the box. The least permeable soil came from an area just southeast of the dam site: the borrow pit. The material was referred to as "cement gravel" or "plastic clay."[38]

Tragedy struck the project early on while the dam site was still being logged. In October 1908, reclamation worker Ray Henry was killed when he was crushed by a falling tree. His death was relatively simple, but its aftermath was not. His suitcase, said to contain well over one hundred dollars, disappeared and soon the Yakima police were searching for it. No relatives came forward to claim his body despite a nation-wide hunt which was complicated by the fact that he may have used a pseudonym. Yakima undertaker A.J. Shaw incidentally discovered that he had a glass eye while examining the body a full two months after his death. This added descriptive feature did not solve the mystery of his identity and Shaw eventually gave up and buried him at his funeral home's expense, five months later.[39]

Before work could commence for the 1909 season, two critical pieces of machinery needed to be onsite and ready to work: a forty-five ton Bucyrus steam shovel and a one-cubic yard Hayward "orange peel" skid excavator.[40] Both were shipped in pieces by rail to Naches. The skid excavator was freighted up to the dam site where it was assembled and put to use all over the dam site, its "donkey" engine powering everything from circular saws to cement mixers.

The steam shovel was more problematic. Its sheer size and bulk—even disassembled—seems to have been too heavy for wagons. Newspaper reports indicate that the pieces were carried on a drag (similar to a sledge or strong, heavy sled) for the first eighteen miles. But the calendar read February and in the middle of the Nile near Benton Creek the freighting teams hit snow. The contraption was somehow switched over to sleds which were then pulled up by horses on a "snow road" twenty-seven more long miles to the lake. The task took eight days.[41]

Actual construction of the dam began on May 17, 1909. Snow still lay in deep drifts as crews got to work. Because the project site was essentially divided in two by the Bumping River, a stout bridge had been built to span the waterway and gain access to the north section. Horse teams were dispatched across the bridge to start digging the main cutoff trench down the center along the length of the dam. The trench would become the solid and waterproof base for the bulk of the dam above it.

The steam shovel, similar to those which were cutting the Panama Canal at the time, was inaugurated by digging the cutoff trench on the south side of the river. Once that was done, the machine was pulled by horses over to the borrow pit where it would remain for the duration of the project, endlessly scooping fill dirt into little trains of dump cars.

Other workers started constructing the dam's conduit. Essentially a giant pipe, the conduit would conduct lake water through the middle of the dam and then to the Bumping River below it. The conduit, with a seven foot inside diameter, had to be constructed early so that the flow of the river could be moved into it. Once the river was diverted, the ancient riverbed could be stripped of its boulders and covered by the dam embankment.

The conduit was built in two phases. Precise wooden forms were cut and placed for the bottom half and concrete mixed. The concrete was then conveyed by hand in little wheelbarrows, which were pushed along narrow plank pathways that wound above the forms.

Crews push wheelbarrows full of concrete to pour into wood frames that will form the conduit by which water will pass through the dam. View is looking east from the lake side on August 17, 1909. (Courtesy of the United States Bureau of Reclamation, Columbia-Cascades Area Office)

At the head of the conduit, heavy five by five-foot iron control gates were levered into place and the gate tower, also formed and poured, started to rise above them. The gates would control the flow of water out of the lake. A little house—complete with windows and white trim—would be added later to the top of the column. It would protect the gate controls and the operator.

At the same time, the 250-foot-wide, funnel-shaped spillway (for overflow reservoir water) was taking shape at the north end of the dam. The approach to the structure was lowered to a precise elevation of 3,426 feet which would be the elevation of the future lake. The largest stones encountered were loaded onto sleds and dragged off to be used later on the facing of the dam. After careful grading, shaping, and leveling by horse and mule teams, forms were built, and rock rubble was spread as a base to prepare for the concrete expanse. The punishing job of pouring the concrete was completed by hand here too, as men pushed loaded hoppers along tracks onto the spillway to be emptied and then refilled again.

At the north end of the dam, workers push heavy hoppers along tracks to place concrete on the wide spillway floor. October 1, 1909 (Courtesy of the United States Bureau of Reclamation, Columbia-Cascades Area Office)

Because of the delays getting the project started and design changes to the very structure of the dam, construction was slowed and by mid-summer the project was behind schedule. In July, the Reclamation Service announced that the dam would not be completed by the end of the season as planned. Even without any complications, a twelve-month construction goal was just too optimistic. The delay must have been a crushing disappointment to the Yakima Valley farmers who had purchased property but could not begin planting crops or orchards without their promised irrigation water.[42] To help compensate, crews were kept working through autumn to wring every workday out of a limited construction season. They were still toiling in October as snow fell on the surrounding ridges.

The Reclamation Service was trying to achieve an important milestone before wrapping up for the season. They wanted to move the river. Once the conduit complex was complete, crews started to build a temporary coffer dam to divert the Bumping River into the tunnel. On October 17, the coffer dam was complete and the Bumping River which with its inhabitants had flowed freely for thousands of years was forced into a concrete pipe.

Workmen were still on the job when warm Chinook winds began to blow at the end of October. The winds began to melt the snow that had already accumulated, and disaster threatened when the falling snow turned to heavy rain. The river rose quickly behind the coffer dam that protected the cleared dam area. The crews who were still on site worked feverishly around the clock, filling wheelbarrows first with dirt and then, as the rains continued, with mud which they dumped on the top of the saturated coffer dam.

The entire project was at risk as water lapped at the brink of the coffer dam, but the men kept laboring into the night. Somehow, the dam held. The rain stopped and the danger slowly subsided along with the water. But a few weeks later the rains returned, and the river surged again. Since the coffer dam could not be raised any higher, this time crews were instructed to cut into the dam at a point where it would not lead to uncontrolled erosion. The emergency measure damaged a portion of the cutoff trench but saved the dam as the water again receded.[43]

Work was concluded for the season. The workers must have been exhausted. As the men and animals moved out, the snows moved in, covering the raw earth with a smooth white blanket.

The dam creating a new storage reservoir at Bumping Lake was the first of six planned for the Yakima Project.[44] The reservoirs together would ultimately impound over one million-acre feet of water. The new lake at Bumping was planned to be a "replacement storage" reservoir to provide water to the Naches River equal to the amount that the Tieton Canal would remove from the Tieton River for irrigation.

This dam would also be of an experimental design. When early core drilling in the substrate revealed unexpectedly loose gravel and coarse sand under the bedrock (the glacial drift deposits there were deep, inconsistent, and lacked binding clay), the Service's board of engineers was forced to modify its plan and come up with a novel solution for the conditions at the site.[45] They would need a deeper and heavier barrier to prevent seepage problems which were already present, even at this early stage. Additionally, there were large boulders in the base which could not be removed or rolled over as would normally be done. The original and standard zoned earth-fill plan was scrapped in favor of one with a "puddled core" of water-sorted fines.[46] The puddled (or hydraulic fill) core would create a vertical waterproofing barrier. This building method had never been utilized before on a large scale and represented a new design at the dawn of modern dam building. Critics derided the concept, claiming that the barrier would fail and wash away, but the engineers were confident that the puddled core would hold back the lake.[47]

Either way, they would soon find out, as the second season began.

Work resumed at the dam site on April 1, 1910. Preparing for the second season was not much simpler than the first. Though the tools and equipment were largely in place, all the food and materials, animals and their feed again had to be transported—and this year there was fourteen miles of snow to traverse below the construction site. After the long winter break, the steam shovel required care and coaxing to get it back running. The heavy canvas tents needed to be erected and the work site again had to be cleared of its mantle of snow.[48] As laborers arrived, they were dispatched to work all over the project.

The conduit's outlet channel had been damaged during the previous November rains with the high flow of water and was repaved with stones—this time mortared.[49] A tall trestle, nearly 500 feet long was constructed of lodgepole pine logs. It would span the river and run down the middle of the length of the dam. Two sets of tracks were laid on its wide deck. To the north, massive timbers were prepared and maneuvered into place at the lower end of the spillway to frame a sluiceway to convey floodwaters into the river below. Soon the bulk of the dam itself would begin to rise.

Early each morning, the first shift of workmen would head out of camp after a full breakfast, leading or riding their teams. The animals were already harnessed and ready to be hooked up to whatever needed to be powered that day.[50] Men were invariably dressed in heavy pants and long-sleeved shirts. Most wore suspenders or overalls to keep their pants up, some wore scarves around their necks, but they all wore hats of some type. Heavy work boots protected their feet.

Each morning horse and mule teams were ridden from their tent corrals in Camp 22 west to the dam site or south to the Borrow Pit where they were put to work in a wide range of tasks. View is of the east section of Camp 22, at the "Knob Hill" location, looking northeast along what is now the Bumping River Road. (Courtesy of the United States Bureau of Reclamation, Columbia-Cascades Area Office)

The big shovel over in the Borrow Pit was fired up in a hissing cloud of steam, ready to dig into a twenty-foot-high bank as it moved slow-ly from north to south along tracks that were laid in front of it. As many as ten trains of six small, side-dumping ore cars continuously pulled up along-side the machine ready to be filled.[51] The horse and mule teams, pulling hard at their collars to get the loaded cars moving, looped back to the dam.

As they approached the site, the animals followed the narrow railroad tracks right up onto a wooden trestle which rose to what would be the finished height of the dam: sixty-one feet.[52]

A Bucyrus steam shovel scoops soil from the east side of the Borrow Pit and drops it into a side dumping car. Trains of six rail cars were pulled by teams to the damsite and then up onto a tall trestle and emptied. (Courtesy of the United States Bureau of Reclamation. Columbia- Cascades Area Office)

The trestle, though seemingly well-built with a strong wooden deck, must have trembled as the heavy horses and loaded trains traversed it. At the appropriate spot, the team driver would release the load of mixed soil and stones over the side of the trestle. The plan was for the larger rocks to roll or be worked off to the sides with the finer material and silt remaining in the center where it was sluiced down with water. This process was repeated over and over as the two sides of the dam slowly piled up.

Water pressure for sluicing was provided by the offsite streams to the north and to the south which were in both cases tapped well above the level of the dam. Black Devon Creek was diverted into a small canal for a half a mile or so until it flowed into a wooden flume that was routed onto another trestle which loomed high overhead in the trees. At the dam site, the water then entered a pipe that was hung underneath the trestle. At the north end, water was diverted across the mountain in a small aqueduct and then into a pipe that then ran downhill to the worksite. That wood stave pipe split and ran along the upstream and downstream embankments. Fifty-foot-long hoses tapped into the pipe every hundred feet or so could reach every inch of rising dam.[53]

Rail lines looped all over the construction site providing the pathways for the steam shovel, cement hoppers, fill-dirt trains, and finally single flatbed cars which were piled with the large rocks or riprap that would cover and protect the front of the dam. These rail lines were constantly pulled up and rebuilt wherever they were needed, the little round ties wearing smooth from the handling.

As the embankment rose beneath it, the trestle was removed from north to south.

Perhaps some carelessness had crept into the operation, but calamity struck at the height of construction on May 25, 1910. After probably hundreds of trips onto the towering trestle, with trusting horses willingly plodding up and across the wooden structure against all instincts of self-preservation, the whole arrangement collapsed. Dryly captioned Reclamation photographs dispassionately describe the destruction as a "disconnection," but the images show at least one dead horse lying among the twisted metal tracks and splintered timbers. Obviously, keeping to schedule was paramount because the trains were running on a completely rebuilt trestle just five days later.

Disaster struck the construction project on May 25, 1910 when the heavily used trestle above the growing dam collapsed as a fill train was traveling on it. The driver escaped injury, but a horse was killed. The photographer's view of the immediate aftermath shows twisted rail lines with the train cars above left. (Courtesy of the United States Bureau of Reclamation, Columbia-Cascades Area Office)

Overview of the progress on the day that the Bumping River was "closed," and the river water was diverted through gates at the base of the dam's gate tower and thus into the conduit running through the dam. Men are already clearing the newly accessible riverbed of its rocks on June 28, 1910. (Courtesy of the United States Bureau of Reclamation, Columbia-Cascades Area Office)

The pace during the 1910 season was relentless. Thankfully, at the end of their eight-hour shifts, workmen could look forward to a hot meal and an evening of reading, visiting, or playing card games in the bunkhouses where they tended to gather. The workers did not collect casually. The camp was clearly segregated into "American" and "Foreigner's" areas with a separate kitchen, mess, and quarters for those who had not been long in the country. Recent immigrants working at the construction site were referred to as "Dagoes," but distinctions were probably made as there were workers from Wales, Ireland, Germany, and Scotland, all working together at the camp. Sander Harlis, the blacksmith, was from Sweden. The bulk of the laborers, at least at the beginning of the 1910 season, were Bulgarians who had immigrated to the United States within the past four years.[54]

Those immigrants built the most permanent structures in Camp 22, the remains of which survive today. Once their camp was occupied,

Camp 22's blacksmith Sander "Sam" Harlis and his assistants at Bumping Lake, 1910. (Courtesy of the Yakima Valley Museum)

it seems as if they quickly longed for a taste of their home country and missed, most of all, good bread. Evidently, they received permission to build a traditional wood-fired oven. Before long, there were at least four beautifully crafted round "beehive" ovens releasing the irresistible aroma of freshly baked bread into the forest. Apparently, the American workers must have envied their counterparts' superior fare because they soon had two stone ovens at their end of the camp, too.[55]

One of the head cooks was a former newspaper man from Detroit and a Rough Rider during the Spanish American War. Dick Darlington was well known in the Naches Valley when he was hired by the Reclamation Service. One of the earliest homesteaders in the Valley, he built the Edgar Rock Lodge in 1904 as his home. He stayed on at the lake after completion of the dam, cooking for the cleanup crews for several seasons. Darlington's domain included his own personal cabin, a large cook shack (with one wing constructed over Black Devon creek for cold storage in the icy water underneath), several subterranean root cellars, tent mess hall, and icehouse.

The immigrant mess hall at the west end of an ethnically divided Camp 22. The majority of the foreign born workers during the 1910 season were from Bulgaria. The "Americans" messed and slept in separate quarters at the east end of the Camp. (Courtesy of the United States Bureau of Reclamation, Columbia-Cascades Area Office)

Darlington oversaw a crew which included a dishwasher, the "bull cook" who split wood, kept the cook fires burning and rang the "gut hammer" triangle at mealtime, and a small army of white-aproned waiters who served meals to weary workers seated on long benches in the mess tents. In Darlington's spare time, he roamed the mountains looking for minerals. In addition to being at the point of discovery on an early Deep Creek claim, he filed at least one other mining claim high on a ridge overlooking the lake.

Amusement as well as education was provided by a branch YMCA facility that was operating at the camp for the second year. Under the direction of John Decker, English classes were given to those who did not speak the language, Bible classes were held, instruction was given in basic banking (which encouraged the saving of money), and a little lending library was compiled. An eight-by-twelve foot stage for the production of minstrel shows, mock trials and shadow pictures was constructed, and a four-piece

East cook shack at Camp 22. The cook may be Dick Darlington, a homesteader from the Naches Valley who stayed on after the dam was completed, cooking for the cleanup crews. The "bull cook" who was in charge of keeping the cooking fires going, is likely on the left. A supervisor sits on the right. (Courtesy of the United States Bureau of Reclamation, Columbia Cascades Area Office)

quartet was put together for accompaniment.[56] The YMCA organized box-ing and wrestling tournaments and enough workers were apparently spared from dam work to clear and level a tidy baseball diamond (claimed by one old timer as being the best field in the mountains). The camp fielded enough teams to conduct a tournament with the championship team at Bumping Lake immortalized by the camp photographer.

All of these "healthy activities" kept the laborers so occupied that gambling was "almost unknown" and there was "no brawlling" [sic] either.[57]

The Reclamation Service was committed to completing the dam by the end of the 1910 season. To meet that goal, they kept crews working long days, then added a third shift which worked through the night under electric arc lights. It was said that "the night shift worked under conditions nearly as good as those of daylight." [58]

To maintain the pace, a full component of men and animals were needed, but the Service from the very beginning had difficulty retaining

Champion Base Ball Team
Bumping Lake, 1910

Dam laborers enthusiastically participated in sports and games during their off hours. A tidy diamond was marked off in a meadow just north of Camp 22 and south of Bumping Crossing where baseball tournaments were held. The championship team posed for this photograph during the 1910 season. (Courtesy of the Yakima Valley Museum)

enough skilled workers to keep the project on schedule due to a tight labor market. To plump up their crews the Service employed a "man snatcher" who trolled for men on Front Street in Yakima.[59] How strongly they were encouraged to stay at this remote outpost with its unending hard manual labor is unknown, but it would have been difficult to get back to civilization once they were loaded on the stage. Assuming they were charged for their transport and the hospital fee, an unwilling worker would have had to stay and work for at least four days to afford the fare back to Yakima.

What is apparent is that the crews available were always assigned to the work on the dam itself while the less urgent work of clearing the reservoir bottom lagged. It seems as if the Service had been holding out for a lumber bid for the staggering amount of standing timber still in place but with nothing forthcoming well into the second season the agency gave up. In July, there was still a thick forest covering much of the area that would be flooded. On August 1, clearing was finally initiated with government crews

Heavily garbed workers dress the last stones and mortar them onto the dam at the edge of the spillway on a snowy November 14, 1910. The watchman, or dam tender's house, shows in the background. (Courtesy of the United States Bureau of Reclamation, Columbia-Cascades Area Office)

doing the work. As with the dam and borrow pit areas, the trees would be chopped down, piled up, and burned.[60]

A small timber camp was constructed about a mile and a half south of Camp 22 for the logging crew and their horses. It consisted of tents (probably on wood bases), some sort of a food storage building, a horse barn, and perhaps other structures as well. The camp was strategically located on the southeastern shore near the greatest concentration of trees that were to be taken down.[61]

Again, work was pushed into the last workable days of the season to finish the project. There was snow on the ground as the men levered the last stones into place along the front side of the dam. At this point, workers had donned heavy coats and gloves to ward off the deep chill. Others put finishing touches on the little dam tender's house next to the spillway.

On one of the first days of November 1910, the outlet gates were cranked shut for the first time. Cold, muddy water slowly swirled around the roots and trunks of the thousands of trees that still stood tall in the new reservoir bottom.

The Bumping Lake dam, an unprecedented achievement of organization and will, was finished.

❦ ❦ ❦

The stumps—and some standing snags—still remain in the lake, more than one hundred years after the dam was completed. Despite concerted but sporadic efforts to clear the lakebed though the years, the skeletal remains of the trees pierce an otherwise picture-perfect mountain lake. A midsummer visitor might come and go without noticing the former woodland, but as summer wears on and the water level of the reservoir drops, time unwinds, and the forest is revealed, one sawed-off stump at a time.

Exploring this drowned forest in the fall after drawdown when the lake is nearly empty is pretty interesting as it is still possible to trace the ancient streambeds in the sand and climb over huge glacial erratics that were stranded at random along the lakeshore 10,000 years ago. But it is entirely different *swimming* through a forest. For twenty years, I waded into Bumping Lake and splashed about, never lingering long because of two discouraging factors: the chilly temperature of the snowmelt water and the presence of shadowy hulks of the leftover stumps. They darken the depths when we paddle over them and frighten us back to shore when our toes brush against them as we tentatively venture out from the shore. They are everywhere.

In the summer of 2007, in an ultimately successful effort to recover from the lingering effects of a rigorous course of chemotherapy, and at Tom's urging, I took up triathlon racing. With one season of competitions already under my belt and a race nearing, I was eager to continue training in the mountains. We ran the trails, biked the dirt roads, and for the first time, we pulled on our wetsuits and goggles and swam across the lake. The stumps, creepy enough above water, became multi-tentacled monsters below. As we swam over them, their long roots, exposed because the forest duff and topsoil were long washed away, looked like writhing arms, stretching out in all directions. The haste or carelessness of those logging crews a hundred years ago created stumps of all different heights so that the more threatening creatures reared their heads way up out of the dark depths towards us like a Loch Ness legend stilled by time. On subsequent swims, once we got used to the beasts and saw them as the corpses of trees, the tallest ones that we had to swim around made for a surreal experience as if we were suspended in space, gliding through a silent, doomed forest.

With the completion of the dam, Bumping Lake was about to be introduced to the world. Jack and Kitty Nelson were its perfect ambassadors. The fact that the area still resembled a construction site with jumbles of rocks, swathes of bare earth, muddy water, and broken trees did not seem to deter visitors. Before long, the new lake and its dam became minor sensations both in eastern Washington and to water engineers around the world.

Almost immediately, local adventurers came to the lake to witness raw wilderness and sample what was soon to become legendary fishing both in the lake and its tributaries. Irrigation professionals from around the world traveled the long route to Washington State and then up the winding roads to witness for themselves the little earthen dam that was proving its critics wrong by successfully holding back the massive weight of stored water behind it.

The Nelson's visitors included water engineers from India, the Philippines, South Africa, Canada, and China seeking first-hand information about impound dams and methods of water distribution. Giants in dam construction like John "Jack" Savage, who designed all the major dams of the West (Boulder/Hoover, Grand Coulee, and Shasta) and Frank Crowe who built Boulder and Shasta dams both visited. The "Father of Irrigation in the Northwest," Senator Wesley Jones, following his initial visit to check out the new dam, became a regular visitor and a treasured friend of the

Nelsons. In time, mayors of Seattle and governors of the state made their way to Jack and Kitty's door as well.[62]

Once the road was opened in the spring of 1912, the regular weekly stage made it easier for visitors to get to and from the lake. Kitty's daughter Frances rejoined her mother and stayed at the lake for much of the summer, as she would for the remainder of her childhood, making trips back and forth to town and hosting friends when they could visit.

Camp 22 remained occupied with a crew of men tasked with finishing work and cleanup at the dam, as well as repairs. The rock paving of the outlet works had washed away with the high spring flow and needed to be replaced.[63] Dick Darlington was still in residence as well, cooking for workers at least into 1915. Since attention by that time had largely shifted to the construction of the other dams in the Yakima Project, only men who could somehow be spared were sent up to Bumping Lake for clearing. The amount of timber on the lake bottom seemed to be interminable.[64]

The parade of visitors, not to mention the regular appearances of miners and trappers who stopped by during their travels in and out of the valley, quickly overwhelmed Kitty and Jack in their little, rough cabin. In response, the Nelsons started building a number of rental cabins near their house to accommodate guests. Less than a year after they arrived at the lake, the couple was already creating what Kitty would soon christen Nelson Lodge.[65]

In March of 1915, the federal Term Occupancy Act was passed, which allowed private development on public lands for the first time. Kitty immediately applied for permission to build a large lodge with a restaurant and overnight accommodations. When approval finally came in the fall, the fact that winter was fast approaching did not deter the commencement of construction.

On October 15th, the entire population of the valley at the time—fourteen people—came together, along with a team of horses supplied by miner Pete Cresci. The miners, prospectors and trappers proceeded to labor through rain, sleet, and snow for days. They worked without pay and claimed to be simply repaying some of the kindness that the Nelsons had extended to them.

In two weeks, they had a rough shell erected, and by necessity departed, promising to return at Christmas to strengthen the structure and continue construction. Unfortunately, nature intervened: heavy snow fell throughout November. So much tumbled from the leaden skies that the unfinished roof was overloaded.

On the eve of Thanksgiving, the entire building collapsed. Thirty feet of snow accumulated on top of the ruin until it became an indistinguishable bulge in the snowy landscape. Jack spent the idle hours of that long winter splitting cedar shakes and cutting new lumber for the lodge from a stand of lodgepole pines across the lake.[66]

In early spring, as the weather started to ease, the local crew of friends returned, accompanied by a light team of horses with burlap bags wrapped about their hooves to help them over the crusty snow. The second time around, now knowing the tremendous potential of snow load, they built a much more substantial building, complete with steel cables, that was described "as sturdy as a railroad bridge." [67] Without any engineered plans or substantive experience, they constructed a sixty by thirty-two-foot, two-story structure, huge for the area, into which the Nelsons welcomed guests for the next thirty-two years.

The next phase of Jack and Kitty's life at the lake had begun.

Chapter Five

UNCLE TOM AND OTHER MINERS

"Gold has been discovered near the road by Capt. McClellan's party. Also copper and brimstone, both in large quantities."
—*The Columbian*, October 1, 1853

"...Richer than the Klondike"
—*Yakima Herald*, January 25, 1900

"Everything present and nothing present in commercial quantities"
—Guggenheim Minerals Report
for Central Cascades, 1949

One of the men who most certainly helped to build the new lodge was already a treasured friend of Jack and Kitty's. Nearly twenty years before, Tom X. Fife[1] had settled in the big prairie three miles downstream from the lake, so he was well established there by the time the Nelsons arrived and became his first neighbors. He was a gregarious man and due to his charitable nature was no stranger to work parties. He would not have missed the opportunity to help out.

I had the pleasure of coming across Tom Fife—or at least his mark—several years ago, on a bright summer morning. My husband Tom and I had arrived early at the Goat Peak Trailhead to hike up to American Ridge. The dew was still beaded up on the vanilla leaf plants when we began, planning to make the long loop back to Normandie in one day.

This trail starts low and passes through a tangled clot of cedars whose long, bare, lower branches reach out like bony, gray fingers. Adjacent to the trailhead is Cougar Flats, open and grassy and one of the few places that we have observed a bear in all of our passages along the road there. The memory of its black bulk moved me more briskly up the trail and we settled into a good hiking rhythm. The trail soon rose in a series of switchbacks. Our breath came quicker but we pressed on, feeling at peace and grateful for our strong legs and lungs that carried us up through the forested landscape. We rounded another switchback, no different than the others, when I lifted my eyes and stopped short. If Tom had been behind me, he would have run into me like a cartoon character piling up in a sight gag.

In front of us was a silver monolith, towering towards the sky, a giant snag long dead, its limbs torn away by wind and weather, its bark gone too, only its heartwood left which was polished smooth with the passage of time. Across the middle of the trunk was slashed a giant "X" that wrapped from one side to the other at chest height. The tremendous wound had not killed the tree. The edges of the cuts were grown over, healed. This was clearly Fife's mark, his "blaze" that he chopped into trees along his winter trails, to signal the way when the snow lay deep on his paths.[2] Tom Fife was not a tall man but standing in front of this tree it was easy to see him here, feet braced as he swung his long-handled axe and sunk it into the thick bark. These were not tentative cuts like the polite Forest Service trail blazes of a short mark over a long one. They were like the man himself: strong and confident, a clear territorial message to all who might encroach upon his forest.

* * *

Tom Fife surely would have felt as if it were "his" forest for he and his father, John, were the first white men to settle in the Bumping River Valley. Tom Fife had immigrated to the United States from Fifeshire, Scotland in 1866 at the age of thirteen along with his step-brothers, Robert and Joseph. Soon after his arrival, he was working deep in the earth in Pennsylvania, mining coal with his father. After several years of back-breaking labor, they made their way west, stopping to ranch in Wyoming and to help build the Tabernacle in Salt Lake City while prospecting for "precious metals" on the side. By the time they arrived in Yakima in 1886, they were itching to get into the beckoning hills, especially into the American and Bumping River Valleys which they had heard might hold metal riches.

There being no trail at the time, they forded the Naches and then the Bumping River many times and finally rode into an open, grassy meadow protected by tall mountain ridges to the east and west. As soon as he saw this peaceful prairie, John, who was now in his 70s with a worn out, pain-wracked body, declared his wish to live out his life there. They continued no further and set about erecting a log cabin with the help of the saddle horses that had brought them there. It was just eight feet by ten feet with a fireplace at one end for heating and cooking. Not long after their arrival, a lone snow goose dropped from the sky and stayed long enough that Tom and his father named their new neighborhood after it: Goose Prairie.[3]

As soon as they were settled, Tom Fife started prospecting the nearby rivers, finding the upper American River the most promising.[4] The quartz ledges and free gold he located were in an area close to the crest of the Cascades near what much later became the Crystal Mountain Ski Resort.

A decade or so earlier, around 1875, Henry "Lew" Tucker and George Gibbs from Yakima had discovered placer gold there at the head of Morse Creek.[5] Before long, the placer gold was collected and the next round of miners started chasing promising looking ore into the ground. Around 1888, Tom's half-brother Robert, bought Tucker's claim and named it Elizabeth after his daughter. Tom Fife christened his claim, located on the head of Union Creek, Blue Bell, in honor of Scotland's national flower.[6]

"Uncle" Tom Fife strikes a heroic pose on the front porch of his original cabin which he built with his father in Goose Prairie in 1887. With him are Mrs. Pembroke Stice and Edith Cockrell. Fife's flair for publicity is already developing in this early photo which shows a prominent name plate over his front door. (Franklin Press, *We Never Got Away*, 1963)

In the winter, because the access trail was obliterated by snow, Fife got to and from the mine site by his tree blazes. He generally worked his claim all summer and fall staying until his supplies, or his strength ran out. Usually by December he would return to his tiny cabin in Goose Prairie.

When hopes were running particularly high, he had the help of other miners who were paid in stock.[7] In the early years, Fife followed a promising vein that inspired them all, but was increasingly difficult to access as it dove deeper into the mountainside. Work with dynamite, picks and shovels was slow and physically exhausting. Still, they bored over 600 feet by hand into the solid rock.

Near the end of one summer season, a miner on the night shift at Blue Bell uncovered a particularly rich streak of ore. Unable to open it up before winter set in, Fife suggested it be covered over so that others would not find it. Though he spent much of the next season looking, Fife never located that elusive ore again.[8]

Just below Blue Bell, Fife built an arrastra to crush the extracted ore. Developed in Mexico, the contraption was a circular rock trench with a pole in the center attached to an arm with a heavy boulder that was dragged through the trench, crushing the ore. Usually powered by a horse or ox, Fife's arrastra was water-powered with a large wooden wheel and a flume directing water into the attached cups. The pulverized mineral-bearing ore was then mixed with mercury which amalgamated with the metal leaving the worthless rock behind. In 1896, he milled ten tons of ore from the Blue Bell. It was assaying gold and silver at a respectable forty-nine dollars per ton.[9]

Other miners followed the Fifes and the number of claims in the area quickly multiplied. Before long, there were eighteen quartz claims bearing gold and silver and even some coal workings.[10] Claimants organized into the Summit Mining District about 1891 but the area was also referred to as Gold Hill or sometimes Rainier District.[11] As deposits were discovered and ore started to stockpile, excitement grew. Publicity was enthusiastic: "Richer than the Klondike" and "A Proven Mountain of Riches" were headlines—and the rush was on.[12]

In the midst of all this activity, Tom's father John became ill. Despite dedicated care by Tom and some Naches Valley neighbors, he succumbed to "dropsy" (probably congestive heart failure) in 1890. Tom built the coffin out of larch boards and with Valley neighbors' help, laid him to rest, along with his favorite hat, in a little plot nearby. Tom was now alone, living in his modest cabin on the Prairie.

If anyone could live well, completely alone in that remote river valley, it was Tom Fife. He was like most pioneers, extremely hard working and resourceful, independent, and seemingly immune to any need for personal comfort. He was motivated by the hunt for buried treasure and had the optimism every miner needs to see himself through another day of elusive pursuit, but he also was in love with the outdoors. He was curious about the plants and animals in the area. Many times, on a jaunt with Jack Nelson, the two would pause to examine some small plant and Fife would share with the younger man his appreciation of the finer details of the tender herb. He enjoyed living in the mountains and loved his prairie, "with all the love a man is able to bestow on land." [13]

Access to the Fife's mines was still via a narrow foot trail and without heavy equipment available, mining was limited to hand work. With the Gold Hill miners actively agitating the state for a wagon road to the Cascade summit, two cities started vying to build that road, and thus benefit from the traffic that was sure to follow the riches coming from the mines. Both Yakima on the east side and Enumclaw (and also neighboring city Buckley) on the west side loudly proclaimed their intentions to quickly put in a road to access the mines.[14] Unfortunately, state funds for construction did not follow so the miners, in desperation, finally "scratched out" a road themselves to get much needed equipment to their mines. This road started at the junction of the American and Bumping Rivers (where the Reclamation Service's road to the new dam turned south), ran west to Morse Creek and from there up to the crest. The miners' road became the first and only access up to the Chinook Pass area for the next twenty years.[15]

The road, as terribly primitive as it was, allowed the bigger equipment to be packed in and resulted in the expansion of the district. Fife got a stamp mill erected below the Blue Bell in Cement Basin but only after raising capital by the sale of stock—at five cents a share—in his newly incorporated mining company.[16]

Tom's brother Robert (Bob) joined Frank X. Nagler and incorporated the Elizabeth Gold Hill Mining Company in 1907. The Summit Mining District eventually totaled hundreds of claims (Robert Fife bragged of 1,000 claims in 1898 newspaper article, but a more realistic number was around 250 total claims) and at the turn of the century the area was home to over 300 miners. For a time, one of the few woman miners in

Washington, Emily "Little Dot" Knight lived and worked in the Summit District.[17]

Despite continuous hyped press, inflated valuations—$118,810,000 dollars by mining engineer Frederick P. Sanford in 1910—sporadic rich strikes and enough equipment to mill the ore, the material coming out of the mines just wasn't valuable enough to justify the cost of getting it transported all the way to the nearest smelter in Tacoma.[18] Mastodon, Comet, Neptune, Ophir, Silver Reef, Warrior's Mask, Blazing Star, Terror, White Elephant, and Little Gem all flamed out. The Fifes hung on, but interest in the district began to fade. Most of the other hard-working miners moved on, one by one, to more promising hills—including those that rose up from little Bumping Lake.[19]

Tom never lost hope in his Blue Bell, but he did move downstream and busied himself with other activities to make just enough money to get by. He logged for some time down on the Rattlesnake where he purchased some railroad land and continued to help newcomers put up their homes. During construction of the Bumping Lake Dam, Tom leased out the entire prairie to a butcher contracted to supply fresh meat to the workmen at Camp 22, asking only for a fence around the land as payment.[20]

After nearly thirty years in harsh conditions, Fife's little cabin in the Prairie was wearing out and he decided he needed to replace it. Around 1915, he took down the necessary trees, cut, and prepared the logs for his new home. Jack Nelson and Richard "Dick" Ball showed up on the appointed day and found the materials so well prepared that they erected the cabin in a single day. The building still stands.

When World War I broke out, Fife, being extremely patriotic to his adopted country, was anxious to join up. When he was turned away by the enlisting officer in Yakima, he assumed that it was because of his teeth (he had only six at this point) rather than his age—sixty-five. Upon his rejection it is reported he said he "wanted to *fight* the Germans, not *bite* them!" So strong were his feelings for the United States that somehow, he obtained a uniform-like khaki shirt and trousers which he would wear with great pride for special occasions. Just after the war, "Uncle" Tom, as he was now known by, finally came up with a plan to give back to his country in a meaningful way.

The Boy Scout movement was developing in Yakima Valley about the same time that Uncle Tom was pondering the future of his 150 acre homestead in Goose Prairie.[21] One day it came to him, and he ran to the lake and tearfully shared his brainstorm with Jack. He would give ten acres of his land to the Boy Scouts for a permanent summer camp. Camp Fife was born from that gift.[22]

In the summer of 1924, troops first gathered on their new plot of land which was "remote and perfect for a troop of husky scouts who like to swim, fish, hunt and make a lot of noise." [23] By July of 1925, the Yakima Lions Club had built for the fledgling camp a large cabin consisting of a kitchen, dining room, first aid room, office and a canteen. The boys slept in tents equipped with steel beds and mattresses but needed to bring their own bedding. Fresh meat and vegetables were delivered daily as was "an abundance" of milk from a dairy down the valley. Mountain spring water was piped from its source directly into the kitchen.

An account of the day's schedule at Camp Fife seems to be written to reassure readers that scouts would not be let loose to run wild in their feral setting:

> "The boys get up at six o'clock every morning and the first thing on the roster for the day is morning exercise. When this is over the boys wash for breakfast. After the morning meal the boys spend a hour on fatigue duty, an army term for cleaning up around the cabin and tents. Then comes three hours of scout training. Noon mess is then served, after which there is a quiet period for one hour. The afternoon is devoted to recreation, which generally takes the form of swimming, boating or games of different sorts. When going boating or swimming the boys are also accompaied by either the scout director, Leon Folsom, or some of his assistants. The evening is spent around the scout council fire, where stories of scout lore are told or scout songs are sung." [24]

All boys were welcome, scouts or not. The charge was $7.50 for the two week session, including transportation.[25]

The Yakima Boy Scouts received a legacy Christmas gift in 1929 of five acres of land adjacent to Camp Fife. Fred Shaw, president of the boy scout council, made the presentation of the deed which increased the camp tract to fifteen acres.[26]

The next addition to Camp Fife was a lodge. The structure would be built from trees cut on the site and though construction began in 1933, three summers would pass before it was complete. In 1935, leftover lumber from some nearby road construction was donated to the project. The lodge's dedication celebration on June 28, 1936, was opened by Walter S. Gallant, director the construction and Scout leader Curtis Gilbert. Selections from the Yakima Drum and Bugle Corps were heard. To accommodate the 115 scouts and leaders who were in attendance for the dedication ceremony, the Boy Scouts borrowed beds from the Nelsons' resort.[27]

In 1937, Kitty sold her adjacent five acres in Goose Prairie to the Simcoe Boy Scout Council for $400 dollars and in 1958, Jack did too (twenty-four acres for $14,250 dollars) allowing Camp Fife to expand many times over. Ira Ford was hired to take care of the camp in 1951 for an annual salary of one hundred dollars. In 1963, a new larger lodge was rebuilt around the original lodge fireplace after the original structure was destroyed by fire.[29] That building then became the Trading Post when a third, even larger lodge supplanted it in 2004. In time, Camp Fife boasted a heated swimming pool, horseback riding, boating, a shooting and archery range, a ropes course, climbing wall, and for a short time its own lake.[30]

Fife's generosity to others—despite his own needs—never flagged. A story that was often told about him was an occasion in which Fife needed a new pair of shoes or boots. He made his way to Yakima, fifty miles from Goose Prairie, purchased the new footwear and started for home. He got a ride to John Anderson's ranch, still twenty miles downriver and from there continued on foot. Halfway home he saw a group of miners heading down from the hills, one of them limping badly. Recognizing that the man's shoes were as worn out as the ones he had just discarded, Fife sat down and removed his brand-new shoes. The stranger protested, but Fife insisted, telling him he had many more pairs—just as good—back home at Goose Prairie.

In fact, Fife seemed almost obsessive about helping others with never a thought for compensation. It became impossible for him to pass by building projects without lending a hand. Fortunately, even when he was older, he was a strong and capable man, or his efforts might have been unappreciated. Instead, many fine homesteads along the Valley road bore the mark of Fife's helping hand. Jack said simply. "Tom had a heart as big as a frying pan."[31]

Even though he was not a large man, standing just five feet seven inches tall, over time, Fife earned the reputation as an omnivorous and voracious eater. Kitty related stuffing and baking a seven-and-a-half-pound Dolly Varden trout for guests at the lodge. Fife ate the entire fish before she had a chance to serve it to the others. When in Yakima, he reportedly would regularly order a dozen fried eggs, a dozen boiled eggs, and "ham to match." Once Fife spied his friend Frank Case's morning collection of eggs. Quipping that he could eat the entire pail full, Case offered it to him. He took the bucket to the local restaurant in Naches and had the cook fry up all forty eggs, which to the amazement of his fellow diners, he ate in one sitting. Another well-known gastronomic achievement involved the consumption of a nuisance bear that a ranger had killed. Fife and one of the Case boys polished it off in three days.[32]

In July of 1922, at the age of sixty-nine, Tom Fife suffered a serious stroke that left him unable to speak.[33] For such a sociable man this handicap was a crippling blow, and one from which he never recovered. Mrs. Margaret Carmack, his neighbor near Rattlesnake Creek, nursed him back to some semblance of health, but in the second week of November he was found in his cabin mortally wounded by a self-inflicted gunshot.[34]

Friends for miles converged in Naches for his service after which his body was driven up to Goose Prairie accompanied by district forest ranger Harry Croxford. Children from the nearby Rattlesnake School had been dismissed for his service, and as the funeral procession passed by the schoolhouse, they dropped flowers along the route in memory of him.[35] He was buried next to his father in the tiny cemetery in Goose Prairie, just as a snowstorm blew in. The old mountain man was dressed in his treasured khaki uniform which he had saved for the occasion.[36]

Tom Fife in his khaki uniform that he wore on special occasions.
Photo dates from the late teens or early 1920s. (Courtesy of Gretta
Gossett Gregg)

Yakima journalist Patty Rose memorialized Fife well when she
wrote that he lived the Boy Scout credo and "…was dedicated to service for

others, asking nothing in return. His philosophy, as well as his life should be a great example to us all." [37]

At the time that Kitty was trying to get her lodge built, events in distant Europe were sending out shockwaves across the Atlantic, the continental United States, and up the Bumping River Valley. By 1915, the Allies of WWI were dismayed to discover that, despite a dearth of all known resources, Germany was producing munitions thanks to their use of a previously overlooked and discarded metal, tungsten. For years, the British had been selling this by-product of tin mining to Germany, happy to get rid of it. Germany was just as happily mixing it with carbon to create tungsten-carbide. Tungsten-carbide was a miracle material, so tremendously hard that it doubled the efficiency of steel armor and shells, made barrels that could fire them, and high-speed tools that could fashion these superior weapons. Suddenly, the rest of the world wanted tungsten too, global production surged, and the price shot up.

In 1915, Dick Ball, who had been prospecting and working mines in the Bumping Lake drainage since 1905, announced the discovery of "rich tungsten ore" up on Nelson Ridge, just east of Bumping Lake.[38] Ball, known locally as Paul Bunyan for his prodigious physical abilities, had owned a dairy farm in the Nile Valley and worked for Lum as crew foreman cutting the first river road at Horseshoe Bend. In 1905 he sold out, preferring mining to cows, and moved up to the mountains.

Upon his tungsten discovery he formed the Ball Mining Company with Jim Simmons and other partners. In their search for heavy equipment, they purchased from the Reclamation Service the old donkey steam engine that had helped build the dam at the lake. Now they could start digging in earnest.[39] The mining complex became known as Keystone. Such was the value and demand for tungsten that the miners planned on working all winter. But the same weather that destroyed the first version of the Nelsons' lodge was to impact Ball's early mining efforts as well.

Snow started falling early in the autumn of 1915 and by mid-November was deep enough that supply wagons heading to Ball's mine bogged down on Bumping Lake Road, just three miles above the American River junction. The drivers, Jack Robillard and Johnnie Martin, both experienced freighters from Naches, unhitched the team from one wagon and doubled up on the first wagon so that a total of eight horses strained to pull the heavy load forward. With Martin walking ahead, the wagon started across the shale-rock slide area but at the same moment the steep snow slope above broke loose and swept the horses, wagon and Robillard toward the river. The wagon overturned on the bank, but the horses were caught in the icy current with one killed immediately. Both men jumped into the river to cut the horses from their tangled harnesses. As Robillard labored to free the last horse, Martin collapsed on the bank, apparently of a heart attack. Despite Robillard's strenuous efforts to revive him, Martin never regained consciousness.[40]

Robillard then mounted the one horse remaining on the scene (the other horses upon being released from their harnesses backtracked to a trappers' cabin and stable on the American where they had spent the previous night) and returned to the trappers' cabin. Leaving an exhausted Robillard tucked in bed, the three trappers went out into the dark night to retrieve Martin's body. From the Nelsons' halfway house, they used the telephone to call Jack and Kitty to tell them of the accident. Jack then needed to inform Ball and the other six miners up at the mine, but weather again thwarted them. A furious storm had moved in and pinned Jack and Kitty down.

Finally at two o'clock in the morning the storm abated. At three a.m., they set off for the mine, each using a "bug" or Palouser[41] to light their way. It took Jack and Kitty three long hours to push through the three miles of deep snow to the cabins below the mine and deliver the terrible news. The miners returned with Jack and Kitty on improvised snowshoes made of cedar shakes and spent the next day at the lodge making seven pairs of skis for them all to ski out on. Their winter's mining was over.[42]

Their determination to get back to work was so great that in March, Ball returned with five of the same men to resume mining. This time they handled their own supplies, which was an immense undertaking. First, they freighted them in five miles to Goose Prairie where they were renting Tom Fife's cabin. They then shuttled the goods to the Government warehouse near the end of the dam (leftover from construction) and from there—because there was still so much snow on the ground—they loaded sleds which they hauled three miles up to the lower cabins.

That was the easy part.

Next, the material was loaded into backpacks and packed straight up, 1,200 feet, to the upper cabins and the mines. One can only imagine how many trips that must have taken, up and down the steep foot trail. But because the calendar read only March and the mine was located up a mountainside at some 4,500 feet in elevation, the winter's snowpack was still deep at the site. To expose the mine, four men—using a crosscut saw—carved out large blocks of the compressed snow that they then heaved out over the cliff's edge.

As is characteristic with most steep mountainsides in the spring, slides were common. Alert to these dangers, two men were posted as look outs to warn the men on the saw of the slides. Suddenly the lookouts shouted as an avalanche started, but Joe Stillwell, one of the saw men, was swept away, along with the saw, and carried all the way down the mountain. When the others reached him, he was unconscious with a tremendous head wound from the saw, which had come to rest beside him.

A runner was sent to the Lake to summon Jack. Jack could do no more for the patient than dress his wound and help sled him back to the Lake and the shelter of the Nelson's lodge. Supplies were gathered there, and the nearest doctor notified. At four in the morning Jack and the miners departed to deliver Stillwell to medical care at the Anderson's ranch, twenty-three miles away. The doctor was waiting for them when they arrived at 9:30 in the evening but could do nothing for the man. He died three hours later.

In July 1916, Yakima newspapers reported that Alfred Simmons had brought a ton of tungsten ore down to North Yakima for the Ball Mining Company.[43] But even that was not an easy trip by wagon due to the previous winter's snows and subsequent spring floods that left the roads nearly impassable. At least one bridge along the route had been washed away and Ball reported that he had to use dynamite to clear log jams on the Bumping River and slides on the road to get his wagon through.[44]

It is unclear how much tungsten was ultimately brought down to the smelter. Documents show that in 1917, additional funds were spent to increase the length of the tunnels and to construct more buildings including an ore mill. Ultimately, over $30,000 were spent on the claim, but eventually the meager veins petered out as they were chased into the earth, and work ended.[45]

Ball later worked for the Forest Service and the State Highway Department and died in an accident while working on the Rattlesnake Bridge in 1923.

Despite disasters, inclement weather, and challenging access, interest in the remote Bumping River Valley continued to grow. In 1913, twenty-two mine owners met in Yakima to organize into the Bumping Lake Mining District. The name would give the area an identity, facilitate promotion and enable the group to secure a governmental geologic survey.[46]

Some of the miners may have originally come into the area searching for the legendary Zockseye's Lode,[47] but many were following enthusiastic reports from others already digging in the ground. Miner Richard McCaffey "Bacon Rind Dick", so named because of his thin stature (Question: "Where is you Dick?" Answer: "Here I is, behind the whip!") came from Butte, Montana and established a mine high on the slopes above Deep Creek. His small cabin was said to have had as its door an opening as short and narrow as he was.

The Nelsons loved to have McCaffey for Sunday dinner but wondered if the bird like portions he consumed were worth the five-mile trek off the mountain and down to their home. Dick entertained with stories of his youth as a jockey and when asked about his weight—never more than ninety-eight pounds—replied that he had a brother who was taller but not quite so "heavy-set." He wintered down in Naches and once, during a baby contest, was voted second prize baby.[48]

Another determined miner in the district was William "Billy" C. Richmond. Richmond had survived a pioneering boat passage through the Grand Canyon before he found his way to the Bumping Lake area.[49] Richmond had made a lucrative placer gold claim up the Rattlesnake drainage which he had located while herding sheep. The profits from that find financed the development of a sizeable strike at the crest of Nelson Ridge near the headwaters of the North Fork of the Rattlesnake.

William Chesley Richmond made a pioneering decent by boat down the Grand Canyon in 1896 before he turned up in the Naches and Bumping River Valleys some twenty years later prospecting for precious metals. He found modest success on the Rattlesnake and then developed the Richmond Mine on Richmond Lake, just over the crest of Nelson Ridge. (photo source unknown)

"Richmond Mine" contained an alphabet soup of minerals: cop-
per, gold, lead, silver, and zinc. However, it required a heroic effort to get
there. Richmond cut an access road from the Bumping River Road, at
Bumping Crossing, up to the summit, which climbed 3,100 feet in less
than two miles. At some point a catastrophic fire took out his mine buildings and shorings, but such was his commitment that he and his miners
continued working on the rock face hanging by ropes.

Several men from Italy made their way into the Bumping River
Valley by way of the coal mines in Roslyn and stayed long enough to
leave their mark on the mining community. John "Joe" Crosetti, originally from Genoa, is said to have helped develop the first coal mine
in Roslyn. He built several businesses there (two saloons, a bakery, and
a butcher shop), got married, and soon had a son. But when his wife,
Margherita, died at just twenty years old and left him with an infant son,
he abruptly sold all of his holdings and left Roslyn.

With baby Victor, Crosetti drifted south and ended up moving
into Dick Ball's old cabin on the banks of Deep Creek just above the
falls.[50] In association with Pat Mullins of Yakima and William Carmack
of the Nile, he developed a molybdenum mine on the slope above the
river and worked it for many years. The claim was later sold to Charles
Huey.[51] The ore pulled from that hole was hand sorted and brought out
on horseback by Tom Fife. The first shipment, totaling five tons, netted
fifty-five dollars per ton at the Tacoma smelter. John and his brother
Frank prized good food and made their own beer and wine (from dan-
delions and elderberries). John also loved to cook with mushrooms and
collected many varieties all over the area. When the crop was especially
abundant, he dried the extra, happily sharing with anyone who would
use them.[52]

Frank Crosetti built a robust cabin just a half a mile above his
brother John's on the Deep Creek trail which stood for many years until it
succumbed to winter snows. Frank was beloved in the community because
of his work ethic. He was said to have hand dug a well in Goose Prairie "just
like a gopher" and though he was a small man, he would regularly do the
work of two or three when he showed up to help clear the Bumping River
Road of snow every spring.

John Crosetti (left) and Ruben Root work on a ponderosa at Cougar Flats near the Bumping River Road. Crosetti was born in Genoa, Italy and was a lover of wild mushrooms, homemade wine, and good conversation. Root promoted Copper City as a great mining center for many years. (Courtesy of Gretta Gossett Gregg)

Peter Cresci was also from Genoa. After immigrating to the United States in 1876, he mined in New York, Pennsylvania, and Michigan before making his way to the new coal mines in Roslyn. He would have joined a substantial Italian population already there. After a year or so, he left Roslyn and established a homestead and timber claim near present day Grandview and got married. But like his friend John Crosetti, Cresci's young wife Mary died soon after giving birth to their first son. The boy, also named Victor, was left motherless at just eleven days old. Though Cresci labored on his farm and taught young Victor how to ranch, mining never left his blood. He spent many seasons in the Bumping Lake District, at one point working a molybdenum claim not far from Crosetti's mine.[53]

Peter Bertoglio was another friend of John's who lived and worked with him in the Bumping Lake mines. His nickname, Six-Fingered Pete, was perfectly descriptive; unlike many with extra digits, Pete had perfect control of all his fingers as well as his extra two toes. He apparently put his extra fingers to good use, as he was known as a master blacksmith who turned out miracles from his primitive forge. Ever resourceful, he made his own charcoal for the forge in a homemade oven and crafted footwear for his fellow miners. It seems that their leather shoes rotted almost immediately in the wet tunnels, so Pete set about fashioning a machine out of cast-off pieces of iron that turned out wooden shoes.[54]

There is little known about the molybdenum claims where Cresci worked, but they briefly received enthusiastic press attention in 1929. Assays conducted by a respected mining expert returned as much as fifty-five percent high grade molybdenum equaling almost $20,000 dollars per ton. The reports created a lot of local excitement. Edwin Fitch and Fred Parker incorporated the Molybdenum Mines Company to develop what was thought to be perhaps the largest and richest deposits of that mineral in the country.[55] The promise was so great that by September the company had filed for water rights on Deep Creek to remove enough water at the falls to run a large power plant to operate mining equipment.[56] Activity continued into 1932 but there is little additional mention of the site after that year. Like most of the rest of mineral discoveries in the region, this deposit was not to become what was hoped of it. The ore, no matter how rich, was of limited quantity and only a small amount was recovered.[57] Whatever physical remnants of these workings remain have long since been enveloped by the forest.

In these most remote settlements, law and order was maintained by the simplest means. Once, when a miner at Morse Creek queried another asking where his claim signs were posted, the prospector pulled out his gun and said, "Here's the sign." Similarly, when uranium was discovered near Deep Creek, the American River Resort was awash with guns as would-be miners swarmed into the Bumping River Valley.[58]

What sustained interest in the Bumping District was the wide variety of minerals being encountered, not in large or easily accessible quantities, but just enough to keep up the hopes of the prospectors and miners, the eternal optimists. Anthracite, copper, zinc, lead, gold (trace), silver, molybdenum, nickel, cobalt, tungsten, antimony, amorphous graphite and even sapphires were found in the ground in and around the valley.[59] Names were promptly bestowed on even the thinnest discoveries, sometimes descriptive, sometimes nostalgic, oftentimes hopeful. Lucky Day and King

Solomon above Copper City, Black Jack (Black Jack was the nickname for zinc) just below Twin Sisters Lakes, Ivanhoe in the Mosquito Valley, The Sure Thing at Keystone above Bumping Lake, The 17th of Ireland above Granite Lake with its arrastra, and Whistlin' Jack Mine near Copper Creek were just a few of the mines being developed in the neighborhood at the time. It seemed that mines were everywhere and that there would be no end to the mineral wealth that could be wrested from the rocky ground.

❦ ❦ ❦

On the Fourth of July, in the mid-1990s, Tom and I made the acquaintance of one of the very last of a long line of miners inhabiting and working the mountainside at Copper City. This small ghost town, ten miles south of the Lake, was once the most substantial mining operation in the Bumping Lake District, but by the close of the twentieth century was a forlorn collection of tumbled down buildings that were steadily composting back to earth. We, with some friends, had hiked in to see the ruins of the old bunkhouse and stamp mill and to picnic on the meadow that offered a great view of Nelson Ridge to the east. At that time, the road up to the site was hardly suitable for even jeeps so we were surprised to see a battered Toyota Corolla parked well up the trail. Next to it was a grizzled man with a big belly who introduced himself as Hans. He said he lived there—at his mine. This statement surprised us, but he certainly looked the part with a long beard, checked shirt, suspenders, blue jeans, and battered work boots. His nearby companion fit in as well: a huge Malamute sporting a red bandana tied around his massive neck.

"This is Benjamin Franklin," he announced as if introducing another person to us. "He is a wolf and wears this kerchief so that he won't be accidentally shot." We looked at the dog again but who were we to argue with a mountain man we had just met? When he started telling us about his pet bear Chrissy which he had saved when he removed an arrow from it and that he could summon with a whistle, we knew he was crazy.

There are different kinds of crazy however, and Hans seemed earnest crazy: friendly, not scary crazy, which is why I suppose we agreed to follow him up the side of the mountain to his mining camp. I was intent on obtaining historical information and we all were curious about his mine.

We straggled behind him on a barely perceptible game trail that went almost straight up the mountain. He cautioned us to step aside here and there to avoid quicksand pits and directed us around invisible booby traps that supposedly protected the path. We were advised to stop with him at prede-termined points to let our bodies adjust to the altitude, in particular to keep our ears from bleeding—all survival techniques that he learned in Vietnam.

The last part of the track cut across a huge, moss covered tailing pile, the blasted rock evidence of a substantial mine from long ago. The camp that greeted us at the end of the trail with multiple tents and ample mining equipment was impressive given the physical condition of the man who was responsible for its construction.

Hans claimed to be a geologist working for a natural resource com-pany involved in exotic metals. He had filed a mining claim on a long-aban-doned site to extract rhodium that he believed remained in the old mine. To do so he had to first reopen the original shaft that had been filled in due to the actions of a creek that ran down the mountain into the entrance. Somehow, alone, he had located the entrance, dug out a huge amount of rock and debris and built new wood supports so that the mine was com-pletely accessible again. Above the opening was tacked an old peeling sign that read "Xenolith." For his comfort, Hans had built an extensive camp that included a roomy sleeping tent in addition to a huge cook tent com-plete with running water courtesy of the creek from the mine. His mining equipment and tools were neatly organized at the mine opening.

Hans encouraged us to check out the mine, which was a wet, black, foreboding hole plunging into the steep mountainside. He further piqued our curiosity improbably claiming that we could find a small hole at the very end of the tunnel from which all manner of water sounds could be heard. Foolishly putting all good sense and caution aside, we all volunteered to go first.

The inside of the mine was unbelievable: like a manufactured Disneyland attraction with an arched ceiling blasted out of solid rock and a gently sloping floor smoothed with fine sand. The tunnel curved away into blackness that the dim light of Hans' lantern could not penetrate. Clearly, we were heading to the center of the earth.

We shuffled cautiously along and encountered narrow gage rails on which a hand cart once rolled on its way to empty the shaft of rock debris and it was hoped, valuable ore. The tunnel seemed to stretch on forever, but it couldn't have been more than a quarter of a mile. When we did reach the end, the wall contained, just as Hans had claimed, a small round hole, at head height. We each in turn put an ear up to the opening and heard to our utter surprise, the sound of a mighty underground waterfall. To me, it sounded as if the torrent was crashing through a space the size of a football stadium.

It is fortunate that Hans did not start ranting about the plight of American POWs or the wife he left behind in Vietnam until *after* we had returned to sunlight, or we might not have ever dared to go in. The discovery of a black assault rifle and his sharing of ever more fantastic stories about giant crystals and even skeletons—of both a cowboy and an Indian—in nearby caves hastened our polite goodbyes. Promising to see him again we hurriedly-cautiously wound our way back down the trail past all the traps and back to the relative safety of the Copper City meadow.

A few days later we returned and prospected with Hans for "platinum" next to Deep Creek which on later inspection proved to be nice pieces of flake graphite. We waved hello a few more times in passing but we never saw Hans again after that summer.

Worse for history was that several years later during a mid-winter thaw, the little creek that dribbled down the opening of the mine turned into a cascade. The deluge completely washed away not only the front of the tunnel but cut in two the massive tailing pile on which Hans had built his camp. Boulders now completely occlude the mine entrance, and it is nearly impossible to tell that there ever was an opening there. Nature wins. Where Hans went, we will never know, but I'm pretty sure he is, and will continue to be, the last of the Copper City miners.

The *first* Copper City miner was James T. "Cap" Simmons who came across some intriguing blue-green ore when he was salting cattle for the Yakima Cattle Company.[60] It was 1899 and he was tromping around the mountains south of Bumping Lake. As one of the first miners in the Summit Mining District and knowing something about colored rock, Cap had the material assayed which showed returns of copper and tungsten.

John Crosetti was a close friend of the Nelsons from the time he arrived in the Bumping River Valley from Roslyn, Washington until he died in 1950. In this March 1927 photograph, "Joe" is standing in front of the original Bumping Lake Lodge. The frames of the tent cabins along the lakeshore show behind him. (Courtesy of the Richardson family)

Cap then turned his findings over to his son A.B. "Bud" Simmons who incorporated as the Copper City Mining Company. In 1905, Bud sold his shares for a tidy sum of $700 dollars to Ruben Root who added these holdings to his own Clara claim nearby. Wholly committed to his new enterprise, Root soon set about extending the Reclamation road seven miles from the new Bumping dam, south to his "Copper City" mining center. In addition to all the clearing and grading, he had to build at least one bridge and cover the low, swampy areas with corduroy. It was a monumental undertaking but without a road, he could not expand.[61]

Root was a brilliant, tireless, and effective promoter who truly and fully believed in the potential of the area and thanks to those qualities he quickly obtained substantial capital for machinery by selling shares in his claim. In 1907, following the blueprint from the Summit Mining Company nearby, he incorporated with other claim holders with the not very original name of Summit Copper Mining Company.[62]

Soon William Carmack along with Pat Mullen, and Manley Dunham filed the nearby Redbird and Bluebird claims, respectively. A great deal of interest was subsequently generated by the Redbird mine when it produced very promising early returns. John Crosetti, his son Victor, Pete Cresci, and Pete Bertoglio all quickly got involved. They built a cabin and spent the winter mining and stockpiling hand sorted ore. In the spring, William Carmack's twelve-year-old son Ralph packed five tons of ore concentrate by horseback thirteen miles down to Goose Prairie where Tom Fife was waiting to haul it to the railroad in Naches. The returns came in at a respectable $55 dollars per ton.

Before long, there were forty-two active claims in the Copper City area. It seems no one was immune to the fever, as an early map shows that even Kitty got in on the action, filing a claim just adjacent to Copper City on Deep Creek.

The steady influx of money, machinery and men into the area was impressive but the ultimate success of the entire operation was based on two premises, both fervently believed in by Root and both unfortunately, flawed. The two critical ingredients were the production of paying ore and a railroad line to the site. The miners got right to the ore part, immediately blasting adits and working feverishly right through the winter to pull mineral laced ore out of the mountainside.

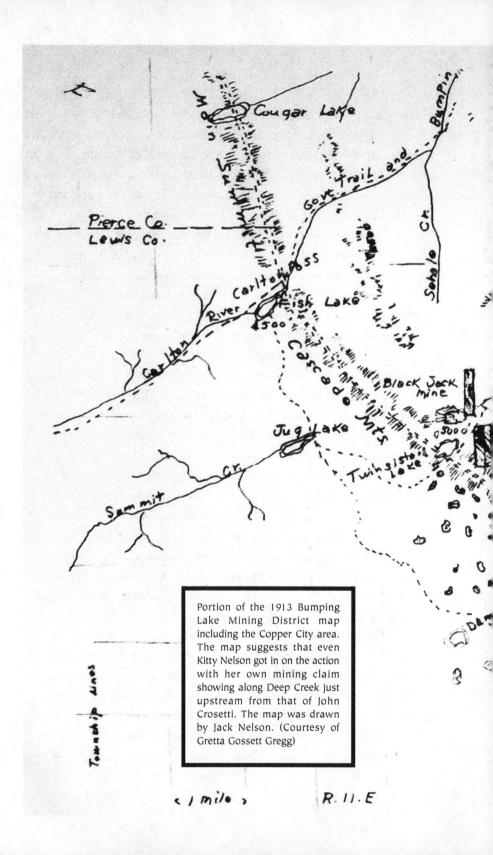

W

Cougar Lake

Bumpin

Gov't Trail and

Pierce Co.
Lewis Co.

Sehala Cr.

Carlton Pass
Fish Lake

River

500

Carlton

Cascade Mts.

Black Jack
mine

Jug Lake

5000

Twin sisters lake

Summit Cr.

Portion of the 1913 Bumping Lake Mining District map including the Copper City area. The map suggests that even Kitty Nelson got in on the action with her own mining claim showing along Deep Creek just upstream from that of John Crosetti. The map was drawn by Jack Nelson. (Courtesy of Gretta Gossett Gregg)

Township lines

‹ 1 mile ›

R. 11. E

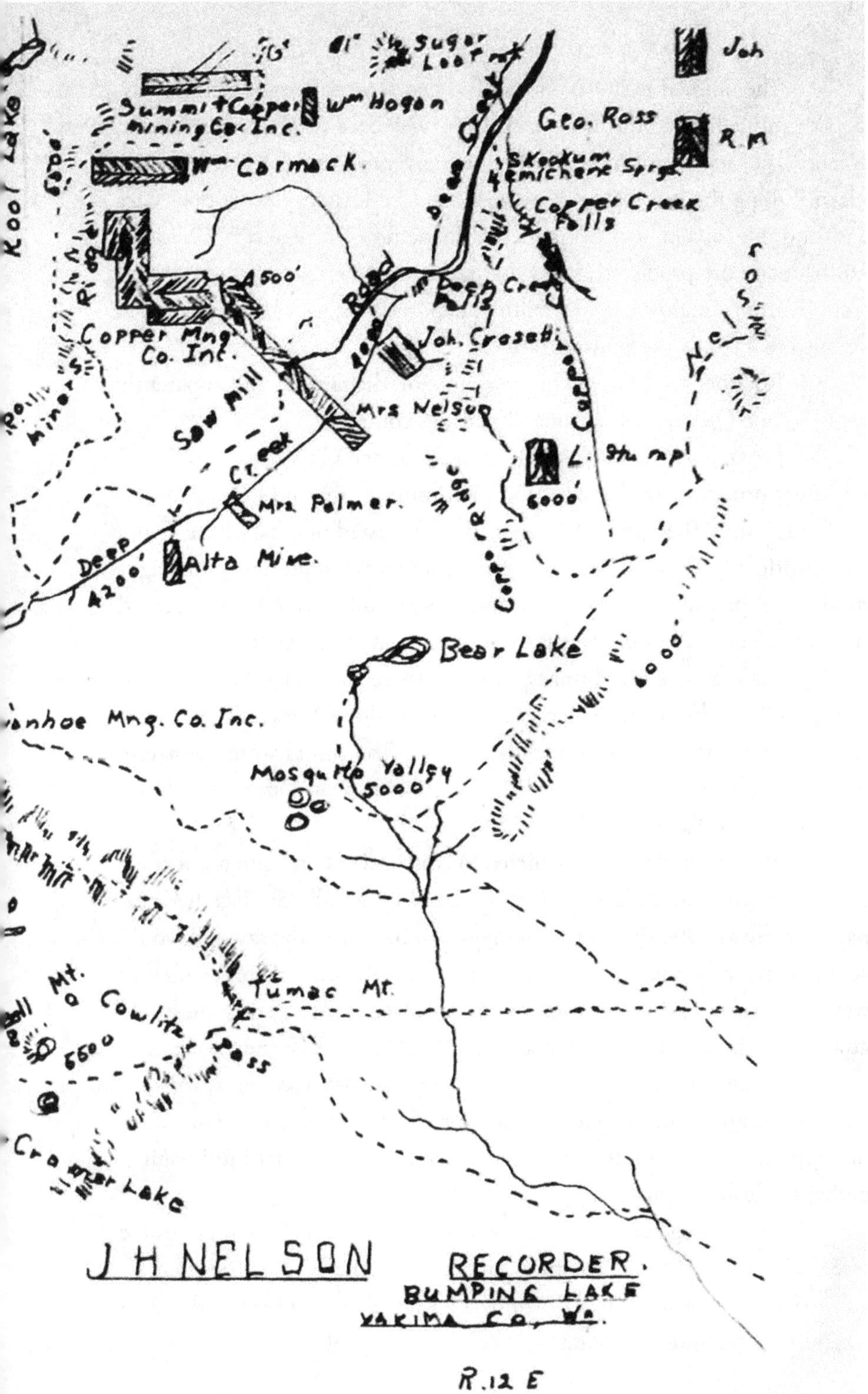

Kootinie Lake

Sugar Loaf mt.

Joh

Summit Copper mining Co. Inc.

Wm Hogan

Geo. Ross

R.M

Wm Cormack

Skookum emichene Sprs.

Copper Creek Falls

4500'

Rock Creek

Copper Mng Co. Inc.

Joh. Crosetti

Saw Mill

Mrs Nelson

Creek

L 9thump!

6000

Mrs Palmer.

Deep 4200'

Alta Mine.

Copper Ridge

Nelson

Bear Lake

6000

nhoe Mng. Co. Inc.

Mosquito Valley 5000

Mt. Cowlitz Pass

Tumac Mt.

6500

Cramer Lake

J H NELSON   RECORDER.
BUMPING LAKE
YAKIMA CO, Wa.

R. 12 E

The railroad part was trickier but necessary to economically transport the mined ore to the Tacoma smelter. Way back in 1892, the Yakima, Nachez [sic] and Eastern Railway Company proposed a spur line from Naches along the Bumping River, up Deep Creek right past Copper City and into the nascent coal fields on the divide near Fish Lake.[63] Without a railroad, any ore produced had to be packed by horseback (later trucked) from the mill site down to the railroad depot at Naches where it was then shipped to Tacoma via Stampede Pass.

Root bet the future of his enterprise on the railroad and apparently never stopped believing that the railroad was coming.[64]

Because of Root's cheerleading, Copper City soon developed into busy mining complex with an upper mining area and lower processing compound. The upper "Clara" section consisted of most of the mines along with at least one large cabin and a cookhouse, built next to a bright meadow. Piped-in running water and a well-built septic system served the camp. The cookhouse was looked after by at least one full-time cook serving hot meals to the hungry miners. There may have been a small stamp mill nearby. To the west and higher up along Miners Ridge, were the dark entrances to the mines themselves. The mines were colorfully named here as well: Sunset, Red Bird, Garibaldi, Iron Door, New Find, King Solomon, Pasco.[65]

The first building constructed for the lower "City" site was a combination sawmill and blacksmith shop. Built by Josiah "Si" Fletcher perhaps as early as 1906, it was in full operation by 1915. The sawmill would supply lumber for the buildings and timbers for the mines. Following that was a two-story bunkhouse that boasted an unusual two-story outhouse attached to the rear of the building for use even in the deep snows of winter when the miners were still in residence. There was also a second story winter entrance above the one on the first floor. The bunkhouse had a dirt floor but apparently had running water and, even though it is hard to imagine, perhaps a flushing spittoon.[66]

Food refrigeration of sorts was provided by a three-foot square screened wooden box affixed to a large stump. The box was covered by gunny sacks that were wetted down by a trickle of water piped to the contraption. As the water evaporated, it kept the box cool.

The bunkhouse at Copper City in the 1920s. The structure's second story entrance was particularly useful in the deep snows of winter. Several unknowns persist in this view including the purpose of the vehicle parked in front and the function of the boxed watercourse running from the building to the right. (Courtesy of the United States Forest Service, Naches Ranger District)

Completing Copper City was an assay office, foreman's quarters, cook's shack (also with a dirt floor), and a house for the engineer that was known as the "Love Nest." [67]

The wagon road connecting the two sites was carefully engineered and well-constructed with heavy timbered bridges at every creek crossing and beautifully built box culverts for the minor water courses. The surface was regularly graveled with the waste ore from the mill so that it was as smooth "as an automobile road."

The biggest investment in labor and capital was the fifty-ton stamp mill which started to rise at the south edge of the clearing in 1934 (though it was said to be on its way to the site as early as 1919).[68] The mill's heavy stamps mechanically crushed the football-sized chunks of ore as they were off-loaded from wagons into the top level of the building. Then, the gravel sized ore was washed and sorted by gravity as it moved down the structure's three levels, with the heavier mineral-laden pieces dropping to the bottom.

Water may have originally powered the operation but later it was supplied by a large two-cylinder diesel engine.[69]

The three-stamp mining mill at Copper City in 1937. Mineral ore extracted from the mines three miles upslope was crushed by the heavy "stamps" in this building as the first step in processing. The ore was then trucked to Naches or Yakima where it was loaded onto railcars and transported over the Cascades to the nearest smelter which was located in Tacoma. (Courtesy of the Yakima Valley Museum)

Hard rock mining is physically grueling and terrifically dangerous work. At the turn of the century, ore was wrested from the adjacent rock by large hand-hammered drills and black powder or dynamite. Because Copper City was so remote, the potential for bad outcomes was higher than for mining centers closer to civilization.

Ruben Root himself was the first mining casualty during one of the very first winters of operation. Root was drilling into rock when a piece of metal broke off the equipment and pierced his eye. Knowing that he needed help immediately, he and another miner set off—on skis— for the nearest doctor. That doctor was in Yakima, sixty-five miles away. Travel was slow due to the intensity of his pain and as his other eye was affected sympathetically, sometimes he was traveling virtually blind. It took eight days to reach Yakima with many of their nights being spent sleeping outside in the snow, there not being many cabins along the route at that time (or now for that matter). There was no saving his eye and Root was fitted with a glass replacement which served him for the rest of his life.

The only other recorded casualty also occurred in winter and emphasized the hazards of working in such a harsh climate. Mankichi "Tommy" Imada (his name has been variously spelled as Omata, Amato, and others) was employed as the cook at the upper Clara site and was reportedly saving his salary to return home to Japan to see his wife. One day, the miners returned to the camp looking forward to a hot lunch and instead were greeted by a cold cook shack. Somewhat annoyed, they searched about and found Imada's lifeless body underneath a pile of snow. Apparently, a substantial roof of snow had formed over the wood pile behind the cookhouse and collapsed after one too many pieces of wood had been removed. Tommy had no chance to escape.

Ira Ford transports a load of firewood by dogsled to the Goose Prairie school. Ira trained the German Shepherds Mike, Boots, and Lady to pull in a harness. This is the same rig that he used to bring Tommy Imada's body down from upper Copper City (Clara site) after Imada perished in the dead of winter. (Courtesy of Betty Jean Ford Gallant)

Jack was notified and arranged for Ira Ford to retrieve the body from Copper City, fifteen miles from Goose Prairie where Ira lived. Ford had the only reliable winter transportation at the time: a dogsled pulled by three large German Shepherds.[70] The snow, moderate in the Prairie, only got deeper the higher they traveled. The second day, the drifts were so deep, it became almost impossible for the dogs to break through. With Tommy's body tied to the sled it took two days for the return trip to American River with everybody resting overnight in Goose Prairie on the way back down.

Copper City continued to grow and evolve with Root at the helm. He added more buildings, enlarging Clara cabin and running a telephone line ten miles up to Copper City from the Lake. He soon had a line strung another three miles up to the Clara cabin and then between the lower buildings as well, probably most importantly between the cook's shack and the bunkhouse.

In 1939, the miners petitioned for and ultimately gained postal delivery service, three days a week in the summertime.[71] Ira Ford packed the mail on his back the long miles up from Goose Prairie which, though a pleasant journey by foot in the summer, was sometimes nearly impossible in the winter. One winter, his load of mail and supplies was so large and the snow so deep, that he hitched his dogs up and lashed the load onto his sled. The first day he made it only as far as John Crosetti's cabin on Deep Creek with one of the three dogs reluctant to pull. The last five miles up to Clara were a battle wills between Ford and the three dogs, especially the last steep two and a half miles, but the mail ultimately came through.[72]

All the needed equipment was in place, with plenty of men—forty at one point—to run it, with comfortable accommodations for them, but the ore rattling down the mountain in the wagons just wasn't of high enough grade to make that long journey to Tacoma pencil out.[73] The minerals were in the ground, but their occurrence was patchy and what veins existed were narrow and hard to follow. Eventually, all the best material that could be reached and removed had been, and a US Geological Survey report in 1942 found little further promise in the mines there. It concluded, "The prospect for discovery and production of any appreciable tonnage are slight." [74]

Wintertime Copper City miners at Clara cabin during the heyday of operations. Charlie Bedford is seated lower right and the others are unidentified. (Courtesy of Betty Jean Ford Gallant)

The report may have been the nail in the coffin for the Copper City Mining Company. After hundreds of thousands of dollars spent, over a thousand feet of underground workings blasted and cleared, approximately 800 tons of concentrated ore shipped over the course of twenty-six years, Ruben Root just could not will any more copper—or gold or silver or tungsten—out of the ground. Out of money and finally out of hope,

Copper City ceased operation in 1942. Root moved back to Milwaukie, Wisconsin and died only two years later, his great dream of riches from Copper City dying with him.

❦ ❦ ❦

  That bright morning on the Goat Peak trail, I took a picture of my husband Tom in front of the big snag, posing him off to the side of the giant scar. I then put my hand on the smoothed edges of the "X," tracing the outline with my fingers. I could imagine the older Tom standing right here, making sure his mark was clear, deep enough to last. Nice to meet you, Thomas X. Fife and yes, your memory and your forest endures.

Chapter Six

A LODGE FOR ALL

"As society becomes more and more mechanized, it will become increasingly difficult for many people to stand the nervous strain, the high pressure and drabness of their lives. To escape these abominations, increasing numbers will seek the primitive forest for the finest features of life."
—Robert Marshall,
The Forest for Recreation, 1933

"Bumping Lake, as a summer resort, is in a class by itself,"
—Professor 0. L. Waller of Pullman,
Yakima Morning Herald, 1918

Every summer when we stay at Normandie at least once a car will pull slowly into the driveway and park. One or two people, usually a little or a lot older than us will move hesitantly up the path and by their inquisitive, open expressions, I know what they are going to say before they speak.

"Is this the old Bumping Lake Resort?"

They have come by feel, by instinct, returning to revisit the site of happy times in an earlier life. These travelers are homing in on a place that looks very different than it did the last time they were here. Their pilgrimage has been precluded by the nearly complete dismantling of the operation and the impressive growth of dozens of trees which quickly took root in the buildings' absence.

I am more than delighted to tell them "yes," and show them around what is left of the resort. In return, these folks share with me captivating stories of their trips here and we walk slowly to where their favorite cabin once stood, the tipped foundation blocks marking the exact location of family gatherings long past. The way their faces soften as they walk about is remarkable to witness. If I am particularly lucky, the visitors are old enough to have known Jack and Kitty and am treated to a precious first-person window into their lives.

Most of the time the introductions are friendly, but the pilgrims' names mean nothing to me. One memorable afternoon, a typical couple delivered themselves up the driveway and the man introduced himself quite deliberately as "Jim *Nelson*." I stared at him, looking deep into his face in an attempt to recognize something of what I had memorized from so many old photographs.

"*The* Nelson?" He seemed pleased at the recognition and my appreciation of his last name.

"Yes," with a big smile. "Jack Nelson was my great uncle. I visited here from Canada when I was just a kid. This is my first time back."

We spent a few magical hours sharing a mutual appreciation of his relatives and our predecessors here. A month or so later my husband and I received in the mail a digital copy of a minute or so of a grainy moving film clip that was taken during his long-ago visit. To this day, it is my most complete and prized glimpse into the past at the resort.

I did not always care so much about the history behind our summer getaway spot, but the more time we spent there, the more I wanted to know. Quite suddenly I had to know more when one summer, I was asked to testify in the Yakima Superior Court as part of the Washington State Department of Ecology water adjudication case. The proceedings involved sorting out the entire county's surface water rights in an epic forty-two-year-long case.[1] To retain water rights for Normandie, we needed to document the history of water use there.

To my surprise, once I started really researching the issue, it became clear that the water system that still served Normandie was much older than the building or the resort and dated back to the beginnings of the dam construction itself. Subsequent research at the Yakima Valley Museum and the Bureau of Reclamation brought to light old construction maps, original documents, letters, and photos that were like the richest gold mine finds to me.

With Tom's help and a 1944 map of the Bumping Lake Resort in hand, I was able to establish not only the locations of each of the rental cabins, but the water lines, roads and accessory buildings that served them. Here were bits and pieces of long-ago vacations scattered everywhere on the ground, in the trees, behind the sheds. There was a chipped teacup, a heavy fire door of an old wood stove, a fishing reel, a broken ski pole, a tiny toy truck. Suddenly, it seemed as if everywhere I looked yielded an artifact that told another story of the resort.

With the assistance of her miner and trapper neighbors, Kitty's big lodge was successfully erected and open for business in 1915. It is remarkable how quickly the resort developed. In less than four years Jack and Kitty went from the test of surviving alone in a little shack way up in a remote wilderness to successfully housing and feeding multitudes of guests—reportedly forty at one time in the summer of 1915.[2]

Kitty hired a cook and a dishwasher (often a husband-and-wife team) to help feed the guests who remained for what we would consider extended stays. Since it took so long to make the journey to the lake, guests would settle in for a week or two with some visitors staying for the entire summer. In those days, no one came up for just the weekend.

The original Bumping Lake lodge as it appeared in 1917. There was a large lobby area, a dining room, and commercial kitchen on the main floor with overnight accommodations upstairs. In 1915, when the lodge opened, there were few other resorts in the state and the facility was busy from the start. Kitty soon added tent cabins and other buildings to accommodate the growing number of visitors from all over the world. (Courtesy of the United States Forest Service, Naches Ranger District)

By the early 1920s the resort was, by all accounts, booming. Initially, the visitors came to experience the novelty of the area and the new lake, but the biggest draw was the fishing. During the early years, before fishers took undue advantage of the abundance there, Bumping Lake was legendary for incredible fishing.

Yakima resident Frank Kappelman described his June trip to the lake: "The fishing is tophole…the Nelson long house is crowded with hungry fishermen every time the meal horn sounds and there is a constant procession of cars each way daily." Jack wrote in his memoir, "I doubt if our lake had an equal on the Continent." [3]

One source of the bounty were the multitudes of sockeye salmon that were trapped in Bumping Lake when the dam was finished. These fish made for easy pickings initially. Bumping River also offered outstanding fishing for salmon, steelhead, and other trout, during this last window of opportunity before the massive dams on the Columbia accelerated the decline and extinction of five of the six salmon species that once ran on the Bumping River.[4]

One group of fishermen took particular advantage of the tremendous numbers of fish in the lake early on. Jack tells of four farmers arriving at the lodge around nine in the morning, hiking a mile to the landing to rent a boat and rowing to the end of the lake. They returned to the lodge at four o'clock with 660 silver trout or kokanee. With no means of refrigeration, waste was inevitable. The same farmers came back some time later hoping to duplicate their success, despite admitting that most of those delicious fish were fed to their chickens.[5]

At the same time the native fish were being heavily fished, Yakima County Game Warden Greenman was ramping up his efforts to stock every reachable body of water with trout (mostly rainbow) with the intention of making the Yakima River and its tributaries a great fishing attraction. The local stocking efforts immediately increased the numbers and diversity of fish in the lake and with consistent glowing press, put Bumping Lake on the sportsmen's map.

The fishermen kept coming and coming.

Of course, the bounty could not last, but for the present, Jack and Kitty took advantage of their location and made sure there were boats to rent and pans to fry the catch for the evening supper.

Another aspect of the resort's success in the twenties was the passage of federal Prohibition laws in 1920. Overnight, mountain and other remote retreats became attractive destinations if someone wanted to socialize and imbibe more publicly than in one's home or a crowded speakeasy. Since technically it was not illegal to drink alcohol, only to make, transport, or sell it, once visitors were in place at the resort, they could feel some freedom to consume their beverage of choice.

Politicians in particular, sought out distant locations to relax, away from the eyes of their constituents. The Nelsons were not only accommodating hosts but discreet ones. In time, a steady stream of legislators and judges from Olympia found their way to the lake, many becoming staples at the lodge.[6] In Jack, they found a fierce poker opponent, entertaining raconteur, and a well-read debater with whom they "could solve all of the problems of our great nation."

The lodge was spacious, with tall ceilings, a huge fireplace topped by a giant bear head and easy chairs arranged in front of the fire. A player piano was installed early on that proved to be one of the most popular attractions with visitors driving up from Yakima just to pump its pedals. Jack reported that it seemed to play from morning until bedtime. In the evening, the furniture was pushed back to make room for dancing. Scattered tables hosted poker games that sometimes lasted until dawn (players reportedly stumbled from poker table directly to breakfast table). A screened porch ran the length of the building on the lake side where visitors could enjoy the endless view. Horseshoe pits on the lawn behind the lodge were well used when the weather was fair.

Eight little tent cabins stood ready in a neat row along the spillway, and more wooden cabins sprouted on the hillside behind the lodge a bit farther from the lake, but with a fine view of it. When they were over capacity, Jack and Kitty rented out their house and slept in a tent pitched in the yard.

Kitty was responsible for the dining room. From that room issued forth a huge variety of mouth-watering dishes that earned the lodge a reputation for great food. Fruit pies, potato pancakes, fish preparations of every style, and fresh bread were some of the delectables fondly remembered by guests. The kitchen crew must have labored hard to keep up with the appetites of the patrons. With three meals being served and only a wood stove to prepare them with, it was a formidable undertaking.

Kitty also employed young women each summer to assist with hospitality chores. Ira Ford's daughter, Betty Jean, who was raised and lived in Goose Prairie, worked for Kitty one summer in the early 1940s helping to clean the cabins, do laundry, wash dishes, and even wait tables. She recalled that Monday was laundry day, with Jack and Kitty both rising around 4:00 o'clock in the morning to start work. Betty Jean and her friend Louisa Taylor rose at 7:00 o'clock. There were sheets and pillowcases by the dozens from all the tents and cabins. The towels and bedding were washed in a wooden barrel tub with a hand wringer and then hung on lines to dry. The girls were instructed to clip the sheets in a particular way so that they could be easily removed and fed into the hand-cranked gas mangle which ironed them flat. For her work, Betty Jean was paid one dollar a day, plus board.

Betty Jean recalls Kitty as being a tough but fair boss who "didn't hesitate to ask questions and expect answers." [7] She was an efficient manager who ran the resort with a no-nonsense attitude. One day Kitty observed Betty Jean washing the dishes and thought she was taking too much time. "These are sturdy restaurant dishes—they won't break," she said. To demonstrate she tossed a dish onto the floor where it shattered. Kitty picked up a second dish and threw it on the floor with the same result. "Thank goodness the third one did not break, or she might have tossed the whole stack!" was Betty Jean's recollection. [8]

Kitty was a resourceful businesswoman who made the most of their outpost in the wilderness. When she had extra bread or milk, she sold it to visitors and cabin owners who were starting to build their own places along the lakeshore. She sold ice as well, which was precious, having been cut in the winter from the lake and then stored in the sawdust-insulated icehouse for as long as it would last. She rented boats and offered pleasure boat rides around the lake for a modest fee: fifty cents per person with a one dollar minimum.

Nelson Lodge was not the only place in the area to get away from prying eyes or protective parents. Roadhouses and Juke joints were springing up all along the Nile Valley Road offering dancing, romantic rendezvous—and alcohol. One popular weekend spot was Eagle Rock which had a dance pavilion built out over the Naches River for dancing under the stars. Couples could take a footbridge which led from the pavilion to a cave-like grotto in the cliff complete with a concrete floor, tables, and chairs. Ice cream and other treats were served there under twinkling Chinese lanterns. Other evocatively named roadhouses were Pleasure Island and Paradise Park. [9] The old Edgar Rock Lodge became known as an informal speakeasy during Prohibition years. Elk Ridge Lodge, also in the Naches Valley, offered lodging, but most outdoor adventurers kept driving until they got to the end of the road, as they "are not satisfied until they get straight through to the lake..." [10]

Soon, an "auto-stage" replaced the old horse stage and made it easier to get to the end of that road. From 1915-1917, at a time before the populace owned their own cars, Walter Purdin and Wade Shockley operated a regular service from Yakima to the Lake which certainly added to Kitty's guest roster. [11] After the auto stage was discontinued, Kitty petitioned for bus service from Naches which would have been a huge coup, but it never materialized.[12]

Jack and Kitty didn't just welcome paying guests. They hosted the Boy Scouts from nearby Camp Fife twice a week during the summer season before the Boy Scouts built their own lodge in 1937. The scouts staged their evening programs at the lake and Jack became a regular part of the ceremony, telling funny or scary stories to the boys. Even after the scouts had their own facilities, Jack continued to join their evening campfire programs. Almost seventy years later, former Boy Scout Ray Foisy vividly recalled Jack's dramatic entries into the firelight and the suspenseful delivery of hair-raising stories he told.[13]

There were many challenges of running a hospitality business in the remote wilderness. Getting and keeping food was foremost among them. Trucks gradually replaced the horse drawn supply wagons, so delivery was eventually a bit quicker. But since the road was so rough food did not always arrive in the same condition that it started in. Kitty's first—and last—delivery of fresh raspberries, even with careful packaging and padding by the driver, poured out of the buckets: red juice with a scattering of seeds. And sometimes things got mixed up. An order relayed over the long telephone line for twenty pounds of *round beef* was interpreted as twenty pounds of *brown beans* which must have posed challenges for the menu that week.[14] Keeping food fresh was the most daunting challenge for the Nelsons. Until they acquired a propane refrigerator, the only way to store perishables was on ice in a box cooler or later an ice box refrigerator. Since their lake ice supply was inconsistent year to year and dwindled as the season progressed, Kitty had to make do with a limited range of meats, consisting of cured ham, bacon, and corned beef. Fresh fish was always a welcome and regular addition to the menu.

To solve the fresh meat dilemma, Kitty started raising and keeping animals. The first purchase was Lily the cow, so that fresh milk could be made available for guests, children in particular. Lily was delivered in the first truck that drove to the lake, which also carried a half a ton of hay for her and the player piano. However, Lily didn't make it to the lake on that truck. Somewhere on the road about fifteen miles from the lake, the road began to give way into the river so the truck driver Al, quickly secured the truck to an upslope tree. He and his helper unloaded the hay to make a platform for Lily to offload and then got the truck moved to a safe location and replaced the hay. They found it impossible to get Lily back in, so Al's helper had no choice but to walk Lily to the lake, which he did, all fifteen miles. These drivers were so unflappable that Al offered to bring Kitty another load anytime she needed something. Lily quickly adapted to her new home and was soon free roaming to graze and returning home at milking time. Occasionally she had to be called or fetched. Kitty could be observed walking on the trail along the lakeshore, Lily following, her cowbell clanging gently as she moved along.

Procuring a fresh milk supply was not as simple as buying and keeping a cow, however. Because cows only produce milk when pregnant or nursing, Lily needed to be bred each year to keep producing milk. Since there were no bulls handy at the lake this necessitated a trip down to the Fontaine's ranch in the Naches Valley for a conjugal visit. Initially, this transport was in a crate in the back of a wagon provided by the Copper City Mining Company and later by truck. Occasionally, by the time she made the long journey to the farm, she no longer would be in the mood to receive the advances of the bull and then would return all the way to the lake to make the journey again the next month. Jack reported that the second visit was always successful.[15]

The ability to store eggs was also limited, making the choice to keep chickens obvious. Kitty suggested a real hen house and apparently Jack obliged as they soon had "a two-room building with good light, feeding room, dusting area, and all whitewashed." [16] It was located on the south-facing hill just across the entrance road for the lodge, so the hens would receive all the sunlight and heat possible in the colder seasons. The chickens did well and provided an occasional evening meal as well as a welcome respite from all that cured meat. An experiment with rabbit keeping was not long lasting. It was difficult to obtain the needed feed year-round.

A gift of two live turkeys one holiday season added to the menagerie. They were appreciated by the Nelsons and their Copper City neighbors for the feast days, but the six live geese given for similar purposes were not as fondly remembered. Jack remarked, "One blade of grass and a drink of water and their bowels moved for a week." He wished that they might be swept over the spillway during their daily swim but that never happened so another dinner invitation to the miners solved the goose problem.

The last addition to the barnyard seems a bit ambitious for the couple who were so busy with other duties, but apparently the desire for fresh meat was relentless. For several years, Jack and Kitty would raise one or more pigs in the summer and then butcher them just before winter.

One pig, Jerry, was particularly friendly, regularly breaking out of his pen to find company in hopes of receiving a good rub. One day, Jack departed early in the morning to repair the phone line which had gone out in the night. He walked down the road nearly fourteen miles before he found the break. While Jack was up in the tree threading the wire through the insulator, he was startled by a noise and surprised to witness the arrival of Jerry to the base of the tree. Jack descended, gave him the desired rub, and returned to the tree to finish his job. Jerry stretched out on the road and napped until it was time to return home. The journey back was a slow one and they didn't arrive until well after dark, due to the 200-pound animal's need for frequent rest stops along the way.[17]

Sometimes the Nelsons had assistance with food supplies when their guests brought fresh food gifts. Most memorable was that from a Major Swabb from McChord Field, south of Tacoma. Swabb and some other fliers had visited the resort one fall to hunt and fish and appreciated the stark paucity of fresh produce that Jack and Kitty experienced as winter wore on. For several seasons in February, he arranged for air delivery of fresh fruits and vegetables to the couple. Carefully boxed and parachuted, green onions, lettuce, vegetables of great variety, and even fresh bananas were delivered by a well-aimed toss out of a low-flying plane. The first package got hung up on a lightening arrester on the way down, but successive produce from heaven drifted gracefully to the snow-cushioned ground.[18]

There were other challenges. The weather regularly impacted access to the Lake, especially in the early years before the road was improved. With only the one road for access, visitation to the lake was completely dependent on that route being passable—and often it was not. Area roads were so rudimentary that they seemed to sustain damage from almost any weather event.

The weather events of the winter of 1915-16 were extreme by any measure. January was the coldest month ever recorded in the Yakima Valley.[19] A massive snowstorm hit the Northwest at the beginning of February that set records that are yet unbroken: twenty-one-and-a-half-inches of snow in twenty-four hours in Seattle and four feet at Bumping Lake. The bridge at Bumping Crossing collapsed under the sheer weight of ten feet of accumulated snow.[20]

Adding to the travel woes, a late-spring hot spell caused rivers to rise above flood stage all over Yakima County. It is little wonder that at the end of June, the Bumping River Road was still impassable. The pathway was a mess: washed out in places, boulders strewn about, and short one bridge. Low on all supplies, the Nelsons were most anxious to get freight in for the season. Furthermore, there was at least one guest stranded at the lodge. Caroline Vance, a friend of Kitty's daughter Frances, had come up with Frances before the June 18-19 flood and now could not get out.[21]

By the middle of July frieght was again traveling on the Bumping road although Dick Ball had to dynamite a landslide before the roadway was clear enough for a wagon to pass. Presumably, Miss Vance was able to return home to Yakima on the auto-stage.[22]

Just two years later, in 1918, the Bumping River Road was out again. This time, an unusually warm and wet December brought rainstorms that filled the lake. Ultimately, the water crested at nearly four feet over the dam's spillway. The downriver flood swept away both Bumping River bridges, cut off train service in Yakima, marooned workers on the Tieton Dam project, and washed out the brand-new road at Horseshoe Bend.[23]

This weather event impacted Jack dramatically. That winter, Kitty had been staying in Yakima with Frances while her daughter attended high school. Jack's plan to join them for the winter holidays was dashed when in the middle of the month rain, rather than snow, started to fall. The level of the lake began to rise ominously. Every day the rain continued. When the skies finally cleared and the temperature dropped just three days before Christmas, Jack's boss telephoned and again encouraged him to come down to Yakima. Somewhat against his better judgement, Jack accepted and left the lake in the capable hands of his friend, the trapper Grover Coleman. Jack had scarcely entered the city limits when the downpours resumed and after two days of precipitation, he felt compelled to get back to his post at the dam headgates. He was worried about the stability of the structure under his care.

Even Jack, who was wise to the vagrancies of weather and travel by now, had little idea how difficult it would prove to return home. From

Yakima, he rode the train (the affectionately named "Sagebrush Annie") to Naches and then caught a ride with the mail stage up the valley. When they rounded the curve at Horseshoe Bend, their progress was halted. The road had been washed out. The stage turned back, and Jack continued on foot, scrambling up over the hills above the raging river. It was still raining.

Just as he straggled into John Stevens' ranch for the night, Mrs. Stevens and Jack watched in awe as the bridge he had expected to cross the next morning was swept past in the roiling waters. When he set out at dawn the next day, instead of walking along the now inaccessible road, Jack again had to clamber along the trackless ridges that towered above the overflowing river.

Later in the day, as Jack approached the Steindorf ranch, he looked down on a sorry sight. Most of the Nile area was flooded, with houses and barns marooned in the middle of small lakes. Jack remained with the Steindorfs for four days while he waited for the Naches River to subside enough to cross, but even then, it was only just possible on horseback. He rode up to junction of the American and Bumping Rivers only to discover that the bridge there had been washed away, too. At that point, Jack sat down to contemplate his next move. If he couldn't cross the river, he would again have to travel cross country without a path of any kind and the remaining twelve miles to the lake were just too rugged. The road, tantalizingly close but on the other side of the swollen river, was the only way home.

Jack decided he needed a sharp ax and more food. Turning his borrowed horse around, he backtracked to the Fontaine ranch, nine miles downriver. He arrived well after dark but was cheered to see Tom Fife who was in residence as caretaker while the Fontaines were in Yakima for the holidays.

As was Tom's way, he immediately insisted on accompanying Jack to help his friend home. The two men spent half the night filing axes and baking biscuits for the next day's journey. Returning this time on foot, they started up the side of the Bumping River looking for a suitable place to cross. At the first narrow spot, they felled a large tree, expertly dropping it slightly up-current expecting its heavy branches to dig into the river bottom and hold. Instead, it was instantly swept away. The next two trees suffered the same fate. The men slogged up along the bank until they located small island in the middle of the river and determined that a tall cottonwood would be sufficient to bridge the gap to it. The other channel looked like it could be forded. The tree dropped perfectly in place but was too small and slippery to walk across. Instead, Jack straddled it and shimmied across to the island with their equipment. He then returned for Tom who shut his eyes in terror and held onto Jack as they both scooted across.

Once on the island, the pair had to face the last river crossing. In what must have been an excruciating act, Jack stripped off his clothes and wearing only his hat and rubber boots, carefully waded through the torrent with their supplies held high overhead. He then plunged back into the current and returned to the island for Tom who didn't trust himself on the shifting boulders of the riverbed. Jack hoisted the man up onto his back and piggy-backed him through the unimaginably cold January water.

What most mortals hesitate to do in the summer, Jack accomplished three times in a winter flood—naked.

The rain continued, unrelenting. The men trudged on to the familiar halfway house which they reached after dark. Jack later wrote that no hotel ever looked better, with its stove and plenty of dry wood, than that friendly cabin.[24]

Jack's ordeal wasn't quite over. After staying in the hut the next day to rest up and dry out, there was still the matter of getting Tom started back to the Fontaine's. The pair returned to the river and located a suitable tree on the near bank to provide passage to the island. Jack then made his way to the other side of the Bumping and felled another tree to add to the undersized cottonwood to create a "real" crossing. With the river behind them, Jack walked with Tom another mile or so before bidding him farewell and turning back for the lake. He managed the log bridges and the last miles quickly, reaching home that evening.

The return journey of sixty-five miles had taken ten days.

In March, road repairs were begun at Horseshoe Bend, but funds were short for the substantial work needed beyond that point. Exasperated County commissioners argued against rebuilding the Bumping River Road in particular, claiming that scarce moneys should be spent on the war effort rather than repairing a "pleasure" road for tourists. Yakima boosters countered that Bumping Lake was Yakima's "only outing spot," superior in every way to Lake Kachess and Keechelus.[25]

The Bumping River Road with Old Scab Mountain in the background. This south facing view illustrates one of the smoother sections of the road. The driver may be Albert Botsford who built the Goose Prairie store and gas station. (Courtesy Betty Jean Ford Gallant)

At the same time the road debate was being waged, Game Warden Greenman planted a half a million Lake Mackinaw trout in Bumping Lake, further enhancing the draw for fishermen. But the road remained unpassable—and the fish unreachable.[26]

By the end of May there was a call for volunteers to fix the road. At the end of June with still no repair work in sight, there came a suggestion in a Yakima newspaper that visitors could ride packhorses to Bumping Lake, there being a "squad of veteran horses…placed at Anderson's." [27] If horses were not your thing, it was possible to hike in by way of the old Spring Flat-Goose Prairie trail which was "shorter than the Edgar Rock trail."

At the end of July, Kitty, probably out of desperation, donated a hundred dollars to the road effort to add to the $1,000 dollars from the Reclamation Service, $2,000 from Yakima County and $1,000 that the auto and mining people finally offered to repair the road and bridges. She also offered to do the cooking for the road crews at the lake end of the work. The Yakima papers put out a call for volunteers to rake stones on the Naches Road, suggesting that "it is an opportunity of a lifetime to have some fun, make it count and display democracy." The fun might have been in enjoying the results of Kitty's cooking which apparently was renowned enough to be a draw to road workers and volunteers alike.[28]

Further complicating access to their resort was America's entry into World War I. Protection of domestic infrastructure was taken seriously and by June, every Reclamation dam had armed guards assigned to them.[29] Two civilian men were hired to guard the Bumping Lake dam along with Jack. With the delivery of firearms and ammunition delayed, one of the men brought his old British 303 rifle "Old Pet" along, which he slung over his shoulder and patrolled with until the official munitions arrived. The men took turns sitting on a plank out on the gate house bridge and kept all vehicles and people off the dam.

Yakima resident Clarence Truitt and his friend Fred Redmon bicycled up from Yakima one day and ignored the "No Trespassing" sign on the end of the dam, pedaling across even as Jack yelled at them. They finally turned back when he pointed the rifle at the pair.[30]

Jack and Kitty had glimpsed a preview of the coming conflict in 1915, a full two years before the United States entered WWI. One evening in May, they were startled by the appearance of two German men at their doorstep, arriving from the west. Mr. Bergin and his assistant Otto, carried heavy packs and explained they had just hiked over Carleton Pass from Packwood, traveling most of the thirty miles in snow. They were employed by the German Imperial government and were in the United States to map, document and photograph all infrastructure, agriculture, and industry of the Pacific Coast from California to Canada in anticipation of German settlement. The two men were in no way secretive about their mission and even showed the Nelsons their extensive notebooks, maps, and large format cameras. They were under instruction to thoroughly investigate all the mountain passes, and so after leaving Bumping Lake the next day and interviewing a family of German descent in the Naches Valley, they turned west and disappeared over Naches Pass.[31]

The road to Bumping Lake was finally opened to "automobilists" on September 21 and Jack wrote that the first wagon with supplies got through only the day before. That date puts a full ten months between the last supply wagon the previous November and the first possible resupply in mid-September.

It is remarkable that the couple attempted any hospitality at all at the resort that season but there are glowing reports of visits there and big fish caught. Outers who somehow made it to their door, "an oasis in the wilderness," could enjoy sitting on "quaint furniture made from local trees and evening dancing on the waxed floor in the lodge" before bedding down in one of the new tent cabins.[32]

Around the time of John Muir in the late 1800s, there began a shift of public sentiment in the United States. Wilderness areas, rather than being a threat (as the home to dangerous wild animals) that needed to be vanquished, came to be regarded as a retreat, a respite from civilization, a place of rejuvenation. Unspoiled tracts of land were good for the soul and for one's emotional well-being. For the first time, wildlands were valued as such and deserving of protection rather than being exploited. Timber barons and mineral kings controlled and exploited vast acreages of the West, treating government managed lands as their own. Recognition was growing that untouched areas were a national resource that was rapidly diminishing and needed to be protected and wisely managed or they could disappear forever. [33]

In the Northwest, so called "Forest Reserves" had been set aside before the turn of the century but were created exclusively to protect timber and water resources.[34] The Reserves had no plan of operation and were simply closed areas and off limits to the public. In 1905, the United States Forest Service was established under the Department of Agriculture with Gifford Pinchot as its first chief. Pinchot, along with Muir and President Teddy Roosevelt, was a national figure leading the crusade to conserve, rather than distribute our nation's resources to the highest bidder. He argued that forestlands had tremendous value and that if properly managed, were a resource that could last forever. Pinchot further advocated the use of the forests and all that they had to offer to all people for "the greatest good of the greatest number of people in the long run." [35] These three conservationists promoted the then-radical idea of public ownership of forests and other resource lands.

Despite strong opposition from lumber and mineral interests, in 1907 the Forest Reserves were renamed National Forests and were opened to the public (grazing, logging, mining, and homesteading continued as allowed uses). Congress soon mandated a policy of multiple use for public forests, including for the first time, recreation. Citizens now had access to the benefits of clean air, exercise, and the beauty of nature and were eager to claim it.[36]

For the first time, Americans were able to enjoy those benefits. With increased leisure time after WWI, many took advantage of the opportunity to explore the country around them—and the National Forests and Parks. It became fashionable to motor to the seashore or into the mountains, to hike, and even to climb. People went out into nature to pose for a photo next to a waterfall, drink from "soda springs," or row a boat across a lake. Explosive growth of car ownership and the expansion of roads into previously inaccessible areas accelerated the growth of outdoor recreation.

The new Forest Service had to scramble to develop a plan to accommodate the crowds that were soon flooding into the forests. First to be built were sanitation facilities to protect visitors' health and fireplaces to protect the forest from fires. Rangers were hired to keep a new breed of outdoor visitors safe, and the land protected. On July 4, 1927, a record number of twelve hundred cars checked into the Current Flats Ranger Station before heading up to the mountains. In Yakima, the newspapers suggested a variety of mountain outings including announcements when the mountain huckleberries were ripening for the convenience of their readers. A 1925 article describes dozens of vehicles parked near Gold Hill with families camped "all over the hill" combing the bushes for the riches of the "berry rush." [37] As roads reached closer to the peak from both sides of the pass, the Mount Rainier area became a realistic day trip option. "Yakima Park" (now called Sunrise) to the west of the divide and Lake Tipsoo on the crest of the range, became favorite picnicking destinations. On weekends, hundreds of cars packed the newly cleared parking lots.

The first forest rangers were a rugged lot. Many were former trappers, prospectors, or herders—tough men who knew the mountains intimately. The Forest Service preferred to hire local men who could handle problems effectively, so they looked for natural leaders who were intelligent and honest. Around these early recruits grew the legend of the forest ranger as a strong and resourceful outdoorsman, polite and preferably handsome. A ranger could handle any situation, day or night, helping out when needed in any sort of weather.

Every forest ranger applicant needed to be "thoroughly sound and able-bodied, capable of enduring hardships and performing severe labor under trying conditions. Invalids seeking light out-of-doors employment need not apply." [38]

Furthermore, applicants needed to be skilled. In order to apply for a job with the Forest Service, a recruit had to go through a three day ordeal and successfully complete such tasks as "felling a tree ten or more inches in diameter with an axe so that it drives a stake into the ground when it falls; tell the boss man what ingredients and how much of each to use in preparing a batch of biscuits; and, pack a horse with all the equipment and personal effects for five days while being timed." [39] Some tests also included a working knowledge of cabin construction in case the need arose in a remote location.

Despite the high standards they were expected to uphold, there was little money in the early budgets for rangers, and these first hires were paid just thirty and sometimes thirty-six dollars a month. Rangers were expected to provide their own riding horse and pack animal as well as their own provisions. Initially, their ranger "stations" were either old, appropriated prospectors' cabins or simple shacks they built themselves. Each had small corral and hitching post and were often located well within the districts which meant lonely living.

The first station in the Naches-Tieton area was up Nile Creek and named "Little Fish," after the only thing in the creek there. The single building at the site was a small dugout, halfway underground with wide gaps in the floor which at least made it easy to "sweep the dirt away between the cracks." Harry Croxford, one of the first rangers in the area, made Little Fish his headquarters for the next thirty years. [40]

Initially, primary responsibilities of the rangers were to count livestock, patrol the ranges, and inspect permits, but their duties soon expanded. Before long, they were protecting fish and game, shepherding the public, and for the first time, starting to try to control and combat fire. In addition to all their responsibilities, the rangers were always on the lookout for grass for their horses. Harry Croxford said finding forage was a constant problem in the high country and that he "followed many a trail to see what he could find." [41]

In contrast to the sightseers who were motoring into the park for picnics and photos, other people were using the outdoors more vigorously. Climbers, both men and women, were conquering nearby peaks in large numbers and making records for long distance hikes and even ski trips.

Winter didn't seem to be an impediment to these new adventurers and the crest of the Cascade Range seemed to be an irresistible obstacle to traverse. Two expeditions set out to cross over from east to west in January of 1925 alone. One was successful and one was not.

A westside resident, Fred Yenny, was returning to Greenwater from Walla Walla when, on a lark, he decided to hike home rather than take the train—in the depths of winter. With a small pack full of snack food but no gear, he strode out of Naches and headed toward the mountains. Before long, he bogged down in deep snow, located an old cabin, and tore off some long shakes to make a pair of skis. Having never skied before, he learned how on the way up American River and fortuitously came upon Jack Campbell's cabin where he was welcomed by the old miner and trapper. Yenny stayed for two days while Campbell helped him make a better pair of skis. Up at Bear Gap, he got caught up in a blizzard, lost his pack and all of his food. After getting disoriented in the storm, he ultimately made his way over Chinook Pass and down Silver Creek to the National Park entrance and onto Greenwater. He skied over sixty miles in just seven days and was without food for two. Though he said he undertook the journey for fun, he also said only a "chechahco" (tenderfoot) would attempt such a trip in winter and concluded that "once was enough." [42]

At almost the same time, two hikers with much more preparation left Yakima on a "mush" to Paradise Inn in Mount Rainier National Park, some fifty miles southwest of their jumping off spot at the junction of the American and Bumping Rivers. Phillip Phillips and Richard Van Vliet packed a toboggan with 250 pounds of supplies and headed toward Chinook Pass in their snowshoes. They too, got caught up in a blizzard and then lost their toboggan when it slipped off a cliff and dropped 300 feet into a canyon. After multiple trips to retrieve the sled and its contents, they got started again but decided to continue without the cumbersome load. They cached the toboggan under a tree and continued with packs. The pair followed Chinook Creek down the west side but having no trail to follow they "spent a day wallowing through snow in the roughest country I ever saw," related Phillips. When it started snowing again the next day and they ran up against a glacier, they decided they'd had enough. They spent a day and half laboring back up to the summit and snowshoed back home. Despite the hardships, they said they "got a few pictures and enjoyed themselves." [43]

A year later, two men from Enumclaw, Olaf M. Berg and Herbert J. Gilbert, hiked from the White River on the west approach to Mount Rainier, up over Chinook Pass and down the American River Valley to Cliffdell. They made the expedition in March, so they traveled most of the distance on snowshoes. The thirty-seven-mile journey took them two days and like Yenny, they had the good fortune to chance upon Campbell's cabin late in the evening after a long day's travel. After "a good night's sleep and breakfast fit for a king," the two departed the "congenial and hospitable gentleman's" home and continued down the American River Valley to a road construction camp where they picked up a ride to Yakima, forty-two miles away. [44]

In the Northwest, adventurers began to coalesce into outdoor clubs both east and west of the mountains. These new groups offered members easier and safer access to the nearby peaks through climbing classes and organized hikes. They gathered for social events as well. The Mountaineers of Seattle, the Mazamas of Oregon, and the Cascadians of Yakima were Northwest clubs that were each inaugurated with hundreds of members. New youth organizations including Camp Fire Girls, Boy Scouts, and Girl Scouts emphasized outdoor activities and skills of the woods that were perceived as positive, wholesome, and very American.

Yakima, even though boasting a population of only 18,539 in 1920, seemed to have produced an outsize number of notable outdoor athletes. Perhaps the allure of the misty green range to the west with its majestic volcanos was a powerful draw to those who were born in the rather featureless sagebrush valley. Claude E. Rusk grew up near Yakima in the shadow of Mount Adams and became a nationally-known mountaineer when he led an expedition to Mount McKinley in 1910. He had already founded the American Alpine Club (1902) and in 1920, cofounded the Cascadians, an outdoors club based in Yakima, which thrives still. As president of that club, he mentored a generation of outdoorsmen and women. [45]

One of his prodigies was Clarence F. Truitt. Born in 1893 and of average stature and unremarkable appearance, his exploits in the mountains seem superhuman. Truitt worked as a manager at a fruit company in the Yakima Valley but spent every free moment hiking, snowshoeing, and skiing in the Cascades. He became the scout master for the first Boy Scout troop in Yakima, #1, which meant he had the excuse to spend even more time outside, overnighting and teaching survival skills and the ways of the woods to his young charges.

In the summer of 1921, Rusk invited Truitt to be part of the first attempt up the east face of Mt Adams. His handpicked group consisted of E.E. Coursen, Wayne Richardson, Clarence Starcher, Clarence Truitt, Rolland Whitmore, and Robert Williams. Many had examined this route and declared it to be impossible but at the end of two days, seven intrepid men, with only two ice axes among them along with five alpenstocks and some rope, stood triumphantly on the top of the peak.[46]

On August 13, 1921, seven climbers from the Cascadian and Mazama mountaineering clubs made the first ascent up the east face of Mount Adams. The feat was considered a significant mountaineering achievement in the United States at the time. Shown in front of their camp before the climb are from left, Wayne Richardson, Clarence Starcher, Clarence Truitt, Robert Williams, Rolland Whitmore, Edgar Coursen, and Claude Rusk, the climb leader. (Courtesy of the Yakima Valley Museum)

Rusk fondly remembered Truitt's enthusiastic encouragement to the other team members, especially during difficult moments. "This is the life!" Truitt would announce, making the others smile, in spite of the danger or their discomfort. The ascent, made on August 13, was considered the signal achievement in United States mountain climbing that year.[47]

The head of the lower Bumping River just behind the dam. This 1923 view shows the old bridge from the construction of the dam along with a telephone line strung above it. Kitty is fishing as usual, while midwinter visitors from the Cascadian Club look around. Clarence Truitt and Pearl Synder are in the center with Max Hiscock and the Nelson's dog on the far right. (Courtesy of the Richardson family)

Truitt seemed to like the challenge of long overland treks in any season. One early expedition was a ski trip in February of 1923 with friends from the Cascadians and Spokane Mountaineers. The group included Pearl Snyder, Max Hiscock, and Rolfe Whitnall from Yakima and Elsa Hanft from Spokane, with Truitt leading. They started at the Fontaine homestead in the Naches Valley, setting out for the Nelson's home at Bumping Lake. The group arrived in the dark at nine o'clock having covered the twenty-two uphill miles to the lake in just twelve hours.

Photos from this expedition suggest a light-hearted jaunt. The skiers are athletic and confident, goofing around as they traverse obstacles along the Bumping River. At the Lake, they relaxed inside Jack and Kitty's home, listening to the radio, and reading. The miner, John Crosetti dropped by for a visit. Back outside, with the Nelsons guiding, they explored the outlet works of the dam and hiked up to the falls to inspect the couple's water system that initiated there. They glissaded back down the mountain, with even Kitty getting in on the fun, long skirt, stylishly tailored jacket, and all.

Another outing in late winter of 1927 was more ambitious.[48] In March, Truitt along with Hanft and James Thompson, started on snowshoes toward Bumping Lake from the river junction. After spending the first night with Jack and Kitty, they set off to the south for Twin Sisters Lakes gaining 3,000 feet in altitude only to find that twenty-three feet of snow had completely entombed the nearby Cowlitz Pass ranger's cabin where they had hoped to gain overnight shelter. Though the party eventually located the structure and tunneled in, they spent much of the rest of the trip sleeping on open snow fields. After crossing the crest of the Cascades, the next morning, they dropped down Summit Creek toward Ohanapecosh Hot Springs. The group crossed the Cowlitz River in a "basket ferry" and followed Skate Creek up to Longmire, then finally ascended to Paradise Inn on the south flank of Mount Rainier. They spent two days in the vicinity exploring and skiing as far as Panorama Point in perfect weather. Reluctantly, the three snowshoed into Longmire to pick up the auto stage to Tacoma. In the end, the adventurers' five day, cross-pass trek totaled just under one hundred miles.[49]

One winter, word came to Yakima that someone at Bumping Lake was ill. Truitt immediately obtained the necessary medication, was driven as far up the Naches as possible, and from there headed for the lake on snowshoes. It was a reported twenty-four miles to the lake, and he made the roundtrip in just over sixteen hours.[50]

He was just warming up.

In the twenties, adventurous explorers were probing some of the last corners of the known world. Evidently, sometime around 1926, excitement about Richard Byrd's upcoming Antarctic expedition reached the east side of the Cascades. Clarence Truitt, along with fellow Cascadian Clarence Starcher, became determined to be part of that expedition. Together with Q.A. Blackburn of the Seattle Mountaineers, they hatched a plan for a trek to prove their fitness and endurance to apply to be part of the expedition.

Their test would take nine days, cover approximately 350 miles by foot, and summit five peaks. They would carry nothing more than a small pack each to sustain them. The 1927 Cascadian Annual suggested that they "made a record for mountain climbing and hiking that…likely has no equal in the experience of mountaineers."[51] Truitt and Starcher started at Cloud Cap Inn on July 3, 1926, and climbed the north side of Mount Hood, descending to Government Camp. They were then driven to Spirit Lake, where they met up with Blackburn and climbed up and down Mount St. Helens. They next hiked forty miles to Mount Adams along the Highline trail through the Goat Rocks and via the summit of Gilbert Peak.[52] They reached the top of Mount Adams on July 6. From Adams, they hiked to Mount Rainier and summited by the Kautz Glacier, descending the Gibraltar route to Paradise. Blackburn left them at this point, and the two Clarences continued, hiking back over the Cascade crest to the Nelson's. They were met by car and driven back to Yakima arriving on July 11.

In their sixteen-pound packs, they carried no bedding and only minimal food. The men supplemented their meager portions with berries and fish they gathered along the way. Truitt estimated they climbed 56,826 feet.[53]

Although they certainly qualified by this remarkable achievement, family emergencies prevented both Truitt and Starcher from joining the expedition. Reportedly, Blackburn ultimately did journey with Byrd to the Antarctic, but the two others remained at home.[54]

Curtiss Gilbert of Yakima was Truitt's close friend and near double. Born just months after Truitt, both men served in WWI, worked in the fruit business in Yakima, had an insatiable appetite for outdoor adventure, and became Boy Scout Troop leaders (Gilbert led Yakima Troop #9) at a young age, deeply dedicated to mentoring their young charges. Tragically, both men also died prematurely in their mid-fifties, cutting short lives of generosity and promise.[55]

Like Truitt, Gilbert possessed bottomless enthusiasm and energy for mountain ventures and arduous journeys. As a young man, he climbed all the major peaks between Canada and California. He encouraged his scouts to venture out into the rugged terrain near and far on countless overnight camping trips. By the time he guided childhood friend Justice William O. Douglas to the top of Mount Adams in 1945, he had already climbed that peak eleven times. Douglas believed that Gilbert knew the Cascades more intimately than any other man in history, white or Indian.[56]

Gilbert's ultimate expedition was in 1946, when he conceived of—and completed—a 10,706 mile countrywide road trip with eighteen boy scouts in the back of an open fruit truck. His laconic journal entries were the genesis of a book about the epic journey titled, *Where's Frank?* by Lloyd Phillip Johnson.

It was not only men who were heading outdoors for pleasure. Women were in the process of throwing off their cloaks of modesty and tradition and putting on pants and boots to hike, climb, ride, and even ski in the spectacular scenery.

Olga Bolstad was one of these early pioneers. In the summer of 1917, the Northwestern Ski Club organized the first ever ski jumping tournament in the Northwest. The competition was held at Paradise on Mount Rainier. There, Bolstad, reportedly just twenty years old, defeated all of her male competitors to win the event and become the first ski champion of the northwest. The Tacoma News Tribune wrote that "she seemed to skim through the air like a bird." [57]

Even earlier, in 1915, the Mountaineer Clubs of Seattle and Tacoma planned a ladies' excursion to circumnavigate Mount Rainier for what was one of the first trips along the brand-new Wonderland Trail. John Anderson of the Naches Valley was the outfitter and guide for the group providing sixty-five horses for the 100-125 women expected for the journey. He had experience. Three years earlier, Anderson had outfitted and led seventy women adventurers, aged seventeen to fifty years old on a twenty-two-day trip to climb Mount Rainier.[58]

Elsie Hanft was one of those women. She seemed to be all over the mountains of the Northwest in the early part of the century. She was born Elsa Augusta Lina Hanft in 1885 in Germany, and was a schoolteacher and dressmaker living in Spokane when she joined the Cascadians. She accompanied Truitt on many jaunts all over the Cascades, but the treks through the Bumping River Valley were the more trifling of her expeditions.

Adventurer Elsa Hanft with Max Hiscock left and Kitty Nelson center in 1923. Hanft, a schoolteacher and seamstress from Spokane, was an irrepressible outdoorswomen. A professional climbing guide on both Mount Rainier and Mount Baker, she trekked hundreds of miles through the mountains of the Northwest on snowshoes and skis. Hanft also joined a scientific expedition in 1926 to explore the little-known Craters of the Moon area in Southern Idaho. (Courtesy of the Richardson family)

One of Hanft's earlier publicized feats was a mountain hiking expedition to traverse 215 rugged miles between the eastern and western entrances of Glacier National Park.[59] Another achievement was a widely hailed first ascent of the north side of Mount Shuksan near Mount Baker. Hanft, along with two guides, made the dangerous route in just eight hours. "I don't get scared," she told reporters afterward. "The more dangerous the climb, the more I like it." During one winter "vacation," Hanft embarked on a ten-day snowshoe trek of 250 miles into the North Cascades—solo.[60]

By the time she joined the Spokane Mountaineers Club in the mid-1920s, Hanft was an expert mountain climber who had bagged twelve major peaks in the United States and several in Europe. She had hiked up and skied down Mount Hood. She had served as a guide on both Mount Baker and Mount Rainier, and reportedly had already summited Rainier more than fifty times. It was she who "really taught us how to climb," said the club's founder, Ora Maxwell.[61]

But Hanft wasn't just an adrenaline junkie. She shared her love of the outdoors not just with other mountaineers but with younger girls through the YWCA. In 1935, she joined the brand-new Wilderness Society. Hanft lugged along a movie camera on many of her travels into the North Cascades and regularly showed reels of her pictures to outdoor groups.

At fifty years old, Hanft was still climbing and was hired as the local guide for the location filming of "Call of the Wild" starring Clark Gable and Loretta Young. She helped manage the nearly one hundred crewmembers and fifty dogs as they rolled the camera on the snowy flanks of Mount Baker. In 1935, no one knew the mountain better than Elsie.[62]

In 1923, Jack and Kitty had seemingly earned themselves a new house. The old Reclamation shack that they had occupied since they first arrived at the lake was torn down. The Bureau replaced it with a spacious cottage with gas lights, a brick fireplace flanked by glass-fronted bookcases, ruffled curtains, and modern, comfortable furniture. They must have felt like royalty. In time, they obtained a radio which brought the world to them via three vacuum tubes and two sets of headphones. In the evening, "we could go to a good theatre, listen to a World Series, a horse race," Jack wrote.[63] With their intense interest in the rest of the world, the radio brought them not only daily news and music but discussion of national and international affairs which they eagerly took in. The couple felt connected to the world and celebrated the successes of the twenties with little idea of what was about to come in the next decade.

Kitty Nelson reads a freshly delivered newspaper in their brand new cottage at Bumping Lake. In 1923, this comfortable government building replaced the old dam tender's shack that had been quickly built in 1909. Hobnailed boots were not allowed inside their new house. Apparently, the Nelson's shared the space with not only a cat but a dog too, both unmentioned in Jack's memoir, *We Never Got Away*. (Courtesy of the Richardson family)

Jack Nelson and visitor Max Hiscock with one of the Nelson's most important possessions: their radio. It was both their source of news of the outside world and their entertainment. Jack was an avid baseball fan and closely followed the sport, especially as he got older. (Courtesy of the Richardson family)

Chapter Seven

DEPRESSION—AND HOPE—
IN THE MOUNTAINS

"I propose to create a civilian conservation corps to be used in simple work, not interfering with normal employment and confining itself to forestry, the prevention of soil erosion, flood control and similar projects...More important however, than the material gains will be the moral and spiritual value of such work. ...I call to your attention that this type of work is of definite, practical value, not only through the prevention of great present financial loss, but also as a means of creating future national wealth."
—President Franklin Delano Roosevelt,
proposal to Congress March 21, 1933

"Bumping, that pristine place where deer and elk dabble in the water in the evenings and where the occasional hungry bear wanders through. Bumping Lake has always been a camping and fishing hideaway, a place for long walks through narrow trails, a place for the solace only a forest can offer, a place where a fairish angler can (still) catch dinner."
—Jim Gosney, *Yakima Herald Republic* August 15, 1991

Our family was at Bumping Lake one summer weekend when I felt as if we were sliding into the past, but not a past I was familiar with. We were slipping sideways into wild west territory, as if into one of those hard-scrabble towns that were slapped together all over the West. Those settlements had sprung up next to a stand of virgin timber, ancient fish run, or a rich vein of ore, and their inhabitants stripped the land of its wealth which was subsequently gambled or drunk away. There were few laws, customs, or respect in those low-value towns. When the treasure inevitably ran out, residents dribbled away and left nature to repair the damage. It seemed like we were in one of those failing hamlets.

In the summer of 2006, the Bumping Lake Marina and Campground, located just a half a mile south of Normandie, had been closed for about two years. The marina had always felt as if it was a struggling enterprise, forever limited by a short summer season and the variable lake level. The latest owners, George and Gail Nolan, had brought in a young couple to run it for the season but soon the general store shelves stopped being restocked, the rental boats ran out of fuel, and the docks themselves began to sink.

The next year, no one showed to open it up, and things really fell apart.

Word had spread that camping was free at the lake and the sites were as full as they ever had been, though this time with no rules. We hadn't realized what a stabilizing force the operating marina had been. As soon as nobody was in charge there, campers went a little crazy—or the people that came up wanted a little craziness. With the Forest Service and Yakima County Sheriff's budgets trimmed yet again, there was no official presence here, only an occasional drive through by various uniformed officers. The result was chaos.

Target practice had always been a favorite activity in the remote clearings across the lake from us, but at this time we heard alarmingly close gunshots almost daily. Campers were taking down trees at will for campfires which were left burning on Sunday afternoons after they pulled out. There were no garbage or septic services.

Harold Webb and his wife Beatrice in Goose Prairie in the late 1920s. Their children, Blanche and Leslie, are nestled in the homemade sled. The Webbs ran the early Bumping Lake Landing for the Nelsons, renting fishing boats to the many visitors who were drawn to the Lake for its legendary fishing. (Courtesy Betty Jean Ford Gallant)

R.A. "Chuck" Hammond was a prolific builder in the Bumping River Valley during the thirties and forties. In 1933, he built Normandie Lodge and a number of the rental cabins for the Nelsons. He built the first summer home on Bumping Lake, the Double K Mountain Ranch buildings, and probably built the original structures at the Bumping Lake Landing (later Marina), which he may have also owned for a time. Besides being a skilled carpenter, Hammond was said to be a dashing lady's man. (Courtesy of Betty Jean Ford Gallant)

This little marina was once a thriving place. It was likely constructed sometime in the late 1920s or early 30s by Chuck Hammond and
Harold Webb. Webb, who ran the marina for nearly a decade, lived in the
winter in Goose Prairie with his wife Beatrice and two small children. In
the summer, the family moved up to the little cabin at the marina.[1] The
facility was simple and consisted of a boat house with rails running down
to the water's edge, floating docks (huge logs with planks nailed to the top),
a log boom, and a perhaps a bait house. Fifteen to twenty boats, hand built
by Hammond, were available for rent.[2] Originally known as Bumping Lake
Boat Landing, and then about 1935 as Hammond's Wharf, the little port
was busy from the beginning.

Early Bumping Lake Boat Landing. This little marina replaced Kitty Nelson's earlier facility
which was closer to their resort. This south-looking view shows the floating restaurant
stranded on the shore by winter's low water. (Courtesy of the United States Forest Service,
Naches Ranger District)

Kitty, never one to pass up a good opportunity, probably owned
the operation, initially. At some point later, she had her son-in-law Dick

Reed, along with Frances, run it. It was known during that time as Reed's Boat Landing. Other owners put up a floating restaurant, leveled little squares along the shore and welcomed campers. A trailer court was installed along with running water and then electricity. A luncheonette served hamburgers and chocolate cake.[3] Kids were drawn to the bait store to buy candy and learned to row in the little aluminum skiffs that bobbed next to the tippy wooden docks. When the lake water warmed, everyone jumped in and splashed around, sporting the latest swimsuit styles, even way up in the mountains.

For decades, fishing was huge at Bumping Lake. Heavy stocking by Yakima County kept populations up after the initial abundance of fish was depleted by irresponsible fishing. In this 1946 shot, fishing boats crowd the dock while Kitty Nelson casts a line into the cold water. (Courtesy of the United States Forest Service, Naches Ranger District)

For the scaly residents below the surface, life was getting a lot more complicated. From the time the first European explorers came upon it, Bumping Lake was considered a fisherman's paradise. But the native fishes' long legacy in the river and lake came to end with the construction of the dam. To compensate for the barrier, a fish hatchery was planned at the lake. In 1913 Yakima County Game Warden Frank Bryant purchased equipment and set up what seems to have been a collection trap for returning salmon at the tailrace of the dam. It was to utilize at least a few of the abandoned buildings that had been left at Camp 22.[4] High spring water in 1914 washed out the river traps but a determined Bryant got enough of the structure rebuilt and hoped to catch at least a few stragglers from the last Chinook run of the year.

The following March, Warden Bryant left the Yakima trout hatchery, hauling a water tank on a wagon containing 200,000 trout fry. They were apparently intended for the Bumping Lake hatchery. He and his three companions expected to travel up to the lake but encountered snow at the mouth of the Bumping River. Taking a cue from the freighters of the past, they loaded the tank onto a sled and dragged it by hand seven miles through the snow up to the lake. Bryant later said that he might have turned back if not for Jack and Kitty Nelson's promise to care for the hatchery that season.[5]

There is no news of the success or failure of the facility, but it was discontinued sometime after 1916.[6] In 1927, there was talk of another hatchery to be built behind the dam, but it never materialized. With abundant fry at the ready in commercial hatcheries, the county started taking the opportunity to stock lakes directly with fish that anglers wanted to hook, especially as local catches declined. Soon the goal of fishery managers was to stock as many of bodies of water with as many fish as possible. Because Bumping Lake was so popular as a fishing lake, over a million trout and salmon fingerlings were poured into its waters in some years and hundreds of thousands in others, to grow fat and be available for sport and dinner two or three years after they were planted.[7]

The problem was, other fish were growing fat too.[8] Over the years, inadvertent as well deliberate releases by individuals in addition to escaped bait fish led to a lake that was teeming with "undesirable scrap" fish. In some cases, these unwanted populations were of the same species that the game department had planted years earlier with the idea they would be favored game fish. Now they were outcompeting and even preying on the more popular fish. Things got so bad that in 1939 and again in 1940 the Yakima Valley Sportsmen's Association members begged for a solution. They asked for additional sucker traps to be constructed near the head of the lake (in the shallows near the present-day Forest Service campground) pointing out that the one constructed the previous year was so successful that it had captured several tons of squawfish, carp, shiners, and other predatory fish.[9]

The traps may have caught tons of scrap fish, but game officials seemed to be looking for a quicker and more thorough solution to problem lakes. H.J. Reynolds, the "leader in scrap fish poisoning," proposed the use of the chemical rotenone in lakes and streams to eradicate unwanted fish. Even though he admitted to the Bureau of Reclamation in 1948 that it "was not all that can be desired for the purpose," he posited that "continued experiments would lead in a few years to lakes and streams of the state to be largely cleared of scrap fish, with the result that state could have better fishing than ever before." The state was in. State fish biologist Robert Rennie explained that though the wildlife poisoning budget for 1949 was already expended, positively something would be done for Bumping Lake by the next year.[10]

And it was. On a cool September day in 1950 at eight o'clock in the morning, fifty-four men in twenty-seven boats, motored away from the shoreline dragging behind them burlap bags filled with a total of 43,000 pounds of the poison rotenone. The powder dissolved as the boats crossed and recrossed their assigned portion of the 1,300 acre lake. The dam's outlet gates had already been closed—and would remain that way for three months—to prevent the poisoning of Bumping River.[11]

Within minutes, fish rose to the surface gasping for air as the poison interfered with their ability to take up oxygen. By noon, the surface of the lake was covered with dying animals. Two days later all the gilled inhabitants of Bumping Lake were dead.[12]

Workers managed to scoop up some of the struggling kokanee and get them into buckets where they revived, but the majority of the multitudes of fish either sunk to the bottom or drifted to the north end of the

lake to pile into stinking drifts. Some of the carcasses were shoveled into
bins and hauled away to be used as fertilizer.[13]

The poisoning of Bumping Lake was the largest fish eradication
program ever conducted in the United States (by many times over) and as
officials would boast later, in the world as well.[14]

Though 800,000 baby trout were planted by 1951, the lake would
remain closed to fishing at least until they grew up. Visitors stayed away
and the lakeshore was quiet.

With the lake closed and no fishing for ultimately three years, the
owners of the marina at that time, Howard and Betty Jean Ford Gallant,
reluctantly sold, pennies on the dollar, to Mack and Molly McDonald in
1954. Through the years, other owners came and went but the lake's fishing
was never quite the same.[15]

Now, fifty years later, the closed marina facilities and its amenities have become some sort of community property, but the community
doesn't manage it well. The generators disappeared first. The little store
was broken into and emptied. Pieces of the floating docks were cut loose
and became fishing rafts for a day or two. Freed from their moorings,
they drifted until they inevitably bumped up against the dam to gather
with the rest of the worn driftwood there. The sturdy picnic benches
which once anchored each campsite traveled all over the forest, popping
up in distant clearings. Most became firewood. Rangers were scarce. The
Sheriff was AWOL.

One particular midsummer weekend was an especially pleasant
one and the Bumping Lake area was full of spirited campers. They crowded
each available clearing along the shore and the closed marina campground.
They took advantage of the flat lake to paddle, float, or motor about on a
wide variety of vessels. Fish were caught, wakes were jumped, shallows were
waded. It was so warm that Tom and I went upstairs to bed that night and
kept the window open.

Tom quickly fell deeply asleep. Just as I was drifting off, I thought I heard a sound like a pebble bouncing off the screen. How strange. I got up and looked out onto the lawn and was deeply surprised to see a figure there, illuminated by the light pouring out of the living room windows. I helloed down to her, and she replied with a question:

"Can you help me? I'm lost and I don't know where to go."

She looked young and vulnerable. I told her to go to the door and I would be down. I went downstairs and paused for a moment before I swung open the heavy, dead-bolted front door.

A doe-eyed young woman, not more than twenty years old, dressed in jeans and a white hooded sweatshirt stood in a pool of light from the fixture above the door. Out of habit, I asked if she wanted to come in. She did. As soon as she stepped through the door, she said,

"I lied to you. I am not lost. I saw the lights of your place, and I came over."

My heart skipped a beat. Two.

My children were here, Tom too, all asleep upstairs. I had let a stranger into our home in the middle of a hot night. Since she was already well inside, I looked her straight in the eye, told her she could sit down and asked her,

"What's up?"

She glanced up, her eyes filled with tears and as soon as her mouth opened, her story poured out. For hours, she talked, and I listened and learned about her life. I came to understand the struggles of someone who has grown up without love, without hope, without self-worth of any kind. Caroline's single mother had neglected her while she was growing up, and now she was caught up in an abusive relationship with an alcoholic boyfriend.

This young woman was trying hard to make life work, toiling at two jobs to put herself through college. She had come up to the lake with the boyfriend and others for a weekend of camping fun. For this group though, fun included lots of alcohol and some number of guns. Her personal plan for the weekend involved one of them. The idea was that this evening, when the rest of the group went out for a midnight swim in the lake, she would stay back in the tent, retrieve her boyfriend's gun, go up into the woods, and shoot herself.

Her dispassionate delivery completely disarmed me. I sputtered objections of all sorts but now things were more complicated, and I was alarmed.

"Do you have the gun?"

"No."

"Is your boyfriend" (who was certainly drunk by now) "looking for you?"

"I don't know."

"Does *he* have the gun?"

She explained that her evening's plan was derailed when the group did not go to the lake as planned, and out of desperation to get away she walked, down the road until she saw our home, a safe haven of light in the dark forest. Seemingly secure behind the heavy log walls, we talked on and on: of the value and promise of living, of ways to get help, to heal, to thrive. She seemed to gain strength from my attention, our words, and a warm—if not tenuous—connection to another person.

But now what? It was the absolute middle of the night. I couldn't let her stay, but I could not imagine sending her back to that cauldron of possibilities at her camp.

At three o'clock in the morning she agreed that she was okay to go, and I walked her out and down to the gate. We embraced, and I sent her down the road with a flashlight and a prayer.

I made my way back upstairs and back under the covers of our bed. Just as I was dropping gratefully off to sleep for the second time that night, Tom sat bolt upright and asked what "that sound" was.

"What sound?" I asked.

"The gunshot," he mumbled, before falling back to sleep.

Early the next morning, I relayed the night's events to Tom before we reluctantly headed toward the marina where Caroline said they were camped. There was no group there, no tent, no fire, but no sheriff either. On Monday I called the number that she had scrawled on a scrap of paper before I let her go that night. To my surprise, a familiar voice answered. I learned that Caroline had broken up with her boyfriend on Sunday and was on a new path by Monday. She assured me that she was better, and she called me her angel. She promised me that she would live, and I finally hung up, grateful that a chance taken on another human being had ended so well.

The rest of that summer remained unsettled. Groups of people kept coming up, camping all over the forest, but seemed more interested in raising hell than appreciating the scenery. The appeal of a place without rules seemed to draw a certain segment of the population eager to follow their own worst impulses without fear of any consequences.[16] We were on guard nearly constantly.

Cooler weather and the fall rains eventually chased away even the hardcore partiers for the season and salvation finally came the following summer when new owners took over the ruined marina and started to enforce rules. Their influence spread like a salve over the area which slowly returned to state of more responsible use.

At Bumping Lake in the early thirties, the hardships of the Depression lurked just over the horizon.[17] The worst of the deprivations were for the most part kept at bay by the resilience and resourcefulness of the rural settlers. The inhabitants at the far reaches of civilization deep in this river valley were already used to making do and providing for themselves. The Nelsons may have suffered a dip in visitors to the lodge, but Jack continued to be employed by the Bureau and would soon have more opportunities for income as the New Deal developed under President Roosevelt.

The few hardy residents of Goose Prairie were self-sufficient, too. The Prairie had started to grow as a community not long after Tom Fife died in November of 1922. Later in his life, Fife had grown close to the family of his friend and attorney, James O. Cull. The old miner named his attorney as his executor and in his will bequeathed his real estate (much of the Prairie) to Cull's two children, Ruth and James B. Within months of Fife's passing, Cull was having the Prairie surveyed and by July had divided up the meadow into "Fife's Goose Prairie Home Tracts." [18] A small plot was set aside as a cemetery where Fife and his father lay at rest. Ten acres were deeded as promised to the Boy Scouts. Some fifty lots of various sizes were readied for sale in the little settlement not quite three miles below dam.

On the new 1923 plat map, Jack Nelson is the largest landowner, holding title to thirty-four acres right in the middle of the Prairie. The Nelsons had purchased from Fife a prime plot with a front row view of the three major peaks on Nelson Ridge not long before he died. The deal had probably been made without much enthusiasm. Back in 1907, the Department of the Interior had ordered the withdrawal of a strip of land around Bumping Lake one mile wide at the normal water line.[19] It would remain under the control of the Reclamation Service. It may have been this set-aside, or a legal case in 1916 between the Department of the Interior and the Forest Service over leases at Bumping Lake, or even that the Service was uncomfortable with the size of Kitty's growing enterprise so close to their dam infrastructure. In any case, the Nelsons had apparently been told that they could no longer operate their resort on the government's lakeshore land.

The news must have been a terrible blow considering how much the couple had put into their business. Apparently, however, they shifted gears and their gaze to the Prairie. Tall newspaper headlines in July announced, "Jack Nelson Will build Big Hotel" along with a summer resort. He would buy lumber for the buildings from a new sawmill in the Prairie which Ruben Root had just begun operating.[20]

Negotiations between the Nelsons and the Service continued and, in the end, somehow, the couple prevailed. Their resort could stay. There was a limit to their tenure though; all the Nelsons' buildings would have to be removed from the property when Jack retired as dam tender. Jack and Kitty would put off that eviction for twenty-four years.

Ruben Root and his wife, Gertrude Erickson Ford Root, were among the first to settle in the newly-laid-out community around 1926.[21] In addition to his dreams for Copper City, Root had big plans for the Prairie. Just before Fife died, Root also obtained a portion of his homestead. But instead of cash, he traded Copper City mining stock for a large parcel of Fife's land on the west side of the Prairie.[22] Root divided approximately fifteen acres of it into forty-five small lots to sell to vacationers. His sawmill would see to those future buyers' building needs.

In the summer of 1927, Gertrude's son Ira Ford moved with his family from Yakima to Goose Prairie, and in 1930 was hired as the foreman at the sawmill. He contracted to buy twenty acres of the Nelsons' now superfluous parcel on which stood Tom Fife's old cabin. He, his wife Bess, and their three children moved into Tom's tiny cabin, adding a small bedroom and kitchen wing to accommodate the five of them. However, late in the same year, the sawmill closed, leaving Ira to provide for his family as best he could in the middle of nowhere.[23]

Because one of the few things that was plentiful during these lean times was wood, Ira supplied cordwood to newly built Whistlin' Jack Lodge, the American River Resort, and others at $3.50 a cord, less a fifty cent stumpage fee to the Forest Service. For that precious coin, trees had to be located, felled by crosscut saw, cut into lengths with a 350 pound drag saw and then split and loaded into sled or truck for delivery near and far; a slow way to make a living.

During the long years of the Depression, Ira also raised foxes and mink in partnership with Mrs. Harriet Karr, ran a trap line, and raised rabbits for a short time before turning them loose on the prairie for lack of food for them.

Some families spread out into the forest to collect seeds from tree cones to sell to lumber companies for replanting. Many probably supplemented dinner with poached game. It has been said that the larger animals helped many families in the eastern Cascade foothills through the hungry years.

In 1935, the residents of Goose Prairie successfully petitioned for mail delivery, and Ira obtained the contract to deliver it. Delivery was three times a week in the summer, but only once a week in the winter, which required skiing to the American River junction nine miles away to meet the mail carrier up from Naches and skiing back with the mail in a backpack. For several summers, Ira carried the mail an additional eleven miles all the way up to those hardy miners at Copper City. The Ford children helped out on the mail run and remember the contract to be a great blessing to the family, at twelve hundred dollars salary per year.[24]

For the rest of this lean time, Ira made money however he could while he and Bess raised their three children in a sublime setting nearly devoid of opportunity and practical amenities. Like most of the structures in the Prairie, their house had no running water, no electricity, no means of modern refrigeration, and little insulation.

The three Ford children, Bob, Betty Jean, and Pat take shelter in the doorway of their one-room schoolhouse in Goose Prairie in 1931 or 1932. (Courtesy of Betty Jean Ford Gallant)

School was a one-room affair in the middle of the Prairie. The parents of the nine children who roamed the Prairie passed a hat in the early 1930s to hire a young teacher.[25] When the other families drifted away downstream in search of a living, the Fords were left with less and less in the hat. Ira lobbied the Naches School District and managed to convince them to absorb the tiny school. By 1936, the student body had dwindled to just four students and the district announced they would close the school. The three-to-four-hundred-dollar cost was too much of a burden for the small district.[26] Yakima stepped in and helped create what must have been one of the country's smallest school districts (Goose Prairie, #122) with a single one-room school, three grades, and between three and five students, depending on who showed up. It was always difficult to attract teachers for the nine-month school year since for most of the time between October and April, the Prairie's inhabitants were snowbound.[27]

By the time the Ford kids were in junior high, the school was closed for good, and they were traveling eighty-six miles a day roundtrip to school in Naches. Surprisingly, there was a bus.

Perhaps because school was such an ordeal to get to, it was not wasted. The oldest son Robert (Bob), went on to college, established a veterinary practice in Yakima and ultimately became the chief veterinarian for the Washington State Horse Racing Commission. The second son, Clarence "Pat," enlisted in the Army Air Force ending up in England for D-Day. Daughter Betty Jean attended Central Washington College (now University) on scholarship and then studied nursing at Swedish Hospital in Seattle and St. Elizabeth's in Yakima.

Despite the hardships, the family loved the Prairie and the children loved growing up there. They had freedom to roam, kept all sorts of animals as pets, and learned to hunt and fish. They rode every creature they could rope, climbed most of the nearby peaks, and learned about life from the animals around them, and death when calamity struck. When they got a little older, they fought fires and blazed out trails in the unbroken wilderness. These wild, barefoot kids were sometimes treated as spectacle by outsiders who drove up to Goose Prairie and more than once were profiled in the Yakima papers as if they were some breed apart.

Life might have been adventurous for the kids, but it was all work for Bess and Ira. Son Bob reported that Monday was washday, (using three copper washtubs, stove-heated water, and a wash board) Tuesday was for ironing, Wednesday mending, Thursday baking (six loaves of bread, one pan of cinnamon rolls and pan of hot rolls) and Friday and Saturday were for cleaning and cooking for anyone who might drop in or be invited by the ever-hospitable Ira. As poor as the family was, there was always room at the table for one—or three—more with several unemployed young men, living off the largesse of the Fords for weeks and even months at a time.[28]

The Ira Ford family poses in Goose Prairie in the late thirties. From left are neighbor Maude Meuller, Ira and Bessie Ford, Ira's mother Gertrude Root, the Ford's son Clarence (Pat), daughter Betty Jean, neighbor and former miner Frank Crosetti, and oldest son Robert (Bob). (Courtesy of Betty Jean Ford Gallant)

The Fords were not alone in taking care of others during this difficult time. Another Goose Prairie couple, the Botsfords, took in a niece and nephew after their parents divorced, and raised them until the eighth grade. Albert Botsford originally came to the area in 1924 to mine at Copper City.[29] He then worked at the Goose Prairie sawmill but chose to stay on after it closed. He and his wife Claudine bought several lots on the river side of the road and in the late-1920s built a store and gas station. Goose Prairie's own post office was established there on June 7, 1928, with Botsford as Postmaster. The mail, secured in a locked bag, was brought up by whomever was traveling up from American River. Seeing a need for housing in the village, Albert also built six cabins which were rented to workers and vacationers.

Fortunately, the Botsfords had a monopoly on retail in the Prairie, or business might have suffered from a wide roaming collection of cats who made themselves at home in the store, complete with using the open fifty-pound bags of flour and sugar as beds and freely licking the cream off fresh milk put out to settle. The milk was sold in thick glass bottles. There being no refrigeration available, perishables were held as best they could be in a dirt cellar while soda pop stayed cold via Bumping Lake ice in a red Coca-Cola cooler out front. Claudine was a stern woman of German descent but was admired for her industriousness. Albert, "Uncle Bun" to the children of the Prairie, was well remembered for his kindness to them, teaching the Ford children to play pinochle and letting the boys drive his car in exchange for helping him cut wood.[30]

The general store and gas station changed hands a few times, and in 1944 it was purchased by Ed and Soria Musetta "Zetta" Bedford. The store was well run under Zetta's tight authority, and she soon was selling baked goods in addition to food and fuel. Zetta was friendly and helpful in the community, but apparently the couple worried about competition from the Fords and their café and had a habit of watching its clientele with binoculars from across the road.

Zetta Bedford stands at the ready in this pretty-as-a-postcard picture of the gas station, store, and post office that she and her husband Ed owned and operated in Goose Prairie. (Courtesy of Betty Jean Ford Gallant)

Families from the Yakima Valley began to buy lots in the Prairie. The McNieces, the Griffins, the Severns, and the Meads were some of the early part-time residents who painstakingly constructed vacation homes on the grassy plain.

🌲 🌲 🌲

In the fall of 1933, a raggedy tentacle of the Depression reached all the way up to the lake to ensnare the Nelsons. One gloomy day, a battered auto pulled up at the resort, its occupants asking for gasoline. When Jack sold one of the men the requested amount, the man told Jack, as he handed over the bill, "That is the last dollar we have in the world." It soon became clear that these two families—one with a very small child—were planning to live up at the lake for the winter, squatting at the empty bunkhouse at Copper City.[31] Their plan was to live off the land and trade marten skins for tobacco at the Goose Prairie store.

Knowing what it took to provision for the winter, Jack and Kitty were horrified at the misplaced confidence that the group possessed. The couple tried to dissuade the families from their ill-advised idea, but they could only be persuaded to settle instead at the abandoned cabin at Keystone, much closer but still three miles south of the dam on the Deep Creek road. In spite of their assurances that they had plenty of stores for the winter, snow had barely fallen before the men were back at the resort asking for food and other necessities. The Nelsons provided them with skis and poles along with food and even books from their ample library.

Throughout the long winter they shared their pantry, including citrus fruits which were vital for the little girl. In March, with plenty of snow still on the ground, Jack and Kitty finally convinced them to return to Naches where the Red Cross was distributing essentials to the needy. Before they could make the exodus out of the valley though, the men returned to the resort for more supplies and announced that one of the women was about to give birth.

Tiding these families over with food and supplies was one matter, serving as a midwife completely another. Transportation was immediately arranged for the group with Ira Ford mobilizing his dog team to take them out by sled that same day and Jack setting up a ride from American River to the lower Valley. The Nelsons helped them pack up and sent the small families on their way, with their blessings and each with a check from Kitty for necessities tucked in their pockets.

By the early 1930s, farming practices were putting a tremendous strain on the nation's midsection. Widespread deforestation and excessive cultivation along with a historic drought, led to the devastation of the Dust Bowl years. Farmers watched their crops wither and their soil blow away, only adding to the misery of the Great Depression.

During his election campaign, Franklin Delano Roosevelt proposed a series of social programs he called a "New Deal." One part of his ambitious plan combined the needs of the unemployed with conservation projects for the benefit of both the individual and the country. This program became known as the Civilian Conservation Corps, or CCC.

In what must be the most efficient fulfillment of a campaign promise ever, FDR proposed, Congress passed, and the president signed the "Act for the relief of unemployed through the performance of useful public works and other purposes," within one month of becoming president (the president had outlined his concept for the CCC before the end of his first *day* in office). The date was March 31, 1933.

Only seven days after the bill that created the CCC was signed, 25,000 young men had signed up. Just ten days after that, the first camp, appropriately named Camp Roosevelt, was established in Virginia. What followed was what program director Robert Fechner called "the most rapid large-scale mobilization of men the country had ever witnessed." In less than three months, 300,000 men from all over the nation had been enrolled, transported, and settled in nearly fifteen hundred camps stretching from coast to coast.[32]

Washington State received its first companies in May 1933 where they were organized into camps to work with various state and federal agencies. There would soon be Forestry Camps (Federal and State), Park

Camps (National and State), Soil Conservation Camps, and Bureau of
Reclamation Camps.

The entire Yakima area benefitted hugely from the work performed
by the CCC boys who lived in the five Reclamation Camps, four Forest
Camps, and one Soil Conservation Camp that were built in the county
over time. The sudden arrival of a young work force at their disposal was a
welcome addition to the Forest Service which had been laboring under slim
budgets and fat backlogs in the previous years.[33] For the first time, district
rangers could imagine getting caught up on neglected projects as well as
getting started on items from their wish lists.

In the national forests, the CCC afforded an immediate and
dramatic increase in the development of recreational facilities. Trails,
campgrounds, picnic areas, shelters, scenic viewpoints, and restrooms
were constructed all over the district. The second section of what would
become the border-to-border Pacific Crest Trail (after the Skyline Trail
in Oregon), was built in large part by CCC enrollees who cut and filled
most of the recently surveyed Cascade Crest Trail. The trail ran the length
of Washington State, from Canada to the Oregon border. That same
path, now part of the Pacific Crest Trail, traces the southwestern border
of the Bumping River Valley.[34]

The first camp in the Yakima area was Forest Camp Nile (F-26) on
Nile Creek, which was still being constructed when it was occupied on May
16, 1933. It was replaced by Camp Naches (F-70) the following summer.[35]
Camp Naches was a large camp with the customary military style barracks,
mess hall, dispensary, shower and latrines, garages and repair shop, offices,
and supply buildings. The camp also contained a horse barn, a sign making
shop, and a sawmill as well as a large recreation room called Enderud Hall.
Built by the enrollees, it consisted of a dance floor, a stage with elaborate
sets, a movie projection room, library, and classrooms. Artist and CCC en-
rollee Vittorio Massimino painted beautiful murals on the walls of Enderud
Hall and the mess hall that were widely admired.[36] Soon, enrollees set about
building a swimming pool, too. It was supplied with fresh water from the adjacent Naches River and included an elaborate water-driven screening system
to keep migrating salmon out of the pool.

The young men arriving at the new camps were from the local area and from all over the country and were per CCC requirements: unemployed, single, and between eighteen and twenty-five years old. For the most part, they were poor, often discouraged youth with no work experience and little education. Without hope and sometimes even a burden to their struggling families, these men quickly filled the company's rosters as soon as they were opened. Pay for the forty-hour work week was thirty dollars a month with twenty-five dollars required to be sent home to families for relief.

Benefits to the new enrollees were immediate. Although the camps were often remote and accommodations were basic with shared barracks and latrines, the health and sustenance of the men were paramount. In contrast to some of their living conditions at home, enrollees had access to running water, heat, electricity, ample clothing, and medical treatment. Healthy diets were carefully calculated, and cooks were well trained and supervised. One newcomer from Georgia, Ed Hill, remembers his first meal consisting of braised sirloin tips, vegetables, potatoes, Waldorf salad, bread with butter and orange marmalade, and ice cream for dessert. He recalled that for the first time in his life he had enough to eat.[37]

In stark contrast to the generally excellent food, the first enrollees were issued leftover World War I clothing that was old and worn *before* it had been put into storage in 1917. "Pistol legged" pants and flared overcoats coupled with blue fatigue hats and newer shoes gave the earliest camps a rather rag-tag appearance. The "olive drab" army uniforms were soon exchanged for CCC specific attire, in part because of the furor that erupted when parents started seeing photographs of their boys in military dress and were certain that they were actually being trained for military service in the run-up to World War II.

Transportation from camp to work projects was by ancient Liberty trucks governed at fifteen miles an hour. The trucks rolled on hard, solid rubber tires that made for an uncomfortable trip in the back of the canvas covered beds. All in the camps celebrated when the old rigs were replaced by new 1933 Chevrolet trucks with pneumatic tires.

Soon the mountains were swarming with young men building things. As early as 1934, CCC crews were finishing overnight shelters at Twin Sisters and probably Swamp Lake, too. Enrollees built a bridge over Deep Creek and cleared the road to Granite Lake and up to Miners Ridge Lookout.[38] Sturdy picnic shelters in a bold, rustic style were built at Soda Springs, American Forks, and Sawmill campgrounds. These and similar facilities at Boulder Cave and Pleasant Valley remain, sheltering happy campers to this day.

By 1939, crews had completed a new high bridge over Copper Creek to replace the old hair-raising lodgepole one. The companies of men would have lived in temporary camps close to each project. Surprisingly, it seems that they were still in camp near Copper Creek as late as December 11 when their new bridge suffered extensive damage due to an earthquake.[39]

CCC men (Co. #932) also built the forest guard station that stands at the junction of the Bumping River Road and Highway 410. Built in 1941, it originally housed forest service and fire-fighting personnel.[40] Just across the road and along American River a tiny building was raised, constructed entirely of exquisitely fitted local stone. It served as a river gaging station.

In 1935, Jack Nelson was tapped to lead Reclamation Camp BR-49, a traveling camp that was located for the summer at Clear Lake, the little reservoir above Rimrock Lake on nearby White Pass. That Jack was hired to supervise a company of CCC boys is hardly surprising, as the program looked for local leaders whenever possible. Jack was already working for the Bureau, and he certainly had the practical knowledge of a woodsman. Jack soon recognized the program's potential to transform delinquent youths into good citizens and felt a personal calling to help make these boys into men. As he spent time with hardened city toughs and naïve country boys alike, he saw what a regular routine, good food, a job to do, and hope could do for a young man's soul.

One of BR-49's projects was to clear 300 acres of water-killed timber from Clear Lake. Like Bumping Lake, the reservoir bottom had not been logged prior to construction of the dam. Floating logs tangled with standing snags and completely covered the surface of the water, creating not only an unsightly mess, but a fire hazard.[41]

The following summer the reservoir was drained to allow the enrollees from CCC Co. 572 full access to the site. Using axes and saws, the boys took the trees down, cleared, and then piled them so they could be burned. The burning crew worked overnight from six pm to six am with a meal and hot coffee at midnight. Jack taught his boys how to fall and to buck, how to put up a spar tree, and how to hang a bull block: practical logging skills that they could take with them.[42]

Once a week, outdoor classes were held. Enrollees learned about motors, welding, carpentry, as well as truck and tractor operation and repair. Traditional indoor classroom education quickly proved to be a dismal failure and was for the most part abandoned. Much of the vocational training was given by LEM's—local experienced men—as they were known in camp, who were invaluable sources of experience to the enrollees.

Jack, always appreciative of the value of athletics, did not neglect them in his camps. He arranged for the construction of horseshoe pits and brought in local horseshoe pitchers to coach the boys. Nearby, a small baseball diamond was cleared and somehow all the needed equipment was obtained. In later instances, he also encouraged the organization of football, basketball, and softball teams. Jack went so far as to rearrange schedules during the World Series so that the boys could listen to the games.[43]

The camps were not perfect. In the early days of the CCC, not everything was well organized or fully functional. Jack's first camp at Clear Lake was unfinished when he and his company of boys from New York and New Jersey arrived. The mountain site was high and remote. Running water was provided by a nearby creek and the only refrigeration available was a burlap covered, water-cooled wooden box. As a summer-only camp, accommodations would have been tents rather than buildings, but only a few of the tent frames had been constructed when the company arrived. The newcomers likely had to make their own mattresses by stuffing sewn canvas sacks with hay before they could bed down.

The mess hall and kitchen were similarly unbuilt, so for six weeks the enrollees cooked and ate outdoors. No one in the company had received any culinary training and the food, despite the best efforts of those assigned to prepare it, was terrible. Soon, the carpenters and then the entire company announced that they were quitting all work until better food was provided. Arrangements were hastily made for the loan of experienced cooks from headquarters at Fort Lewis until some of the company could be properly trained.[44]

For three summers, Jack worked wonders with the boys in his charge. They toiled again at Clear Lake and Rimrock Lake before moving on to more reservoir clearing projects at Kachess and Keechelus Lakes. The second summer's companies of boys came from Indiana, Ohio and several southern states.[45] Jack had farm boys from the Midwest and moonshiners from the south, but with outstanding officers, a mess sergeant, and fine boys to work with, he "had a camp that clicked." The men set a record for work accomplished that summer.[46]

The majority of the boys from the south had never been to school or at least not long enough to learn to read or write, so Jack encouraged them to visit his quarters at night when he could read their letters from home out loud to them and write their dictated replies. Often, he would come across boys working in their bare feet despite having been issued sturdy work boots. They told Jack they were more comfortable that way.

Years later, Jack would remember many of "his boys." Moon Mullins, with a round face and "quite prominent air-cooled teeth through which a constant smile shone," was one. He was the smallest boy on his crew, but a hard worker. Jack made him the water boy and later he worked on the burning crew.[47] Mullins was a Southerner and joined up after his mother shot and killed another woman over her husband. Subsequently, their house burned to the ground when his father accidentally tipped his pipe onto the casket lining of a relative's open coffin.

Freckle-faced Cecil, from West Virginia, was remembered for his physical capabilities and leadership. He had worked on his father's "patch of ground" and joined the CCCs after his abusive father threw a singletree (a crossbar attached to a horse-drawn plow) at him—and didn't miss.

Another dependable worker was tall and strapping Farrell, from Brooklyn and of Irish descent. He was a prodigious reader who hurried to the library in the recreation hall every evening as soon as supper was over. As he worked outside during the day, he peppered his supervisors with obscure questions born of his previous night's study.[48]

As he came to know these young men and understood their childhood privation, Jack showered attention on them, trying to make up in part for the lack of love and guidance they had been given as children. He gave credit freely to the other supervising men in the camp for their influence on the boys, for their patience, their education, and their generosity. Under Jack and other supervisors, the boys recognized the value of hard work and satisfaction from a job well done.

But Jack's deepest gratification came from sharing his love of the great outdoors. He relished witnessing the transformative power of Nature on these young men. Like a schoolteacher of today, Jack recognized the restlessness of these young men who seemed to need stimulation from noise and activity. Under his watch, they learned to focus and allow their minds to quiet. Over time, the rough boys matured into thoughtful men.

Jack believed, just as Justice William O. Douglas wrote twenty years later, that nobility of the spirit could be gained from good work in the outdoors. Douglas' friend Dr. George Draper wrote that "Man is at his worst when pitted against his fellow man. He is at his best when pitted against nature." As one CCC man from a tough part of Brooklyn learned, "There's no use getting sore at a tree." [49]

For Jack, it was tremendously fulfilling to see the results of his efforts in the lives of these young men. He later wrote that his time with them was the most rewarding of all the work that he did in thirty-five years of service with the United States government.[50] The Civilian Conservation Corps boys repaid Jack's care with their confidence, their friendship and a lifetime of letters sent back to their mentor far away in the mountains of Washington State.

🌲 🌲 🌲

It is summer, I was deep in the forest and totally confused again. I had explored the remains of Camp 22, the old dam construction camp, and thought I understood the layout. I'd drawn a map of what remained and reconciled the foundations, pipelines, root cellars, pit latrines, stone ovens, and such with the original construction map from the turn of the century. But as I moved north away from what was once "main street," I kept coming across new discoveries that were messing with my map. Here was evidence of buildings where there should be none. There were poured concrete footings in contrast to the simple rock foundations of Camp 22 and, seemingly, sophisticated plumbing as well. As I moved farther north through the trees, I found trenches everywhere, crisscrossing the sandy ground. What *was* this?

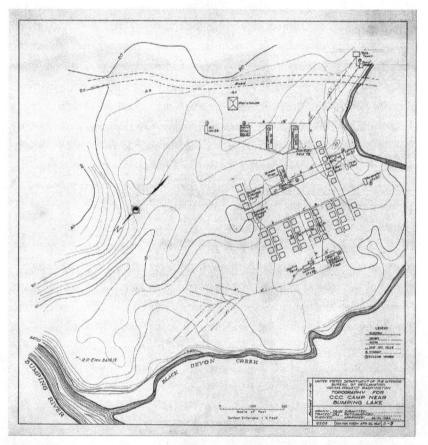

This beautiful hand-drawn map depicts Civilian Conservation Corps (CCC) Camp BR-67 at Bumping Lake. Located just below the dam and tucked into a curve of Black Devon (Barton) Creek, the camp was never fully completed and occupied. Begun in 1941, it was one of the last CCC camps to be constructed before WWII caused the program to be terminated. (Courtesy of the United States Forest Service, Naches Ranger District)

A visit to the Yakima Valley Museum research room a few days later uncovered a beautifully drafted map of a CCC camp tucked into a gentle curve of Barton Creek, not far from the Bumping Lake Dam. The location was exactly the area I had been exploring just the week before. This camp, BR-67, both established and terminated in 1941, was the last camp to be built in Yakima County before the program was ended on the eve of America's involvement in World War II.

🌰 🌰 🌰

A CCC Reclamation Camp had been recommended for Bumping Lake as early as 1937 primarily to take another stab at clearing the debris and timber, both standing and floating, that still plagued the reservoir. But it wasn't until 1941 that a camp was finally approved.

In April, nine men from Company No. 1297, originally from New York State, were sent ahead to Bumping Lake to clear the area for the camp. The spot that was chosen was adjacent to old Camp 22 and overlapped it in the area along Barton Creek/Black Devon to the east of the Bumping River Road.[51] The construction crew set about clearing the site and then building the foundations and frames for thirty-four, sixteen-by-sixteen-foot pyramidal tents, six wall tents for officers, three educational storage tents, and a dispensary storage tent. Rigid structures would include a combination mess hall and kitchen, a technical service office, army office, maintenance shop, generator shed, oil house, pump house, bath houses, and officers' and enrollees' latrines. An old storehouse from the dam construction days would also be utilized for the new camp.

The structures were arranged in neat rows with the latrines located a discreet distance back toward the trees and the oil and generator sheds a safe distance away from the rest of the camp.

When the members of Company No. 6459 arrived to occupy the camp on August 4, 1941, it was still being built, and they were put to work on that construction. Few men could be spared for the project work of reservoir clearing but the crew did manage to rebuild the old mining road south to

Copper City and clear at least nine acres of timber in the lake bottom before the camp was closed for the winter in October. It was still unfinished.[52]

With the bombing of Pearl Harbor in December, the tidy little settlement at Bumping Lake never was reoccupied, and in September 1942 the buildings were turned over to the Navy.[53] The larger structures were dismantled to be shipped to Alaska, but a number of the smaller ones were moved over to the growing collection of buildings at the Nelsons' resort.[54] Even the water and oil pipes were removed but their open trenches remained, for others to stumble into some sixty years later.

While Jack was busy transforming CCC boys into men, Kitty was just as busy transforming their resort into one that could accommodate the next generation of vacationers. A new road was helping bring those visitors to her.

The roadway was a long time coming. In 1931, after thirty-eight years of political wrangling, fits and starts of funding, construction and reconstruction, the trans-mountain highway over Chinook Pass (Highway 410) was finally completed.

Serious efforts to build a wagon road locally to join the two halves of the state began in the 1850s at Naches Pass. In the 1890s, attention shifted to a new route just south in the Chinook Pass area when it was imagined that such a route could be completed in a few months for a few thousand dollars. The development of the Summit Mining District further flamed interest on both sides of the state for a local east-west connection. When the much-ballyhooed mines didn't immediately produce, Frank Nagler and Robert Fife, founders of the Elizabeth Gold Hill Mining Company and desperate to keep interest and development growing, jumped into road building.

Fifteen miners put down their picks in 1910, and with axes, shovels, and sweat widened almost sixteen miles of trail from the Bumping River junction along the American River and up Morse Creek. The men roughed out a narrow road that was sufficient to get their heavy mining equipment through, spending $15,000 dollars of precious mining capital on the route.[55]

Nearby cities and local citizens did not have the capital necessary to build across the formidable barrier of the rocky crest, so they appealed to the state for funding. Construction money was approved on and off through the years but what monies were appropriated were often diverted when other projects took priority.[56]

In 1914, the state focused funding and attention to cutting the eastern approach to Chinook Pass starting at the point where the Summit miners' road had left off (northwest up Morse Creek). Seattle contractor Samuel Normile was awarded the contract for $66,631 dollars for the arduous, six- mile route. When an expected steam shovel was not available, Normile had to rely on manpower alone, without even horse teams to assist with grading. Apparently, all the heavy work cutting across the flank of Silver Mountain was done with picks, shovels, and wheelbarrows—and wagonloads of dynamite.[57]

Normile's contract also included constructing a log bridge over Morse Creek. It balanced on thirty-foot cribbed piers with the road deck a soaring seventy-five feet above the crashing stream. It must have been built more solidly than photos suggest since the bridge survived three major floods (1916, 1917 and 1921) and heavy auto traffic until it was finally replaced by a steel span in 1929.[58]

The road work contracted to Normile was completed by the time snow started falling in September. The dirt roadbed ranged from seventeen to thirty feet wide and maintained a reasonable six percent grade up to Lake Tipsoo at the summit of the Cascade crest. Unfortunately, there was not a corresponding roadway up the west side to the pass and it would be years before that route was started. Critics decried the Normile Grade as a road "from nowhere to nowhere." [59] Though it was not a connecting highway yet, it certainly *was* a road to a gorgeous picnic spot with a spectacular view for any eastsider who had the means to make the trip.

When auto and commercial traffic exploded in the second decade of the 1900s, demand ramped up for a road connecting Yakima to Enumclaw or another west side city. Though there were sections of primitive road and some bridges in place in the Twenties, most of the east side route was still either a rutted wagon track or footpath that petered out as it reached toward the divide.

Morse Creek bridge in 1923. Built by Samuel Normile's crews in 1914, this wooden bridge consisted of thirty feet of stacked log cribbing supporting its car deck a full seventy-five feet above the falls of the creek. To drive over it must have been either exhilarating or terrifying depending upon one's confidence in the road builders. Highway 410 travelers today cross the stream at the same place, on a replacement steel span not built until 1929. (Courtesy of the Yakima Valley Museum)

While the little-used Normile road section slowly washed away, debates as to what route the road would take—and via which pass—slowed progress. Countless road surveys, pass inventories, and route maps were developed as debates over the road's location raged for decades at the local and state level. Along the Cascades' backbone, Carleton Pass, Cowlitz Pass, Rainier Pass, Bear Gap, and Naches Pass were all considered. Over time, the route would be named State Road No. 1, State Road No. 5, McClellan Pass Highway, Naches Pass Highway, and Pioneer Highway. When the focus finally shifted in the 1920s from the need for a commercial trans-mountain connection to a scenic and recreational one with access to Mount Rainier National Park, Chinook Pass became the obvious choice. In the decades since, travelers fortunate enough to cross at Chinook Pass are treated to an unparalleled view of Mount Rainier and its breathtaking surroundings.

Many local residents were involved in different stages of this marathon of road building including the Ira Ford family. In 1927, Ira and Bess were hired by the road contractors Meyers & Goulter to cook for one of the road crews rebuilding the long stretch from the Bumping River junction west up to the Pass.[60] The family lived in a tent house next to the road. Ira delivered supplies from Yakima to the camp which was next to the American River about two miles above the Bumping River junction. At the end of the summer, the family moved into the cook's shack which was constructed of single pieces of lumber covered with tar paper. Having nowhere else to go, they stayed on after the road crew departed for the winter and tried to stay warm.[61]

The next summer, a caterpillar tractor and steam shovel were brought in to speed the progress on the road. Another firm, Wilburn and Stone from Seattle held the contract to improve part of the section including the Union Creek and Morse Creek bridges. Reportedly, they were bankrupted due to the heavy rock work in the area.[62]

In 1928, a concerted effort was made to conquer the last few miles of forbidding cliffs immediately west of the pass itself. Fortuitously, sufficient state funding was also available. The end was finally in sight. However, the sheer face at the west summit was by far the most difficult section of the entire route—it is not surprising that it was not tackled for so long. The solid rock removed from both sides of the summit amounted to two and a half times the material taken out of the two-mile-long Milwaukee Railroad tunnel built under Snoqualmie Pass to the north.[63] Almost three more years of blasting and clearing were required to cut the west switchbacks and lower the elevation at the summit to obtain a manageable grade.

During the last rushed months of construction, crews worked night and day to try to get the route passable for the summer season of 1931. The weather did not cooperate with record rains in June slowing down progress to such an extent that the planned summer opening became impossible. Nonetheless, the first auto traversed from west to east on July 15th when enough rubble was pushed aside to squeeze a car through. It was loaded with State supervisors and contractors.[64]

Meanwhile, the last preparations for a long-awaited public celebration at the junction were being made. Lake Tipsoo would be the site of a symbolic mock wedding between Miss Peaches (Betty Hollum) from Yakima and Mr. Cream (Arthur "Barney" Lind) from Enumclaw. There would be speeches and bands and free peaches and cream for all celebrants. The day dawned rainy with heavy fog at the summit but in spite of the inclement weather, an estimated six to eight *thousand* people made the drive from the east and the west sides on September 13th. Eight hundred vehicles were turned away at the east side entrance after the flowering meadows around the lake were filled with cars.[65]

The opening of the Chinook Pass Highway, dubbed "the queen of the mountain routes"[66] stirred new interest in Mount Rainier and the central Cascade Mountain range especially from western Washington residents. Kitty advertised in the new promotional tourist guides and alongside travel articles in the newspapers. The highway opened up a whole new market to the Nelsons' resort with the rapidly growing cities on the west side of the state now a much shorter drive away.

There was no more room along the lakeshore for additional tent cabins, so the resort continued to expand up the slopes behind the original 1915 lodge next to the spillway. There were already wood cabins dotting the hillside in the early twenties, and in the early thirties the Nelsons had Normandie built. It would soon be both their home and the center of the "new" resort. For Normandie, they hooked into the same water system that supplied the lower resort. Telephone wires soon stretched across the road and looped through the trees to connect the buildings.

At about the same time, they erected several matching log cabins just above Normandie.

These were the next generation of rental cabins for the resort. "Minnesota" was the largest with two stories, "Mark Hopkins" sat closest to the lodge and was also two-storied, and "Maine" sat just across the drive. Each had a sitting area, kitchen, separate bedrooms, and a small bathroom. An outdoor shower house served all the cabins. Jack kept an ample supply of wood stacked in front of each cabin to fuel the wood-burning stoves inside, the only source of heat and cooking for the buildings. Each cabin had a parking area and in a small clearing, a wooden picnic bench for outdoor meals.

Then, in the early forties, four more cabins appeared on the hillside to the west of Normandie. Of a completely different style, they were clapboard buildings painted red with tidy white trim around the windows and the doors: classic CCC style. Because of Jack's association with the camps, it is likely that the ever-enterprising Kitty managed to obtain the CCC boys' services to build the cabins for her.[67]

They were christened Larch, Idaho, Pine, and Illinois. Two other large rental cabins were added just east of the expanded resort. The uncreatively named #5 cabin was reportedly originally from Camp 22 and dragged over to a spot just north of the spillway bridge. It had been hastily built in 1910 for the temporary dam construction camp and was a bare bones rental. "Spring" cabin was built onsite at the head of the old river gauge road and was a popular rental. This cabin got around: it was later moved to a clearing just south of the resort and then up above Normandie with the rest of the rental cabins.[68]

For the next fifteen years the Nelsons presided over this expanded empire with twenty-two buildings making up the mountain getaway. It was a lot to keep up.

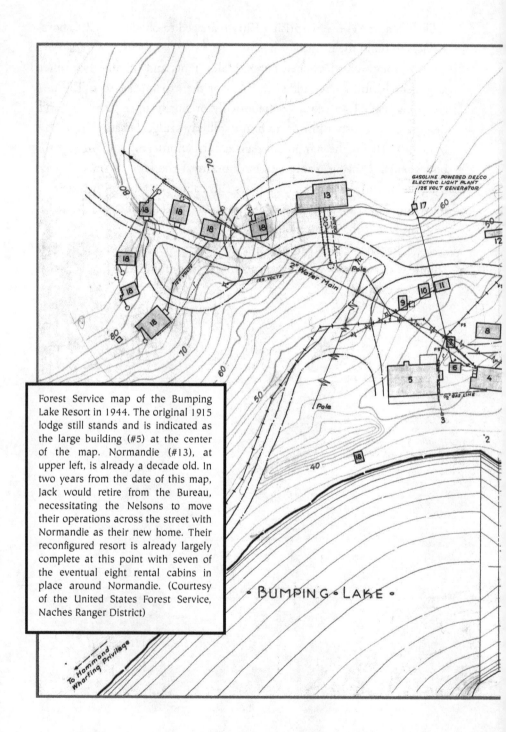

Forest Service map of the Bumping Lake Resort in 1944. The original 1915 lodge still stands and is indicated as the large building (#5) at the center of the map. Normandie (#13), at upper left, is already a decade old. In two years from the date of this map, Jack would retire from the Bureau, necessitating the Nelsons to move their operations across the street with Normandie as their new home. Their reconfigured resort is already largely complete at this point with seven of the eventual eight rental cabins in place around Normandie. (Courtesy of the United States Forest Service, Naches Ranger District)

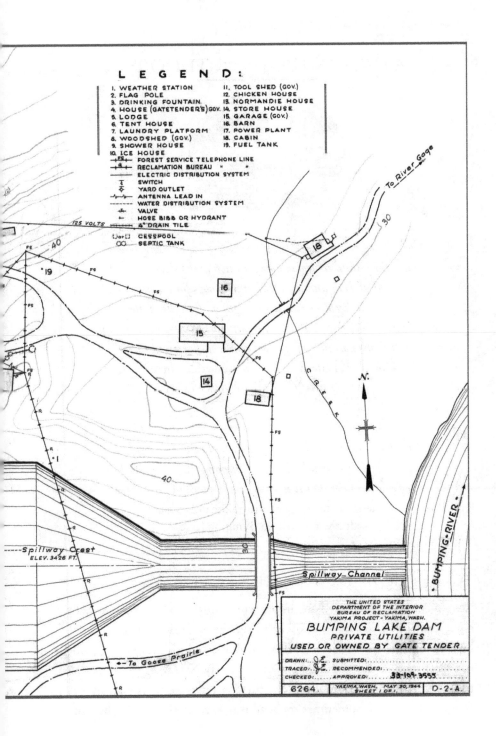

LEGEND:

1. WEATHER STATION
2. FLAG POLE
3. DRINKING FOUNTAIN
4. HOUSE (GATETENDER'S) GOV.
5. LODGE
6. TENT HOUSE
7. LAUNDRY PLATFORM
8. WOODSHED (GOV.)
9. SHOWER HOUSE
10. ICE HOUSE

11. TOOL SHED (GOV.)
12. CHICKEN HOUSE
13. NORMANDIE HOUSE
14. STORE HOUSE
15. GARAGE (GOV.)
16. BARN
17. POWER PLANT
18. CABIN
19. FUEL TANK

FS — FOREST SERVICE TELEPHONE LINE
R — RECLAMATION BUREAU "   "
—— ELECTRIC DISTRIBUTION SYSTEM
⊥ SWITCH
⍏ YARD OUTLET
ANTENNA LEAD IN
WATER DISTRIBUTION SYSTEM
VALVE
HOSE BIBB OR HYDRANT
125 VOLTS 4" DRAIN TILE

CESSPOOL
SEPTIC TANK

To River Gage

N.

CREEK

BUMPING-RIVER

Spillway Crest
ELEV. 3426 FT.

Spillway Channel

To Goose Prairie

THE UNITED STATES
DEPARTMENT OF THE INTERIOR
BUREAU OF RECLAMATION
YAKIMA PROJECT - YAKIMA, WASH.

BUMPING LAKE DAM
PRIVATE UTILITIES
USED OR OWNED BY GATE TENDER

DRAWN: SUBMITTED:
TRACED: RECOMMENDED: 33-109-3555
CHECKED: APPROVED: 33-109-3555

6264.   YAKIMA, WASH.   MAY 30, 1944
         SHEET 1 OF 1.   D-2-A.

Chapter Eight

A NATION HEADS OUTDOORS

*"Miss Olive Rand struggled along on two lanky slabs of wood,
with turned up ends and a pair of simple loops for harness which
quite failed to keep the runners straight or, for that matter, to
keep them on her feet at all. She explained that the slabs were skis
and that she had in a misguided moment, borrowed them."*
—Joseph T. Hazard on a winter snowshoe trip to
Longmire, Mount Rainier, in 1912

*"It is hard to believe that any place could be as beautiful as
Nelson's is now. It is wonderful here. Bumping Lake is all right in
spring and summer, but it is a marvelous place in the winter."*
—Clarence Truitt by phone to Yakima newspapers
after winter trip to Bumping Lake

Visiting Bumping Lake in the winter qualifies as an adventure by
any measure. There is no quick way to get there. Chinook Pass is buried
by snow and so, from Seattle we drive over Snoqualmie Pass, make a long
loop east through Yakima and head up the frosty Naches River Valley. We
then continue up the Bumping River Road as far as we can until our way
is blocked by drifts. Sometimes the road is plowed all the way to the dam;

other years the asphalt disappears at Bumping Crossing, a mile and some short of the lake (clearly, we are not winter-hardy, as were Jack and Kitty).

At this point we have to switch to skis for the rest of the journey. Children, gear, dog all pile out of the car, and we stuff the last of our supplies into our backpacks. Even though we always pack conservatively, we are so top heavy that when we hoist our loads, we sway dangerously on our narrow cross-country skis as we get underway. Poles are a blessing.

One year, we enlisted our Great Dane to help transport our weekend supplies and somehow hitched him up to a long toboggan. Not trained to pull, he panicked when he glimpsed the loaded sled gliding behind him and bolted. Before we could stop him, our provisions were liberally scattered all over the dam.

The ski across the dam is an orgy of views, the most exhilarating being the long vista south across the frozen lake and into the Cougar Lakes basin with its crenulated peaks. We glide off the dam, over the spillway bridge, and as we swing around the last bend, we strain to catch sight of Normandie. Most years, the building is barely visible under a thick blanket of snow. We struggle up the drive and to the area where the door usually is. With the drifts well past the windows, we have to dig our way in. Six snow steps are usually sufficient to get us down to the door, but additional excavation is required to get the door open. The kids make snow angels or wage snowball battles while we shovel.

There is no real refuge inside. Without the benefit of even weak winter sun, the interior of Normandie is frigid. It is warmer outside. With all of the snow shutters bolted, it is as dark as a tomb as well. Soon, lanterns brighten the main rooms but can't chase the shadows from the corners. We gather around these islands of light. Though we are quick to create illumination, we can't do the same for warmth. It will be a full twenty-four hours before the roaring fireplace and wood heater sufficiently heat the heavy log walls so that they keep the outside cold at bay. By day two, we can take our jackets off inside, but the snow that we tramped in on the floor of the unheated dining room remains frozen.

With limited resources, we keep meals simple, cooking in a big pot on the embers in the fireplace for the novelty of it and boiling water on the stove for nonstop hot drinks. We all sleep on the floor in the living room, jostling for the spots closest to the sources of heat.

The reward for our efforts is scenery out of a fairy tale. An already delightful landscape is made pristine by the virginal snow that covers everything. The snow sparkles and crystalline icicles hang like ornaments. We explore this magical world on skis, marveling at fantastic wind carved sculptures along the lakeshore, swirling mists fronting the mountains, and a giant frozen waterfall hanging suspended at the end of the spillway where water trickled over in the fall. It is luminescent turquoise.

As noticeable as the captivating scenery is the overwhelming quiet. Billions of stacked snowflakes absorb every sound the moment it is created. Nothing bounces back to our ears and the result is a profound stillness to wrap yourself up in.

I do not take any of this for granted. Our children, the landscape, the cold, the warmth, my husband. The sum is almost overwhelming.

Here are trees and mountains and lake and white snow binding it all together. It is a place outside of time.

In the twenties, a new winter activity was gaining popularity in the Northwest. Local residents had always snowshoed to get around and by 1913 travel by "skees" was being reported at Bumping Lake.[1] After World War I, increased interest nationally in outdoor activities and Nordic influences led to the introduction of ski jumping, downhill skiing, and ski racing. Recreational skiing as sport quickly gained popularity in the favorable conditions of the Cascades.

Unlike the bank-busting sport of today, skiing during the early years was a simpler affair. Local residents early on skied out of necessity on homemade skis, made from barrel staves or slats cleaved from a scavenged log. The first recreational skiers made do with the same or, if they were lucky, a pair fashioned by the old freighter John Anderson. He would sometimes craft skis for visitors when they stopped in at his ranch in the

Naches.[2] Ira Ford made skis for himself and his family utilizing a home-made steamer which he used to create a perfect curve at the tips. His and wife Bess's skis were purely utilitarian: they never skied "just for fun."[3] Jack certainly would have made his and Kitty's as well.

Early skis were generally between seven and fourteen feet long and had simple leather loops or straps as bindings.[4] For balance, turning, and braking, skiers carried a single, stout wooden staff similar to alpenstocks that climbers were using at the time. Later, a pair of lighter ski poles outfitted with rawhide baskets replaced the staff.

Attire was similarly primitive. For warmth, skiers usually wore wool sweaters or a thick coat and baggy pants tucked into heavy leather boots. None of the attire was waterproof or even particularly comfortable.

Before long, ski enthusiasts started to organize into clubs which began to cobble together basic facilities near their favorite slopes. In the old Summit Mining District just under Crown Point, a warming hut was made from the remains of a ramshackle miner's cabin. Nearby, Cascadian club members dragged an old circus wagon up to the head of Morse Creek and made it their clubhouse.[5]

The first facilities were extremely primitive by our standards to-day. Originally, there were no lifts of any kind. Skiers were obliged to walk to the top of any slopes they wished to shush down and warmed themselves between runs next to bonfires of gathered wood. Despite the lack of amenities, skiers loved the conditions and dramatic scenery the Gold Hill area offered— "as beautiful as any to be found in the Northwest"—and soon displaced the last of the prospectors hanging on there in their old shacks.[6]

Around 1938, Yakima Scout leader Clarence Truitt took over the Gold Hill warming hut for a Boy Scout ski facility. He brought in Chuck Hessey and Marion Madder (soon to be Hessey) to teach his boys downhill skiing and even hired them to make an instructional ski film. After the second World War, which dispersed many of the skiers, the Hesseys and others assumed responsibilities of the cabin. The Cascadians continued to base their winter skiing activities there for the next ten years, making regular treks across the pass to the Crystal Bowl area for its exciting terrain and dramatic views.[7]

By the 1930s, Yakima area skiers had begun to organize and were promoting the development of a local ski facility. The newly formed Yakima Valley Ski Club, under the leadership of Charles A. Ranking, chose a little hill just west of the confluence of the Bumping and American Rivers for one of the first downhill ski developments in the state. It would be called the American Ridge Ski Bowl.[8]

CCC Company 932 (stationed at nearby Naches Camp F-70) was authorized to build the facilities and worked in conjunction with the Forest Service and ski club to drain a swampy area at the base of the bowl, clear the run, and build a ski jump along with a three-sided warming hut. Oliver Klingensmith was the CCC superintendent who supervised the construction in 1935 of a handsome lodge along with an unprecedented twenty-seater outhouse that is said to be the largest in the world.

The Civilian Conservation Corp (CCC) crew who constructed the American Ridge Ski Bowl pose in front of the newly finished lodge on or around November 13, 1935. This sturdy building sheltered a generation of hardy skiers at the Ski Bowl until the White Pass ski area was developed in the 1950s. The lodge and its famous outhouse still stand today. (Courtesy of the United States Forest Service, Naches Ranger District)

The construction of the American Ridge Ski Bowl was a complex CCC project which utilized skills from crews learning trades in four

different classes. The Lodge itself was built by men in a carpentry training class using lumber milled on site by another crew. A masonry class
constructed the stone chimney while a logging crew cleared the slope for
the ski run.[9]

With ski traffic now funneling through their city, boosters with
the Yakima Chamber of Commerce were anxious to promote the new
ski center and sponsored ski tournaments at American Ridge complete with ski jumping and gliding contests cheered on by thousands
of spectators. Not surprisingly at this remote outpost, many of the
contests in the first years were won by locals who had been skiing up
and down the mountain sides on "boards" for a living. Local trapper,
Harry Griffin won several races even though on the last one, one of
his skis was broken. Slim and Tex Ballinger were two competitors who
skied to the American River tournaments from their mines on nearby
Miner's Creek.

In January 1937, the Yakima Winter Sports Club opening tournament at American Ridge attracted thirty-three skiers from Seattle and
Tacoma competing in jumping, downhill and slalom, including two
members of the 1936 U.S. Olympic ski team, Don Fraser and Darroch
Crookes. Area newspapers claimed that between 3,000 and 5,000 spectators gathered to watch the events.[10] The Pacific Northwest Ski Association
was soon holding tournaments at the American Ridge Ski Bowl but in-
sufficient snow in 1938-39 forced them to move the contest up the road
to a spot half a mile up Morse Creek. Dubbed "Quartermile" by orga-
nizers (Quartermile sounded closer than "Halfmile"), the new downhill
course was ambitious for its time, dropping 2,500 feet in a mile and a
half. The next few years saw the tournament expanded to two days with
the downhill races at Quartermile and slalom and ski jumping held at
American Ridge.[11]

In 1945, the addition of a much-anticipated rope tow erased the
single file line of skiers trekking up to the top of the bowl that looked
just like the endless column of miners trudging up Chilkoot Pass on their
way to the Klondike.[12] The earliest versions of local tows were reportedly
fashioned out of a long loop of rope encircling the back wheel rim of a
motorcycle chained to a tree.[13]

The American Ridge Ski Bowl was a popular local destination for skiers during the War years. The ski jump and the longer runs were on a broad hill behind the photographer in this image. (Courtesy of Betty Jean Ford Gallant)

American Ridge Ski Bowl remained the local skiers' choice until the early 1950s when the White Pass highway was completed, and the White Pass Ski Resort was developed. White Pass had more runs and better access but more importantly, its 4,500 foot elevation meant a much longer ski season than the ten to eleven weeks that American Ridge could typically expect to eke out at 3,000 feet. Skiers abandoned the single rope tow at American Ridge for the superior terrain at White Pass but the old ski lodge, along with its remarkable outhouse, still stands at the edge of the little bowl, the old runs overgrown with tall trees. The entire area, along with many ghosts of skiers past, is available year round as a Forest Service rental facility.

Kitty wasn't the only one expanding her vacation facilities in the Bumping Valley area in the 1930s. Even though there was a great depression on, other mountain folks were managing to get things built, even without the help of the CCC. Clearly, there existed a shared hope that better times would return, and the vacationers would too.

Two more roadhouses with overnight accommodations went in, both downriver from Bumping Lake. The first was Whistlin' Jack Lodge, named after the hoary marmot of the high country. Built next to the Naches River by Charlie and Mildred Rodgers, the facility originally served the overflow of families staying in the new vacation community of Cliffdell. The building may have initially been called Wapato Lodge but by 1930 or 1931 it had been renamed Whistlin' Jack.

Whistlin' Jack Lodge opened in the community of Cliffdell in the Naches Valley in the early 1930s. This postcard photo was taken in the 1940s when the entrance sign indicated that the facility was not only modern, but AAA Club approved. (Ellis postcard, Cyr family collection)

The American River Resort also opened in the early thirties at the intersection of Highway 410 and the Bumping River Road. The building, complete with a restaurant and store, was constructed on the foundations of an earlier planned grand hotel that never made it past the pouring of the foundation.[14] Owners Charles and Alice (Manny) Walls soon added a gas station and a handful of rental cabins. The addition of a large bunkhouse to house groups completed the resort which served a pre-motorhome vacationing public.[15]

The American River Resort, located at the junction of Highway 410 and the Bumping River Road, was also opened in the early 1930s. The facility consisted of a day lodge with a restaurant and small store in addition to separate rental cabins. Almost no one drove past the building without stopping, if not for a meal, then for last-minute camping items or perhaps an ice cream treat to break up a long drive into the mountains. (Clark postcard, Cyr family collection)

The American River Resort was a favorite stop for travelers heading into or out of Bumping Lake. Early on, some skiers enjoying the Ski Bowl stayed at the Resort and walked to the slopes, but after the skiers migrated to other venues the operation struggled, hampered by a short summer season. In 1966, the lodge burned to the ground along with the bunkhouse nearby.[16] The Forest Service did not issue a new lease. The beautiful fireplace and chimney remained standing for many years, a monument to both hard work and summer idyll.[17]

Structures were starting to go up at the lake, too. After twenty-five years of relative seclusion, Jack and Kitty were soon to have neighbors as a result of the approval in 1937 of the Bumping Lake Summer Home Tract. Lots were quickly leased, and Chuck Hammond was back at work at the lake building the first home of the Bumping Lake Tract (#13, approved October 28, 1937) for Mr. and Mrs. Arthur Karr. Cabin #1 was soon begun as well. Before long, the sound of hammers was echoing down the lake as vacation cabins (and dreams) were banged together.[18]

Partly as an attempt to encourage citizens to get into the National Forests, in 1915, Congress had authorized the Forest Service to offer small parcels of land for lease for hotels, stores, and summer homes. Leases started at five dollars per year. By the 1930s, the policy had taken off and the Naches Ranger District had become particularly enthusiastic about the program, ultimately platting thirty-one home tracts throughout the district. The Naches District is home to the second highest number of summer homes in the nation at 531 cabins in thirty-two tracts.[19]

The Edgewater Summer Home tract which is located along the Bumping River Road below Goose Prairie, had been surveyed earlier, in 1928, along with many of the American River Valley tracts. Another summer home tract was surveyed for Bumping Crossing that was never realized. It would have consisted of eight cabins arrayed on the east side of the river on the flats called Snooks by some old timers. Also never constructed was a small airfield suggested for an area along the road near the old ballfield.

The Nutley family from Yakima, in a bid to escape the summer heat in their hometown, built the next cabin in the summer home tract, which was truly a family affair. In 1938, Ben and his wife Lorena, after years of vacationing at Bumping Lake (including rentals at the Bumping Lake Resort), asked their children if they would like a cabin at the lake or a swimming pool in the backyard in Yakima. They voted for a cabin. Ben designed the building himself and then hired Harold Webb to cut lodgepole pines from the large stand across the lake. The logs were notched and stacked to create a twenty by twenty-six foot log frame. The family then hired Mr. Jimenez to build the fireplace with the children helping to gather stones for it. Family members took over from that point with the two sons, Jack and Van, along with aunts, uncles, and cousins building out the rest of the structure. With each adding what they knew best, the floors, staircase, windows, doors, trim, water system and finally the roof were installed. The two-story cabin, a long labor of love, was finished in 1940.[20]

In all, fourteen summer homes would be built along the west shore of Bumping Lake.

There is little mention of the Bumping Lake Resort during World War II and Jack wrote nothing of it in *We Never Got Away*. However, Ranger Horace Cooper announced restrictions to travel in the National Forest as early as April 1942. Travel was limited to the main roads, lakes were only open to fishermen who had registered at a ranger station, and all enemy aliens were excluded completely except on the Naches highway and official campgrounds.[21]

Responsibility to keep the forest lands safe was also imposed upon the Forest Service fire lookouts stationed on the mountain tops. Before assuming her post at Raven's Roost (in nearby Little Naches), Betty Jean Ford was told she was expected to inspect the permits of anyone she encountered—while remaining courteous and helpful. Furthermore, she was advised to be alert at all times. "Keep a record in your diary of all Air Crafts flying over your area; time, direction traveling and if possible, type and number of motors," her letter from the Naches Ranger Station instructed. "If any objects are dropped from an Air Craft or if an enemy plane is sighted call the Naches Ranger Station immediately and give the above information." [22]

Effects of the faraway war doomed one of the Nelsons' few attempts to convenience themselves. By 1942, the couple had endured thirty winters at the Lake. By Jack's own admission they spent more than five months each year on skis and were as isolated as they had been when they first arrived. Though a few Goose Prairie residents were fashioning motorized vehicles for winter travel, snowmobiles were not yet commercially or widely available. Jack and Kitty heard about a promising snow machine then being built in Durango, Colorado called a snow plane. The Price Snoplane had an enclosed cab, three wide runners and a large rear push propeller powered by a sixty-five horsepower engine. Jack figured it would be perfect for getting around in snow conditions similar to those of the Rockies. Unfortunately, they were unable to purchase one in 1942 and restrictions on manufacturing during the war prevented them from buying one the following year as well.[23] For the rest of their winters in the mountains, the couple never did get off of their skis.

Gasoline rationing and shifting priorities during the war meant there was surely a dip in visitors to the resort, and those years were probably quiet ones for the couple. If the dam was closed to travel as it had been in the previous world war, then the Nelsons would have been very much on their own.

The couple did have good communication, however. By 1940, the Bureau of Reclamation had supplied a radio telephone for the daily

operation calls (although the original telephone lines were still operational). Soon the Forest Service would install their own line as part of fire suppression efforts. Three phone systems served the Nelsons in 1944 and an
additional line ran down to the marina.

The dam itself and equipment was regularly inspected and maintained by Bureau work crews. As early as 1927, when the dam was only
fifteen years old, problems with some of the concrete work started to arise.
Excessive cracking and "soggy" concrete were noted in the gate tower and
the conduit through the dam. In addition, the control gates at the bottom
of the tower were not well aligned and had been difficult to operate almost
from the beginning. It took all of Jack's not insignificant strength to adjust
them. At some point a small motor was installed to move the gates. Over
the years, the failing portions of the dam infrastructure were repaired and
replaced.[24]

As the twentieth century neared its halfway mark, momentous
changes were shifting the Nelson household. Within just a few years, Jack
would retire, the couple would move across the road into Normandie, and
they would celebrate a second wedding of their daughter, Frances.

In October of 1946, after almost exactly thirty-five years of continuous and faithful service to his government through the Bureau of
Reclamation, Yakima papers celebrated the occasion of the original dam
tender's retirement. It might have been a difficult transition for him. His
name had become synonymous with the lake, and no one knew more about
the area than he and Kitty. Overnight, the rhythm and order to his life
changed. No longer would he raise the stars and stripes to greet the dawn
or relay the daily meteorological data to the Bureau.

Jack not only had to relinquish those responsibilities, but also
turn over the dam tender cottage and "his" reservoir to his replacement,
Clarence "Pat" Ford.[25]

Pat Ford was a worthy successor. Raised in Goose Prairie and in-
culcated in the ways of these woods, he was already working for the Forest
Service as a Forest Guard when he applied for the dam tender position. He
was just twenty-two.[26]

Ford may have been young, but he had a wide skill set. He was a mechanical prodigy who could rebuild any machine with his eyes closed. As a kid, he had repaired the transmission of a 1919 Model T truck that Jack had given the Ford boys when he upgraded to a 1936 Dodge pickup. He diagnosed a recurring bearing problem on the new school bus they rode to Naches. And when he returned from the war—after having served as a mechanic—he built a novel machine for traveling across the snow. It had tracks in the back, steerable skies in the front and an old Indian motorcycle engine for power. The vehicle resembled the early snowmobiles being invented in other snowy climes around the world.[27]

Jack and Kitty pose on Ed Bedford's homemade snowmobile which is perched in front of their nearly buried cottage. Kay Kershaw smiles from behind while Bedford poses proudly in front in this mid-1940s photo. It is unknown how well this vehicle worked, but he was not the only one tinkering around with snow machines at the time. Pat Ford also developed two snowmobile prototypes that he tested out in the deep snows of the area. (Cyr Family Collection)

His next project was more ambitious, involving the renovation of a World War II military surplus Weasel. These versatile vehicles had been designed for winter warfare with a powerful engine, long tank treads, and room for a crew of four. They could go anywhere in any condition and once the snow clogged the roads, Pat Ford piloted his Weasel all over the Valley. He retrieved stuck vehicles, freighted mail and supplies, and delivered guests and their luggage to the Double K Mountain Ranch in Goose Prairie in the winter months.

All winter, Ford pushed the Weasel to its limits. One time he used the vehicle to take some hay to an elk which had become trapped in deep snow after failing to migrate to the lowlands.[28] While heading back home over the lake, the machine broke through the ice. Ford grabbed his two-year old son, Billy, and jumped off the Weasel as it began to sink into the icy water.[29] Grabbing a tree from shore, he jammed it in the front of the vehicle and ran home with Billy in his arms. He returned with a cable which he just managed to attach to the nose of the Weasel before it sank, eighty-five feet to the bottom of the lake. It took much of the winter and the help of his brother-in-law, Lucky Gallant, to winch the Weasel from the lake bottom, repair it, and drive it around the south end of the lake, including a hair-raising crossing of the Upper Bumping River.[30]

Ford returned to Goose Prairie from the front in Europe, with a wife. Doris was a Royal Air Force flight sergeant from London who it is said, made an admirable adjustment to mountain living when she moved with Pat first to Goose Prairie and then up to the dam tender's cottage on the edge of Bumping Lake. Once their two children were of school age, Doris and the children moved to Naches for the school year. In order to see them, Ford drove down every weekend, and brought them back up to the lake for the weekend when it was convenient.

One Friday in the middle of winter, with the Bumping River Road closed by snow, Ford skied the eleven plus miles down to American River where his car was parked. To his dismay, the engine would not turn over. Faced with no good options, he opted to get the car running—somehow. He retrieved a battery from an old flashlight he kept in the car and rigged it with a wire to the coil. In order to ensure that it would start, he decided to warm the oil. With no fuel and only snow available, he stripped off his long underwear, pushed them down into the gas tank to soak them in gasoline, brought them out again, and ignited the clothing underneath the oil pan. When the underwear had burnt out, the oil and even the battery was warmed and with the flashlight battery assist, the engine started on the very next try. His brother Bob claimed that "This was certainly another example that you don't have to be crazy to live in the mountains, but it sure helps."[31]

A DUKW on Bumping Lake. After returning from service in WWII,
Goose Prairie native Pat Ford got the job as the second dam tender
at Bumping Lake when Jack Nelson retired in 1946. To cope with
mountain living and to facilitate his responsibilities at the lake, he
purchased and refurbished not only a surplus Army Weasel but an
amphibious Army DUKW (know later as a "Duck"). Pictured motoring
past a floating boat house in 1948, is Pat, his mother Bessie, sister
Betty Jean, Pat's new wife Doris Ford, and friend Carl Birley. The
Bumping Lake dam is visible in the rear. (Courtesy of Betty Jean Ford
Gallant)

Flush with the success of his Weasel, Ford graduated to a Duck
(originally known as a DUKW which was a manufacturer's code). Shortly
after the War, he purchased the surplus Army amphibious vehicle in Yakima

for $750 dollars. He drove it up to the lake, refurbished it, and tooled around Bumping Lake while he was the dam tender. What may have been a novelty at first turned out to be quite useful: the Duck was much more effective hauling drifting logs out of the lake than the standard-issue Bureau of Reclamation skiff.[32] In winter, he attached a blade to the front of the vehicle and plowed the road with it.

At some point in the early 1950s, Pat, always tinkering and always improving upon systems, undertook his most enduring project. The nidus of the idea is unknown, but Pat designed and installed a hydroelectric power plant for Normandie. The new system revolutionized Jack and Kitty's lives and benefits ours still.[33] Until then, the Resort had generated electricity by an assortment of gas and diesel generators that were noisy, smelly, and expensive to run. As a result, electricity was only available for limited hours (lights went out at ten o'clock) and the rest of the time the buildings were dimly lit by kerosene or gas lanterns.

To construct the power plant, Pat tapped into the infrastructure that was originally put in to supply water for the construction of the dam forty years before. This was the diverted stream that supplied the water to dam tender's residence at the spillway and to the Bumping Lake Resort (Normandie and the rental cabins). Near the top of the system, Pat would need to create a collecting point for water to keep the supply pipes full. He built a sturdy cedar-shingled house a quarter of a mile upslope from the resort, right at the bend of the old wagon road that led up to the rockslide. He laid a six inch iron pipe that ran downhill towards the resort and then behind past Normandie. In a recently-erected shed, he installed an 1889 enclosed Pelton wheel to which he hooked up an old World War II generator. As planned, the generous fall down the mountainside created plenty of head pressure in the pipe which propelled pressurized water into the cups of the Pelton wheel. When everything was hooked up, the spinning water wheel ran the belts which powered the generator and created electricity. Suddenly, the Nelsons had abundant, free power to light their home day and night, winter and summer alike.[34]

Pat's installation freed the Nelson's from the expense of generators forever. The system has endured and for the ensuing seventy years has quietly converted flowing water to electricity to power our lives.[35]

Upon Jack's retirement, the Nelsons had to move from their government cottage by the spillway. Per the Bureau of Reclamation, all of the Nelsons' many resort-related buildings and equipment would need to be removed from the government land along the spillway. The small empire Jack and Kitty had built there was beginning to look a little "shabby" an internal report revealed, and the agency wanted the area cleaned up.[36]

The original resort's big lodge (the one built back in 1915) had settled badly over time and could not be moved, so it would have to be dismantled. The couple started clearing out the building, selling the venerable player piano—for twenty dollars—and getting rid of the extra furniture. Many of the smaller buildings, like the icehouse and storage sheds, were moved up to new spots on the hill and continued in use. Much of the summer of 1947 was spent clearing out and cleaning up.

By the end of the season, the dam tender's home and a few storage buildings were the only buildings that remained next to the spillway. The land was regraded somewhat, but an attractive landscaping plan drawn up by the Bureau for the area seems to have never been installed.

The Nelsons settled into Normandie, described by a reporter as a "log cabin dream home."[37] The second version of the Nelsons' resort would be called the Bumping Lake Resort (the original was known as Nelson Lodge). Normandie contained the resort's office where guests checked in and was front and center, with the rental cabins perched comfortably on the hill behind.

Once the big lodge closed, Kitty's life was somewhat simplified. She no longer had the responsibility of running the restaurant, the kitchen, or changing out the upstairs guest rooms. From now on, all visitors would take care of themselves in their rental cabins, bringing their own food and cooking on the wood stoves that anchored each kitchen.

Kitty also would have had more time to indulge in her very favorite pastime: fishing. With her own boat at the ready, she went out onto the water almost every day without fail. Eastern Washington newspapers pronounced her one of the best fishers in the country and their accolades were not empty hyperbole. In 1920, she landed a record Dolly Varden trout at eight and a half pounds. As Kitty maneuvered the leviathan into shallow water, the leader broke. Reportedly, she went right into the water after it. She also reeled in eighteen cutthroat trout that day.[38] Kitty almost never came back with an empty creel, and so renowned was her ability that fishermen would covertly follow her boat to try to discover her secrets.

Normandie Lodge, built in 1933 and the Nelson's last home, as it looked at eighty years old. Almost all of the building is original, including the roof, and most of it has been restored. (Susan Cyr photo)

By the next summer, the lodge was finally emptied. After thirty-two years of sheltering friends, guests, and dignitaries from all over the world, the venerable building was taken down. Much of the wood was surely recycled, since milled lumber was always a valuable commodity so far up in the mountains. The propane lights that illuminated the main room were given to the Nutley family for their cabin, where some still operate today.[39]

Of the old building, Jack reminisced, "Within its walls, hundreds of friendships were made. Thousands of memories came down with the weather stained logs. And within its walls we had a million laughs." [40]

Two years later, the "new" resort was the site of Frances' wedding ceremony. Her first marriage to Richard Reed (their wedding ceremony in 1926 had also been celebrated at the lake) had ended in divorce, but not before they had a child, a boy named Billy. Kitty doted on her only grandchild, spoiling him with treats and calling him "darling" whenever he visited. Now Billy was grown up, and Frances was to be married to Emmett Higgens from Yakima. Their ceremony was on August 17, 1949. The witness lines were inscribed with the loving signatures of J.H. Nelson and Kitty Nelson.[41]

Chapter 9

FIRE IN OUR FOREST

*"Today we understand that Forest fires are
wholly under the control of men."*
—Gifford Pinchot, *The Fight
for Conservation*, 1910

"...Man's efforts have been puny in the face of nature's forces,"
—Elers Koch, Supervisor, Lolo National
Forest, *Journal of Forestry*, 1935

Even though we understand that fire is a natural part of the forest ecosystem, there is absolutely nothing like a forest fire to make you sit up and pay attention. After years of blissfully but somewhat mindlessly heading up to Bumping Lake for weekend relaxing, reality bit. Tom and I had been busy growing a family—three cherished children—and a few small businesses so that the mountain getaway was more precious than ever. The kids loved going up and roaming around relatively unsupervised in the ever-fascinating forest. Their grandmother Virginia was the consistent presence in the kitchen, issuing dish after steaming dish of mouth-watering meals three times a day for the family and friends who were regularly invited.

It was during this period when we were investing in our future that we really started pouring our energy into Normandie's future as well. Much of our free time and any extra money in our household budget went not to our own home's needs, but to the lodge's. Maintenance could not be put off in the severe conditions of the Cascades where one year's neglect could mean the ruin of an old building.

We replaced and repaired, repainted, and repointed. Tom rewired and replumbed. It never seemed to be enough—the building was so old and so in need of attention that it seemed to suck up every bit of energy we threw at it. But miraculously, over time, Normandie started to shine. The foundation was leveled and strengthened, the windows re-caulked, cabinets straightened, floors sanded, ceilings sealed. The bathroom went from icky to shiny, the furniture was overhauled, and even the chimney got scrubbed. And year after year, we continued to haul loads of old accumulated junk to the dump in Yakima.

All of our work was done in consideration of the historic nature of the structure and its role in the past. We restored rather than rebuilt and in time applied for national historic status for Normandie and the outbuildings that represented the remains of the Bumping Lake Resort. Washington State recognized the site as historically relevant and forwarded our seventy-five page application on to Washington D.C. for their consideration. The application was approved, and Jack and Kitty's old home was added to the list of historically important sites on the National Register of Historic Places.

With every day spent there, every drop of sweat and every hour of our time invested, our emotional attachment to the building grew. What started years before as affection became a love affair. We loved Normandie and everything that came with it.

One day, I caught myself whispering goodbye to the cabin, telling it to be good and stay out of trouble while we were gone (actually willing trouble to stay out of it). It was when I found myself talking to a building that I began to consider the depth of my feelings towards this inanimate pile of logs. Such love of place is not unique of course, but I was still surprised at the extent of my emotions.

There were many reasons to love this corner of the woods, but I suspect much had to do with the reassurances that come from the continuity of life: in our family and in nature. Every year without fail, morel mushrooms poke through the duff in June, ospreys crash-dive into the lake for fish in July, huckleberries grow fat and sweet in August. The family was another year older, problematic for Grandma Virginia but the opposite for the thriving kids. We made the cabin retreat into a utopian world where we distilled life down to the basics. We practiced what we thought was good in life and pruned away distractions. It was there that we were able to turn our backs on the mundane aspects of life like paying bills, fixing the car, driving to the grocery store. Bumping Lake was where we were most happy.

Then, on August 5th, 2010, at the apex of my appreciation for this place and all that it represented, a hot bolt of lightning hit a tall snag on a sunbaked ridge high above Boulder Creek. Thousands of lightning strikes were recorded in the National Forest that crackling summer day and this was one that stuck.

We first saw smoke from the trail while hiking back to Bumping Lake from Cougar Lakes. We managed to make a 911 call on an otherwise unconnected cell phone. Not only had this fire already been reported, but it was assessed and assigned a name, we were told by the officious sounding voice on the other end. My heart began to race as we got closer to the cabin and could see flames flickering on the mountainside, a mile or so south of Normandie. They were mostly low but occasionally flashed into giant flares as individual trees caught fire and seemed to explode, shooting orange vortices of embers swirling into the sky.

But since the fire was several ridges away from the cabin and didn't seem to be moving in our direction, we eventually drifted inside to make dinner, checking outside occasionally. Without smoke or any visible evidence of fire, we went to bed and slept deeply, recovering from our long hike.

We would have been much more alarmed if we knew what the Forest Service Fire Chief saw when he arrived early the next morning. Although still small, the Boulder Creek fire held tremendous potential. It was on a steep slope in a dense area of the wilderness forest that had not burned in hundreds of years. And it was upwind of all of the homes along

the lakeshore. Normandie in particular was in the dead center of the projected path of this conflagration.

It had been an uneventful summer until that day. Sure, there was
the omnipresent dark cloud of the proposal of a new dam that would, if
built, completely submerge us, but the last effort had died for lack of funding several years ago. With the present economic situation, it seemed like a
distant possibility. There were other threats like the chance of destruction
by a falling tree and damage by vandalism, but these seemed rather exis-
tential compared to the absolute reality of a forest fire around the corner.

In fact, the biggest disturbance in our family life lately had been a
shift in fare. Usually, our days in the mountains ended with some sort of a
feast featuring Tom's masterwork on the grill. It might be a fresh salmon, or
Virginia's specially marinated pork shish kababs. This summer though, had
featured vegetables and more vegetables to accommodate the swelling ranks
of vegetarians in our family, with the oldest Cici disdaining even eggs and
dairy, leading us all in a pretty complete dietary revolution.

The immediacy of the fire struck at the heart of one of our most
primal fears. We cannot control, cannot reason with, or mitigate an out-of-
control forest fire. This one has been thrust upon us without warning to, at
least for now, shift our entire life focus.

When you fall in love with another by opening your heart, you take
on the risk of unrequited love and a broken heart. When you fall in love with
a place, you can only hope it will remain there until your return so that you
can spend time with it again. To that end, we undertook every precaution to
ensure Normandie endures: securing the windows with heavy shutters and
double dead bolts on the doors to keep out bad guys, grooming relationships
with our landlord the Forest Service and our protectors at the Sheriff's office,
removing dead trees when they threaten the cabin, clearing accumulated
fuels, prepping thoroughly for the snows of winter. Maintenance, leases,
taxes: all were given in return for the privilege of continued visits to this place
so steeped in stories and experiences—the essence of our lives together.

Time at Normandie has always embodied the best in what I want
our family to experience and our kids to represent. Our visits there celebrate

time well-spent together, building the bonds of family and unconditional love. We've cultivated a deep appreciation of nature, the seasons, and the intricate, interconnected web of life on earth. We have led an active life, using our bodies vigorously and with gratitude; hiking, biking, swimming, paddling, climbing, running, all before a backdrop worthy of a travel poster. It is a place with the time to do something new: whittle a bow out of a Yew branch, create fairy houses out of twigs and moss beside a tiny stream, fashion picture frames and maybe even furniture out of cast-up driftwood from the lake's depths. It is a place to have time—of days with space for a game to be played, a meal to be savored, a good book to be read, a path to be followed—without a specific goal or purpose in mind. It is a place of laughter, kisses, shared adventures, dear and treasured.

I would do anything to protect this spot, preserve it for our future and that of our kids and their children unborn. We have done everything we can to build the foundation of a family heritage but the building in which we gather is really only an arrangement of dead logs on cold stone within a vast forest.

Now the ultimate menace has come and is lurking, like a monster under the stairs, the worst imaginings in a nightmare. It is over the ridge unseen but is moving, coiling, unpredictable. It is ready to strike, paralyze and devour us all if we look away, even for an instant.

So, we don't look away. All day, we ride out onto the dam, lean on our bikes, and watch the growth of this beast, a living organism to us not unlike an agitated serpent or a furious bear. Fortunately for us, this young creature is having a hard time developing. Cooler weather and low winds are holding it to the upper ridge for now, where it circles, growling.

🌰 🌰 🌰

If Jack and Kitty faced a similar threat, they did not write about it and there is little mention of any major fire in recent history in the valley.

The closest to the resort was probably a small blaze that started next to the road between the marina and the Nelsons' and spread upslope. Betty Jean Ford Gallant related that everyone in the vicinity quickly joined the successful effort to put the fire out before it grew completely out of control.

Earlier, there is a newspaper mention of Reclamation Service employees fighting a large conflagration, five by two-and-a-half-miles in area, during the time the dam was being built.[1] It may have been that fire that blackened the trunks of the giant Douglas firs scattered along both sides of the Bumping River Road above Bumping Crossing.[2]

That anyone was attempting to combat the fire at all was somewhat unusual. At the time, the wilderness was still the enemy to be conquered and forest fires were not unwelcome, being a handy way to clear away some of that pesky timber. Settlers did not hesitate to start fires to help them open up homesteads and travelers sometimes ignited trees for the thrill of watching them torch the sky.

Mary F. Lewis of Packwood wrote in her diary in August of 1906, "Albert Bellows set fires on his place Sunday. Fires got away and burnt Tom Bivins' and Al's barns up and all of their fences."[3] Early outdoorsmen were careless with fire, igniting trees in order to have light to set camp by or setting up campfires beneath trees. Mountaineer Claude Rusk describes a man who was obsessed with lighting trees on fire in remote parts of the forest. This fellow hiker believed that the utter destruction of all forests would be a beneficial to mankind—an opinion shared by many others, Rusk lamented.[4]

Native people were still burning specific areas of the forest in the second half of the nineteenth century and soon a new group was as well. Sheep and cattle men regularly set fire in their mountain ranges believing that fires would improve the grass the following year. Sheep herders sometimes burned pastures behind them in order to keep out others. So many of these fires got away, that early travelers in the Northwest described haze so thick from smoke that they could scarcely see one ridge to the next.

Fred Plummer, writing about forest conditions in the Cascades, noted in 1903 that "not a year goes by since 1865 but fire has not burned or reburned some area." At this point, forests were still relatively open.[5]

In 1905, when Forest Reserve lands came under the jurisdiction of the Department of Agriculture, management of timber resources and protection of the watershed were the Forest Service's primary goals.[6] The scenic qualities of a green forest were secondary, and recreation was not yet recognized as a forest use. It was not until 1908 that the Forest Service began to formulate anti-fire policies in order to preserve the potential lumber on their lands. At that time, local rangers were expected to respond to reports of fire in their jurisdiction and gather resources to fight them. In the more remote reaches of districts, a ranger might rely on locals or send in whomever he could find.

Bob Ford of Goose Prairie recounted several instances in which he was sent into the timber to locate distant smoke. In 1934, when he was just twelve, Ford accompanied Albert Botsford up towards Old Scab Mountain on Nelson Ridge. They found a lone tree burning which Botsford cut down and extinguished. When Ford was older, he and his brother Pat were asked by Ranger Horace Cooper to locate a blaze that had been spotted south of Mount Aix. They rode there on horseback with fire tools which included a five gallon rubber bag to pump water onto the fire. This time, a small clump of firs had been ignited. They were able to put the fire out.[7]

Within a decade, a federal fire protection study resulted in a plan to develop a region wide fire detection system with forest rangers coordinating firefighting efforts. The infrastructure would consist of strategically placed observation stations built on ridges and high peaks to cover the views of the entire district.[8]

The first lookout in the Naches District was built on Mount Aix around 1920. Naches ranger Harry Croxford hired Clarence Brown to break a trail and Fred Hall to pack supplies and construction materials to the distant mountaintop. The trail construction was hard and slow. Hall ended up relaying the equipment each day to the end of the path again and again as it inched upward towards the timberline, twenty days in all. Jack Robillard was hired to string the telephone line.[9]

Soon, pack trains were winding their way all over the district, horses and mules laboring under loads of cement and lumber to construct spindly fire lookouts on each of the highest peaks. Bald Mountain was built in

1931, Goat Peak on American Ridge, Miner's Ridge and Edgar Rock in 1933 and '34, Raven's Roost in 1934, Little Bald Mountain in 1936, and then Timberwolf Mountain too.[10] These stations were staffed all summer long by sharp-eyed spotters who scanned 360 degrees of forested mountains during the daylight hours, alert to the most tenuous column of smoke. To avoid false alarms, they had to know the location of each forest camp and habitation.[11]

In National Forests all over the West, staffed fire lookouts were connected to distant ranger stations by telephone. This extensive system was a boon to communication in the forested wilderness. Presumably, this dapper and composed ranger is not in the middle of a fire emergency. (Courtesy of the United States Forest Service, Naches Ranger District)

But locating a birthing fire was of no use without communication of it, so telephone lines were installed connecting lookouts to each other and to ranger stations. Hundreds of miles of galvanized wire looped among trees, up and down ridges and valleys all over the forest.[12] In a spasm of technology and apparent funding, a line was even put in all the way up over Carleton Pass south to the Davis coal mine, and over Naches Pass to the new ranger station at Greenwater, in 1913.[13] At intermediate points along the line, hand-cranked phones in locked boxes were nailed right onto trees. Rangers could access them when on the move.

Over time, additional trails were cut to gain access into the forests, with the goal of getting expanding firefighting crews within two miles of any fire by trail. These Forest Service trails were all marked with the same blaze to identify them: a two inch slash set above an eight inch vertical one. These pathways to the lookouts and the supplementary access trails became the backbone of an extensive hiking trail system throughout the Cascades—their blazes still evident today.[14]

Bob Ford poses in front of the American (Ridge) Fire Lookout on Goat Peak in an undated Forest Service photo. (Courtesy of the United States Forest Service, Naches Ranger District)

Lookout living was lonely, often with only mountain goats for company. A typical lookout building was a fourteen-by-fourteen-foot box of windows with shutters over them to keep out the sun's glare. Often perched up high on wooden legs, there were long stairs or ladders to reach a hatch in the floor. The little structures had steep roofs and an exterior catwalk all the way around. A rangefinder stood in the center of the room with kitchen space, counters, and a bed along the walls.[15]

During World War II, able-bodied men were in such short supply that Betty Jean Ford of Goose Prairie was hired to staff the Raven's Roost and later Miner's Ridge Fire Lookouts. She was only seventeen years old, but so familiar with the area that the Forest Service made a hiring exception for her age. During the war, for security reasons, no travel was allowed beyond the Bumping Lake Dam, so visitors were especially scarce. Betty's father Ira packed in her supplies and mail. Water was from a stream about a mile downslope and required an uphill haul, so she relates that she used it wisely. "I did the dishes and then mopped the floor with the same water."[16]

All day, fire trucks have been rumbling across the dam and disgorging crews of fresh faced firefighters into the clearing next to the spillway. They set up yellow tents as if they are going to stay for a while. Because this blaze is within the wilderness boundaries, it is classified as a "resource fire" and is allowed—very specifically—to burn. However, since the summer homes along the lake, the marina campground and Normandie lie just outside of that boundary, firefighting policies get a bit tangled. The Forest Service has declared its intent to protect the buildings here that are threatened by the wildfire even though they will not fight the fire itself. We, not surprisingly, have mixed feelings about this policy.

Just as a doctor becomes a hero to the family of a sick child, the fire's Incident Commander, George Marcott is fast becoming our family's champion. Lean and rugged from a lifetime of working outdoors and as handsome as a leading man, he's at least got the looks of a superhero.

George introduced himself on his arrival and quietly took charge of the growing population of firefighters, quickly winning our confidence. Whether he knew it or not, George was the man with the power to save a significant part of my heart. He alone assessed this baby wildfire, recognized its potential, charted its likely growth, and drafted the plan to mitigate its effects.

His strategy was to prepare the entire area on this side of the lake for the arrival of the fire. He ordered the muscled crews not to kill the fire at this time, but keep it at bay, and once it arrives to control its spread by preparing with water. Long hoses lines with sprinklers punctuating their lengths were laid all over the area, encircling Normandie. The plan was to soak the periphery of the building and grounds seventy-two hours before the anticipated arrival of the flames, not only wetting the physical fuel but also raising the ambient humidity in the area to limit fire's intensity.

A crown fire is what we want to prevent. We pray that this fire stays low, out of the top of the forest where it could leap from tree to tree in a frenzy of flames that can throw embers as much as a mile ahead of the advancing edge.

Upon inspection of our vegetation and the water system installed courtesy of the hard-working crew, George declared this "Easy," and Tom and I looked at each other with something resembling hope. His next words were not as reassuring. "Of course, I would still take out anything precious with you when you leave."

We spent our last days putting up our own sprinklers to supplement those already soaking the ground, pulling hoses this way and that, trimming trees, hauling branches, and raking up every last fir needle from the ground. It was hard work, but it felt good to be doing something—anything—to prepare for the incoming storm. If the fire does miss us, there will be nothing lost, as the dead branches should be cleared and the new hoses we bought will serve us well here and at home.

More Forest Service fire crews arrived. It had been a week since the fire started and we were on first name basis with the leaders: Tim, Torrie, and Cody. We met Brandi who would be providing security, since suddenly the whole valley was closed. They, along with George and the crew chief, discussed the historical importance of the buildings here, of their pending inclusion on the National Register. I was relieved that they seemed to appreciate the significance of the site and were dedicating themselves to protecting it, but I could only hope that their confidence was not misplaced or simply projected for our benefit. Mostly, I hoped that they would not have to prove the effectiveness of their systems and fire plan.

As much as I acknowledge the role of fire in this ecosystem, I do not want it here. Even if the cabin is spared, I cannot bear to think of the dancing twin flowers, splendid trilliums, cheeky bunchberries, and the layers upon layers of delicate greens that lace up the space from ground to sky, being incinerated.

        🌲 🌲 🌲

In 1910, a collection of catastrophic wildfires, later known as "The Big Burn" or "Big Blowup", consumed parts of the Northwest and put to rest any lingering debate over the adoption of Teddy Roosevelt's novel plans to protect national lands through firefighting. In August of that year, in the midst of an intense drought, gale-force winds picked up and lightning started to strike the dry forests.

The result was walls of fire that swept across huge swaths of Montana, Idaho, and parts of Oregon and eastern Washington. The entire city of Wallace, Idaho was destroyed as were many smaller towns. Terrified residents fled in panic. The resulting smoke drifted all the way to New England.

The fledgling Forest Service, newly charged with fighting fires, was challenged on every front. With little equipment, no experience, and almost no men, rangers attempted to deflect the firestorms from settlements and high-value timber and keep crews safe at the same time. Rangers found men wherever they could to press into service. Prisoners, immigrants from work camps, and Buffalo Soldiers from the 25th Infantry alike were handed a shovel or a bucket and told to kill fire: 10,000 men in all.

By the time the fall rains finally extinguished the maelstrom, three million acres had burned, and eighty-five lives had been lost. Seventy-four of them were firefighters.[17]

The great fires of 1910 were so traumatizing to the entire nation that an aggressive policy of fighting all fires, everywhere, became enshrined Forest Service policy: *Every fire would be extinguished by ten o'clock in the morning the following day, or the day after that…*[18] The result of that policy is that one hundred years later, forests are ripe for disaster.

The ecologic role of periodic, low-intensity fire has been disregarded for so long that western forests have become congested with dense stands of trees, heavy with underbrush, and clogged with downed logs. Crowded trees are more susceptible to disease and insect infestation. Recently, the proliferation of the bark beetle, white pine blister rust, and budworm has produced scores of dead trees, dried out and inert, that stand in endless waves like giant, ready matches. The inevitable result of this gradual buildup of accumulated fuels is massive, high intensity wildfires that incinerate everything—even the earth.

🌲 🌲 🌲

In part because of its diversity of conifers, the Bumping River Valley forests have fared much better than many areas in the West with only scattered patches of insect killed trees but there are still more skeletons in the forest than we have ever seen. Our firefighter hero George doesn't mention this component in the implementation of his fire plan.

All day, crashing roars followed by earth-shaking thuds have been moving closer. The revving whines of multiple tree-felling chain saws close in. Our quiet forest has become a hub of activity and industry. Three huge Forest Service rigs, painted a familiar and reassuring sea green, are parked between our sheds, and an ATV zips up the drive. Orderly lines of men and women, hard-hatted and military-like in olive and ochre, march up our trails. We have been completely and fully invaded.

Some firefighters haul brush—the bodies and limbs of understory trees they cut yesterday—down to the road to a growing pile of forest slash.

The heaps are destined for the maw of a massive woodchipper that is slowly grinding down the road toward us. Others hook up even more sprinklers along the endless hose lines, tying down their tall tops at four points to steady them. They are testing some now, having charged the line from the new hookup into our main water pipe. When the sprinklers jerk to life, the now familiar rat-tat-tat sound signals the crews' retreat away from the arcing sprays glittering in the morning sun. Cody comes up to ask if I am aware of any other dead trees around other than the last three that he has identified. "No, those are the only ones."

Normally, the angry sounds of tree felling are heart wrenching for me. This time, they are hopeful, even reassuring. While the fire continues to brood on the ridge, the forest along the lake and around the cabin is being cleaned up, cleared of extra fuel. The crews are taking down all the trees less than six inches in diameter. They are so deliberate, with care and respect for the life here, that I am given hope for the future even in the face of destruction.

All this focused activity, which started six days ago and will continue after we leave, is to protect us and our few precious buildings. If not for the dam and the other cabins here, none of these crews would be here, camping and eating and working. The fire could burn at will, in the wilderness, to do its own cleaning, rejuvenating work. Instead, since this narrow scrap of civilization is here, we are once again changing the course of nature, bending it to fit our wishes—or at least trying to.

Just like the dam. The original one wrecked an ecosystem, but gave life to the Yakima Valley, and is the reason for us being here at all. While we hate the damage inflicted by the dam, we recognize its role in our history and will continue to fight any attempt to build a new one. How selfish we are!

I am selfish about this fire as well; wishing it away, willing to ignore its benefits for the preservation of everything I treasure.

So, we watch, and wait.

We wait from afar, utterly helpless to impact the course of the beast. The entire Bumping River Valley has been evacuated and since we cannot return, we hang onto the daily online summary of the fire's progress. We pray.

Day after day, the conflagration continues to burn but stays high on the ridge. It spreads slowly to the north and then to the south. The wind swings, and the fire changes direction again.

Finally, after six interminable weeks of pacing, shifting, inhaling, and exhaling, the Boulder Creek monster has turned on itself one too many times. With the last available fuel consumed and no wind to push it into new pastures, it diminishes and then dies.

Far away at home in Woodinville, we hear the news and exhale, too. Normandie is safe. The legacy of the forest is secure. For the first time in weeks, we sleep well.

Chapter Ten

THE DOUBLE K GANG AND
THE BATTLE FOR A WILDERNESS

*"But of all the marvels, and all the beauties, and all the majesties
of this region, these forests of giant trees are chief. Forests in
which you cannot ride a horse…forests into which you cannot
see, and which are almost dark under a bright midday sun…"*
—Samuel Wilkeson, Northern Pacific
Railroad Report, 1869

*"Any fool can destroy trees. They cannot run away; and if they
could, they would still be destroyed—chased and hunted down
as long as fun or a dollar could be got out of their bark hides…
God has cared for these trees, saved them…but he cannot
save them from fools—only Uncle Sam can do that."*
—John Muir, *Atlantic Monthly*, 1897

*"There is a spiritual value to conservation, and wilderness
typifies this. Wilderness is a demonstration by our people that
we can put aside a portion of this which we have as a tribute
to the Maker and say—this we will leave as we found it."*
—Senator Clinton Anderson, New Mexico, 1963

The side of a mountain at night is not a good place to be if you had not planned on it. Yet there we were in the dark, propped up against the angular boulders of a rockslide, faithful dog Karma at our side, unable to go on.

Tom and I thought we had prepared well for this hike. The plan was to climb the Pear Butte Trail south and take a smaller trail east to Bismark Peak, the only mountain in the area we had not yet summited. We would return the same day to Normandie for a cold beer and dinner. Since there would be a lot of climbing and seventeen miles to traverse, we wanted to travel light. Still, we filled our small packs with most of the recommended "Ten Essentials," which I concede I had always considered overkill for our day hikes and symptomatic of the over-cautious safety culture that has developed in our over-sanitized and over-litigated country. In went our jackets, high calorie food, compass, matches, knife, band-aids, map and water. We carried more water than usual because there would be no streams to refill our bottles once we were off the valley floor. Because of the weight of the water and because I brought my larger camera, there was not room for sunscreen, emergency blanket, or signaling devices. And we didn't pack any food or extra water for Karma.

But what a glorious trek! Within an hour of our start, we had decided that this was a new favorite trail. An expected trudge up through an occluded forest was instead an orgy of spectacular vistas. We stopped often to scramble up rock formations for even better views than the trail offered. As we gained height, Bumping Lake revealed itself behind us, Mount Rainier's majestic bulk reigned to our right, Mount Adams and the shell of Mount St. Helens rose in the south, and to our left we slowly attained a view of our target: sculpted Bismark Peak. At 7,585 feet, it is the second tallest peak on the Nelson Ridge chain, its graceful apex looking like a dollop of granite whipped cream. It seemed far away and very high above us, but we pressed on, buoyed by the scenery surrounding us.

We saw our first elk just before lunch, a massive bull with a small harem of cows that dashed into cover below us as soon as we spotted them. After traversing the ridge south, we turned east and tramped along another ridge towards Bismark.

Right after a much-needed lunch break in the meager shade of an ancient, twisted white-bark pine, we spotted a bachelor herd of elk in a meadow to the south of the trail. It was a scene that I suppose would make a hunter's blood course: at least a dozen bulls, each one with a magnificent rack of arching antlers, lounged in the emerald meadow below. Some were sleeping, nestled in hollows in the green with their knees tucked under their chests and chins nodding. Others nibbled at the thick grass, and one lifted its muzzle and scratched his back with the tip of his own antler. Their sleek bodies were rounded with muscle and fat and their coats gleamed in the sun. We watched them through binoculars until they caught our scent, then rose one by one to trot off together into the trees, leaving only a cloud of dust hanging in the air for us to remember them by.

Part of a group of fifty elk after unloading in Yakima stockyards, January 1913. Yakima sportsmen hoped to expand game hunting in the surrounding mountains and donated funds to transport the animals from the Yellowstone, Montana to the city. The animals were released in the Naches Valley (near Buckeye Ranch) and did so well that by 1927, the first elk hunting season in Yakima County was opened. (Courtesy of the Yakima Valley Museum)

These animals are the descendants of an experiment by the Yakima County Game Commission over one hundred years ago. Eager to have more big game in the area, Yakima Valley sportsmen raised money by subscription and imported forty-two cows and eight bull Rocky Mountain Elk from the North Yellowstone area. The animals traveled by railroad west to Naches making several stops for feeding along the way.[1] They were then hauled fifteen miles by wagon up the river to the Buckeye Ranch, where they were held in corrals for three weeks while they settled. The animals were released in January 1913.[2]

The experiment was wildly successful. The small herd adapted so well that their numbers soon overwhelmed the available range, and they became a nuisance to Valley farmers. Elk began marauding orchards and crops especially during the winter when they migrated down to lower elevations. Haystacks proved to be especially irresistible to the hungry beasts and farmers started to protest. By 1927, Jack believed there were more elk than deer in the area.[3] The same year, the county Game Commission opened the first hunting season but depredations on farms continued, and angry famers resorted to shooting animals outright when they raided their properties.

The "Elk War" of 1949 resulted in at least ninety animals being killed. In time, the population was reduced through hunting which continues today in part by lottery. The herd in the Yakima basin is heavily managed to maintain their numbers at about 12,000 animals roaming 900,000 acres of public land. Losses to farmers have been reduced by the installation of hundreds of miles of high fencing and by the regular winter feeding of animals at several feed stations in the Naches and Tieton areas.[4]

A little further on, we broke out of a copse of fir into an amphitheater-like cirque, backed by cliffs and carpeted in chartreuse moss. Rivulets of spring melt seeped from the slopes and collected into tiny streams which trickled around shiny stones and collected into singing creeks. Everywhere, the moss was pocked by late summer wildflowers: little alpine speedwell, yellow and pink monkey flowers, nodding penstemon, purple lupine and delicate buttercup. The meadow was framed by the sharp spires of subalpine fir with their short, drooping branches which better shed the deep snows of winter up high. Those trees, along with stately mountain hemlock

rule at these high elevations. White rhododendrons mixed with huckleberry bushes filled the spaces in between. The views, already tremendous, only
expanded as we continued to climb and soon, we could see much of this
part of the state and into Oregon with the north-south string of volcanic
peaks signaling portals to the center of the earth.

We kept climbing, a long arc of up and down ridge trail bringing
us closer to our target. At a very late three o'clock we stopped, looked again
at the map and decided to press on to the top of the mountain, still at least
a half a mile away. But I was surprisingly tired. The early steep trail had
worn out my legs, it was a hot day, and the last ascent looked to be above
the timberline on the southwest shoulder of the mountain, completely exposed to the late afternoon sun. At 6,800 feet, the faint trail, which had
been hard to follow for the last two miles, disappeared altogether and we
were left to scramble up the loose scree and outcroppings. I told Tom to go
ahead to the top, that I would stay here with Karma who, distrustful of the
shifting rock, was unhappy with the prospect of continuing.

Tucked within the boulders where we rested, cute wild buckwheat
was blossoming, its pompom flower heads sitting up on long stems like little orange balloons. Spreading phlox opened in lavender mats like colorful
scarves laid down on the rocks. A large hawk wheeled and called and far
below the whistles of marmots echoed off the cliffs.

During that break, I came to completely understand the powerful
allure of the top of a mountain. I knew it was getting late, that there was
a very long return hike, and that I was worn out. But the summit was so
close, it would be a shame to turn back with the goal so near. With renewed
motivation, I started climbing again, at times now with hands and feet, so
steep was the slope. At fifty feet short of the top, I passed Karma off to Tom,
who was coming back down having attained the peak. With his promise
to wait at a small cave, I continued up and up, resting every few steps until
there was no more up and the rounded peak was mine. How magnificent
was the view in every direction and how pleased I was to have made it, only
wishing I could share the achievement with Tom, I quickly took some photos, returned back to him and we shared the marvel of the place.

We now had a big decision to make. We could return on the cir-
cuitous route by which we had come with some significant climbs along

the way, or we could take a short cut along the spine of the Nelson Ridge due north to the familiar Mount Aix trail and drop back to the valley floor not far from our parked car. We had a clear view of the route we would need to travel but there were two problems we were confronting: there was no mapped trail along the ridge, and we were completely out of water.

I had sucked the last drops out of my pack just before the summit, and Tom somewhat earlier, having shared his water with Karma. We were at the farthest point away from home and it was after five o'clock, with less than three hours until sunset.

We succumbed to the challenge and the intrigue of the unknown, mutually agreeing that the shortcut route along the backbone of the range was our best choice. Cutting across the rock field that covered the west flank of the mountain, we followed a narrow path, certain that others had blazed a trail before us. We soon found ourselves on the knife edge ridge itself, looking back at the sheer north face of Bismark Peak. A steep drop-off to the right was part of a huge bowl that gathered snow melt to become Hindoo Creek which tumbles east and joins Rattlesnake Creek further down. An equally sheer drop to the left ended in cliffs that framed the headwaters of Copper Creek which we had crossed early in the morning on the way to the trailhead.

We continued along the thin ridge as it was the only way to traverse. Soon we dropped slightly below the crest when it became too narrow to navigate but then the footing changed as the rocks became larger. We were at the birthplace of the mountain where ancient basalt slabs were being uplifted by the collision of tectonic plates and thrust diagonally up towards the heavens. These jagged edges of broken stone were heaved up and lay in wait like giant teeth of hungry dragon, ready to tear at us, to slash us as we tried to clamber over them. Not a single step was level, and nothing was secure. We scrambled and slipped. We gripped serrated edges of rocks while our feet probed for the next foothold and cursed when our feet slid. The sun, though dipping, was still ferocious on the bare ridge and the sweat that dripped from us did nothing to improve our grip.

Each time we achieved a high point, there was another dip and then an incline up to another peak along the ridgeline. What looked like a short distance on the map multiplied as we went up and then back down. Our progress was incremental as we inched over small cliffs of loose rock which dropped away to the valley far below.

Our lack of water was starting to get noticeable to both of us by now. In addition to our cracked lips and dry mouths, swallowing was getting more difficult with what little saliva we had. I kept pushing back a slow tide of dizziness lapping at my brain as long as I could, but Tom's budding headache was getting worse, and he was starting to wane.

Karma soon refused to go on, so spooked was she by the rocks that we sent crashing down the mountainside. I could not persuade her to continue. She kept bolting back towards the safety of the trail we had come from or back towards anything that was not the razor-rocked hell that we had led her into. I finally picked her up and lifted her over the worst sections while Tom scouted the route ahead.

Whenever he could, Tom was tracing mountain goat trails, less than six inches wide, that crisscrossed the ridges here. We had seen a mountain goat a few hours earlier on the way up Bismark. He was a rugged creature, as blocky as the basalt chunks he was meandering across. This was country he was made for, his long white coat, while excessive for today, served him well in his alpine home. Each small foot had two soft hooves that were flexible and padded to better grab the rocky terrain. This mature male sported a pair of sharp, black horns. We were relieved when he continued on his way after a pause to look our direction as we recalled a hiker who was gored to death by a billy not long ago out in the Olympic Mountains.[5]

But the problem with following goat tracks is that the animals are superbly adapted for mountain traversing with those grippy feet, a low center of gravity and exquisite balance. Though the trails offered the only somewhat stable ground and were better than no path, the goats were vastly more athletic than we. Inevitably, a trail we were following would abruptly end, the user having simply jumped to the next spot, leading us to reconnoiter a more human way through. Again and again, we were led to the end of a trail when the path evaporated, the path makers having simply leapt over a crevice, up a rock face, or down a ragged cliff.

There were some treats along the way: we came across gatherings of mountain goat nests, small areas of dirt that were pawed into soft depressions and were surrounded by hoof prints of every size. Clumps of white mountain goat fur caught on some of the low windswept trees that managed to cling to the ridge. They fluttered like cottony wings as we walked past, and I was tempted to gather the soft wool that was in such contrast to this hard land.

Finally, as I drew yet another time on my long-empty bottle in hopes that some stray drops had collected there, we spied a small patch of snow not far above us. We scrambled to it and greedily scraped at the grainy corn snow, eating as much as we could but feeling the need to push on, too. We filled every container we had with the stuff and trudged on, the trail junction that we could plainly see on the mountain face to the north never seeming to get any closer. We absolutely needed to get off the ridge before the sun set. That imperative had not originally been apparent but now the earth was making quicker progress away from the sun than we seemed to be able to make across it.

Just when we thought we were on the homestretch to that trail, we hit another obstacle. We had clawed our way to the top of a rib that branched off of the main ridge, expecting to see our trail goal right in front of us. Instead, there was another huge bowl in our path. We were exhausted, sick, and completely demoralized. The sun was out of sight over the ridge above us and we could not imagine another push now. But we couldn't stay here either. We were out of water and food. The sides of this bowl were too steep and loose for us to traverse. We did not want to go straight down and across the bottom for that meant another huge climb up the other side. We were left with just one other option: climbing up the rib to the top of another peak along the ridge and traversing that to the trail intersection.

At this moment of decision, somehow, I dropped my camera. Without emotion, I watched as it somersaulted down to the bottom of the cirque and lodged against a tree, several hundred feet below. Since it was in its case, I was sure that it had survived and, as it was full of spectacular photos of our day, I couldn't leave it. While Tom shook his head in dismay, I edged down to retrieve it, and much more slowly trudged back up, the still-working device slung carefully over my chest.

We tried to gather some kind of enthusiasm to continue. Karma was limping when we started again.

When we finally made the Mount Aix trail, we didn't even have time to celebrate. It was eight o'clock. The sun was setting in a glorious show behind the peak of silhouetted Mount Rainier. As we started down, Tom remarked that we were in "the pink," the luminous alpenglow that we enjoy watching develop along Nelson Ridge at sunset. We both would have been happy to be at home observing it from the behind the security of the windows of Normandie. Instead, we hurried down the golden trail as fast as we could, racing the last, waning rays of the sun.

With more than four miles to go, there was no hope anymore of getting back to the car before dark, and since that most important essential, a light source, had been left at the cabin, we had only Tom's cell phone, its battery diminished by picture taking, to light our way.

But we had another asset it turned out. As the remaining twilight faded and we plunged into the forest again below the ridge, we found ourselves able to follow Karma's raised tail, its white tip a little waving beacon in the dark. She led us, never missing a switchback as we wove our way back and forth down across the mountain's face; never leaving us behind even as we got slower and slower with fatigue.

Finally, it was so dark we had to turn on the phone. The battery was at eighteen percent. Not daring to use the flashlight feature for its energy consumption, Tom used only the light of the screen to illuminate the trail. If I followed a close step behind, I could anticipate the terrain by watching his dimly lit feet. Down and down we stumbled, like a pair of blindfolded drunks.

I fell off the narrow path first, but the ground was soft and forgiving and I clambered back up to the trail and continued. When Tom stepped off the edge next and tumbled, I started to worry about us getting hurt, my concerns from the high ridge traverse returning. He came back up with only scratches but as we went on, we tripped over unseen roots, lurched off of hidden boulders and collided with overhead branches.

Not once, did Karma take a false step off the main trail even when we were sure she had led us onto a meandering game trail in the dark. We wisely stopped questioning her and just followed, the precious phone off whenever possible to preserve whatever energy was left inside its slim battery.

We were grateful it was not a chilly night with cold to add to our discomfort, but Tom was still sweating in spite of the cooler conditions. He was losing water far faster than he could suck it out of the meager snow that was melting in our Ziplock baggies. When we reached a rockslide, he stopped and suggested a rest. It couldn't get any darker, so we sat, rooting through our packs for any overlooked food or water. Our gathered snow had been pretty much consumed or shared with Karma, but I found some forgotten cheese slices. Tom was so nauseous that he could not eat so we gave everything to Karma and tried to find a smooth spot on the rocks to lie down for a moment.

The plan was to nap for just a few minutes and hope that the over-due moon would rise, helping us on our way. Instead, Tom in spite of his jacket, started shivering uncontrollably and we were forced to continue on, to keep him moving and hopefully warm. Just when we thought we might have to stop again we heard the faint sound of the stream which we knew crossed near the bottom of the trail.

We rushed forward to the welcome sound. When we reached the creek, we drank, and drank some more, nearly delirious with gratitude for the delicious liquid. Our pace quickened as we finished the last half mile of the wide open trail to the road and then the car. We gave Karma extra caresses before gently lifting her up onto the comfort of the back seat for the short drive home under the rising full moon.

Every step that we took and almost all of what we could see during that fourteen-hour hike was within the boundaries of the William O. Douglas Wilderness. This area was established in 1984 when President Ronald Reagan signed into law the Washington State Wilderness Act. Named in honor of one of our country's most influential United States Supreme Court Justices, it was proposed and promoted in large part by two little old ladies in tiny Goose Prairie, population eight.

The women were not really old when they originally conceived of the idea of a wilderness area in 1960, but they certainly were by the time they saw it finalized. In 1984, they were gray haired and wrinkled and did not look like the change agents they were. At an age others were putting their feet up, these two women were still feisty, outspoken, and knee-deep in a variety of local conservation projects.

To outsiders, Kathryn Kershaw and Isabelle Lynn were an unlikely pair to permanently change the land use map of Washington State.

Kathryn "Kay" Kershaw was born in 1906, the only daughter of the lower Naches Valley pioneers Ed and Ora Kershaw. From childhood, Kay was interested in all things outside and nothing domestic. When still a child, she could run a horse-drawn mower and binder and in her free time pruned fruit trees in the family's orchards. "Everyone who met her agreed that she should have been born a boy," said Jack Nelson.[6] Kay was an all-around athlete, raced motorcycles, skied competitively, hunted big game, taught swimming, and loved to climb as well, summiting nearby Mount Rainier and other Northwest peaks. She became one of the first female pilots in Yakima in her young twenties, piloting the early "flying tin cans" that had started appearing in the Valley. But above all she was a consummate horsewoman who was completely at home on the back of a horse, broken or not.

Kay met Pat Kane in Walla Walla just before the war when they were both engaged as welfare workers. Pat was dark haired, friendly, and enthusiastic. Soon, the two young women were exploring the mountains by horseback. In winter, they set out on skis, relishing the adventure and ruggedness that Oregon's Wallowas and Blue Mountains had in such abundance.

When Kay returned from an overseas deployment with the Red Cross during World War II, she was determined to make a living and build a career outdoors and asked Pat to join her. They conceived of a mountain ranch where they could host guests in a rustic but comfortable setting and introduce their charges to the pleasures of the high country. Kay could lead pack trips into the wilderness while Pat would fill hungry bellies on their return.

Kay had known of Goose Prairie since childhood when her family regularly traveled through on their way to the Nelson's lodge. Jack and Kitty had taken an early interest in Kay and ignited her infatuation with mountains and the natural world. The little settlement proved to be a perfect location for Kay and Pat's imagined ranch. Goose Prairie sat in the middle of a wild, untouched wilderness with hundreds of alpine lakes, glacier carved cirques, and views of the Cascade's magnificent volcanic peaks from Mount Baker to Mount Hood within six miles of the Prairie.[7] The Prairie was at the center of a spider web of trails which accessed these high country jewels. Kay and Pat also found the ideal climate there with nearly rain-free summers for packing trips and abundant snow cover for winter sports. Goose Prairie was perfect.

With the assistance of both their families, Kay and Pat purchased seven acres of Tom Fife's original homestead and started to build the Double K Mountain Ranch (coined after both their last names). They began with a tent in 1945 and soon built a small winter cabin. Next, the women got to work on the main structure: a six-thousand-square-foot, three-story building with accommodations for twenty-two guests, a commercial-sized kitchen, and plenty of comfortable public space for relaxing. Chuck Hammond was hired to build the lodge, but Kay and Pat worked right alongside him. The women split thousands of yellow cedar shingles for the roof and Kay dug the seventeen-foot-deep well by hand. A huge coal furnace in the basement would keep the rooms cozy and two generators were installed in a separate building for electricity. A generous barn with corrals was constructed to shelter the horses that would soon carry guests to the nearby ridgetops. The Double K Mountain Ranch opened for business on the first day of 1947.

The opening made a splash locally and established Goose Prairie more firmly on the recreationalists' map. A feature article in the Seattle Post Intelligencer dubbed Kay and Pat as "The Smart Set." Posed photos show the attractive young women "duded out" in western hats, plaid shirts, kerchiefs, jeans, and cowboy boots. Their "unusual" guest ranch would be regularly profiled in newspapers and magazines just as Jack and Kitty's was a generation earlier. In interviews, Kay made sure to mention the tranquil mountain setting and the steak and martini pack trips. Even on the trail, "We don't forget the Happy Hour," Kay would add.[8]

Kay Kershaw and Pat Kane make shingles by hand for the Double K Mountain Ranch. Shingles were split from a block of cedar using a froe and a heavy club. No strangers to manual labor, the two women worked alongside Chuck Hammond to construct the buildings for their guest ranch. (Courtesy of the Museum of History and Industry (MOHAI)

Kay and Pat made a great team.[9] Kay took care of all of the infrastructure needs, tending to the well pump, the generators, dropping trees, and fixing fences, while Pat took over guest care: bookings, rooms, and food—the latter being prepared using a massive, double-oven wood-fired stove.

Since Pat didn't have any experience cooking for large groups and good fare was a prerequisite to any hospitality business' success, Kitty took it upon herself to make sure the cuisine at the Double K was up to standard to bring visitors back. Kitty invited Pat to copy all of her trusty recipes for use at the Ranch and made sure Pat assisted her in the kitchen so she could fully absorb Kitty's hard-earned culinary skills. Because the Nelsons' old lodge had just shut down (with Jack's retirement), Kitty passed on to the Double K all of her sturdy dishware that had served countless meals to guests for thirty years. It was still being used at the Ranch in the 1970s.

Despite the pleasant setting and the efforts of the hosts, success came slowly to the Double K. Winter access was problematic in the deep snows and not everyone could—or wanted—to stay the minimum one week visit.

In the summer of 1948, Kay and Pat got word that Supreme Court Justice William O. Douglas was staying with a group of friends at a guest ranch down in the Naches Valley. In an effort to drum up business by word of mouth, the women invited the Justice, who was a well-known public figure, to stay at the Ranch as long as he wanted, for free. Douglas and his buddies promptly took Kay up on her offer. At the Double K, Douglas found privacy and liberal hosts who let him do whatever he wanted as long as he followed their rules. Douglas loved it.[10] It was a perfect hideaway, seventeen miles from the nearest phone, fifty-five from Yakima and a state away from his family in Oregon. "It's the Secret Valley," Jack Nelson said.[11] And it was.

His friendship with the proprietors of the Double K would last for the rest of his life.

Kay Kershaw, Justice William O. Douglas, and Pat Kane sit on the steps of the Double K Mountain Ranch building in the late 1940s or early 1950s. (Courtesy of the Yakima Valley Museum)

❧ ❦ ❧

Jack and Kitty were still new at the lake in 1912, in their original Reclamation shack, when a lanky, freckle-faced boy knocked on their door, soaked and cold from a surprise summer rainstorm.[12] Raised in the city of Yakima, but already a great lover of the outdoors, the young hiker was on his way to Fish Lake on Carlton Pass. As a youngster he had taken to the hills to explore and to strengthen his skinny legs. Now, he was venturing further and further into the Cascades, on solo overnight trips and week-long excursions with his brother or a friend. With his horseshoe rucksack dumped on the porch, and his blond hair plastered to his forehead, Kitty warmed him with hot coffee as he dripped water onto the clean floor of her kitchen. Recognizing an appreciative audience, Jack sat him down and soon had him enthralled, regaling him with tall tales and the secrets of the woods. The boy was captivated and would become a life-long friend of the Nelsons. For the next fifty years he would return to their door again and again as he hiked and rode through the Bumping River Valley.

The boy's name was William Orville Douglas. In time, he graduated from Whitman College in Walla Walla and then Columbia University Law School. Following two highly effective years as the chairman of the Securities and Exchange Commission, President Roosevelt appointed him to the United States Supreme Court at just forty years old, where he served for thirty-six years, the longest serving justice in the history of the Supreme Court. In the course of his career on the Court, he wrote a record 1,164 full opinions, including 486 dissents. His approaches to the First Amendment, Equal Protection, privacy, and religious issues have become mainstays of American law.[13] Columbia University, in conferring him the honorary degree of Doctor of Laws, wrote that his judicial contribution shaped an "original and profound vision in the role of law." [14] During his time on the bench Douglas published forty-one books and countless articles, married four and divorced three women, survived three impeachment campaigns, and became one of the most influential environmentalists in the country.

Douglas felt strongly that the boy makes a deep imprint on the man.[15] His formative visits with Jack and Kitty, Tom Fife, and other locals were not forgotten as Douglas became an increasingly passionate conservationist.

Jack's contribution to Douglas' environmental consciousness is unmistakable. Over the years, Jack mentored young Douglas on the ways, mysteries, and inhabitants of the forest, further kindling his appreciation for the outdoors and the value of unspoiled nature. From Jack, Douglas absorbed a wilderness philosophy honed by experience and polished by the teachings of John Muir. Their conversations were not just philosophical musings. Jack and Douglas discussed their shared experiences with CCC boys who had been empowered by their exposure to nature, miraculously transforming from tough kids to thoughtful young men by immersion in the mountains. Both men shared their examples at length in their first books.

Douglas wrote prolifically and included in his biographies are descriptions of boyhood adventures in the Cascades. He experienced both spiritual as well as physical benefits from his journeys.[16] Like Jack, Douglas believed that man's best qualities are developed in nature. When confronted by the immensity and power of the forces of the natural world one finds serenity, humility, and dignity.[17] Furthermore, Douglas felt that all people had a right to experience these wild places. As the natural world became increasingly threatened during his lifetime, Douglas became a leader in nascent environmental movement, effectively activating for the preservation of wilderness that could provide for an individual's salvation.

In addition to his appreciation of the unspoiled landscape, Douglas was deeply interested in the natural history of the area and studied the trees, shrubs and especially the wildflowers that flourished in the Pacific Northwest. On a packing trip, it was not unusual for him to stop in the middle of the trail, dismount, and carefully pick, examine, and pack away a new specimen for later study. He sometimes brought a flower press along in his saddlebag.[18]

Yakima native Naydene Nutley Maykut met the Justice high on Nelson Ridge when she was solo hiking in her early twenties. She was delighted to meet the famous figure whom she deeply admired. He greeted

her and proceeded to tell her by name which wildflowers she might encounter on her way along the ridge.[19]

The Bumping Lake area continued to be an important physical
and emotional retreat for Douglas, especially as his personal life became
more complicated and conflicts within an increasingly conservative
court escalated. After he lost two beloved cabins in the Northwest to
wives in divorce settlements, he was in the market for another mountain getaway. His choice was easy. Douglas bought eight forested acres
in Goose Prairie right next door to the Double K Ranch. He had the lot
cleared of trees, seeded his own prairie in front, then had neighbor Ira
Ford supervise the construction of his chalet-style home. It was finished
in 1965. Douglas called it Prairie House. Even though it was of a modern style, the interior was clad in knotty pine, and it featured built-in,
floor-to-ceiling bookcases and a basalt fireplace in the living room—just
like Normandie.

Ira Ford built a small barn for the Justice's two horses, King and
Willows. They were stabled there, at the ready for trail riding for the rest
of his life. Douglas hired Ford as caretaker for his home (and horses) at a
hundred dollars per month, a responsibility he held for nineteen years. As
Douglas got to know Ford, he increasingly admired the man's abilities and
experience. "He can build a barn or a fence or make an engine run or repair
a vacuum cleaner…He can also cut your hair, and if you are trusting, fix
you a drink." [20]

Though Douglas loved his new mountain home, when he arrived
in Goose Prairie from D.C. he would inevitably drive first to the Double K
before going to his own Prairie House. Much of the time he wasn't writing,
he spent with the "Double K Girls" Pat and Kay, holding forth from his
favorite chair in the kitchen with a drink or a beer in hand.[21]

But life at the Double K revolved around packing trips into the
high country: Big Basin on American Ridge, Cougar Lakes, Twin Sisters
Lakes, Mount Aix, Blankenship Meadow, and Douglas eagerly took part
in any rides that he could. Even though he grew up hiking, not riding,
Douglas fancied himself a cowboy, at home on the back of a horse. Kay tells
a different story. "Bring 'em back alive was my motto. But it wasn't always
easy keeping him alive." [22]

Kay Kershaw leads a group of riders through a sub-alpine meadow near Cougar Lakes. This is part of the area that Kay and Isabelle Lynn proposed for protection as a federal wilderness area in 1961. (Bob and Ira Spring photo, courtesy of the Roger and C. Alice Matson family)

Nonetheless, Douglas valued nothing more than escaping to Goose Prairie, then escaping further still to the most remote reaches of the trails above Bumping Lake—truly one of the last frontiers of the United States. There, drinking bourbon and telling tales around the flickering campfire and surrounded by friends, he could laugh and be himself. In the mountains, away from the press and his political enemies, he was renewed.

It was late in the summer of 1970, on a pack trip to the Hindoo Basin, that the extent of Douglas' desire for solitude became legend. The Justice, with a group of ten friends from around the country led by Kay, had spent a long day riding from Goose Prairie up to the high country. They were making camp in a scenic clearing on Nelson Ridge and were looking forward to cocktails and dinner. Just as the bottles were being opened, some hikers were spotted tromping up the trail towards their camp. These interlopers presented an astonishing sight. Each of the three men wore a business suit and leather dress shoes. Each carried not a pack, but a briefcase.

The men were attorneys seeking an emergency appeal to the Supreme Court for a group of Vietnam protesters who had been arrested. The men were making an individual appeal to Douglas as the supervisory Justice of the Ninth Judicial Circuit. While they organized their papers on a nearby stump, Douglas sat on a large rock to listen. The others poured another drink while their dinner sizzled over the campfire. Douglas heard their arguments but was furious for the intrusion. Rather than issue a hasty decision, he said he needed to think over their petition and told them to come back in the morning for his answer. They asked to stay there overnight, but having no gear or provisions, Kay turned them down. Thoroughly dejected, the three attorneys turned and headed back down the long, switch-backing trail by moonlight.

When they returned the next day, the camp was empty. They found only a note on the top of the stump, weighed down by a rock. On it was a single word. It read "Denied." [23]

Three years later, court responsibilities again intruded into Douglas' summer break. At the end of July 1973, the Nixon administration expanded the Vietnam War by bombing neutral Cambodia. Opponents of the war sued to block the bombing offensive and were initially successful but then lost on appeal. The only avenue left was to find a Supreme Court Justice willing to issue a stay until the full Court resumed in the fall. They needed to find Douglas, who was by now deep in the woods at Prairie House. Legend has it that lawyers from the American Civil Liberties Union called Doug Williams, the owner of Whistlin' Jack Lodge. His was the nearest telephone since there was no phone service in Goose Prairie. The attorneys dictated—over the open party line—a detailed message to Douglas. Williams personally delivered his notes to the surprised Justice who, at once, drove back to Whistlin' Jack, fourteen miles down the road. He returned the attorneys' call using a pay phone in the middle of the parking lot.[24]

Douglas immediately convened a hearing at the Yakima County Courthouse to hear arguments from both sides. The courtroom was packed, and it buzzed with national media as well as local citizenry curious to see the battle over the Vietnam War play out in their town. After the hearing, Douglas started drafting his ruling. By evening he was dictating it to his office staff in DC by a series of phone calls placed from roadside payphones as he hop-scotched his way back up to the Prairie.

Douglas' order to stay the bombing was issued late Friday, August 3. His opponents on the Supreme Court were ready for his ruling. Within six hours, Thurgood Marshall conducted a vote of the Justices by telephone and overturned Douglas' order.[25]

Although his actions did not stop the bombing, Douglas did manage to, in the middle of the summer recess and 2,700 miles from the Washington DC, at least symbolically stop the war, if only for a few hours.

In the summer of 1952, two guests arrived at the Double K Ranch from faraway Washington, DC. Isabelle Lynn, national director of publications at the Red Cross and her friend Frances Rummell were inspired to travel across the country after reading William O. Douglas's new bestseller, *Of Men and Mountains*. In an early chapter, Douglas described the verdant Cascade Range that beckoned to him as a youngster in Yakima:

> *"All in the Valley looked to the Cascades for health and sustenance. The mountains furnished water, and water was more precious than gold. Hence, we were utterly dependent on the snow-capped ridges that lay against the western horizon. They became the symbols of our hopes and aspirations."* [26]

His passage extolling the virtues of the area around Bumping Lake might have hooked young Isabelle:

> *"Lush bottom lands along the upper Naches, where grass grows stirrup high—succulent grass that will hold a horse all night. A deer orchid deep in the brush of the American River Trail. A common rock wren singing its heart out on a rockslide above Bumping Lake. Clusters of the spring beauty in the damp creek beds along the eastern slopes of Hogback Mountain. The smell of wood smoke, bacon, and onions at a*

camp below Meade Glacier. Indian paintbrush and phlox on the high shoulders of Goat Rocks. The roar of the northwesters in the treetops in Tieton Basin. Clumps of balsam fir pointed like spires to the sky in Blankenship Meadows.[27] *The cry of a loon through the mist of Bumping Lake. A clump of white-bark pine atop Darling Mountain—gnarled and tough, beaten by a thousand gales. A black, red-crested woodpecker attacking in machine-gun style a tree at Goose Prairie.*" [28]

Goose Prairie! They could go there and experience first-hand the wonderous scenes Douglas had painted in their minds.

After a rewarding vacation and a return visit to the Ranch the next summer, Isabelle decided to move to the Northwest. She quit her job and she and Rummell both moved to Olympia, just across the mountain range from the Double K. In 1955, Pat decided to return to charity work after nearly ten years in Goose Prairie. Isabelle asked if she could help at the Ranch. "Can you cook?" asked Kay. At the moment of her affirmative answer, another dynamic partnership was formed, if anything even more effective than the last.[29]

Tall and long legged, with a huge grin and an easy laugh, Isabelle towered over the diminutive Kay, ten years her senior. Isabelle proved to be an effusive host and a gifted chef. Word soon spread of irresistible food at the Double K: garlic roasted lamb, gingered fruit salad, and carrot cake that guests begged for.

The Ranch thrived. The transition from Pat to Isabelle seems to have been seamless. The "new" Double K Girls were brash and confident; they rolled their own cigarettes (with one hand, on horseback, at a gallop), expertly dropped trees, and made their own rules. Guests were expected to participate in the Ranch activities and be on time to dinner (late comers faced an empty plate or a solid scolding).[30] There were no second helpings.

The Double K Girls looked like they had walked off the set of a western movie. Invariably, they wore well broken-in boots and jeans (Levi's 501 with a button fly), a checked shirt, a scarf or bolo, and if they were riding, a fine quality felted cowboy hat. Even though she could heft a thirty-six-inch chainsaw without thought and regularly walked through the kitchen casually sharpening a huge chef's knife, Kay was not manly. She and Isabelle were never seen without red lipstick or their hair well permed (they did each other's).

The pair, also known as the Blister Sisters for their caustic wit, screened prospective guests who enquired about availability.[31] They carried on lengthy mail correspondences to ensure visitors would fit into the ranch setting and be able to carry on an interesting conversation. A college degree was preferred and adults only, please. By the time they were granted visitation, appreciative guests from all over the country—and the world—made the most of their stays, letting go of conventions and inhibitions alike. Drinks and spirited conversation flowed.

Guests gather in the kitchen with Kay Kershaw and Isabelle Lynn in this 1959 promotional photo at the Double K Mountain Ranch. From left is the ranch's wrangler, guest Pat Keller (seated) and Helen Argash (standing) with Kay on her right. At center is the "housegirl" with Isabelle on her right talking with Alice Matson. Guest Anna Katan is seated in the foreground (with Lucky the Springer Spaniel) while Paul Ozman stands at right. (Courtesy of the Roger and C. Alice Matson family)

Nothing was too good for their guests. Both women had exacting standards and a keen eye for detail. Wanting just the right ambience in the living room, the fireplace was laid only with white pine that would produce an exciting pop as resin blisters exploded. Horseback rides and pack trips were choreographed with spectacular vistas dramatically revealed and rest stops perfectly spaced. The laundry was never hung when guests were in camp. There was always a bouquet of fresh wildflowers on the piano. The building was spotless, inside and out.[32]

Isabelle had in her pantry delicacies from all over the world with which to work her magic: friends and repeat guests brought gifts of the best their region had to offer. Russian caviar, European cognac, French brie, Greek olives, maple syrup from Vermont, fresh California citrus—all were all hand delivered to their door. One childhood friend of Kay's would regularly drive over the mountains with a huge king salmon, caught that morning in Puget Sound and packed on ice. Their bacon was custom cut in Naches. The fruit Isabelle sliced into her famous fruit salad was always at the absolute peak of ripeness and flavor since Kay had a standing order for the best of what the most talented farmers in Yakima Valley could grow. Tiny biscuits, the size of quarters and fall-apart flaky, were baked every day and always out for snacking. Foraged wild mushrooms rounded out the exceptional fare.

There were no mixes or prepared food. All was from scratch, even the mustard and mayonnaise Isabelle slathered on the hearty sandwiches packed for the day rides. Furthermore, no guests would eat the same meal twice, no matter how long they stayed.[33]

All of Kay and Isabelle's unceasing effort was toward a single goal: for their guests to experience the majesty of the wilderness, to understand it and to be moved by it. Their truth lay in the value and preservation of the unspoiled landscapes. Not unlike missionaries, the women shared all that they knew and loved of the country in hopes of offering the salvation of this nature to others.

Guests were transformed at the ranch in other ways. They arrived as city slickers and departed, after the deliberate tutelage of Kay, Isabelle, and the wrangler, with a slight swagger.[34] The staff challenged their charges to push past their self-imposed limits. After a stay in the mountains visitors took home a confidence born both from the constant praise and affirmation they received at the Ranch and the perspective they gained with exposure to and being part of something far bigger than themself—raw nature.

But Kay and Isabelle were doing something almost unheard of for the time—and the place. In conservative eastern Washington, they were a gay couple, "daring to live a life that few women would or could have chosen." [35] They were building a hospitality business deep in the wilderness, without utilities or modern conveniences, braving the elements year round, shouldering the workload almost completely themselves and pushing back a cultural bias against women running a guest ranch.[36]

The fact that they did it so well did not go unnoticed. Just as in the early days of the Nelson's successes, the Yakima papers enthusiastically profiled the couple which further elevated the status of the ranch and helped keep the guest rooms full.

Then, around 1956, Kay and Isabelle's idyllic Eden was shattered by the sound of chainsaws and bulldozers. Although there were clear-cut parcels all over the rest of the Naches Ranger District, commercial logging was moving into the Bumping River Valley for the first time in history. Perhaps without any public notice, the Forest Service finalized a timber sale on eight acres around Chipmunk Creek. The site was just a few miles down the road from Goose Prairie.[37] An access road was bulldozed in and after the timber was cut and the logs were hauled out, what was left looked like a war zone. Eight miles of logging roads slashed across the mountainside, discarded trees were scattered about like spilled matchsticks, piles upon piles of half burned slash marked the slopes, and the unstable, clear-cut inclines seemed ready to erode.

The Double K Girls were horrified. They simply could not accept the complete destruction of a virgin forest and the violent intrusion into the otherwise untouched river valley. The totality in which the trees were taken, and the blatant waste left behind felt immoral to them. Kay and Isabelle's naïve assumption that the Bumping River area was somehow immune to logging was gone as quickly as the trees were. They would never trust the Forest Service again.

Angry and galvanized, Kay and Isabelle began to take action to halt any further logging in "their" forest. First, they challenged the local ranger district and complained to the Snoqualmie Forest supervisor about details of the sale. The regional forester in Portland assured the Double K Girls that there would be no more timber sales in the area.[38]

But within two years, new sales were being negotiated by the Forest Service in the Bumping River Valley. Each operation would require the construction of new logging roads for access to the ancient trees. One sale, speeding to approval was just beyond Copper City, the old mining center along Deep Creek to the south of Bumping Lake in an area of particularly massive old growth hemlocks. Most galling was that all of the timber sales being considered were within the so-called Cougar Lakes Limited Area established by the Forest Service in the 1940s.[39]

Kay and Isabelle might have been incensed, but they were fighting an uphill battle. Commercial logging was extensive all over the ranger district—and the entire region. Although the Forest Service had set aside some wilderness areas in the northwest as early as the 1930s, these areas were roughly defined and lacked clear protections. Increased national demand for timber after World War II marked the beginning of a substantial resource management policy shift. When the Forest Service was created, its management goal was Gifford Pinchot's idea of multiple-use. The Service was to steward the public land's basic renewable resources—watershed, timber, range, outdoor recreation, and wildlife—on an equal priority basis. By the 1950s however, priorities had clearly shifted towards maximizing the extraction of timber—at the expense of all of the other supposed uses. Because private logging companies had exhausted almost all of their supply before the War, the timber industry lobbied hard to obtain timber from public lands to keep their mills running. In the Northwest in general and Oregon in particular, industrial logging on public lands only accelerated through the next forty years.[40]

In the 1960s, logging methods and equipment changed. Selective logging was gradually replaced by the cheaper practice of clearcutting in which every tree, whether usable or not, was taken down. This new method of harvest was particularly hard on the land, especially for the health of the watershed and for animal habitats. In the Northwest, where much of the terrain is steep and rugged and adjacent to a waterway, that meant that logging and their attending access roads were impacting especially fragile ecosystems.

Clearcutting of the forest is much like bottom trawling in the ocean in which the substrate is destroyed in the process of fishing and the by-catch is equal to or greater than the desired species which is then discarded; dumped dead or dying back into the sea. The resulting erosion and runoff from the roads invariably silted up nearby streams and rivers and warmed those same bodies of water that were newly exposed to sunlight. Where clear-cut lands *were* replanted, previously diverse ecosystems of multiple species of forest trees were replaced by just one or two market species.

But inexpensive and high quality lumber was needed for the expanding United States economy and for export too, and so clearcutting of the land continued. Most people did not live near lumber sources and so as a whole, a majority of the citizenry, when asked, was in favor of a continued supply of building material from their forests. In 1960, Congress passed the Multiple Use and Sustained Yield Act which validated the Forest Service's legal right and management preference for resource extraction.

Ultimately, as more and more trees were taken down, especially on the deep green slopes and valleys of the lower foothills, the public in the Northwest started to take notice especially as clear-cuts started to encroach on recreational areas. Nationwide, a growing consensus was shaping that the environment was being exploited and was limited in its capacity to absorb abuse and to provide resources.

In response to the continued depredations on federal wild lands throughout the country, the Executive Secretary of The Wilderness Society, Howard Zahniser, drafted a conservation bill in 1956. If it could be passed by Congress, the Wilderness Act would set aside specified areas for permanent preservation, where commercial development, road building or resource extraction would not be allowed. The land would be left in its primitive, roadless state for the health of the ecosystem and for future generations to enjoy.[41]

In Washington State, the North Cascades National Park was proposed as part of the pending Wilderness Act. Public comments to the proposal suggest the feelings that many had toward the Forest Service and the changing local landscapes. "I feel that the machinery of the Forest Service is out of control, running away with too much, too fast, and that no one is at the wheel who is thinking about what the end result will be," wrote a science teacher in Bellevue, Washington. Others commented on "the insatiable appetites of the forest industries" and a resident of Portland "want[s] to see this area preserved because the Forest Service hasn't left us much in Oregon."[42]

By the time the Bumping area timber sales were being considered, a national debate over two incompatible uses of the same land was being vigorously argued. On one side were the conservationists who saw the proposed Wilderness Act as one of the only ways to protect the remaining rich forest environments they valued so highly. On the other side, the timber industry saw the same bountiful forests as a resource that should be utilized. Old growth forests, containing the most wood mass and best quality lumber were the most valuable—and the most attractive for cutting. Under the legislation being considered, all Forest Service lands outside of future wilderness boundaries would be made available for commercial logging, so the stakes were huge, especially in Northwest where the aggregate value of timber was so high.[43]

With only two land use designations being considered for Forest Service land, it became abundantly clear that the only way to protect the primeval forests in the Bumping Lake area was by a wilderness designation. With the help of Zahniser, Kay and Isabelle drafted a proposal to establish the Cougar Lakes Wilderness Area. Co-sponsored by the North Cascades Conservation Council (NCCC) and submitted to the Forest Service in 1961, it was subsequently endorsed by the Wilderness Society, the Sierra Club, the Mountaineers, and the Federation of Outdoor Western Clubs. Over time the effort also gained the endorsements of the Mazamas, the Cascadians, the National Parks Association, Summit Magazine, and the Dude Ranchers Association.[44]

The proposal enlarged the original Cougar Lakes Limited Area from 90,000 to 125,000 acres, adding acreage to the east along Nelson Ridge and the Rattlesnake Creek drainage and land along American Ridge while dropping the large area north of Chinook Pass Highway.[45] The proposed wilderness would border Mount Rainier National Park to the west and include both the pastoral subalpine meadows in the Cowlitz Pass area as well as the rugged and dramatic glaciered cirques along Nelson Ridge. The developing Pacific Crest Trail ran for twenty-eight miles along the western edge of the proposed area.

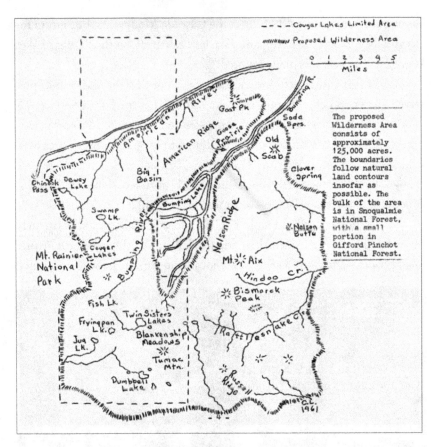

Map showing the original proposal for the William O. Douglas Wilderness as conceived by Kay Kershaw and Isabelle Lynn. Initially named the Cougar Lakes Wilderness, it included the previously defined Cougar Lakes Limited Area. Carmelita Lowry drew this map in 1961 and it was published in the North Cascades Conservation Council's newsletter, *The Wild Cascades*. (July 1961: Volume V, Number 7) (University of Washington, Special Collections, Double K Mountain Ranch Records)

Supporters extolled the unspoiled environment, the variety of the scenery, and the spectacular views of Mount Rainier and other major peaks that the land offered. "The area has something of everything the Cascades have to offer," Isabelle wrote.[46]

Despite an initial positive reception locally and in the Capitol, the proposal soon languished. Part of the problem was that the area was so remote that it had become an afterthought in a larger struggle. The North Cascades Study Team had been put together to make recommendations about both parks and wilderness in the Cascade Mountains, but group focused on the North Cascades and Glacier Peak areas, so the Cougar Lakes Wilderness area was virtually ignored.[47]

Logging interests were increasingly protesting the addition of preserved areas and before long there were rumors that the Forest Service was considering declassifying the Cougar Lakes area altogether as "compensation" for lands that would soon be off-limits to logging in other proposed wilderness areas and the North Cascades National Park.[48] That land use change would immediately open the thickly forested slopes of Miner's, American, and Nelson Ridges to commercial logging.

Fortunately, the Double K Girls had a prominent and extremely powerful ally on their side. Their friend, William O. Douglas, the nature loving Justice, felt as protective of the local landscape as Isabelle and Kay.

Isabelle Lynn, William O. Douglas, and Kay Kershaw pose on the same front steps of the Double K in the summer of 1969. (Courtesy of the Yakima Valley Museum)

The three had only grown closer over the years. During the summer months, they were next door neighbors in Goose Prairie and visited constantly. As best friends do, the Girls and Douglas volleyed friendly insults back and forth, shared inside jokes, teased each other, and laughed nearly constantly.

They were playful and affectionate, in marked contrast to their collective public personalities which could run to the combative and irascible. When Douglas returned to DC, the friends continued communicating through frequent letters which always ended with affectionate salutations.

At this time, Douglas was increasingly using his public position to advocate for the preservation of natural lands. In his first books, Douglas movingly described majestic wild landscapes, but by the 1960s he was sounding the alarm about the threats to those same places through logging, road building, and pollution. He reminded the public through magazine articles, books, speeches, coverage in and letters to the media, and even his judicial opinions, that America's irreplaceable natural heritage belonged to them. He challenged citizens to be informed and to get involved because, as he pointed out, for too long the public resources belonging to all had been exploited for the economic gain of the few.[49]

He went further. In his landmark dissent in Sierra Club v. Morton, Douglas philosophized that nature, without a voice, a lobby, or financial backing, should have rights, just as corporations and ships already enjoyed. Those who would sue on behalf of the natural world might have legal standing and could speak for the inarticulate members of the environment.

Douglas wrote,

> "The river…is the living symbol of all the life it sustains or nourishes—fish, aquatic insects, water ouzels, otter, fisher deer, elk, bear and all other animals, including man, who are dependent on it or who enjoy it for its sight, its sound, or its life. The river as plaintiff speaks for the ecological unit of life that is part of it. Those people who have a meaningful relation to that body of water—whether it be a fisherman, a canoeist, a zoologist, or a logger—must be able to speak for the values which the river represents, and which are threatened with destruction."

> "The voice of the inanimate object, therefore, should not be stilled. That does not mean that the judiciary takes over the managerial functions from the federal agency. It merely

> *means that before these priceless bits of Americana (such as a*
> *valley, an alpine meadow, a river, or a lake) are forever lost or*
> *are so transformed as to be reduced to the eventual rubble of*
> *our urban environment, the voice of the existing beneficiaries*
> *of these environmental wonders should be heard."* [50]

Douglas was pushing the United States closer to a cooperative land ethic espoused by Aldo Leopold which enlarged the boundaries of the community to include the soils, waters, plants, and animals, or collectively, the land.

The dissent made waves on and off the court. That and his book, *A Wilderness Bill of Rights*, published the following year, established Douglas firmly "as the leading judicial champion of the environment." [51] Michael Nelson, environmental philosopher at Oregon State University goes further, writing that Douglas' dissent was "the cornerstone of a new environmental ethic, one premised upon empathy with the human and non-human world alike. "[52]

Once he heard about the timber sales pending for Bumping Lake, Douglas immediately jumped into action. He contacted local Snoqualmie National Forest Supervisor Larry O. Barrett, USFS Chief Forester Ed Cliff, Secretary of Agriculture Orville Freeman, and United States Senator Henry "Scoop" Jackson and lobbied all of them hard.

Douglas then alerted regional and national conservationists, John Osseward of the NCCC, and David Brower, Executive Director of the Sierra Club. From the Forest Service, he demanded a halt to the proposed sales and road building until they could be reviewed by an impartial board and discussed by public hearing. [53]

Douglas helped set up connections and served as a liaison between the "Double K Gang" (Kay, Isabelle, Eileen Ryan, Carmelita Lowry, Harvey and Betty Manning, and other local advocates) and political leaders in DC and in doing so helped create a powerful grassroots lobby in Washington State.

The Double K Gang had to do something quickly to increase the profile of the area. Despite Kay having led long pack trips into the spectacular high country around the lake for years, the area was still so unknown that it was easy for far-away bureaucrats to trade it away. So, the Double K Girls organized more pack trips—called field studies—so that interested parties and those making land use decisions, could see in person what was at stake.

Kay led the first of the field studies in August 1961. She guided the president of the Wilderness Society Harvey Broome, editor of *The Living Wilderness* magazine George Marshall, Naches District Ranger F. H. "Spike" Armstrong, Supervisor Barrett, and other guests on a horseback trip up into the rugged Mount Aix region in the eastern part of the proposed Wilderness Area. They rode along the sharp ridges and gazed out at the long vistas.

Later the same month, Douglas arranged an all-day ride with Barrett and Armstrong up through the Deep Creek drainage, Twin Sisters Lakes, and Blankenship Meadows to showcase the pastoral landscape of the southern section of the wilderness area.

That excursion did not go as planned. Instead of grandiose scenery, the group rode up the trail into a landscape of destruction near Copper City. The previous fall, a windstorm hit the Northwest mountains hard. Thousands of trees were blown down in the Bumping River watershed. Not wanting the toppled trees to go "to waste" the Forest Service planned a salvage sale for the timber. In anticipation of the sale, Barrett had authorized access roads to be bulldozed into the virgin forest. Massive trees were down and slash was shoved into rough piles. Mud was already sluicing into nearby Deep Creek, a formerly pristine, crystal-clear stream.

Douglas was enraged and it is hard to imagine the rest of the ride was pleasant. Barrett was unmoved by either of the scenic tours however, and though the Double K Gang protested, they soon learned that the salvage would proceed.

The conservationists took issue with several aspects of the sale, in addition to the land damage that they had witnessed. The first was that the sale site was inside the Limited Area and well within the boundaries then being debated for the Cougar Lakes Wilderness Area. The new road construction instantly excluded the entire sale area from ever being part of any future Wilderness Area.

There were also questions about the quality of the wood being taken out, with the Double K Gang claiming that much of the timber was worthless because of rot and blister rust damage.[54]

Lastly, though the sale was claimed by Barrett to prevent economic loss (of the downed trees), he reportedly accepted a bid of $7,000 dollars for the timber but then was obligated to credit $30,000 dollars for the road construction costs.[55]

Despite the questionable economics and environmental damage of the Copper City sale, Barrett was soon negotiating three more sales within the area. ("He's not called "Logger Larry" for nothing!" quipped Lowry.) One was on the Upper Bumping River near Swamp Creek which would require construction of a new, five-mile-long road along the Upper Bumping River. Another was just west of the earlier Chipmunk Creek sale off the Bumping River Road, and the last was a large salvage sale near Rattlesnake Creek on the east side of Nelson Ridge. Apparently, he saw absolutely nothing wrong with these sales, claiming that the aesthetic values of the area would not be affected especially when viewed from far away. As for their locations inside the proposed Cougar Lakes Wilderness Area, his remark was that "the high country is all that matters in a Wilderness Area" since the timbered valleys below are of "great economic value."[56]

These three sales were ultimately cancelled as a result of pressure from William O. Douglas and others.[57]

It seems as if losses to the Forest Service for timber sales were common. Road building and other costs made the expenses of sales very high— often more than the timber was worth to the highest bidder. The Forest Service was able to show aggregate profits because of their accounting procedures in which certain costs were not included and records were not kept for individual sales.[58] The General Accounting Office had questioned the economics of timber sales for years and in 1995 demonstrated that the agency sustained one billion dollars in losses in timber sales from 1992-1994 alone. In 1997, under pressure, the Forest Service for the first time in its history, admitted that logging expenditures exceeded revenues in the previous year by fifteen million dollars.[59]

The fallout of the Copper City sale was as if Barrett had kicked a hornets' nest. The Double K Girls, not reticent to begin with and now coached by an equally aroused Justice, were seized with a greater sense of urgency and even more energized to fight. Douglas, in a blistering letter to Barrett in September 1961, typed on United States Supreme Court letterhead, wrote, "...I hope every year on July 27 (the date Barrett let the logging contract go through) there can be a pilgrimage to Copper City so that the people can be reminded of the monstrosities sometimes committed by an uncontrolled bureaucracy." [60] Soon, national conservation groups were calling for the establishment of Cougar Lakes Wilderness Area as well as a halt to further timber sales in the area. [61]

Barrett's actions reverberated all the way to the Capitol and only confirmed Douglas' belief that the only way to save the last remaining wild places was to get land use decisions out of the hands of the Forest Service. In particular, he was concerned that the power to save or destroy lay in the mind and mood of an unelected bureaucrat. [62] Douglas argued the point in 1960 in the National Parks Magazine:

> "Great issues of social security, power dams, reclamation, soil conservation, price controls, quotas for farmers, and the like are debated in Congress. Yet the issue of whether the people will be left a rich wilderness area or a dust bowl of stumps, serviced by roads, is left to the whim or caprice of a bureaucrat... if roads are to pierce this wilderness, the people should decide it after fair debate. It is their inheritance that is at stake. God made it, and it is among the loveliest of His creations. If it is to be protected, changes in the basic law governing national forests must be made. These sanctuaries need the mantle of protection that only an Act of Congress can give them." [63]

In 1964, the long-debated Wilderness Act finally passed both houses of Congress and was signed into law by President Lyndon Johnson. But, to the surprise and utter disgust of the Double K Gang, the Cougar Lakes Wilderness was almost completely passed over. The Bill included a National Park for the North Cascades and generous wilderness areas around Glacier Peak in the Central Cascades but proposed just a tiny area around Mount Aix on Nelson Ridge for wilderness protection. By the time all of the boundaries were negotiated, even that small area was dropped, and the Cougar Lakes proposal essentially disappeared. With over 100,000 acres of prime timberland opened up, the Forest Service started marking trees for cutting.

Kay and Isabelle did not give up. They reorganized and redoubled their efforts. They lobbied bureaucrats, called congressional offices, and wrote countless letters, keeping interest up and pressure on.

Carmelita "Mad-dog" Lowry, who had fallen in love with the Cascade Mountains during visits from her hometown of St. Louis, Missouri and Eileen Ryan, a schoolteacher in Seattle who had worked as a wrangler at the Double K in the fifties, became pivotal players.[64] The women coordinated strategy, engaged additional conservation groups, and diligently kept up correspondence both locally and nationally. As writers, they kept proponents informed through newspaper articles and the NCCC newsletter.

On the other side of the country, Douglas also ratcheted up the pressure, calling the Secretary of Agriculture, writing editorials, and constantly urging action. He told the Double K Girls that since the Cougar Lakes area was being ignored, they should get all the conservation groups "hollering." He even wrote an article for the National Geographic magazine. The editors did not publish it, calling the piece too controversial to which Douglas replied, "But what the hell isn't, that is worth talking about?" [65]

Finally, in 1971, Republican Representative John P. Saylor of Pennsylvania introduced an Omnibus Wilderness Bill to Congress including the Cougar Lakes area.[66] On December 11, Senator Jackson from Washington introduced his bill to the Senate, and Representative Mike McCormack did the same for the House, but neither survived the adjournment of Congress.[67]

Another effort to move the proposal forward may have been initiated in 1972 during a "secret meeting" at the Double K. One midsummer day, several unfamiliar cars rolled into Goose Prairie and made a right turn onto Ira Ford Lane. The well-dressed men who emerged were United States congressmen and public agency chiefs. They mounted the Ranch house's broad front steps where they were greeted by William O. Douglas and his two mountain sidekicks, Kay and Isabelle. Senator Scoop Jackson, Representative Mike McCormack, the Lt. Governor to Governor Dan Evans (or perhaps his representative), Howard Zahniser from the

Wilderness Society, Supervisor of the Gifford Pinchot National Forests Ross Williams, the Naches Ranger District Ranger Robert C. Cole, and reportedly the Supervisor of the Snoqualmie National Forest Donald R. Campbell all settled into the big chairs in the living room.

The ranch's wrangler, Tim Franklin, was put on security detail, charged with making sure no one—especially the press—stepped onto the grounds. For the entirety of the meeting, he circled the property keeping a sharp eye for any interlopers.

What some of the most powerful men in forestry and conservation traveled so far to discuss is unknown. It seems likely that they would have been deliberating the proposed Cougar Lakes Wilderness. The conversation might have covered logging issues in the proposed area as well. It seems as if the swap of the Naches Ranger District from the Snoqualmie National Forest to the Wenatchee National Forest which occurred the following year was simply a management issue, but it too may have been touched on since all of the players were in place on that date.

In any case, the outcome seems to have been a positive one as after the meeting, all of the attendees were in good cheer sharing lively toasts all around.[68]

Unfortunately, there would be no breakthrough on the Wilderness from that meeting. For the next decade, political wrangling, the passage of more management bills for public lands, aggressive lobbying by the timber industry, new reviews of roadless areas, and fierce debates over the balance of wilderness verses available timber land, all bogged down the advancement of the wilderness bills. With inaction from Congress, progress on the Cougar Lakes Wilderness stalled, and the entire Bumping area remained open to logging. There were no clear protections on the land.

Douglas continued to fight hard for all that he believed in on and off the bench, even as his health started to fail him. A series of surgeries in the summer of 1968 laid him up. Complications kept him in bed at Prairie

House where his young wife Cathy cared for him. When he was unable to travel to Yakima for a checkup, Douglas convinced someone in the Air Force to give a helicopter pilot in need of more flight time permission to fly his doctors to him at Goose Prairie. The National Guard set up a makeshift field-phone line to the house.

In 1972, Douglas was still driving to Whistlin' Jack Lodge to make phone calls. He would careen down the road in his battered brown Dodge Dart and bomb back up, not recklessly, just fast. He also tended to favor the middle of the road much to the chagrin of the local sheriff, Steve DeVilbiss, who appealed to Kay and Isabelle for help. The plan they hatched to coax Douglas out of the driver's seat involved the Ranch's wrangler, Tim Franklin. At the Girls' urging, Douglas agreed to let Franklin drive him the fifteen winding miles back and forth to Whistlin' Jack. During these outings, the twenty-year-old from Pennsylvania and the crusty Justice talked incessantly—not of politics, but how the Bumping River flowed, what the beaver did, which wildflowers were blooming, what was happening right here in the mountains. *That* was what was important to share.[69]

Tim Franklin had come across the country to work for Kay at just nineteen years old and returned to the Double K for two more summers. He instantly bonded with both Kay and Isabelle and eagerly soaked up all of the practical woods skills and life wisdom they offered in such abundance. They—and the surroundings—had a profound influence on the young man. "I have raced stock cars. I have driven 200 miles an hour but those three years there were more exciting," he asserted in 2019. He believes that everything important he learned in life, he learned from the Double K Girls.

Franklin was introduced to William O. Douglas the first season. Like the Girls, Douglas' powerful personality seemed to have two sides, depending on whom he was interacting. If one was closeminded, intellectually lazy, or bigoted, Douglas could be curt, uninterested, or outspoken to the point of rudeness. On the other hand, if a person was perceived as curious, earnest, thoughtful, or hardworking—all qualities he admired—Douglas was a fatherly, generous mentor.

Having spent hours with the Justice, Franklin came to know

the relaxed, off-the-bench side of the man. At ease he was charming, and Franklin recalls his eyes would positively twinkle. He describes Douglas' personality as overwhelming. When Douglas ran his hand through his hair and his smile broadened, whomever was in the Justice's company was completely at his mercy.

And Douglas was generous with his powerful persona. He had a way of making a person feel as if they were exceptional, even while they were conversing with a nationally famous supreme court judge. In conversation, Douglas had a habit of listening closely, then repeating back what he understood the speaker to say, in a way that was both more eloquent and insightful—while giving that person full credit for their signal wisdom.

He could also bestow his strength on others. The Double K house girl, Mary Worbeck, was a diminutive young woman, rather unsure of herself and generally timid. Apparently, during the course of the season, Douglas had passed on to her practical advice to foster her self-confidence. One day she returned breathless to the Ranch house after picking up the mail at the end of the lane. She explained that she had encountered a big black bear on the way back. She had grabbed a big stick and shook it at the bruin which then ran off. "I did just what the Justice told me to do, and it worked!" she exclaimed.[70]

On New Year's Eve 1974, a massive stroke left Douglas partially paralyzed. He pushed on, remaining on the bench and continuing to head across the country to the other Washington for the summer recess. Having outlived all the other New Deal justices, he was loath to give up his liberal influence and was trying hard to outlive Gerald Ford's term so that the president would not be nominating his successor.

In late summer 1975, Douglas was so incapacitated that his son Bill Jr., Kay, and Isabelle decided to act. They called Douglas' old friend, San Francisco attorney and author Charles Reich, and asked him to come to Goose Prairie.[71] Reich and the others spent three days trying to convince Douglas to retire. It didn't work.

Douglas returned to the Capitol determined to continue serving. When he could no longer follow verbal arguments or take coherent notes on the cases being heard, he finally, with great reluctance, wrote his resignation letter to the President of the United States.

"He didn't go easily into death. No, he fought it all the way" recalled the Double K Girls.[72] On January 19, 1980, William O. Douglas took his last breath. With it, the brightest mind, and the most powerful voice ever to argue for the preservation of the Bumping Lake area, its clear streams, pristine meadows, and saw-toothed ridges, was gone.

It is hard to overstate William O. Douglas' impact on our nation's judicial system and his legacy of environmental protection. The Washington Post's tribute to Douglas eloquently summed up his historical significance and the synthesis of his convictions:

> "...Douglas' love for the land should not be put in separate chapters or paragraphs. The two (environmental crusades and defense of free speech) are actually inseparable. The unifying concept is the necessity for space, a cause that Douglas has championed with equal fervor on the trail and on the Bench....In Douglas' view, the expanses of nature are as precious as the liberties protected by the first amendment. Therefore, the claims of nature should be equally recognized in court. This reasoning seemed to lie behind Douglas' famous dissent in Sierra Club v. Morton, also known as the Mineral King case—an opinion which many lawyers regard as quixotic, and which many environmentalists have memorized."[73]

It was only the persistent involvement of the environmental community and the Double K Gang that kept the bulldozers at bay for thirteen more anxious years. As frustrations mounted, Carmelita Lowry used humor to keep their spirits up, writing "How did life get so complicated? All I want is a little old wilderness area."[74]

Timber sales were pending, and one had been proposed for the Bumping Lake area in 1982 when Joel Pritchard, United States Representative from Seattle (and inventor of the game of Pickle-Ball) teamed up with Representative Mike Lowry (no relation to Carmelita) and introduced their bill for two sections of new wilderness designation to the north and south of Highway 410. Mike McCormack did the same in the house.[75]

The Pritchard-Lowry bill was finally adopted and signed into law as part of the Washington State Wilderness Act by Ronald Reagan on July 3, 1984. That Act included, finally, the Cougar Lakes Wilderness Area.[76]

Twenty-four years had passed since Kay Kershaw and Isabelle Lynn wrote their original proposal.

Isabelle Lynne and Kay Kershaw with Lucky III stand proudly at a trail entrance of the newly protected William O. Douglas Wilderness. The designation took twenty-four years of effort from the time the two women originally proposed it. (Courtesy of Tim Franklin)

When the Cougar Lakes wilderness area was finally endorsed by the President's pen, it had a new name. The flower-filled meadows, wandering brooks, glacier carved cirques, dramatic rockworks, and magnificent old growth groves were christened the William O. Douglas Wilderness, a fitting tribute to the man who, along with his dear friends from the Double K Ranch, worked so hard and so long to see it protected.[77]

*   *   *

The creation of the William O. Douglas Wilderness saved the entire Bumping River region. Because of it, all of the area around the lake, its surrounding ridges and high country terrain, have never been and will never be, stripped of the very life that makes the forests. New roads will not carve up into winding river valleys where tender meadows lie. Logging companies will not make notebook paper out of majestic hemlocks. Ecosystems supporting both common and endangered species will have a chance to continue birthing, reproducing, and dying in their intricate dance with one another. And my children and grandchildren and those of all others who enter here, will still encounter nature as it has evolved from the beginning of time.

Chapter Eleven

THE TWO SIDES OF A DAM

*"In six years, the Government has reclaimed 250,000 acres.
The water for this work comes chiefly from streams rising
in mountains. To maintain the supply of this water, it is
essential that forests be maintained upon the mountains.
To this end, National Forests are indispensable."*
—F.H. Newell, Director, United States
Reclamation Service, 1908

*"Wild rivers, like wildernesses, are scarce and getting scarcer.
The temptation to build reservoirs is great. The trouble is
that acre-feet of water for irrigation or for power have a
predictable market price, while wilderness use does not."*
—William O. Douglas, *Wilderness Bill of Rights*, 1965

*Water's everything. Without water, you're not going
to see anything out here but sagebrush."*
—Brad Carpenter, hop farmer, 2018

"So, how do you feel, as a cabin owner, about the Yakima Basin Integrated Plan?" asked Anita Kissee from TVW. Six months before, a Seattle Times investigative reporter had asked a similarly loaded question to a few cabin owners gathered in the filtered light of the Sanctuary where we were surrounded by immense trees. We were enveloped by thousands of years of collective life and breathed in their immortality along with their oxygen.

The Yakima River Basin Integrated Water Resources Management Plan (IP) was unveiled in 2012. The result of a collaboration between the Bureau of Reclamation, Washington State Department of Ecology, the Yakama Nation and environmental groups, the plan is the latest attempt to reconcile water uses in the Yakima watershed. The complex plan was hailed as a grand compromise between disparate interests.

The Integrated Plan proposes to do a lot of things: to increase water storage, enhance fish habitat and improve the efficiency of infrastructure. It is supposed to correct historic wrongdoings by retrofitting the five storage dams with fish passage. Its comprehensive and cooperative approach is admirable except that it includes one unsurmountable liability. The Bureau of Reclamation wants to build a new dam—right in the middle of the Bumping River Valley.

The new dam would be constructed at Bumping Crossing, a narrow spot in the valley, about a mile downstream of the present dam. Its height has been adjusted downward in this latest plan, but it is still projected to be 138 feet high and would stretch across the valley approximately 3,300 feet at its crest. The new barrier would increase the capacity of the reservoir five-fold, from 33,700 cubic feet to 198,000 cubic feet. The surface level of the lake would rise by sixty-five feet, inundating over 1,900 acres of woods.[1] The majority of the land to be drowned is late-succession old growth forest.

The resulting reservoir would fill much of the present river valley, submerge everything that currently exists along the lakeshore, and cut off road access beyond the dam.

I ponder the reporter's question and try to concisely articulate the immorality of what was being proposed. How do you begin to tackle the Mount Everest of that query? How does one reduce the significance of an ancient forest into a string of words? The water plan's new dam would destroy everything I know and love at Bumping Lake—including Normandie.

Before that day with reporters, one of our tasks was to give testimony to legislators in Olympia at one of many committee hearings held in the capitol. Our earnest but necessarily short speeches were an attempt to make utterly indifferent politicians care about an area they had never seen or even wanted to. The committee members seemed far more concerned about the appearance of their coalition and the progress they had made towards providing more water to farmers in Yakima Valley than the continued existence of an insignificant little valley somewhere up in the mountains.

Back room deals had already been cut to make all of the included interest groups happy without regard to the cost or logic of the plan. Previously hostile conservation groups like American Rivers, the World Wildlife Federation and the Nature Conservancy were asked what it would take to get them on board. For only the promise of money for restoration of fisheries habitat elsewhere, these environmental groups traded away the Bumping River Valley to irrigators.[2]

The primary goal of the Integrated Plan is to ensure all water rights holders receive seventy percent of their full water allotment, even in drought years. According to the Bureau of Reclamation, the only way to achieve this is to add more surface water storage. The agency has proposed building two new dams: one at Wymer Canyon and the replacement dam at Bumping Lake. But since no mandatory water conservation was written into the plan, all water users in the Valley will be able to continue using water as they always have.

Under water laws written when the West was still the frontier and water seemed unlimited, entitled water rights holders are encouraged to consume their allotment of subsidized water and do so however they wish. Some growers run inefficient overhead sprinklers on their orchards, even at noon on ninety-five degree days. Leaks in wooden conveyance canals and earthen subsidiary ditches are not always repaired. Miles upon miles of uncovered aqueducts and canals—some so old they are made out of wooden staves—evaporate precious water into the hot summer air. Some orchards are planted with fruit varieties not suitable for high summer heat and are cooled daily by vast arrays of water misters.[3]

Since the Bureau of Reclamation continues to heavily subsidize the cost of the water, and water rights holders are guaranteed delivery of it, there is no incentive to conserve.

In the vast Yakima Valley, water is squandered in another way. Most of the cities in the valley were built on previously irrigated farmland. When development replaced agricultural land, the irrigation systems were left in place and modified to supply water for landscaping, gardens, and small farms. To this day, most of the city's water departments maintain *two* water delivery systems: one for potable water and one for irrigation.[4] The irrigation water is offered at far below market rate (with one local user admitting he felt it was practically free).

That is why in Yakima, with annual rainfall of eight inches, expansive lawns, sports fields, and golf courses continue to glow green into the depths of September. In contrast, suburban yards and public parks in western Washington have long since withered to straw during the normal dearth of summer rains. Ironically, in water-rich Western Washington, water is too expensive for most residents and municipalities to continue soaking their thirsty grass.[5]

What began as a program to grow food on arid lands, has developed over time into an upside down system that rewards waste and encourages irresponsible water use and development in both the agricultural and urban sectors.

And so, we are yet again, where we were in 1914, when individuals saw the miraculous results of mountain water, realized the potential of that precious liquid on their land and wanted more. Farmers and other water users—all of us—will always want more water and the Bureau of Reclamation, an agency that exists solely to provide it, is eager to prove its relevance by complying.

The biota in the watershed has no voice and little tangible value and so is the pawn to be sacrificed for the greater good. How dare anyone stand up for the luxury of wilderness, old trees, and a few animals when industry and a peoples' welfare are at stake, when there is a need?

The thing is, there are much better ways to satisfy that need.

For four hours, oceanographic scientist Miles McPhee, his wife Saundie, and I answered questions, gave our views on the plan and generally tried to not mess up or appear selfish or ignorant, as the camera rolled, and the storm clouds of the future roiled on the horizon.

Our job was to articulate what made the area unique and to make people care. But how do you generate compassion for this faraway place? It was nerve wracking to speak out with so much at stake, knowing we were challenging powerful interests. What a responsibility I felt: to my family, to the heritage of Normandie, to the other cabin owners, to the ancient forest, the rest of the Bumping River Valley, the Northwest and—indirectly—the world, to preserve this priceless corner of the universe.

As I get miked up, the thin wire threading down my shirt and around to my back, I try to keep fear pushed away. I don't think about a new dam. I don't think about the tidy campgrounds flooded, the countless trees drowning, miles of hiking trails washed away, Normandie rotting under thirty feet of water or what it would take to say goodbye to all of this. Instead, I smooth my hair, take a deep breath, and try to speak to what my mind knows and my heart feels.

Conservationists were not always at war with irrigators. The pioneers of irrigation in the west developed their projects with the understanding that watershed vegetation directly affected their water supply. They argued that forests absorbed rainfall and increased the level of ground water, that tree cover slowed snow melt in the early months of the year which reduced spring flooding and saved water for summer months when supplies ran low. They understood that trees retarded soil erosion and silting in irrigation ditches and reservoirs. Irrigators recognized these basic concepts, and in an effort to safeguard the watersheds, played a major role in the establishment the Forest Reserves and National Forests at the turn of the century. Irrigation groups spent the next few decades vigorously defending the protected forests from timber cutting, livestock grazing, and fire in order to protect their water supply.[6]

In the industry magazine, *Forestry and Irrigation*, editor Thomas Elmer Will sought to strengthen the association's mission:

> *"Our land is the heritage of all people, living and to come... This heritage must be preserved by wise use and transmitted, unimpaired to the generations which must follow us."*[7]

The same year, in 1907, Senator George C. Perkins of California succinctly summed up the equation: *"...without our forests, there would be no irrigation."*[8]

At the turn of the century, the American Forestry Association and the National Irrigation Association were all about conservation and sustainability, it seemed. So, what happened?

In 1902, the Reclamation Act was passed, and the United States Reclamation Service was born. The romantic—and lucrative—notion of making deserts bloom was overpowering to those in control of seemingly endless empty lands in the West. The eastern part of the country had benefited for decades from federally financed infrastructure projects by the Army Corps of Engineers. Now it was the West's turn.

From the beginning, the agency was politically driven. Every Senator and Congressman wanted an irrigation project for their district, regardless of logic or suitability. Within just one year, five major projects were approved. By 1907, twenty-four projects had been fast-tracked for construction, at least one for every state in the West. In the rush to approve, little attention was paid to the economics, climate, soil, production, transportation, and markets involved.[9]

Dams were built, canals were dug, reservoirs filled, and water was delivered. Agriculture developed, and cities grew. During the 1930s, the New Deal meant that the Bureau grew again with sometimes huge public works projects proposed to put citizens to work and build infrastructure. The idea was to spend money, not necessarily to spend money well. Staff ballooned from a few thousand in the 1920s to twenty thousand by the 1940s.[10]

To broaden Congressional support for ever more projects and expand perceived beneficiaries beyond just irrigators, Reclamation proponents touted flood control benefits along with the economic development potential from electrical generation of multi-purpose dams.[11]

As long as Congress was willing to keep funding the projects, no one wanted to stop. A competition developed between the Army Corps of Engineers and the Reclamation Service with Reclamation seemingly in a race to dam every major river in the West as many times as possible. They nearly did it.[12]

By the end of the first quarter century, Reclamation was the largest water storage, diversion, and transmission project builder in the nation.[13] It was very good at building dams.

But there were problems. Construction costs were supposed to be repaid by users but early on farmers had trouble keeping up their payment schedules. The Service adjusted the repayment periods from ten to twenty and then forty years. Still, average repayment from 1902-1980 was less than 14% of construction costs. Taxpayers were picking up the tab for almost all of the irrigation schemes in the West.[14]

By 1923, the situation was so bad, with cost overruns and unmet projections, that the agency was investigated by Congress, completely reorganized, and renamed (the United States Reclamation Service became the United States Bureau of Reclamation). Debts were forgiven, and an unbowed Bureau of Reclamation wasted no time hurtling into the future. Gone were simple single purpose dams. Moving forward, the Bureau would propose huge multi-use projects with the idea that construction costs would be covered in large part now by the sale of electricity from hydroelectric dams.[15]

Politics continued to drive the consideration of projects with states "taking turns" getting projects—whether they made sense or not. By the 1960s, the Bureau was running out of places to dam but was eager to develop big new projects to keep the agency's large workforce busy, its funding in place, and maintain its bureaucracy. Over time, the pace of dam building actually picked *up* with 203 new dams being built between 1930 and 1970.[16]

And still, the costs were not being repaid.

By the 1970s, because of the glaring inefficiencies of past projects, the Bureau was required to calculate benefit to cost ratios before a project was green-lighted. Projects that would cost more than they would be worth would be illegal to build. This mandate has led to exaggerating benefits and underestimating costs, sometimes vastly.[17]

Today, the Bureau has long since fulfilled its mandate to build irrigation infrastructure. In addition to being the country's largest water wholesaler, it is the nation's second largest producer of electricity with fifty-eight hydroelectric power plants. It owns 600 dams and reservoirs and benefits from a secure multi-billion dollar annual budget.[18]

Depending on how small you count, our country is home to an unbelievable total of 84,000 to two *million* dams, from small diversion structures to geology-bending mega-dams. 14,000 large dams disrupt waterways in the West alone.[19] We have been damming and diverting water since the time of the Puritans, at an average rate of one dam per day since the signing of the Declaration of Independence, says Dartmouth College geography professor, Frank Magilligan.[20]

"Water storage is a big part of the reason people can live in areas where it does not rain," writes journalist Heather Hansman.[21] As a result of Reclamation projects, the state of California produces more food than most nations. Phoenix, in the middle of one of the driest spots in the Southwest, has blossomed into the country's sixth largest city. Yakima County leads the state in market value of agricultural products. The benefits of the projects to the economies of the West are profound.

But after centuries of ignoring the environmental consequences of dams, their ecological impact is now well recognized and widely accepted. Dams cut a river's ecosystem in two, disrupting the flow of nutrients and sediment downstream and the migration of animals both upstream and down. Flood-absorbing wetlands are lost under slack water reservoirs; sediment buildup behind older dams can increase river flooding. Where dams are in place, the health of the river is upended, the watershed fractured.

Bumping River is no exception. The Upper Bumping River gathers snowmelt and spring waters from the high country to the southwest of the lake along the divide. The cold water tumbles down broad Bumping Falls and then slows as it flows into the lake. The lower Bumping River begins at the dam itself, coursing through the concrete outlet channel only yards away from its historic riverbed. It continues down the valley, passing Goose Prairie and joining with American River eleven miles away.

But the rivers are no longer connected. The dam is an absolute barrier to the passage of anything but water itself. Without a fish ladder or other means of transport up and over the barrier, any fish that manage to return to the head of the lower river are trapped at the foot of the dam. They are unable to access the tributaries above the lake making the forests above the dam forever deficient of the rich nutrients that the fish previously delivered in their very bodies.

Understanding the full cost of dams is leading to a general change of attitude toward them. Unused dams that have aged out of relevance are starting to be removed all over the country. In Washington State, where dams have been taken out, the newly released rivers have quickly rebounded with life.[22] Salmon especially, waste no time pushing up into their former ranges, almost as if they had not been denied access to them for generations. They have just been waiting.

Back at the Double K, Kay and Isabelle—though certainly deserving of a rest after their long fight for the William O. Douglas Wilderness—didn't put their feet up. As the Wilderness Bill was being passed in 1984, finally granting protective status over the land they knew and loved so well, the Double K Girls were already well onto the next battle.

Just as conservationists learned that as long as there was a tree standing, there would be a logger eying it, it seems as if as long as there is fresh water running down a river, an irrigator will try to gain control over it.

The Bureau of Reclamation was back again, looking for more water.[23]

In opposing the Bureau's proposed 223-foot-tall dam, Isabelle made the identical arguments that are being made today against the same zombie proposal: the substrate under the new dam site was unsuitable for the weight of a taller dam, the new reservoir wouldn't fill due to the limited size of the watershed, and the Bureau was padding the recreational benefits of a new lake and underestimating costs to create a positive benefit to cost ratio.[24]

❦ ❦ ❦

The parameters have not changed in thirty years—except that the trees have gotten larger, the ecosystem more mature and the habitat even more irreplaceable due to the inexorable loss of other areas to development, logging, and fire.[25]

One year after the Yakima Integrated Plan was released, in an effort to get unbiased benefit-cost (B-C) figures, lawmakers in Olympia called for an independent analysis that examined each of the projects included in the plan independently. The State of Washington Water Research Center's report to the legislature in 2013 is damning. The report recognizes positive benefits for all of the fish passage projects (installing fish passage on each of the project's existing dams creates huge benefits in terms of fish returns) but negative benefit-cost ratios for each of the storage projects.

Specifically, the costs of building a new dam at Bumping Lake would be so high, and the returns so low (in terms of increased water supply) that the taxpayers could expect a return of about eighteen cents for every dollar spent.[26] Even though no business in America would ever undertake this kind of project with those numbers, the replacement dam at Bumping stayed in the Integrated Plan.

The research center's analysis did not even consider the costs of lost recreation, the cabins, the campgrounds, marina, or importantly, the loss of the forest.[27]

These numbers are why even though a new dam has been proposed and studied nearly continuously over the past century, in Democratic and Republican administrations, in strong economies and recessions, in drought years and in wet, the Bumping Lake dam has never been replaced.[28] After each multimillion dollar study, hundreds of pages of analysis, and hours of public testimony the result is the same: it does not pencil out.

We cannot dam our way out of our looming water shortages. Our water resources have largely been developed and are currently being utilized at their limit and sometimes clearly past. The only way to possibly have enough water for future needs is through the more efficient use and delivery of our current supply. Four-fifths of the water that the Bureau delivers is for agriculture, so reforms have to start with those users. The most effective solution would be to reconsider the antiquated water rights laws of the West which blatantly encourage waste.[29]

However, since political compromise on this contentious issue seems very unlikely, there are instead reasonable adjustments to reduce demand that are realistic, doable, and can be undertaken immediately.

Conservation of existing diverted water is the most obvious. The Bureau's own reports show significant savings can be gained with improvements in irrigation and conveyance efficiency.[30] In the Yakima Valley, growers utilize a wide range of on-farm irrigation methods from primitive open field flooding to modern high pressure drip irrigation. The Kittitas Irrigation District for example has only twenty percent of its irrigated land in sprinklers or drip irrigation. In contrast, the Roza District is at ninety percent. Fortunately, upgrades of wantonly wasteful older systems are finally starting to be funded. The implementation of these conversions has contributed to an overall reduction of diversions over the past several decades, but upgrades are expensive, so progress has been uneven.[31]

The conveyance infrastructure that gets water to the farms is just as wasteful. While some large canal relining and replacement projects have already been undertaken, as of 2010, the amount of water being leaked and evaporated out of the canals each year from the six largest districts in the Yakima Project was nearly twice the entire proposed storage from a new dam at Bumping.[32]

Market-based reforms will also help alleviate potential future water shortages. Active water markets which allow transfers of water between all sectors (agriculture, municipalities, state, and other buyers) are an effective way to decrease demand and increase efficiency by getting water to the users who most want it. Studies have shown, and practice has proved, that robust and well-run water markets can save as much water in a district as is usually perceived as needed. Voluntary water markets have already been established or planned for a majority of western states. Water transfer mechanisms are starting to be studied and tested in the Yakima basin.[33]

New dams to create more storage has been the Bureau's knee jerk reaction to the agriculture industry's cry for more water for over one hundred years now. The response has rarely been for better stewardship of the resource being supplied already. Bumping Lake has always been the farthest away, the least familiar, and the least developed of all of the Yakima reservoirs. It has always been the easy answer for the question of more water. It is only when critics expose the dismal economic numbers and the impracticality of the site, and public sentiment is roused over the loss of irreplaceable forests, that the scheme is dropped. But like a malicious phoenix, the proposal rises again and again, for each new generation of fiscal realists and conservationists to fight.

With each round, dam proponents have become savvier, are spending more money, and are learning how to pitch and spin the controversies. This time they are gathering former opponents under their tent by offering them whatever they ask in return for their support. And for the latest plan, the Bureau is adding the excuse of global climate change to continue to pursue their obsolete dam-at-all-costs course.

Just as the Forest Service served the needs of timber industry, the Bureau of Reclamation serves the powerful agriculture lobby. Even though the Bureau by its own admission knows that reforms are needed instead of more infrastructure, the agency is like a huge ship, the momentum of which is carrying it toward the rocks even after the captain has corrected course. Maybe the agency is not willing to admit what the rest of the developed world knows: that the era of dam building has passed, and it is time for different answers.

There is too much at stake not to continue to fight just as our predecessors did. William O. Douglas prepped the Double K Girls for political and personal battles by telling them that "if [they] never received a poison letter, [they] weren't accomplishing much…" [34]

So, with the help of the rest of the Gang and others like Loren and Margaret Strain in Goose Prairie and David Ortman with Friends of the Earth, the Girls kept speaking out and penning letters to editors and testifying to committees. And since they really didn't care what others thought of them—that they were too vocal or aggressive or pushy for women to be—they became politically powerful and ultimately successful in the arena that mattered the most: their legacy. Because they did not back down and could ignore hate mail and personal insults and persist for years, they got not only the Wilderness established but shot down the proposed new dam at Bumping, too.

They never gave up and we won't either. We will continue in tribute and in fairness to those fierce women and dedicated men who fought before us and who were not afraid to say what they believed in and speak out even if was uncomfortable, hard, made them unlikeable, or just plain wore them out. Feelings are a small cost to pay for being true to your beliefs. In the end, I think it boils down to which version of our sweet earth you believe in: either this world is ours to exploit and use up or it is in our care to cherish, shepherd, and to pass on intact to the next generations.

Chapter Twelve

THE CURIOUS SIDE OF PARADISE

*"People believe in these things because they like to
believe in them, and it keeps on going because people
like it. And why not? It's a charming story."*
—Ian McTaggart Cowan, *The Future of Wildlife Management*

*"Penetrating so many secrets, we cease to believe in the unknowable.
But there it sits nevertheless, calmly licking its chops."*
—H. L. Mencken, *Minority Report*, 1956

Late fall holds less promise for me than the rest of the seasons here.
The warmth of earlier days has been blown downriver by damp winds. The
sun stays ominously low all day, not able to completely chase the frost crystals from shifting shadows. By now, the dominant groundcovers, grasses,
and vanilla leaf have been drained of all chlorophyll. They are now ochre
and sienna, curling and crumbling back to the earth. Songbirds are heading
south. The mushrooms, so abundant only a week ago, are now either nibbled down to nubs or composting back into the duff.

The huge cottonwoods that cluster along the shores of lake and
river are dropping their saffron leaves one by one all day; they fall like
a gentle, golden rain. The deciduous larches are shedding their needles

too and soon the forest floor is bright yellow around the denuded trees, their bare trunks standing like lamp posts casting a circle of light on the ground around them. All the leaves and needles along with the lifeless perennial growth are weaving the blanket that will protect not only the plants' living roots from the killing cold to come, but also insulate the countless animals that have burrowed in the ground to survive. Ground squirrels and chipmunks are dug in, along with snakes and salamanders. Miniature Western toadlets, which just weeks before slow-motion-hopped all around the cabin causing us to pause our own footfalls as we walked, have covered themselves up as well. Many of the insects have disappeared. Even the bears have hunkered down. Though there are many still in the valley, elk and deer are nowhere to be seen: the calendar is well advanced into hunting season, and they know it. This time of year is like a long, slow inhalation, with all of nature preparing and waiting for the first tentative snowfalls that are the preamble to serious weather and the full onslaught of winter.

I passed through this suspended landscape in late October in the form of a run with our dog. I had no expectations other than to get some exercise. I would need to keep moving to stay warm, since even though I had waited until midday to venture out, the low sun was occluded by leaden clouds. A cruel wind was picking up and sweeping across the remains of the lake. I made a loop through the Sanctuary and cut west through the thin lodgepoles toward the lake. At this time of year with lower water, the fringing mudflats are like a morning newspaper, with clear reporting of the movements of the animals that are still about.

Just two weeks before, Tom and I had walked along the shore looking for lost lures and other items of interest which become exposed as the water level drops. Before we even reached water's edge, we were met by a small man in a tall, knitted cap who eagerly greeted us.

"Do you want to see an amazing trackway?" he asked.

"Um, yes," we replied, not knowing what a trackway was but happy to see anything considered amazing. We followed him toward two other figures who were bent over intently studying the mud along the shore.

"Look—here it is!"

We followed his gesture to observe a looping track of perfectly impressed and beautifully defined bare footprints. Human footprints—or so we thought.

"Aren't they beautiful? Clearly a juvenile and perhaps a female."

Tom and I looked at each other, eyebrows mutually arching.

"Do you see how the footprints are *in line*, heel to toe, not parallel like ours? And how they are pushing off from the center of the foot, and not the big toe?"

It was about now that it dawned on us what was happening. This group was on the trail of Sasquatches. The other two were photographing the tracks and this guy was now preparing to video a section of the trackway. They were calling back and forth excitedly. I shot Tom a warning look, willing him not to start laughing out loud.

"Why would anyone be outside barefoot in this cold? And in the mud?"

I resisted replying that yesterday had been a warm, sun lit day, and I could imagine it. In fact, we probably would have been barefoot without shoes had we ventured to the water's edge. The group was electric with excitement, recording, measuring, and we were witnessing a major discovery.

"These rival the London Trackway," the man exclaimed.

We examined the tracks too and agreed that they were beautiful, and in line. Indeed, the mud was so fine that every detail of the impression was perfectly delineated down to the whorls on the footprints themselves. I didn't see any indication of hair, but then again, I didn't know if juvenile Bigfoot had hairy feet, so I kept quiet. We shared as much enthusiasm as we realistically could, congratulated them on their find, and moved on down the shoreline after taking a few photos of our own. We heard them calling to each other for a long time.

Another fall day, I did not notice Sasquatch track lines but saw many other prints. The biggest bird footprints I had ever seen made it look like a small dinosaur had landed at the lake, but instead told the story of a great blue heron hunting, walking slowly along the shallows and intent on any movement that would suggest a meal. Tiny bird tracks crisscrossed the heron's and made just one line as this little shorebird ran heel to toe. Webbed prints of the Canada geese were no longer as apparent as they had been just a week before, but in their place, I saw what had to be otter tracks: little dog-like prints but wider and with the giveaway clue of a long mark where the animals dragged their tails as they loped about. Suddenly, the tracks were everywhere and droppings too.

I looked around again and now I was not alone. Karma, who had moved on ahead, was staring intently at a point twenty feet offshore where two small logs appeared to be floating. But wood does not leave strong triangular wakes and these shapes were moving quickly in her direction. It was the river otters themselves! After thirty years of seeing only their tracks along both the river and the lake, here was a pair, not crashing away into the underbrush, nor winging away at my approach, but heading straight toward us. In a nice role reversal, Karma lost her nerve at their unswerving approach and backed up, heading up the bank a safe distance while the larger of the two leapt gracefully onto a rock and peered at her. Its body was long and lean, its coat glossy and dark above and silvery gray below. The animal's pale throat set off its dark eyes so that it looked intense, intelligent. As Karma sidled closer to me, the otters followed in the water until they were right in front of us. They dove and surfaced, arcing smoothly through the waves. They watched us for a time and then, their curiosity sated, swam slowly away. As chilly as it was that day, I knew these animals would adjust as the temperatures dropped and would not hibernate or migrate like most of the rest of the mammals up here. They would continue playing and hunting, and in due course would swim beneath solid winter ice to hunt.

Lately, Bumping Lake has become a Sasquatch hotspot. The videos that we witnessed being filmed that lovely autumn day became a minor internet sensation and have brought even more hopeful searchers to the Valley. Dozens of accounts have been generated over the last few years. Even mainstream newspapers like USA Today, list Bumping Lake as a destination for bigfoot hunters. With only one road and so many square miles of untouched wilderness, the mountains seem big enough to hide a mystical beast.

Elusive oversized primates seemed to have lurked around the fringes of cultures and populations of the northwest since prehistoric times. Indigenous inhabitants described "Hairy Man" legends to missionaries as early as 1840 and ancient pictographs in several states depict furry ape creatures alongside more familiar local wildlife like lizards and beavers. Modern day curiosity about such a creature was stoked in 1967 by the now iconic film of a huge dark figure striding away in some grainy footage from northern California, known among enthusiasts as the Patterson-Gimlin film. Roger Patterson was the man behind the camera and Bob Gimlin appears on horseback in the minutes before the creature materializes. Both men were from Yakima.

Two years after the track line discoveries, I found myself chatting with an older gentleman near the end of the dam. After a few minutes, he shared that he was there to look for evidence of Bigfoot. This spry octogenarian grew up on the Yakama Reservation and, though he is eighty-five years old, he comes up to the lake at least once a year since it is great place to find tracks in the fall when the lake draws down. One night near his campsite he had an encounter with what he believes was a Sasquatch, but never saw it.

When I was leaving, I asked his name and he said Bob. "Bob Gimlin—you'll find me online."

The Bumping River Valley, like other remote places, seems to be a perfect place for imaginations to run wild, or perhaps the senses to become more acute.

In 1947, respected businessman and experienced pilot Kenneth Arnold was flying his plane from Chehalis to Yakima on a clear June afternoon when he was startled to see nine large, shiny objects flying in formation near Mount Rainier. They were moving at a high rate of speed on a north to south course along the crest of the Cascades close to American Ridge and very nearly over Bumping Lake. He could see all the aircraft clearly as they flashed and dipped in the sun. From his cockpit, using known landmarks below and his watch, he clocked the mysterious objects' speed at an astonishing 1,700 miles per hour.

The next day when Arnold landed in Pendleton, Oregon, he relayed what he had seen. He was sure that the Air Force would have an explanation, perhaps involving the testing of an experimental aircraft. In a brief statement to a reporter, he described the objects as what a saucer might look like if it was flung into the air. A short article in the local paper was picked up by the Associated Press and quickly caused a sensation across the country and then the globe. The press coverage referred to the objects Arnold had seen as "flying saucers." With that first-ever description of unexplained spacecraft, the modern era of UFO sightings, alien encounters, and men in black suits was born.[1]

Another mystery unfolded just a year earlier when the new wrangler for the Double K Ranch, Lionel Claude "Joe" Blackburn, rode out into a snowstorm to help look for a missing deer hunter. Having spent his life in the mountains, the twenty-eight-year-old was so familiar with the area that his wife was not even particularly worried when he did not return for supper. She finally filed a missing person report several days later. The lost hunter and Blackburn's horse, minus its bridle and saddle, both eventually found their way back to the Prairie, but in spite of the determined efforts of ninety searchers, no trace was found of Blackburn.[2]

Nineteen years later, in 1965, another twenty-eight-year-old man, Wagner M. Robinson, disappeared while hunting elk in the Goose Prairie-Bumping Lake area. On their third day combing the woods, search teams did not locate Robinson, but they finally found Joe Blackburn. One of the searchers came upon a skull and a lone cowboy boot which was confirmed to have belonged to the missing wrangler. There were no clues to what had happened to him, and no cause of death was ever determined. He was only three-quarters of a mile from his home in Goose Prairie.[3]

Robinson left a wife and four children back at home in Lakewood, Washington when he set out on his hunt. Even though search teams eventually totaled 200 people, he has never been found and his trail has long gone cold.[4] At least two people believe that he is still out lurking in the forest somewhere. A letter was sent to the Yakima Sheriff's office in 1967 regarding a supposed sighting of Robinson in the Goose Prairie Cafe, not far from where he disappeared. Thirty-three years later, Mark Cliff, the owner of the Cafe, claimed that Robinson sat down for a meal and left without finishing when he saw his missing person poster on the wall of the café.[5]

These two men were not the only ones to lose their way. Dozens of people, primarily hunters, got themselves lost in the mountains surrounding the lake. Most were found within a day or two or walked out themselves. A few did not. One elk hunter who was lost for four days and three cold nights on the remote slopes near Mount Aix credited his survival to commando training that he received in Vietnam.[6] A pair of teenagers from Selah survived for six days in the snow along Nelson Ridge. They were rescued from the bottom of a hundred-and-seventy-five-foot ravine by helicopter.[7] Randall James Sutey of Richland was only nineteen when he went missing in November and was not found until the following spring when the snows finally melted and revealed his remains.[8] Only a few months after Sutey's body was found, another elk hunter, Donald Czerwinski was lost and did not make his way out before he died of hypothermia.[9]

That there were so many lost is not surprising. Kay Kershaw described the terrain in an interview: "This is rough steep country. It's not for kids. We get nine months of snow and three months of damned poor sledding." [10] In November, when all the men died, clouds roll in reducing visibility dramatically and temperatures hover right around freezing even in the daytime.

Sometimes the losing of oneself was more dramatic. In the middle of winter around 1984, a bank was robbed in Yakima and the suspect sped away up Highway 410 toward Chinook Pass, which was closed for the season. A lone responding officer followed, knowing the man's car would eventually run out of gas or be blocked by snow. When the car finally sputtered to a stop on the Normile Grade, the man jumped out into the deep drifts. The officer waited for backup, expecting an easy arrest. Instead, the suspect disappeared into the wilds and, despite a massive manhunt, no sign of him—or his remains—was ever found.[11]

The legend of the sheepherder "Hindoo John" Sinclair still endures even though his tragedy unfolded over a century ago. Originally from Delhi, Hindoo John had served with the British Army in India before signing on as a groom for a load of horses bound for San Francisco in the 1880s. The passage by sail dragged on for four months.[12] John drifted north to Washington and found work with the Cameron Brothers tending sheep in the Upper Bumping area. He was a well-liked and reliable herder.

One summer day in 1895 or 1896 John's packer George Jackson headed to the upper Rattlesnake drainage near Mount Aix to re-provision him. Jackson arrived to discover a massive pile-up of 1,130 dead sheep, and no herder. Something had panicked the animals and caused them to "bunch up" and suffocate. Since his horse and belongings were missing, Jackson concluded John must have abandoned his herd and returned to Seattle.[13]

Hindoo John, like so many other men who roamed the valleys and ridges of the frontier, prospected on the side. Gold had been found near Naches Pass recently and news of the Alaska Gold Rush fueled gold fever in most men. Before he went missing, Hindoo John had packed several loads of rich quartz ore down to a friend's home on the Nile without, not surprisingly, revealing the location of his find. Maybe he had made a strike or found fantastic riches and was busy pulling money out of the ground. Still, to abandon his charges was uncharacteristic of the proud and conscientious man that his friends knew.

The next summer, two young boys on a fishing expedition to the upper Bumping drainage decided to visit the scene of the catastrophe. To their surprise, under the scattered bones of the scores of sheep, they found Hindoo John's skeleton (inexplicably missing his left hand). He had died trying to protect his charges, after all. The source of his fine ore has never been located.[14]

Another mystery that involved death, skeletons, and missing persons was discovered at the time the Reclamation crews were cutting the road into the lake for the construction of the dam. Several of the road crew wandering about in the forest came upon the skeleton of a packhorse. The poor animal's remains were still tied to tree from which all the bark had chewed off as it starved. Its pack was still in place with its contents intact, but a wide search did not turn up a corresponding skeleton of a man. The assembled force of searchers found only a single snowshoe.[15]

Jack and Kitty may have rolled their eyes at the sensational accounts of flying saucers in their neighborhood, but they could not have ignored the next development of the new atomic age. One morning in the middle of June 1955, a man urgently knocked at their door. A short time later came another, and then another. They were all asking the same thing: "Where's the uranium?"

The previous September, a weekend prospector named Tom Hendrix had come across a little mineral spring near Copper Creek known locally as "Skookum Lemochene" or "the animals' health spring," for all of the game trails that led to it.[16] Thinking perhaps the unusual water could be bottled and sold, he proceeded to take a sample. As he investigated, his Geiger counter started clicking and as the needle swung over the gauge, he forgot all about the water and hurried instead to file a mining claim on the land.

As a result of heightened tensions building at the commencement of the Cold War and the belief that the government was buying uranium, hills all over country were alive with men and women toting, not gold pans, but Geiger counters. As soon as word got out about Hendrix's strike, the trickle of would-be miners became a flood. Within three days, eighty claims had been filed with the Yakima County Auditor. Every available tract within a three-mile radius of the little pool had been marked with claim stakes. The rush was on.[17]

The claims never came to much, however, and within three years the Atomic Energy Commission announced that it would not buy any more newly-discovered uranium stores.[18] The frenzy collapsed as quickly as it had built. The little lemonade spring, gouged and defiled, remained, gathering cloudy water which does not seem to be radioactive. Today, frogs kick across the shallows and animals still come from all over the vicinity to drink its special water.

Chapter Thirteen

FISH AND OTHER NEIGHBORS

"…in this country the quantities [of fish] taken and that might be taken, are beyond calculation. As they penetrate farther into the interior, they afford an almost inexhaustible supply to the Indian tribes of the country as well as the whites…"
—Reverend Gustavus Hines,
Wild Life in Oregon, 1881

"The people of the Valley must take their choice between game fish and big red apples. If they must have the fish, the government might as well go out of the business of operating storage dams."
—Charles H. Swigart, Reclamation Service Project Engineer,
after an inspection trip to Bumping Lake,
Yakima Herald, October 18, 1911

"Fish are a forest product."
—Andrew Tanentzap, *Forests Fuel Fish Growth in Freshwater Deltas*, 2014

September is a delicious time of year at Bumping Lake. In warm years, the memories of summer linger in the air like the scent of a tree-ripened peach. We hike, work, and play in comfort with the sun still on our shoulders. At the same time, reminders that the season is closing are unmistakable. Mountain ash berries start to orange up, the vanilla leaf plants dry perfuming the forest, and huckleberry bushes—neon green all summer— start to burnish copper and cranberry.

But the best part of September is that the Kings come home. Despite all odds, despite all the dams, nets, hooks, boats, and pollution; despite even the sea lions and orcas, and the Bumping Lake dam itself, a few Chinook salmon (as king salmon are also known) somehow make it all the way back here. Within yards of where they wriggled free of their eggs, they are about to complete their life cycle. The giant fish have already made a left turn out of the Columbia River into the Yakima, a second left at the Naches River and a third at the Bumping. The higher the fish climb, the tougher the go. They have negotiated switch-backing fish ladders, jumped spillways and falls, pushed past log jams and rock dams. Finally, they have muscled over the cobbles of Bumping River, passed under the Bumping Crossing bridge, and climbed their way one more mile further to reach 3,400 feet above sea level for a final rest in the spillway pond, a little below the dam. They cruise in slow circles with the gentle current, waiting. Though their original spawning grounds are up beyond the dam and seventy-five feet underwater, one hundred years later they still swim up to within sight of that barrier and in the few accessible gravel bars left to them, they prepare for their final feat before they die. In the clear water, under shallow riffles, they make love.

We start looking for the fish to return in August, wondering each year if there will be enough individual miracles—nets slipped, predators evaded, obstacles leapt—to allow the return of any of a once mighty run of salmon. Every year is a question mark with so few individuals returning to perpetuate the run.

It is mid-month and Tom and I do not wait any longer. We head down to the river on a honey-soaked evening, the air so still that the cottonwood leaves aren't even rustling. The usual wind out of the south has whispered away and the lake is mirror calm. The day's earlier heat has quieted even the animals. There is no sound at all except our footfalls on the gravel road.

We walk down the smooth concrete spillway onto the giant timbers that form an elevated river for Spring's overflowing snowmelt, long since drained away. The sluiceway hangs above a large pond on the river where a hundred years of seasonal waterfalls have dug a deep pool some seventy-five feet across. The river slides briskly into the pool on our right, spinning off bubbles and spiraling whirlpools until it smooths and slows in the deeper water. To watch the water is to be hypnotized. Ripples join up and then break apart forming undulating patterns as they alternately reflect sky and trees. To our left, the river continues on, spilling over a rim of rounded rocks and continuing jauntily down towards the bridge at Bumping Crossing, past Goose Prairie and Soda Springs to join the American River, eleven miles away.

As we sit, feet dangling over the edge, ten feet above the surface, we own an excellent vantage point, not only of the river and pond but all the way up to Nelson Ridge across the valley. The evening's last light is turning the ramparts rosy pink. We study the dark, emerald green water. Insects circle crazily above the surface and touch down occasionally, only to take off again. Suddenly, there is a flash and a splash as a slip of a fish, a young trout most likely, leaps up after a mayfly and crashes back down on its side, like a miniature whale breaching.

A great blue heron, nearly three feet tall with impossibly long legs, stealthily stalks the shallows across the pond, eying the ripples for motion underneath. Clearly unsettled by our arrival, after a few minutes it gives up and with a what I could swear was a sigh and an eyeroll, takes off and swings past us. With its long straight beak and narrow gliding wings, it looks more like a pterodactyl than any modern bird.

Though I am listening for it, this evening I can't hear the distinctive melody of a dipper, a bird that has charmed generations of naturalists. John Muir waxed poetic about this rather drab gray songbird with a remarkable lifestyle. Both Jack Nelson and William O. Douglas wrote fondly about their experiences with the "water ouzel" as it was popularly known.[1]

It is hard not to fall in love with the little bird, once you learn where to find it. Jack declared that its songs added cheer to even the fiercest winter days, but that is only part of its appeal. To watch one is to marvel at its evolutionary example, for the American dipper is a songbird similar to a robin, but it swims.

Its diet consists almost exclusively of aquatic insects that live on the beds of streams. To get at their tiny prey, the dipper uses its strong wings to propel it around underwater. Long claws grab tightly to the submerged substrate keeping it in place as it is feeds. When it dives, little flaps close over its nostrils and transparent nictitating membranes slide over its eyes allowing it to see under water as well as it does above. Rounding out its suite of aquatic adaptations are solid, rather than hollow bones which make it less buoyant and more submarine-like, a layer of down to ward off the chill of the water, and a special oil gland to waterproof its feathers.

The real surprise is how it feeds.

I sat on a boulder next to Deep Creek once and watched a dipper dive over and over again, not into a calm pool or gentle ripple, but into the very most turbulent part of the stream. There the flow contracted between two big rocks and ripped the avian equivalent of a Class V rapid. Into this torrent, the little bird would launch itself, disappearing head-first, only to pop up again, twenty or even thirty seconds later, down-stream. It would fly back, preen for a moment, belt out a little tune or dip a few times, before diving back in. The way it threw itself into the current and then bobbed back up looked like nothing else but play, which I knew it was not, but surely there was some amount of pleasure in this bird's pursuit of a meal.

I never tire of observing the incongruity of a songbird that sings like a nightingale and swims like a penguin.

Another evening, I was back down on the river looking for kings but didn't see them. The waning day was breathless again. The sky was the color of ripe fruit but losing the blush fast. As I turned to head back home, a large moving log caught my attention. With a thrill, I focused on the water. Out of seemingly nowhere, a large beaver was paddling straight toward me, its wide, flat tail trailing at the surface and its nose just high enough out to the water to breathe.

What a superb animal.

It circled the pond then headed toward the swift current where the river enters. I wondered how it would get across. Without slowing, it gracefully dipped its head and dove underneath the swirling water. When it surfaced on the other side, it slowly made its way up the river and disappeared from my view. I turned again to leave, elated with this first ever sighting when another brown shape drifted towards me. From the left shore, also leisurely swimming, was a baby beaver, not two feet long. Since I am female, I could have squealed at its appearance: big head, round body, and all, but since I am also a biologist an "ah" was all that came out with my spontaneous smile.

But no dippers entertain Tom and me today. No kingfisher or swallows either, which were keeping, per their custom, to the airspace above the dam. We heard only the gentle water sounds of the river.

Finally, both at the same time, we see it. An olive green torpedo shape materializes out of the jade depths. We can see the black spots on its back and a wash of deep coral on its sides. As pleased as we are to see the magnificent fish, I am crushed to see only one. What good is one?

Perhaps this is just the beginning of the run but nonetheless, it is sobering to reflect that this river once ran thick with fish and now it seems that they will be counted on a few fingers. As we hold our breath, we see a second shape, nearly three feet long, join the first, and they both slide almost imperceptibly forward in the dark water. Three, then four more cylinders appear. Six have returned! The fish rise slowly up and back down circling with the spiraling current, appearing and disappearing like a mirage. Their existence almost *is* a mirage, and we remark again about the unlikely persistence of both their short term (four year) and long term (last one hundred years) survival in the ever-inhospitable world we have remade for them.

The fish will be our neighbors for only a short time. We will visit them nearly every day. For now, they remain in the pond staging, circling, and waiting for the incoming river water to chill, signaling the time to move upstream to the narrow strips of spawning grounds left on the river.

I could watch forever, but it is getting dark and there has been no thought of dinner. As we tromp back to the welcoming lights of

Normandie, we are raised from our quiet reverie by a penetrating sound that rises to a pitched, resonating whistle. It is a bull elk, bugling from across the river; the first clarion call we've heard of the coming season.

❧ ❧ ❧

Bumping River is a beautiful waterway, as rivers go. It is wide and splashy and vocal and bounces over smooth cobbles as it rushes downhill out of the valley. The river's constant movement makes it seem alive, like an animal, and of course it is full of life, but most of it is hidden. Mountain whitefish and trout lurk in the deeper pools while little river dace and a total of five species of sculpin skulk along the river and lake bottoms. Though we don't often see them alive, pretty blue-green crayfish are abundant. They seem to be the preferred prey of river otters based on the quantities of shells on the shore.

The river wears a thick cloak of woven greens along its banks where the trees lean in close and overhang in sweeping washes of their branches. There, the water is dark and mysterious. Shadows shift and secret water animals pause. In that shade, where the mists of the river waft over them, tender flowers and ferns spring from crevices that crease moss covered rocks. In open places, sedges grow thick on sunlit banks, mostly laid over by the footfalls of the otters trailing their long tails.

I do not know the river here as I know the lake and the forest, but our friends that live next to it and consider it their neighbor can hear the change of pitch through the seasons and read its mood through its voice. They see the changes of color of the water as it deepens, slows down, or warms up. They can tell what is happening upstream, what is flowering or falling, by what the river brings. Sometimes the river changes dramatically, like the American River did after the Norse Peak Fire: so much soil washed into the streams that the bouldery bottom disappeared completely under the chocolate-colored silt.

If I were a fisherman, I would love to fly fish on Bumping River as I see some people do. Just like in *A River Runs Through It*, all life on the river would be poetry and wisdom. As long as I was standing in that cold, clear water and listening to the sound as it slipped over the smooth stones, everything would be perfect.

The earliest European immigrants to the Northwest could not imagine that the vast stores of timber and masses of fish that seemed to thicken the water of the rivers could ever be depleted, but scarcely a century and a half later, virgin forests are scarce, and the greatest wild salmon run on the planet, the Columbia River Chinook, is almost extinct.

At one time, salmon swarmed up every waterway in western North America that connected to the Pacific, from the Sacramento to the Yukon. The Columbia River was the superhighway for all six species of salmon that headed to spawning grounds spread over an area the size of France. Salmon swam through deserts and up mountains. The returning fish followed scent molecules zeroing in on their natal streams like bloodhounds on a trail. Some fish traveled a round trip of 8,000 miles by the time they reached "home."[2]

One major tributary to the Columbia River is the Yakima. In the past, the Yakima River system was likely second only to the mighty Snake River in returning the greatest mass of salmonids in the Pacific Northwest.[3] As a tributary to the Yakima, the Naches watershed also supported all the salmon species and, as the largest, was the most important fisheries river in the Yakima Basin. The Bumping River, tributary to the Naches, supported spring, summer, and fall runs of Chinook salmon, sockeye salmon, Coho salmon, and steelhead.[4]

In 1886, a somewhat misinformed reporter, writing for the *Northwest Magazine*, described fishing in the Bumping River and Bumping Lake, journeying to the then-faraway lake before the dam was built and before the region was very well known. Mr. Farmer wrote:

> *"Bumpin [sic] Lake, at the head of Bumpin River…*
> *is one of the finest fishing resorts in the West. By pack trail,*

the distance from here (North Yakima) is forty-five miles. The
lake is a beautiful sheet of water three by seven miles. Up to
midsummer, trout and salmon trout are fairly banked along
its shores, and from that time through the fall the famous
redfish may be taken in great abundance."

He then goes on to describe the famous fish, "The
body of the red fish is somewhat the shape of the bass, its
meat is of a deeper red than the salmon, it has a ferocious
head and the teeth will snap off the stoutest line. The meat
is excelled by that of no fish in the world. This fish is never
seen in the streams. It lives at the bottom of the lake until the
proper season for it to make its appearance, remains up to a
few weeks and returns to its home in the bottom. It is found
only in the Bumpin Lake (sic), Washington, Wallowa Lake,
Oregon and the red fish lakes on the heads of the Payette and
Salmon Rivers, Idaho. No account of this variety is given in
sporting works." [5]

The fearsome fish was the sockeye (or red) salmon.[6] Settlers soon
discovered that sockeyes *did* occur in streams, traveling like other salmon
from the ocean upstream to spawn. Bumping Lake was perfect habitat for
them. The fish spawned in the upper Bumping River and the lake served as
the necessary nursery for the young fry. The lower Bumping River seethed
with them in the late summer as they fought their way up to the lake. But
the great run was doomed.

When the dam was completed in 1910, the river was closed off and
the young sockeye in the lake were trapped. With no way out, they managed to survive without migrating, subsisting on the rather meager plank-
ton available in the lake ecosystem rather than the ample banquet of the
sea. The slim little fish, known as kokanee, are permanently stunted.[7] Their
pale peach flesh is a pallid reminder of the deep red coloring of the muscu-
lar athletes that once leapt waterfalls and climbed massifs. Kokanee complete their lifecycle by spawning in the Upper Bumping River and rearing
in the lake. Presumably, they don't miss their ancestors' ocean going ways.

For several years after the dam closed off the river, curious onlookers gathered below it, where the lower Bumping River begins, to watch the waters turn red with the churning of returning sockeye. The fish had journeyed to within a mile or two of their birth-place but, thwarted by the dam, they circled and leapt, unable to go further. With each following year, fewer fish returned, and in five years there were none. The glorious, gaudy sockeye would never run in the Bumping River again.

Soon the abundant sockeye runs in the rest of the Yakima system would be extinct too, declining from an estimated 200,000 fish returning to four nursery lakes (Bumping, Kachess, Keechelus, Cle Elum) to none. Each run was snuffed out as the Yakima project dams were completed, one after another.[8]

Newcomers to the Northwest in the mid-nineteenth century were overwhelmed by the staggering numbers of salmon in the rivers—and how delicious they were. Upon tasting fresh salmon during his journey here in 1853, Theodore Winthrop was one of the first to advertise to the nation, "feeling the exquisiteness of his coloring, grilling him delicately, and eating him daintily." Writer Thomas Wolfe visited the Northwest in 1938. After pulling a huge salmon "out of an ordinary-looking creek," he wrote home about the "country fit for Gods."[9]

Another writer, William Baillie-Grohman, described the salmon situation at the turn of the century:

> *"Though I have never performed the feat of walking across a stream on the back of fish, which many old timer will swear he has done, I have certainly seen fish so numerous near the spawning grounds that nowhere could you have thrown a stone into the water without hitting a salmon."*[10]

Businessmen quickly recognized the stupendous value of the resource that returned like clockwork from hostile seas into accessible rivers and swam right into waiting nets. Entrepreneurs wasted no time taking advantage of the abundance which is estimated to have been between ten and sixteen *million* animals entering the Columbia River from the Pacific Ocean every year.

They could not get the fish out of the river fast enough. Nets were effective but had to be manned. So before long, "fish wheels" started showing up on the Columbia. The first was installed in 1867 and was the just the beginning of fifty years enthusiastic overfishing. The contraptions (also called salmon wheels) were mounted either on a barge in the river or on the shore and had baskets instead of paddles which tipped the fish into holding pens or onto the shore. Since the wheels were powered by the current, they were able to run all day and all night, scooping fish up and out of the river without rest, tons at a time. They were so effective that they could wipe out an entire run of salmon in a single season. Soon, there were seventy-nine spinning on the Columbia and its tributaries.[11]

Recognizing the potential for total extinction, fish managers called for restraints, but the wheels kept turning, pulling the lifeblood out of the river at a rate of 20,000-50,000 fish each day.

To process the mountains of fish coming out of the water, canneries were built adjacent to the wheels which packed the life of the river into tin cans as fast as the fish could be removed from the water. Twenty-five canneries packed the shores near the mouth of the Columbia in the town of Astoria, Oregon alone.[12] Tinned salmon was a sensation in London and was soon shipped around the world as an inexpensive and nutritious food product. By 1883, the canneries on the Columbia River were packing forty-three million pounds of salmon a year, enough for four pounds of fish for each person on earth. On the Columbia River, "the biggest Chinook run the world had ever known…was a bounty that tested the very limits of greed."[13]

There could have been enough for everyone had there been any restraint, but once the first harvester started, no one wanted to be left out. The result was like a land grab or gold rush, and as with the buffalo or passenger pigeon, the exploiters thought the resource was inexhaustible.

As fish wheels were installed higher on the Columbia, fishermen were moving further towards the sea attempting to get the fish before they were funneled into the scoops of the wheels. New innovations to gillnets were effective, catching fish by snaring them just behind the gills as they tried to swim through the vertical seine. Soon, there were hundreds and then nearly 3,000 gillnetters in small boats snagging fish upon their return to the mouth of the river.[14] The deployed nets created a virtual wall in front of the fish.

Both industries blamed each other when inevitably, the catch started to drop. Under the brand-new initiative and referendum system adopted in Oregon, each industry wrote proposals to ban the other's fishing practices as early as 1908 and a public, increasingly alarmed by the salmon being fished out, passed both. But industry friendly courts ruled against both initiatives and prevented them from being enforced. It was not until 1927 that Oregon banned fish wheels and Washington did not get around to outlawing them until a very late 1935.[15] By that time, all runs were in steep and irreversible decline.

And then came the big dams.

Begun in 1934 in the depths of the Depression to help employ out of work Americans, the Grand Coulee Dam, a massive 550-foot-high curtain of concrete, was begun. The plans did not call for a fish ladder. At its completion in 1942, it pinched the great river in two. Overnight, more than forty percent of Chinook salmon spawning habitat was closed off forever. The addition of the Chief Joseph Dam, slightly downstream of the Grand Coulee, successfully and permanently eliminated almost fifty-five percent of spawning habitat.

These huge dams eliminated salmon runs in many ways. Even where upstream passage (such as fish ladders) was included for returning adults, downstream passage of young fish was often neglected. Juvenile fish, only two to six inches long, were just expected to negotiate their way through conduits or over spillways but were often injured or killed in the process. Hydroelectric dams complicated the problem since it was assumed that young fish would survive their ride through huge turbines. Spinning blades and giant pressure changes often either cut the tiny slips of life into pieces or imploded them. (Even adult fish that successfully negotiate fish ladders are sometime swept to their death after being pulled into the swift current leading to the turbines.)

The placid water that piles up behind dams is not benign either. Each reservoir creates new habitat as the river water slows and warms. Warm water can be lethal to salmon of all ages and slack water allows new predators like lake bass, to thrive. These fish prey heavily on smolts as they try to find their way downstream through lakes that have been around for a tiny portion of the species' life on Earth.[16]

Even small dams kill salmon. Minor irrigation diversion dams often disrupt upstream and downstream passage of fish and can trap returning salmon in one-way watering ditches. Early loggers built splash dams on streams to create small temporary reservoirs into which they dropped downed trees (fifty-six of them between 1880 and 1910 on the western Washington portion of the Columbia River alone). Once the pools were full of logs, the log dams were dynamited, and the resulting flood would be strong enough to sluice the logs down to a larger river for collection. The practice was efficient for loggers but brutal to fish habitat. [17]

One reason the dam builders did not worry more about accommodating fish passage was because of a promising new technology: fish hatcheries. In the late 1800s, animal husbandry was growing production on farms and the same principles were thought to apply to fish as well. Not understanding salmon's varying and complex life cycles, biologists assumed they could utilize the free range model. Fish farmers could release smolts out to the free range of the ocean and harvest them when they returned as adults. Artificial propagation would supplant falling harvests and perhaps even grow the industry. Rather than dealing with the causes of overharvesting and lost habitat, hatcheries would make up for the damage. Humans could now outproduce nature.

It would soon become obvious, however, that salmon were not cows.

United States Fish Commissioner Spencer Baird predicted in 1875, that the artificial propagation of salmon would work so well that it would eliminate the need to regulate the commercial harvest. The first fish hatchery on the Columbia was completed in 1877 and thirty years later hatcheries were turning out thirty-four million fry into the system. But the Chinook returns continued to decline.[18]

Hatcheries were turning out fish without any understanding or study of their effect. The first studies in the 1920s were disappointing. They showed no correlation between increased hatchery releases and increased returns. A ten-year Canadian study concluding in 1936 showed no difference between the efficiency of natural production and hatchery production. The

Canadian government subsequently ordered all hatcheries in the country to be shut down, declaring them an obvious waste of money. In the United States, that study was studiously ignored.

There are several problems inherent with artificially hatched fish. Fry raised in concrete raceways and fed pelleted feed at regular intervals behave differently from their wild cousins. They outcompete wild fish for available food but quickly become prey as they dart around for their next meal without regard for the safety of cover. A much more insidious problem is that of gene dilution of wild populations that have been keenly adapted to their home streams. It became clear, and is now widely accepted, that hatchery fish pose substantial risks to wild salmon population's fitness and long-term production.[19]

This new understanding has led to a sea change in fisheries management shifting it from production to ecosystem management. Supplementation may still be the best answer for saving wild runs—but by using native stocks for breeding and releasing fry directly into streams rather than hatchery pens. Locally, the Yakama Nation is trying innovative breeding programs that seem promising. The Nation has been closely involved with laudable efforts to rehabilitate river habitat and open up historic spawning habitat. Their biggest hope right now involves righting an historic wrong at the far reaches of the Upper Yakima watershed at Cle Elum Lake.

On a sunny July day in 2013, a single wild sockeye salmon, all fiery crimson and green, swam up to the tailrace of the Cle Elm dam. It was the first sockeye to return in nearly a century. Four years before, the Yakama Nation had started transplanting adult fish from the Wenatchee and Okanogan Rivers into the reservoir in anticipation of the construction of fish passage over the old dam.

Funding for this long-awaited recovery came as part of the Yakima Integrated Plan. One goal of the plan is to construct fish passage on all of the five dams in the valley. Cle Elum Lake, with over forty miles of pristine but inaccessible upstream spawning habitat, is a great place to start.[20] Construction has already begun on downstream fish passage there: a complex twelve million dollar helix drain and tunnel in the center of the lake allowing out-migrating young fish to enter the device at varying reservoir levels and safely navigate the elevation change through the dam. Final upstream passage for returning fish is still in the design stage.

Returns have varied since 2013 and more recently rising temperatures in the mainstem of the Columbia have led to significant die-offs of returning fish. But the Yakamas are committed to the restoration of the run and all of the pieces seem to finally be in place with the ultimate goal of a self-sustaining population there by 2030.[21]

There is hope returning up the rivers on the backs of these fish. I imagine a future when we might see the water run red with sockeye or flash silver with mighty Chinooks. But since the river still runs empty for now, we gather joy from observing the animals that are here and imagine their numbers building as the lifegiving fish return again.[22]

Happily, there are a surprising number and diversity of animals, large and small, that still thrive in the Bumping River Valley. It is heartening to encounter one after another, the animals that Jack mentions in his writing, decades and in some cases, a century later.

Jack especially loved birds and wrote lovingly about them as "feathered bits of God." He certainly would have observed how the flash of a scarlet tanager could brighten a gray day and would have happily listened to the almost comical "yank-yank" call of the busy, red-breasted nuthatch as it filtered through the forest. He admired the handsome elegance of a pair of harlequin ducks that nested next to the river; "the lord and lady of the river" he titled them. Jack noted rare sightings of red crossbills along with more common ones like rufous hummingbirds. He even reported the first and only sighting of a Black Oystercatcher in Eastern Washington. Jack's bird list, a reflection of decades of careful observation, named almost ninety species.[23]

Jack was not alone in his appreciation of birds. The National Audubon Society was formed in 1905 in response to alarming depredations of bird populations. Millions were being slaughtered for their plumage, primarily to decorate women's hats. The new organization's board pressed President Theodore Roosevelt to establish reserves where birds would be protected from the ravages of the feather trade. In 1909, the president by executive order conferred protection on many federal reservoirs including Bumping Lake.[24]

In 1916 T. Gilbert Pearson, acting president of the National Audubon Society and noted conservationist, traveled across the country to visit the government reserves. He must have met Jack and Kitty when he visited Bumping Lake that August, but the occasion is not documented.[25] The lake's birds were not protected long. President Warren G. Harding revoked the protections by special order in July of 1921, only months after he took office.[26]

So many animals are inconspicuous and easily hidden in the interwoven trees that a casual visitor to the forest might assume it devoid of life. But when you spend time and become familiar with the landscape, clues begin to emerge that betray the presence of many beasts. With enough attention, the forest gives up its secrets. Evidence of animal passage is everywhere. Here is the blue feather of a Stellar jay and there are the droppings of a bobcat. A red-naped sapsucker has left lines of little holes in a riverside alder and more dramatically, a black bear has torn apart a rotting log to get at the ants inside. A large hole in the ground has a worn path to its entrance and is obviously well used, but what animal lives there? Nearby is a young tree, its bark scraped red by a buck in velvet, and far overhead, a golden thread traces the drifting course of a traveling newborn spider.

Sometimes we only hear the local residents, without seeing sign of them. Though giant elk are hard to miss, especially in the open fields of Goose Prairie, once hunting season begins only their sounds remain. In the waning light of fall, unseen bulls circle Normandie, thrilling us with their haunting calls. At times, we can track them through the woods by sound as they single-mindedly follow cows during the height of the rut.

We always hear little pikas long before we see them. These hamster-like creatures live in rocky areas at high elevations and when alarmed call out with a high pitched "eeeeek" to warn others of danger. We have a resident population on the rockslide near Normandie where we observe their charming arrangements of cut grass, which have been carefully laid out on flat rocks to dry. All summer, the little rodents harvest forage for winter meals, giving it its nickname "little haymaker."

Cougars live here, too, but are pretty much invisible. Occasionally we encounter their broad footprints, and their screams are frightening enough to melt our insides, but in all our time here I know of only a few sightings. Certainly, we have been seen and possibly tracked by them but with a cougar, it's a one-way viewing. Fortunately, the population here is more interested in preying on other animals than us.

Black bears reside in the valley, but we observe them most often these days only on our glowing computer screen. Our game camera captures the ebb and flow of life along a popular trail nearby and has photographed assorted bruins, including a mother and her cub. Sometimes the animals venture closer. Years ago, a hungry young bear scrambled through an open window and tore apart the inside of our parked car. The aftermath of its scavenging looked like a shark attack.

Longer ago, bears were more plentiful, and sheepherders had trouble with them marauding their herds. The Goodwin brothers reportedly shot and killed eleven bears in the few miles between Fish Lake at Carlton Pass and Bumping Lake.

During the time of the operation of the resort, all garbage was trucked to one of two dumps: one at the old baseball clearing just southeast of Bumping Crossing and the other at the old Borrow Pit. These local sites served the marina and area campgrounds, too. Local bears quickly learned what day was trash day. Visiting children vied for spots on the truck carrying the rubbish so they could watch the bears emerge from the trees and squabble over the manna delivered from above.

Gray wolves, long exterminated in the west, have after a hundred years been sighted again in the Bumping River Valley. All seem to have been only traveling through; none have settled. However, the terrain is rugged and remote and the game sufficient enough to support wolves here again.

You never know what you are going to witness. Recently, a pair of iridescent turkeys strode right down the driveway. Over the lake, a massive bald eagle chased a fish-bearing osprey in cartwheeling loops for fifteen minutes as the family watched, spellbound by the aerial acrobatics. A few days later, a peregrine falcon impassively glanced over us from an old snag. On the Bumping Lake trail, we once observed a pair of short-tailed weasels looping across the boulders above. They made a dotted line of warm brown against the blue gray expanse of the rockslide. I am happier to see them out there than near Normandie where one fateful summer a weasel wiped out an entire family of rather tame golden-mantled ground squirrels that had made their home underneath our front porch.

A relative of the weasel, the American marten, dwells in mature conifer forests and is seen less often. One day at the waterfall above Normandie, daughter Cici was surprised and delighted to see a marten leap by with a mouse in its mouth. It vanished as quickly as it appeared. Perhaps soon we will be graced with a glimpse of an even rarer mustelid: the fisher. Extinct in the United States due to heavy trapping (for its luxurious fur) and loss of its mature forest habitat, fishers have recently been reintroduced to Washington State. Regularly since 2008, individuals have been relocated from British Columbia and are now successfully reproducing in the Olympics and in the Cascades.

Yet another relative of the weasel that may be making a tentative comeback in our area is the wolverine. Survivors of the Ice Age era, wolverines are one of the rarest mammals in North America. These powerful carnivores were hunted and poisoned to extinction in the United States so the crags and cirques around the lake have been empty for years. But the surrounding ridges are perfect habitat for wolverines whose huge feet enable them to tramp across their preferred terrain: snow. In part thanks to the dedication of several conservation groups, wolverines are returning to the lower forty-eight. Individuals have been steadily moving south in Washington, following the crest of the Cascades—peaks that offer them the deepest snow and cold. Lately has come the exciting news that a pair or two may have found habitat to their liking in the highest ridges nearby and stayed to raise young.

Many invisible creatures physically shape our neighborhood. Pocket gophers leave evidence of their wintertime activities all over our front yard. When cold weather prevents the little rodent from burrowing in the frozen ground, they simply shift up into the snow. To insulate their thoroughfares, they line each snow tunnel with earth. In the spring, the melting snow gently lowers the intact tunnels onto the ground for us to observe and trace their serpentine winter homes.

Another animal whose industry is readily apparent is the pileated woodpecker. It is remarkable how much wood this large bird can excavate on its quest for an insect dinner. A particularly buggy snag (standing dead tree) can be riddled with rectangular holes as big as a fist and be surrounded by an impressive berm of heavy woodchips. The leftover holes make excellent homes for a variety of other forest creatures from owls to flying squirrels.

Douglas squirrels also give away their presence by their dining choices. A squirrel's preference for conifer seeds leads it to harvest the green cones before they ripen and the seeds fall out. When masses of cones start to plump up on the trees in late summer, the squirrels are extra busy and the ground around fruiting fir trees is liberally littered with snipped branchlets bearing heavy cones. The cones are either dragged away and cached in the ground where they are kept moist for later consumption or pulled apart where they fall. Squirrel middens, tall piles of cone scales and cores under trees, betray the little animals' favorite feeding spots. Sometimes, caches are forgotten, and a tree family sprouts. A cluster of same-sized tree siblings in the forest is the physical remnant of a long ago squirrel's labors.

There is so much to search out and enjoy. There are frogs and toads and giant salamanders and newts. There are snakes and bats and beavers. And flying squirrels and ground squirrels and red squirrels. Who knew there are seven species of shrews living here, one mole, and even one shrew-mole?

Even the bugs are interesting. One of the more remarkable is the giant water bug that occasionally flies around at night in search of a new body of water. It is as big as a bat and its swollen front legs make it appear as if it clawed its way out of a horror movie. There are huge antlions with glassy wings, great ash sphinxes with five-inch wingspans, and little snake-flies: harmless bugs with an articulated neck so their little heads turn left and right to track us. Also here are heavy Polyphemus moths that flare their wings to flash startled blue eyespots, fuzzy yarn moths, and marginated burying beetles. There are ghoulish horsehair worms and zombie moths. The list goes on and on.

The point is that everything that should be here is here and there is a lot of 'should' because there is such variety of terrain. There are rivers, streams, lakes, bogs, swamps, and meadows high and low; there are forests dry and moist, first succession to old growth; there are talus slopes, felsenmeers, hanging valleys, high elevation ridges, caves, deep canyons, a wide river valley. There is a habitat for everything.

❦ ❦ ❦

Tom and I have gone down to the spillway to view the Chinooks as often as we can for several weeks now but the day that I decide to photograph them underwater in the pond, they seem to be gone. A short trek upriver provides the answer.

In the shallows, a broad back and tail fin break through the surface, and then another, huge bodies looking like sharks on a hunt. As I watch, the fish, all rusty and turquoise now, circle each other, splash, slide downstream, and shimmy back up. Occasionally, a male chases off another and then returns to a female's side escorting her upstream. I am surprised at the amount of energy they still have, but passion has clearly taken over as the waters break and flash with courting fish.

Within a few days, spawned-out bodies are evident underwater. Here is a pair, a three-foot-long male and equally massive female, caught side by side between rocks, their golden eyes staring blindly, like a piscine Romeo and Juliet in eternal embrace, while the cold current passes over them. Yellow cottonwood leaves float past. A bald eagle, perched on a fir high overhead, eyes me, waiting. There is no sadness here, only relief for another generation completed and hope for the next to come.

Chapter Fourteen

AUTUMN

"*Let me grow lovely, growing old—so many fine things do, laces
and ivory, and gold and silks,…there is healing in old trees,…
why may not I, as well as these, grow lovely, growing old?*"
—Karle Wilson Baker, 1923

"*Stone markers, piled up by the trail crew to establish
the path…to each his own, whether it marks the
trail following us or the trail ahead.*"
—Mike Hiler, *Buckskin Larch
and Bedrock*, 2010

Tom and I are getting older. We're in our mid-fifties all of a sudden
and wondering, as all of us are, just how the years have passed so quickly,
even while we *were* paying attention.

We spend each summer at Normandie now, living a long-held
dream that had bounced about for many years. When the kids grew up
and left, we sold the house in the suburbs, let go of Tom's dental practice

and my art studio and started some new adventures. We can now live three long, languid months in the mountains. No longer do we feel we have to pack all we can into our days here. Instead, we stretch out and roll about in the pleasure of being here. I research and write, and Tom builds and fixes things. We hike together, swim and kayak together, bike together.

One day we decide to try to tackle the route to Miner's Ridge by mountain bike. We haven't been to the top in two years; it's the hardest ride around. Originally a route to the mines around Granite Lake and to the fire lookout on the ridge above, it is the steepest, roughest road in the Valley, hospitable now only to sturdy off-road Jeeps. The road was rebuilt long ago by the CCC with culverts, water diverters and ditches, but over the years the surface has devolved into a treacherous minefield of stones, logs, and washouts. In places, the path is so jumbled that I laugh that such chaos is even called a road. It takes all my strength to pedal up and over the rocks. Some of them shift as my tires hit them and all seems lost until I somehow lurch forward again—or tip over. It's exhausting.

Since the route is so steep and the going so slow, I have the time to observe my surroundings. We started at lake level in sparse lodgepole pines, but as we climb, we enter pure stands of statuesque hemlocks. They rule until we gain enough altitude for the introduction of noble and then subalpine fir, then finally white-bark pine.

As we pedal up the mountain, we roll back time, but not in years, which I am sure we would take, but in months. We began our ride in mid-summer, amidst pearly everlasting twinkling on the side of the dam but now we are approaching spring with a waltz of purple: lupine, aster, heather and even a few larkspur. Sleepy-looking columbine nod their scarlet heads in the sun along with a few spotted tiger lilies. With the discovery of delicate, white avalanche lilies a little higher, we push back to the break of spring when snowbanks recede and these beauties unfurl in the wet earth. A single golden glacier lily blooms and clear yellow wood violets brighten the deep shadows.

The higher we ascend, the more compressed the season is as well. On the alpine ridges, some plants finally break their long dormancy as late as July when their cover of snow finally melts. The new growth is immediately blasted by summer sun unfiltered in the clear air. Here, tender shoots unfurl, bloom, and set seed within a few short weeks.

Yet the variety of blooming plants that thrive in the high altitude is astonishing. In the harshest of environments, the windswept talus slopes of mountain ridges, life persists. One summer, when the conditions were perfect for wildflowers, we marveled at the abundance we encountered on an afternoon hike. On a single broad slope near Mount Aix, all the common alpine species—phlox, lupine, asters, stonecrop, and paintbrushes—were opening. Scattered about were silver mounds of sky pilot, their fuzzy heads of lavender blossoms begging to be stroked. Stalks of slender blue penstemon glowed an indescribable blue-violet and mountain sandwort looked like flocks of tiny seagulls flying high above dark green foliage. Saxifrages, cinquefoils, arnicas, daisies, fleabane all competed for precious soil space between shifting scree not unlike the multitude of life forms crammed together in a healthy tide pool along the seashore.

Our reward at the top of the ridge is a sweeping view of all the volcanic peaks from Oregon to the North Cascades. Behind us are the sculpted points of Bismark Peak and Mount Aix, to the south is shattered Mount St. Helens. Overwhelming all of it is the colossal bulk of Mount Rainier to the west. Our appreciation of the impressive results of geology plus time is cut short by the mosquitos and fierce flies that drive us back to our bikes and down the road again.

The journey back down is no easier than the way up. I can't relax for a moment with so many rocks rearing up to meet me. I know how quickly the downward momentum of my bike can be stopped by a boulder while a body continues headfirst over the handlebars. Soon, my hands are sore and my triceps are aching.

Fortunately, a distraction provides a rest. From the heavy foliage, a bird song rings out and I stop to try to identify it. The trilling melody is new to my ears and brings a smile to my face. Could it be a winter wren? My pounding heart is lifted, and I am reminded again how just right things seem to be here. All is aligned, nature is intact. As I start again, a sudden explosion of movement and different sound nearly causes me to crash into the trees. I have disturbed a small family of sooty grouse. Their fat, camouflaged bodies vanish just as quickly as they appeared.

We arrive back to the valley floor beat up, exhausted, and happy. A short detour takes us to the day- use area of the Bumping Lake campground for a quick jump in the lake—clothes and all. The beach is crowded today with boisterous families of all colors, ages, shapes, and sizes.

Pop-up canopies have unfolded to make shade for picnics, and boxy coolers are scattered about dispatching cold drinks. I hear three languages spoken. While I love the quiet days when we have the lake to ourselves, I can't help but feel pleasure for all who are here today enjoying the surroundings. For Bumping Lake is, and has always been, an inclusive place, welcoming all to dip into its cool water.

During the long, sweet summers here, I have time to reflect on my own life with the perspective that has come with the passage of time. Much of my understanding is cycle of life stuff, of identifying with my parents and their roles with us, their children, and their own passing. My world fell into place the day I gave birth to our first child. As I gazed at Cici, I identified with, in absolute clarity, every mother who has ever existed. The unexpected rush of protectiveness and devotion blindsided me, and I have never been the same since I looked into the open eyes of that new life.

Now, I am in the kitchen prepping yet another dinner for our grown children and the friends they have gathered here, happily giving my time while they are out floating or exploring or rock hunting, to create a great experience for them—just as Tom's mother Virginia did for all those years when she packed endless grocery bags with ingredients to feed us and all the friends we brought along.

The bedrooms, benches, and bathrooms are full again with the kids' college roommates, boyfriends, girlfriends—just as it should be—and exactly as I am sure we imagined when we birthed and grew our children. Nothing causes me a quicker smile than to see a pack of young people swinging down the driveway, towels over their shoulders, flashlights in hand, or loaded packs on their backs, heading off for another adventure. I don't mind staying in to start a loaf of bread or maybe a pie. I don't mind washing all the sheets and towels and doing all the extra grocery shopping.

It is a toll happily paid to have them here, sharing time in the place that is at the center of our hearts, that they now love as much as we had always hoped they would.

❧ ❦ ❧

Kitty and Jack did not fill their home with children but instead with other families—treasured friends they had made so effortlessly over the years. It seems as if the majority of guests who came to the resort left as friends. As much as the couple loved the solitude of quiet nature, Jack admitted that "they liked people" and those people kept returning to warm their souls at the couple's hearth.

It is remarkable how deep and sustained their friendships were. In a time that letter writing was starting to wind down, Jack kept up regular and frequent written correspondence with individuals all over the country. In his conversational letters, he wrote as if he was in the presence of that person, sometimes signing off, "It has been fine visiting with you for a little while."

Many bonds lasted for lifetimes and over generations. Jack and Kitty became close to his Reclamation boss John S. Moore early in the century, often hosting his family, including John's mother, at the Resort. The families remained intertwined as the Moores' children grew up and married. Son George and his wife Barbara were dear to the couple and Jack continued to write tender and humorous letters to them until just days before his death.

The Nelsons were tremendously loyal, too. When the couple's close friend Ed E. Sickenga passed away, it was the middle of winter and the snow was deep. Regardless, Jack traveled all the way to Yakima on snowshoes—sixty miles one way—to attend his funeral.[1]

By this stage in their lives, the pair had long settled into a comfortable routine with a fair division of labor. And there was so much labor. Even though much of the Nelsons' energy was directed to meeting the daily needs of their steady influx of guests, the summer months also meant that they needed to prepare for the long winter. Jack chopped and stacked wood incessantly, though in later years he did have teenage boys help split firewood[2]. Kitty had to put away a cellar's worth of food for the dark months. She spent hours in the kitchen preserving food: canning, jamming, and drying. She also continued to fish.

To guests, the couple always seemed to be cheerful, but the turn of the calendar pages towards October 10th (when Jack's original boss Crownover advised them to be ready for winter) must have been an unrelenting burden.

By all accounts, they still loved each other. Jack sung Kitty's praises privately and publicly, declaring that "Kitty is a marvel and because of her I live with beauty indoors and out." She reportedly could call him down with a word and called him "Sap." In 1951, a reporter described the couple: "Jack and Kitty have a rare companionship. Each is so proud of the other that one sees through their close communication in an instant and their thoughts and speech mesh into one. With Kitty, the whole success of their unusual life rests with Jack, for Jack, it's all Kitty."[3] In another article, Jack summed up their mountain existence: "Living isolated as we did must be predicated on good health and a companion who likes it as much as you do."[4]

Kitty and Jack Nelson at Bumping Lake on the eve of the Spring/Summer season in 1944. (Courtesy of Betty Jean Ford Gallant and the Yakima Valley Museum)

❦ ❦ ❦

Little Goose Prairie had matured too. Vacation homes dotted the area, but many lots remained unbuilt, giving it a rather open feel. Since the community exists on privately held land, the houses are more diverse than the strictly regulated cabins on surrounding Forest Service land. As a result, the village looks a little tousled, not unlike Bill Douglas' hair after he roughed it up upon his arrival to the Prairie.

Though most of the rest of the country is electrified by now, power lines do not run up the Bumping River Road. The phone lines that Jack so diligently repaired have long since been pulled down.[5] There is no natural gas utility, no cell phone service, and certainly no internet. Water and septic services are the responsibility of homeowners.

By the second half of the 1940s, some of the first summer cottages in the Prairie had already changed hands but many will remain in the same families for generations. James O. Cull's children still held title to ten lots two decades after they were willed to them. Boy Scout Camp Fife was flourishing even though it would not expand to its full footprint for another decade or so (with the purchase of Jack Nelson's big parcel).

Several of the miners from the old Copper City area owned lots in the settlement, perhaps to retain a tie to the country they had come to love as they toiled along the surrounding ridges and among the towering trees. Former officer of the Copper City Mining Company Dr. John Nywening, and Ray Dimmick who worked as a cook up at the Clara camp, both held title to land in the Prairie. Herb Teeter stayed in the community too, marrying Alice Sandberg and helping Ira Ford build Ford's Café.[6]

John Crosetti, his days as a hard rock miner over, sold his claim on Deep Creek to Charles Huey and moved to Goose Prairie. He became the caretaker at Boy Scout Camp Fife and lived with his dog Bingo in a cabin just across the road from the entrance of the camp. When the Bumping River Road was paved, his home was moved closer to the river, where it still remains. John died in 1950 and his body was returned to Roslyn to be

interred in the Independent Order of Oddfellows section of the old cemetery. He lies next to the bones of his beloved wife, Margherita.

In 1946, the same year that Kay bought her acreage for the Double
K, Catherine "Alice" Matson and her husband Roger purchased three lots
adjacent to the Double K land. Alice soon set about designing her dream
mountain cabin; she may have had the help of the same architect who drew
up the plans for the Double K Ranch house, A. Tito Porreca.[7] The resulting
cabin was a gracious, pine-paneled work of art with modern touches and
massive "Heatilator" fireplace. The Matson family visited often and was
soon tightly woven into the fabric of the community.

The youngest son Marc Matson was twelve when the cabin
was built and growing up spent most of his summers there. He worked
as a wrangler at the Double K and got to know their neighbor Justice
Douglas well. One summer, Marc was hired as the lookout at Goat Peak.
The easiest mode of transport there was by horseback and once he arrived, he would turn the horse loose for it to make its way back home to
Goose Prairie.[8]

Ray and Winnie Rasmussen bought seven lots from Ira Ford in the
early 1960s after they moved out of the old Keystone Ranch cabins. Various
family members built their homes on those westside parcels among the
trees. The Rasmussen's son John and his wife, Betty Jean Gallant's daughter
Janet, dragged two cabins on rollers from near the river up to one of the
lots, nailing the buildings together themselves and making a home.

The Paulson family hailed from Grandview, Washington. Over
time, four of the seven siblings built homes in Goose Prairie. One daughter, Bernadine and her husband Robert Bosler, purchased four acres right
in the middle of the Prairie from Ira Ford. Ira built their cabin which takes
in expansive views and is especially magical at dusk when it is routinely
surrounded by dozens of grazing elk.

The Boslers became friends with Kay and Isabelle as well as Justice
Douglas, socializing with them when they all were in residence. Their
daughter Melissa treasured time with the Double K Girls, sharing books
and wide-ranging discourse and, in time, was introduced to Douglas.

Melissa, like so many who met him, was immediately captivated
by his personality and his charm. The justice seemed to truly care about the

opinions of young people and would listen intently to what she had to say. He would ask penetrating questions in return.

"He became a mentor to me and was one of the biggest influences in my life," she said.

Melissa came to understand that Douglas saw parts of the world in black and white. One summer while he was relaxing at the Prairie, most of the rest of the justices were still at work at the Supreme Court in DC. They were watching films and deliberating pornographic evidence in their capacity to define obscenity and protection of free speech in the aftermath of the Roth v United States case.[9] To Douglas, it was all protected free speech. He told Melissa, "They always complain about how much work they have. Yeah, it does take a lot of time to explain gray." [10]

Goose Prairie may have reached its zenith as a community with the addition of the Ford's Café in 1957. Ira Ford had built five rental cabins about five years earlier. When the vacationers arrived, Bess was responsible for cleaning and laundering all the cabins. Ira built the café with the help of former miner Herb Teeter. They cut, hauled, and peeled the lodgepole pine logs that made up the walls and Ira's son Pat helped pour the concrete floors. The debut of the café increased Bessie's workload still further when she became the cook and waitress for the operation. She rose before dawn to make pies for the day and then started cooking for breakfast customers, not finishing until the last supper customers settled their bills.

There are still Fords in Goose Prairie. Ira and Bess remained, and both passed away peacefully at an old age with Ira dying just one month shy of ninety-nine years old. Two of their three children eventually moved back to the little clearing in the woods where they were raised. Bob, after he retired, built a log home in Goose Prairie where he lived out his life with his second wife Sharon, who still lives there.

Betty Jean Ford married Howard "Lucky" Gallant and raised their two daughters at Rimrock Lake where Lucky was the reservoir superintendent for twenty-two years. After Ira died, Betty Jean and Lucky moved back to the Prairie, renovating and making improvements on his house where she still lives. Betty Jean is a great-great grandmother now. Two of her great-grandsons, Cooper and Chase, are the sixth generation of their family to live in Goose Prairie and to work at Boy Scout Camp Fife. Well

into her nineties, Betty Jean only occasionally complains that it is difficult
to garden with a walker. With no television or internet, her entertainment
is the antics of the elk and deer which graze outside her windows along with
the birds that swoop down to her feeders. Her daughter Janet lives with her
now and makes sure her visitors are poured a glass of lemonade, though
Betty is perfectly capable of hosting her many guests.[11]

There was a gradual evolution at the Double K Ranch, too. Kay
and Isabelle no longer organized fourteen-day pack trips, preferring more
manageable three- and five-day excursions. By the sixties, the Ranch was
successful enough that the girls took winters off, soaking in the absolute
silence of the snow-muffled prairie. In the early seventies, after the last
guests left in the fall, Kay and Isabelle and the wrangler Tim Franklin could
head out on overnight pack trips to their favorite high mountain meadows,
just for fun.

But as they were nudged into old age, Kay and Isabelle worried
about the future of their operation and were having trouble finding a successor for it. They reluctantly sold the last of the horses, but soon the bur-
dens of maintaining the operation became overwhelming. With no friends
or family willing to take on the operation of the Ranch, they listed it for
sale. However, Kay and Isabelle were demanding and particular sellers who
would not let their baby go to just anyone. And since they couldn't really
bear leaving, their list of buyer qualifications grew longer.

Finally, Kathleen Tresham Anderson, whose husband Tom oversaw
nearby Camp Fife, passed their interviews and the Double K Ranch was
sold. Kathleen Anderson was a Presbyterian minister from Yakima who
had long wanted to operate a retreat center, and for the next five years she
and Tom, along with the enthusiastic assistance of their young daughter
Katy, make a go of it. The property was spruced up and guests once again
enjoyed the mountain setting while they relaxed, recharged, and dined on
great food.[12]

Kay and Isabelle were eighty-three and seventy-four years old in
1990 when they said goodbye to their last guests at the Double K. It had
been forty-three years since they opened their doors. Soon after, they packed
up their guestbooks and a few boxes of mementos and moved into a little
concrete block house with a concrete yard in Yakima. It must have been a

difficult adjustment, but they put on a good face in Christmas cards that they faithfully continued to send out to friends. At least they had each other. And then, as they both struggled with illness, the yearly cards stopped.

Isabelle died on March 25, 1996, and not long after, Kay was diagnosed with an aggressive bone cancer. Kay passed away on July 19, 1996, just days before an already planned "Homecoming" event to commemorate Isabelle's passing. Instead, friends, family and neighbors gathered on the appointed day at Prairie House, right next door to the Ranch, to remember *two* unforgettable women. Their ashes were scattered together on the grounds of the Double K Mountain Ranch. Today, tall Ponderosas circle the cemetery in Goose Prairie and shade the modest stone marker honoring them. The inscription conveys the hope that they are "never to be forgotten."

The last decades of the twentieth century brought conflict to Goose Prairie as residents fought to keep the development of their community appropriate to its mountain setting. In the spring of 1982, Jerry and Sally McCulley, the owners of the Goose Prairie Café and some land behind it, applied to rezone their property. The initial request seemed to be reasonable, and the Yakima County Planning Commission gave preliminary approval.[13] But neighbors soon learned that McCulley planned on replacing their seasonal trailer hookups with thirteen permanent homes on their two-acre parcel. Six and a half homes per acre would have amounted to urban high densities in the middle of the otherwise rural prairie.[14] Kay Kershaw pointed out the absurdity of introducing city development into an area that provided relief from city stresses.[15]

The inaugural home of the planned development was built just north of the café before residents organized and successfully fought the rezone at the county planning office. "First Cabin" was prominently carved over the entrance of the large log home. The second cabin was never built.

Just six years later, another development proposal sent the community down to Yakima en masse to protest. Several years after William O. Douglas died, his widow Cathy put Prairie House up for sale. State Representative Georgette Valle, D-Seattle proposed turning the home into a memorial to the Justice.[16] Other supporters, including Senator Brock

Adams and the Naches Ranger District, grew the idea into a larger institute where wilderness studies, workshops, and classes could be held. Participants might be housed at the Double K which was also for sale.

By the time the community was briefed on the proposal, it included suggestions to buy additional adjacent properties for parking and other facilities which raised fears of property seizure by eminent domain. Local opposition was strong. Neighbors worried about potential traffic, crowds, noise, and worst, the probable need for power, telephone, and other infrastructure that residents had no wish for. Some thought Douglas had already been honored enough. Others pointed out that had Douglas been alive, he would have howled at such a development in his quiet hamlet.[17]

Nearly 200 property owners showed up in Yakima in March of 1989 and railed against the House bill. Within a week, Representative Valle had backed away from her own legislation and at the same time commended Goose Prairie residents for their passion and their example of civic engagement.[18] Subsequently, the Trust for Public Land proposed a scaled down meeting center for the site but by then the community sentiment had so soured on any public use of the property that the Trust abandoned its plan. The cabin and land were later sold privately. Prairie House remains a vacation home with the present owner restoring the building and grounds to honor the man who built it.

The biggest loss to the Prairie in later years was the closure of the Goose Prairie Cafe around 2010. The Cafe was the last commercial establishment and the hub of the community where residents regularly gathered over coffee to share gossip and news. The Fords had sold it in 1961 to Hank and June Pletcher.[19] June upheld the reputation of outstanding pies at the restaurant that Bessie Ford had cultivated. By 1966, the cafe was renamed Wil-Lees after new owners Wilma Beach and Leona (Lee) Holeton. Jerry and Sally McCully followed in 1980. Denny and Darlene Sveen from the later 1980s are remembered fondly for their friendliness and for Gus, their pet cougar that had the run of the house and could knock over the sofa with a rub of its haunches. He was raised by the couple and fed fresh meat butchered from local roadkill.[20] Mark and Margo Cliff purchased the Cafe from the Sveens and were foreclosed on, but not before regaining a reputation for excellent pies.

❧ ❦ ❧

Bumping Lake continues to fill and empty regularly with the seasons, but in contrast to most areas which become more developed, the skyline around the lake has seen only losses. The last Reclamation buildings on the spillway clearing were intermittently moved away until the site was bare except for a single storage shed.[21]

Further south, Bumping Lake Summer Home #17 burned to the ground when careless friends of the owners borrowed it one weekend in the 1950s and left a cigarette on the couch. The toppled chimney and some pieces of melted glass are all that remains. Cabin #1 is gone now too, victim of a ferocious windstorm that tore through the south end of the lake around 2010 and dropped trees like a pile of spilled matchsticks on top of it. Not long after that, Cabin #5 was crushed by a huge fir that toppled over. It has been rebuilt.

Over time, the dam has seen renovations and safety improvements by the Bureau. Major repair work occurred in the 1990s with the installation of interceptor drains, replacement of the outlet gates and operators, gate house, and spillway. About the same time, the Forest Service shut down the Bumping Dam Campground. This popular campground was wedged in between the Bumping River and the dam with great access to each. When it was closed, the site was regraded and has infilled with lodgepole so that hardly a trace remains. The gravel road across the top of the dam was finally paved in 1996.

The fortunes of the Bumping Lake Marina see-sawed through the years as new owners made changes and then sold out after they tired of the relentless maintenance demands. Carl and Audrey Kunz operated the marina in the late 60s and 70s and sold to Gary and Donna Clayton around 1980. James and Jacquie Bond from the Naches Valley purchased the facility from them in 1988 and made many improvements to the buildings, docks, and campsites during their ten years there. The Bonds sold to George and Gail Nolan in 1999 who ran it for several years (and for a time, blessed the lake neighborhood with an espresso machine) until

they developed cash flow problems. Unable to sell, the marina was shut-
tered about 2004.

Bill and Mary Garoutte took on the unenviable task of putting
the place back together after it remained vacant for three years, and chaos
reigned. Their first job when they purchased the shell of the marina in
2006, was to restore order. Bill, with a broad, white smile and sparkling
blue eyes looked friendly enough but his no nonsense crew cut and the
nine-millimeter Glock he packed left little doubt that he meant business
once his boots hit the ground. Within weeks, the troublemakers had fled.

The Garouttes poured resources, sweat, and fresh ideas into the
little resort and made it shine. They hauled away wreckage and garbage,
cleared downed trees, and rebuilt the little store. They installed new docks,
poured a new boat ramp, constructed buildings and bathrooms, put in
showers and generators. They dug a replacement well, bought new rental
boats, reconstructed the road, and even rebuilt the shoreline. In 2009, the
old store was razed after being sliced in two by a winter-felled tree. It was
replaced by a new structure farther back from the shoreline.

By the 1950s, the years were starting to pile up on Jack and Kitty.
Their bodies were thickening and every year the lines on their faces were
deeper and Jack's trousers rode higher on his belly. Fortunately, they had
remained healthy with only a few exceptions over the years. One snowy
February, Kitty had a gall bladder attack so severe that she needed surgery.
With no other way to get out, Jack used to quip that she skied down to
American River "with her ski pole in one hand and gall bladder in the other!" [22] One winter, Jack had an episode of "quinsy" (a peritonsillar abscess)
that required lancing. Jack was too ill to ski out, so a doctor from Yakima
skied up to the lake with two companions to treat him. Otherwise, the
couple did not suffer illnesses that they could recall. [23]

The Bumping Lake Resort remained full. Even though it had been
running virtually unchanged for forty-five years, the little cabins remained

popular because they were clean and comfortable—and because of the charm of their hosts. Even city slickers, newly competent at building fires and hiking rugged trails, returned home after a weekend of mountain living with fresh confidence because of Jack and Kitty's skillful hospitality. Through the years, the Nelsons made a "hobby of people." Jack admitted that their secret pride was how many guests returned through the years. "Friends were our proudest possessions," explained Jack.[24]

And the guests kept returning. In 1960, Jack and Kitty were eighty and eighty-two years old, still running the resort, and trying to keep up with the workload as everything got more difficult and took longer. But they couldn't close the doors on their guests and friends.

For the Tyrells, the Cyrs, the Olds, the Rolphs, and so many, many others summer would not be complete without a week—or a month—at the lake with the Nelsons. The Nelsons' best friends—State Representative Cecil Clark, his wife Catherine and their three boys—were in and out of the cabins all summer long, and the Double K girls were regulars for a chat or a meal. Relatives and friends still gathered around Normandie's kitchen table to feast on Kitty's favorite dishes. The couple apparently so loved sharing their favorite spot on earth with others, that they never got around to retiring.

"Kitty and [I] never thought we would get old!" Jack wrote in a letter to Eileen Ryan in the early 1960s. "I wish we were young again and could do it all again."

The couple seemed content. William O. Douglas described a visit to Normandie a few years after Jack had retired. He and Jack lingered outside at twilight to watch the last light flush scarlet on the peaks of Nelson Ridge, then retired inside to visit in front of a crackling fire. They watched the glowing sparks fly up the back of the fireplace. In *Of Men and Mountains*, Douglas recounted what Jack shared with him after they sat for a while in companionable silence:

> *"When man can look at mountain peaks*
> *with a deep sense of his own littleness and still*
> *have faith—*
> *"When man can learn how to make friends*
> *with others and how to keep friends with himself—*

"When man can hunt birds and deer
without a gun—
"When the moonlight on a mountain lake
or a snowcapped peak breaking through storm clouds
brings calm and peace like the thought of one much
loved and long dead—
"When man knows how to pray, how to hope,
how to love—
"When man can find the time to stop and
look at the grass and trees and mountainsides and
come to know them and call them friends—
"When man can see the handiwork of the
Creator in the bluebells, spring beauty, and avalanche
lilies and in the water ouzel, winter wren, and
woodpecker—
"When man can feel the sense of eternity
even in the wind that blows from the northwest
off Rainier—
"Then man has found contentment and
harmony and peace." [25]

Jack attributed the poem in part to another, but Douglas closed his chapter writing, "That is indeed what I learned when I sat as a boy at the feet of Jack Nelson in the wilderness at Bumping Lake over thirty years ago." [26]

In early 1960, Kitty started having heart problems. She was admitted to the hospital and get- well wishes poured in from around the country as word spread that she was unwell. Lyle Hall, the longtime mail carrier, delivered daily reports of her condition to neighbors up and down the Naches and Bumping River Valleys.

In April, Kitty suffered a massive heart attack and was rushed to the Yakima Valley Osteopathic Hospital. Her heart was found to be so damaged that it was clear she would not survive. Kitty's family and the Clarks stood vigil at her hospital bed as she passed away peacefully on April 30, 1960.

A few days later Jack wrote, "Every day of every year the unconditional constancy of Kitty's courage was an inspiration to me." [27] Part of Jack
died with Kitty. After she was buried, he did not smile as much. The great
joy of his life had slipped away.

Reluctantly, Jack put the Bumping Lake Resort up for sale. Ed
and Eileen Nelson (no relation) bought the establishment in 1961 and
through an arrangement allowed Jack to live there in the summertime. He
spent winters down at Whistlin' Jack Lodge with the owners Bill and Helen
Williams.

After only two years, personal problems and mismanagement intruded and the Nelsons could not make their payments. [28] Jack was forced
to foreclose on the new owners. He then sold the resort to Weldon and
Dorothy McIntyre who lived and farmed cucumbers in Wapato. Since
they couldn't get away from the farm in the summer, the McIntyres hired
Lynne and Elda "Mom and Pop" Turner to run the resort, which they did
well. The Turners were capable and likeable, and the little cabins were full
once again. [29]

After the resort was sold to the McIntyres, Jack moved into a little
cabin at Whistlin' Jack where he lived for the next few years. He watched
baseball on TV, received friends, and wrote letters to a wide range of
acquaintances. The Clarks lived in Cliffdell, too, and could help see to
his needs.

With the Turners at the helm, the Bumping Lake Resort stayed busy,
but the entire facility was slowly fading with each passing year. Normandie
looked cluttered and tired. The cabins were perilously neglected. [30] Paint
peeled, and screens sagged. Instead of stacking chopped wood neatly at each
stoop as Jack had done for nearly half a century, large piles of logs were uncer-
emoniously dumped near the cabins. The chaff from guests splitting all that
firewood began to pile up dangerously. Prolific deer mice, once discouraged
from habitation, became so abundant in the rentals that one guest recalls
flipping the sheets several times a night to clear their beds of the animals.
Handfuls of the creatures would be flung off and would hit the floor running—only to return to the inviting warmth of the covers later in the night.

The Forest Service, as the resort's landlord, first asked, and then
demanded repairs be made to meet the standards of the commercial lease.

But McIntyre was increasingly unwell and unable to make the required improvements. The buildings continued to deconstruct. Faced with dangerous conditions and ultimately a failed water test, in the fall of 1972, the Forest Service pulled the lease. McIntyre would be able to continue on as a private lessee but could not rent to the public. The resort was finished.

McIntyre sold the rental cabins and one by one they were jacked up, hauled across the dam, and reincarnated as vacation homes in Goose Prairie. A few years later, Don and Virginia Cyr purchased the few remaining buildings, including Normandie. The family, longtime visitors to the resort, could now call Normandie home and still do so today.

What Jack and Kitty built was appealing in part because it appeared to never change. Guests could return year after year—even from one generation to the next—and while the tumult of city or national life might seem destabilizing, the little resort at Bumping Lake felt locked in time. But the Nelsons knew as well as anyone that change was inevitable.

Lately, many of our favorite walks have become an example of change. Familiar pathways have been increasingly rendered unrecognizable by the wreckage of a tree fall. The violence of the event is remarkable, and in striking contrast to the usual moss-softened vignettes that flank the trails. It is not possible for a large tree to come down in the forest without collateral damage: a single tree will often take down several others as it crashes through the understory, exploding and splintering wood along the way. The result looks like the aftermath of a bomb blast.

Initially, we could rationalize away the death of these magnificent monarchs as those that were killed by the tiniest of threats: the western spruce budworm and the pine bark beetle.

Both deadly pests have been becoming more prevalent lately. In the early 2000s, without winter cold sufficient to kill the overwintering larvae, the budworm thrived. For several years in a row they flourished, eating all the year's new growth on tens of thousands of drought-stressed Douglas and Grand firs across the Northwest. Unable to survive the assault for multiple years in a row, thousands of trees slowly died while we watched, feeling completely helpless except for futilely swatting as many of the adult moths as we could when they swarmed in mid-July.[31]

A completely different way to kill a tree is the bark beetle's breeding strategy. The female beetle burrows through a pine tree's bark and chews her way to the inner phloem where she lays her eggs. A fungus carried by her specialized mouthparts turns the phloem spongy and nutritious for her larvae but eventually kills the tree.[32] A healthy tree can produce pitch to fend off beetles, but pitch production is limited by drought conditions which have become more common. With no cold winters lately to check their growth either, the little black beetle has inflicted destruction on stands of white and lodgepole pines up and down the river valley.

But particularly ominous are the number of otherwise healthy-looking and most certainly live trees that are coming down in the forest. As we walk, we see youthful firs, hemlocks, and cedars snapped off mid trunk, as if a careless leviathan passed through randomly breaking trees in half much as I might thoughtlessly step on delicate flowers in a meadow.

Other young trees are uprooted from the ground, seeming to have given up on the effort to live and having just laid down instead. Still others are simply folded mid trunk, bent over in a permanent genuflect.

Not all the trees coming down are young, either. We arrived at Normandie one spring to the scene of a potentially catastrophic near-miss. A mature hemlock, at least seventy-five feet high and part of the landscape in the front yard for at least as many years, crashed down sometime over the winter. It miraculously threaded the space between the lodge, the garage, and the toolshed and came to rest just short of the propane tank. A few feet in any direction and the huge bulk would have ruined any one of the buildings. This was not a tree we thought to be unhealthy and had no reason that we could discern to fall.

We don't understand this kind of death and its increasing regularity. Recent research points to rising temperatures affecting survival rates of trees even in mature forests.[33] These ruined trees lead me to acknowledge with growing dread that we humans have surely overplayed our hand and just haven't yet digested the full extent of our loss.

On these forest walks, when I get particularly gloomy or close to despair, my heart can be buoyed by a sign of healthy life pushing back. It might be a thick stand of conifer seedlings elbowing for room in a new patch of sunlight cleared by one of the fallen elders, an inky swarm of fat tadpoles wiggling in the shallows by the spillway, or the chattering racket of an annoyed kingfisher, its presence an indicator of the health of the lower part of the food chain. One spring day, a little flash of white caught my eye among the exposed roots of a shore-side pine. This time it was not a gum wrapper or other bit of trash, but two halves of a porcelain white eggshell, the size of a child's fingernail, empty now yet so full of promise for the life hatched in the branches above.

Lately, the trees seem to be doing better. Because of the diversity and maturity of the forest trees here, they have withstood the stand-killing infestations and disease that have ravaged entire forests in many parts of the West. The giant ones stand tall and serve as a repository of seeds to repopulate other damaged areas. The forest seems as tangled and wild as it was when Jack first gaped at it over a century ago.

At the end of 1964, after fifty years of living beside Bumping Lake, Jack's Christmas cards were mailed from Yakima. His last one was co-signed with Kitty's daughter Frances, but he subsequently moved again and to live with his niece Jean Boyd and her family in their little house on South 22nd Avenue. At the time, he was publicly stating that he "would rather live in a hollow log then spend his retired years in a crowded city."[34]

On August 18, 1965, just weeks after her sixty-fourth birthday, Frances died in Yakima.[35]

Fortunately, Jack did have a project to keep him going. For years, friends had encouraged him to write a memoir, and he was finally doing just that with substantial assistance from Jean. With her typing, he finished the manuscript, and with William O. Douglas' help, lined up a local publisher. *We Never Got Away* was published in late 1965 to warm reviews in the local press and a glowing forward written by his old friend Bill, the United States Supreme Court Justice.

On Saturday, November 6th, the Double K along with Cecil and Catherine Clark and Eileen Ryan hosted a book signing party from four to six o'clock in the afternoon. Jack's closest friends were invited for an intimate celebration of the completion of his long-awaited book. Jack was feted and toasted. Although he was a month over eighty-five and quite frail, he reveled in the gathered company.

Two weeks later, on November 19, 1965, many residents of the city of Yakima lined up in front of the Bon Marche department store downtown. They looked forward to having the celebrated "Sage of Bumping Lake" inscribe their own copies of the new book at a widely-advertised book signing event at the store.

He never made it.

Jack died at Jean's home on 22nd Street early in the morning of the event. When he did not come upstairs for breakfast, Jean descended to his basement apartment and found him at peace, lying in his bed, having quietly passed away.[36] His death certificate reads cerebral thrombosis. He was eighty-five years old.

Jack Nelson, guardian of Bumping Lake, philosopher and poet, storyteller and mentor, and above all, lover of nature, was gone.

We Never Got Away was a gracious and fitting farewell. In its pages, Jack told the world how much he loved Kitty—and how much he missed her. He shared what he had learned from fifty years of living in the forest and what he wanted us to know of it.

Fifty years on, his book charms a new generation of readers curious about the heritage of this place. Some of them, like me, are moved by his words and adopt his ideals to become fierce protectors of these wild spaces.

The Nelsons' legacy is the William O. Douglas Wilderness: every stone and every tree, every bud and bug and leaf, every soft meadow and crashing waterfall; all of it protected forever. Without the Nelsons' mentorship, one influential jurist and two resolutely effective women would not have had their nascent interest in the natural world cultivated into a passion. Their unflagging efforts saved this place and changed the nation.

Jack and Kitty must have been aware of their profound influence, and I trust they knew that they would live on, that their impact still drifts along the ridges and skips above the lake and winds between the trees.

I like to imagine Jack returning for a visit here. I would take him by his calloused hand and show him through Normandie, proudly pointing out repairs and upgrades that we have made over the years. He probably would like the big propane heater that replaced his wood burning one, and he would be amused to see the same heavy iron pokers leaning against the fireplace that he used long ago to stir the embers. I know he would be pleased to see Normandie standing tall.

Then we would go outside, the screen door banging shut behind us. Jack might have a hard time at first orienting himself, since the trees have grown so much in fifty years. Seedlings that were once beneath his boots now share space with clouds. Dense stands of trunks form ramparts that close in the views so that what was once open resort grounds are now pocketed glades. The trees obscure the leveled spots where cabins once perched. Mosses and twining Prince's-Pine smooth over the once prim delineations of roads and walkways. The foundation blocks of the old cabins that were left behind now look like crooked tombstones sinking into the earth.

But he would suddenly recognize the largest trees in the yard and exclaim how tall they have grown. As Jack did before he left a half a century ago, he would put a hand on their rough bark and reminisce about this one or that, like they were old friends. We would then gaze out over the lake and I'm sure he would recite his names of the peaks to me: Old Scab,

Buffalo Hump, Baldy, The Castle, Snaggle Tooth, Sugar Loaf; familiar un-
dulations of the horizon that delineated his world.

❧ ❧ ❧

Tom and I walk into the twilight of the Sanctuary. As we sit under
the enormous bulk of one of the ancient trees, we marvel at the miracle
of its furrowed bark, delicately fanned needles, and intricate cones, all assembled from disparate molecules under our feet. Their trunks are resolute
columns rising, not like those of men by force and struggle, but slowly and
inexorably through the vigorous life within. We know that underneath us
shadowy fungal networks connect the trees in a web of symbiotic relationships and communication.

I have to stop and shake my head and wonder at the perfection of
all of this life—and its persistence. What a world! My gratitude to be able
to be here and appreciate it all threatens to overcome me. As we stand up,
Tom puts out his hand, pulls me close and we dance, slowly turning underneath the wide branches of the wise ones.

As I observe the remnants of our own brief history here and ponder the small monuments we might leave behind, I acknowledge that even
the things I cherish will not last forever. I hope Normandie will, but so little
is left now of earlier lives that I can imagine a not-so-distant future when
the compilation of lumber that was once a trapper's cabin is no more than
compost for seedlings, when the tenuous tracing of rock courses that was
once an immigrant's oven are smoothed over by duff, when all the mine
shafts have filled with rubble, when the tallest trunks carrying old cracked
insulators and the last ancient snag bearing a giant "X" blaze has crashed to
the earth, that no trace at all remains of the indomitable pioneers who lived
and loved in this land.

What *will* endure is the happy history we have made here: the
shared memories of meals taken, of stories told, of laughter and games and
friendships made and kept, of hands held and smiles creased; of the bonds

of family ratcheted ever tighter by time shared in a cabin in the woods, awash in nature untamed.

The love kindled and carefully nurtured in the cradle of these mountains still smolders, bridging generations and stealing into the future in our children, and certainly beyond to theirs, not yet born.

ACKNOWLEDGMENTS

This book is graced with the contributions of many, many kind people. It is with great appreciation that I thank everyone who so freely and generously shared their knowledge, family histories, and photographs so that this volume could be as complete as we all could make it. This would be a thin read without your contributions.

First and foremost, among those generous souls is the late Betty Jean Ford Gallant who patiently answered and re-answered my unrelenting questions and freely shared her volumes of curated photo albums with me. Tim Franklin opened my eyes to Double K Ranch life—and made Kay, Isabelle, and the Justice Douglas come to life. The wise members of the PNWWODS helped guide my more difficult scholarly research. Morris Uebelacker led me to a whole new level of understanding of the historical activities of the Yakama peoples in the Bumping River Valley.

This narrative would have been as tangled as the forest here without the talents of my editors, Simon Firth, Elizabeth Roderick, and Roland Summit. Many generous readers helped make valuable corrections to various sections of the manuscript including Kelsey Doncaster (Bureau of Reclamation), George Marcott (fire history), Robert Danielson (road building), Jan Gallant (Goose Prairie), Mike Hiler (Forest Service), Tom Hulst, Mike Hoge, and John Concillo (all experts on William O. Douglas). Other valued readers were Steve Summit, Lynne Davison, Jo Gershman, Cici Cyr, John Cyr, and Chris Maykut.

A special shout out to Gretta Gossett's daughter Gretta "Smiles" Gregg, who enthusiastically shared precious photos and research notes, Kelsey Doncaster who years ago opened a library of incredible dam construction photographs, Rose Ferri who kindled the idea for this book while researching national historic listing for Normandie, Jackie Whitnall Cox for sharing her remarkable family's photo collection, Stan Boyd for the same, and Lee Watts who helped ferret out long-buried genealogical information on countless individuals. So many others shared stories or photos or answered questions including Jim Nelson, Robert Croy, Ruth and Chuck

Koreski and Angela Couchman, Miles and Saundie McPhee, Michael McLean, Carl Burkholtz, Bonnie Moore, Dan Haller, Pat Ford Jr., Michael McLean, Gary Jackson, Ruby Montana, John Ashbaugh, and a bunch of new Facebook friends with deep love for the area.

I love our Bumping Lake and Goose Prairie neighbors who have so much accumulated knowledge of the valley and so freely share it. A few of those special people are Ray Foisy, the entire Nutley and Maykut clan, Nancy and Phil Cooke, the Mayos, the Sanfords, the Burkeys, the Bonds, the Garouttes, the Wilsons, Melissa Parsons, Dee and Harlan Petersen and Doug Matson, Tom Rutter, Loren and Margaret Strain, the Richardson family, the late Bob Ford, and his wife Sharon Ford.

A number of local institutions have been most generous with their collections, uncovering from their files what I consider great treasures. First and foremost are the generous folks in the archives at the Yakima Valley Museum especially Director Emeritus John Baule who helped dig up beautiful long-lost photos from their extensive collection of ephemera. Mike Hiler and Jo Miles have been great sounding boards. Other valuable information came from the Yakima Valley Genealogical Society, Yakima Public Library, University of Washington Special Collections, Nile Valley Women's Club, and the United States Forest Service Naches Ranger District office, especially Jacquie Beidel and Karen Burkholtz there.

My gratitude also goes out to the incomparable members of my treasured art critique group, the Painters of Bumping Lake. Rebecca Bush and Jo Gershman were invaluable when it came to book design and formatting. The Yak-Writers writing group strengthened the manuscript with their eagle-eyed editing and spot-on suggestions.

To all of you and those who I have neglected to mention, I say thank you again. I reserve my deepest appreciation for my husband Tom, and my children Cici, Kiwi, and Clark, who suffered through years of musings, draft readings, and the near complete loss of my company as I rambled along mountain trails in my head—even as I walked the same trails next to them.

NOTES

CHAPTER TWO

[1] The significance of the building's name **Normandie**—and its unconventional spelling—is unknown.

[2] Jack Nelson, *We Never Got Away* (Yakima, Washington: Franklin Press, 1965), p. 2.

[3] It could have been a **family connection** that brought Jack to Yakima from Seattle. Jack's maternal uncle, Peter Croy owned a pharmacy back in New York. It seems as if there was a Croy's drugstore in Yakima as well. (Croy, 2012)

[4] In her **divorce suit** before superior court, Kitty petitioned that "without just cause or reason, [Thomas] deserted and abandoned her on December 15, 1905, refusing to make any support and failing to furnish any suitable lodging for herself and her children." (Yakima Herald, 1907)

The **City of Moxee** started as a large experimental farm testing the viability of crops like tobacco and sugar beets to the area. The Moxee Company was founded in 1886 by Gardiner Greene Hubbard, the first president of the National Geographic Society and father-in-law of Alexander Graham Bell, and others of the Bell and Hubbard families. One of their most successful crops was hops (first grown elsewhere in the Valley in 1872), now one of the most important crops in Washington State. Yakima Valley grows more than seventy-five percent of all hops in the country. In 2015 and 2016, the Valley produced more hops than any other agricultural area in the world, edging out (the entire country of) Germany for the first time in history. (Wilbur, 2009)

[5] The **City of Yakima**, a rough town at the turn of the century known for rampant prostitution and gambling, was shamed into action after the typhoid epidemic drew national attention. Already an important food producing center, concern was growing that the disease could be exported with the apples. The city hired epidemiologist Dr. Leslie Lumsden to make recommendations to help stem the epidemic. Within a year, public programs, new ordinances, and the creation of a city-county health department lowered the disease rate by 90%. The city's turnaround became a model of rural health reform. Dr. Lumsden used the metropolis as an example of the importance of rural health to agriculturally-dependent urban areas and demonstrating that infection was an interstate problem that required federal assistance and funding to solve. (Casner, 2001)

[6] Nelson, *We Never Got Away*, p. 4.

[7] Ibid.

[8] Ibid., 24.

[9] Ibid.

[10] **Nelson Ridge** was named after early pioneer John B. Nelson (not Jack Nelson) who settled in the Naches River Valley in the early 1860's and prospected all over the area. Fifes Peaks to the north of Highway 410, were originally named Jasper Peaks in honor of John's oldest son.

[11] Nelson, *We Never Got Away*, p.135.

[12] Ibid., p. 9.

[13] Rosalie Ferri, *National Registry of Historic Places: Jack and Kitty Nelson's Bumping Lake Resort* (National Park Service, 2012), https:/www.nps.gov/nr/feature/places/pdfs/13000211.pdf

[14] The basalt block **fireplace** was expertly crafted by Jimenez who likely would have stayed onsite with his family for a week or so while he, with their assistance, constructed it. The massive firebox and three-story chimney would have towered over the cleared building site.

[15] **As early as August 1911,** when the reservoir was in its very first year of operation, R.D. Holt chairman of a North Yakima water committee was reporting that water supplies were short and that the Bumping Lake Reservoir should be enlarged. ("Bumping Lake Reservoir is not Large Enough," *Yakima Herald*, August 11, 1911)

[16] *Bumping Lake Enlargement, Yakima Project: Environmental Impact Statement* (Bureau of Reclamation, 1979), p. 9.

CHAPTER THREE

[1] A second **Forest Service campground** at the Lake, the idyllic Bumping Dam Campground, located on the backside of the dam adjacent to the spillway, was closed down in the mid-1990s. The huge trees came down and the area is now filling in with a thick grove of lodgepole pines.

[2] The **Siskiyou Mountain ranges** win the global prize for conifer diversity. As a result of rugged terrain, complex geology and soils, strong moisture gradients from the Pacific Coast inland, and the general lack of glaciation, the area is home to more than thirty conifer species, of which seven are endemic. In one particular location, dubbed the "Miracle Mile," biologists have identified an astonishing seventeen species within a single square mile. (Olson, 2020)

But the Siskiyous span two states and stretch for 3,225 square miles. In contrast the Bumping River drainage is just sixty-eight square miles. In contrast to the Siskiyous, the valley was fully glaciated during the last Ice Age meaning the area has had less time to evolve novel species.

[3] Bumping Lake area **plant counts** were compiled from plant surveys conducted by the Washington Native Plant Society from 2005-2013.

⁴ This last period of **glaciation**, during what is sometimes more broadly called the Ice Age, lasted from 22,000 to about 15,000 years ago.

Bumping Lake during glacial retreat may have been much larger than it is now. In 1953, Agatin T. Abbott documented lake sediments along the Upper Bumping River more than a mile above the present lake. (Abbott, 1953)

⁵ Patrick T. Pringle, *Roadside Geology of Mount Rainier National Park and Vicinity* (Olympia: Washington State Division of Geology and Earth Resources, 2008).

⁶ Gretta Gossett, *Beyond the Bend; A History of the Nile Valley in Washington State* (Fairfield, Washington: Ye Galleon Press, 1979).

A. J. Splawn, *Ka-mi-akin Last Hero of the Yakimas* (Portland, Oregon: Kilham Stationary and Printing Co, 1917).

⁷ Ibid.

⁸ Noah Oliver and Corrine Camuso, "Cultural Resource Evaluations of Howard Carlin Trailhead Park," City of Cle Elum, Yakama Nations Cultural Resources Program, 2017, https://cityofcleelum.com/wp-content/uploads/2018/09/Howard-Carlin-Project-Report-5.26.17.pdf, retrieved September 10, 2021.

Captain George B. McClellan's 1853 expedition documented that the Yakama people used twenty-three kinds of roots and eighteen different berries. (Lloyd, 2018)

⁹ Before the **Yakamas obtained horses** from the Nez Perce, travelers had to drag their housing materials by hand. Horsepower immediately expanded their summer foraging ranges and ease of travel. With time, the Yakama peoples bred superb horses and became exquisite riders. Horses became central to festivities and some chiefs owned hundreds of them, signifying great wealth. (Williams J. , 1913)

¹⁰ E. N. Anderson, "Northwest Coastal Traditions: Indigenous Relationships with Plants and Animals," Krazy Kioti, March 10, 2019, http://www.krazykioti.com/articles/northwest-coast-traditional-indigenous-relationships-with-plants-and-animals/, retrieved September 10, 2021.

¹¹ H. Dean Guie, *Tribal Days of the Yakimas* (Yakima: Republic Publishing Company, 1937).

Splawn, *Kamiakin.*

¹² **Huckleberries and blueberries** are "fire-followers" tending to flourish after light burning. As the bushes age and get crowded, soil nutrients are reduced, productivity declines, and the berries tend to become less sweet. Native peoples learned exactly when and how often to burn to maximize productivity of their "crop." (Anderson E. , 2019)

Huckleberries were so vital that their harvest was celebrated with an annual ceremony and feast in August called "wiwnumi" (berry month). Hundreds of people would gather in the lowlands socializing, gambling, horse racing, and storytelling before heading up to the berry fields to pick. (Lloyd, 2018)

[13] Morris Uebelacker, *Land and Life in the Naches River Basin: A Cultural Resource Overview*, United States Department of Agriculture, Forest Service, 1980.

[14] Cheryl A. Mack and Richard H. McClure, "Vaccinium Processing in the Washington Cascades," *Journal of Ethnobiology, Volume 22(1)*, Summer 2002, pp. 35-60.

[15] Morris Uebelacker, interview by author, December 10, 2020.
     By the time the **Nelsons** settled on the shores of Bumping Lake in 1911, the collapse of the culture of the **Indigenous** people in south-central Washington was nearly complete. Few, if any, Yakamas were still making the trip to harvest at the lake. Over many years, Jack repeatedly retold a Yakama legend of a deadly serpent that lived in the dark lake waters. His erroneous claim that the native peoples stayed away from the lake because of this monster became a widely accepted fact.

[16] **Lodgepole pine** is a first succession tree, the first to colonize a burned or otherwise disturbed area. Some of the seed-bearing cones require the heat of fire to open. The resulting seedlings can tolerate full sun and the dry mineral soils of recently burned areas. The young pines grow quickly in the sun. Other tree species follow, growing in the shade and moister soils with higher organic matter provided by the lodgepoles.
     In the flatlands to the **east of Bumping Lake**, there are very specific boundaries between the lodgepole pine stands and the older mature forest. These verdant patches are impossible to miss as one drives through the relatively barren lands of the formerly burned areas.

[17] The **origin of the name Bumping** is unknown. It seems as if the lake was named for the river but had many names before Bumping was settled on. Preston's map of Oregon and Washington west of the Cascade Mountains dated 1856 shows the lake as *Lake Plehnam*. On Asher and Adams' 1873 map of Washington, the lake is named *Tanum* or *Ghost Lake*. The Northwest Transcontinental Survey Preliminary Agriculture Map for Yakima Region of 1881-82 identifies *Tanum Lake* and *Bumping River*. J.K. Gill's 1889 Map of Washington refers to it as *Georgia Lake*. In 1894, it is back to *Tannum Lake* and *River*. The Summit Mining District map published in the Seattle Post Intelligencer in 1899 refers to *"Bumpkin" River*. Miners in the 1890's apparently called the lake, *"Bumping River Lake."* A 1912 Washington State highway map labels the river *Bumjung*. Both the lake and river are labeled *Bumping* on the USGS map from 1900. By 1923, Edmond S. Meany in his *Origins of Washington Geographic Names*, wrote that "Bumping Lake seems to be well established on the most recent maps." (Meany, 1923)
     The **original Native American names** for Bumping Lake are misleading. Sometimes Indigenous names were generic and among the earliest explorers there was much misunderstanding with local languages as well. Many locations were dubbed "Tanum," "A-tanum" or a derivative (especially referring to salmon spawning areas) in addition to the Bumping area and there are other meanings of the word. Historian and author Dean Guie wrote to Jack in 1943 that Tah-num means "rising up of waters" and referred to Cowiche Creek but may have some reference to Bumping River. (Guie, 1943) Early settler A.J. Splawn wrote that Bumping Lake was called "We-nat-put, Wah-tum." Some believe that Bumping could be an English translation of *nacheez* which means turbulent or rough water. (Gossett, 1979)

David Longmire told the story of the **naming of Bumping River** to L.V. McWhorter who recounted that two old-timers, upon observing the rugged surface of the river as it tumbled down remarked on the broken character of the water and how it seemed to be "bumping along." (Nelson, *We Never Got Away*) Jack Nelson sometimes claimed the name referred to an old fisherman who lost his footing and went bumping down the river. The original meaning of the name is likely to remain a mystery.

William Dennison Lyman, *History of the Yakima Valley, Washington, Vol. 1: Comprising Yakima, Kittitas and Benton Counties* (S. J. Clark Publishing Company, 1919), https://www.sos.wa.gov/legacy/images/publications/sl_lymanhistoryyakimav1/sl_lymanhistoryyakimav1.pdf, retrieved September 10, 2021.

[18] Dorothy O. Johansen and Charles M. Gates, *Empire of the Columbia: A History of the Pacific Northwest* (New York: Harper and Row, 1967).

[19] Craig E. Holstine, editor, *An Historical Overview of the Wenatchee National Forest Washington,* U. S. Department of Agriculture Forest Service, Pacific Northwest Region, 1994.

[20] Gossett, *Beyond the Bend*, p. 207.

[21] Jack Nelson, *We Never Got Away*, (Yakima, Franklin Press, 1965), p. 45.

[22] Ibid., p. 44.

[23] Gossett, *Beyond the Bend*, p. 208.

[24] "Mount Rainier Wonderland: Administrative History, National Park Service, July 24, 2000, https://www.nps.gov/parkhistory/online_books/mora/adhi/chap5.htm, retrieved September 10, 2021.
"Nisqually Entrance Historic District," Wikipedia, August 4, 2019, https://en.wikipedia.org/wiki/Nisqually_Entrance_Historic_District, retrieved September 10, 2021.
Five years after it was constructed, Chief Clerk of the Interior Department, Clement S. Ucker saw **Oscar Brown's cabin** and thought it "the ideal cabin for the National Park Service." He asked for a photograph and a drawing of the floor plan along with its approximate cost. He then distributed the documents to other park superintendents with the suggestion that it be adopted as the model ranger cabin. The National Park Service Rustic architectural style that developed and spread throughout the country in the ensuing years had its roots right here in the Park with Ranger Brown. (Mt Rainier Wonderland, 2000)

[25] Gossett, *Beyond the Bend*, p. 82.

[26] Other **historic names persist at Crystal Mountain Resort**. Two mines in the adjacent Summit Mining District were christened Forrest Queen (J.R. Forrest was one of the owners along with James A. Farrell) and Black Diamond, which are two of the many named runs at the present ski resort.

[27] Nelson, *We Never Got Away*, p. 44.

[28] **Theodore Winthrop encountered Captain McClellan** and his camp somewhere near the junction of the Little Naches and Bumping River. Earlier in his journey he had come across a solitary horse in the forest. The miserable animal was stuck on its back wedged against a downed tree, but Winthrop and his Klickitat guide managed to rescue it. When they met the general, they returned the government-branded horse which the expedition had left behind. (Winthrop)

[29] Gossett, *Beyond the Bend*, p. 33.

[30] Theodore Winthrop, *The Canoe and The Saddle* (Portland, Oregon: Franklin-Ward Company, 1913), pp.113-114.

[31] Kit Oldham, "First emigrant wagon train crosses Naches Pass through the Cascade Mountains in the fall of 1853," *History Link*, January 15, 2003, http://www.historylink. org/File/5053. retrieved September 10, 2021.
    Lucile McDonald, "The First Crossing of Naches Pass," *Seattle Times*, November 1 and November 8, 1953, https://www.nachestrail.org/media/pdf2/MCDONALD_1853_ Roadbuilding.pdf, retrieved September 10, 2021.

[32] Gossett, *Beyond the Bend*, p. 119.

[33] With the **Treaty of 1855**, the Federal government purchased from the Indigenous bands in the greater Yakima area over eleven million acres—about one-quarter of the future state of Washington—for the promise of $200,000 and retention of traditional hunting and fishing rights on that land. In return, all of the disparate groups of Native peoples would have to relocate from their traditional villages onto a single designated reservation located to the east side of Mt. Adams. (Meyers, It Happened Here: Treaty of 1855 took land, created the Yakama Nation, 2017)

[34] George W. Fuller, *A History of the Pacific Northwest* (New York: Alfred A. Knopf, 1948).

[35] Paula Becker, "Yakima Indian War begins on October 5, 1855," *History Link*, February 26, 2006, https://www.historylink.org/File/5311, retrieved September 10, 2021.

[36] Cassandra Tate, "Gold in the Pacific Northwest," *History Link*, December 6, 2004, https://www.historylink.org/File/7162, retrieved September 10, 2021.
    Part of the **federal government**'s effort to solve the "Indian Problem" was to send native children to boarding schools where they would be indoctrinated into western culture and "civilized." One of the first Indian schools in the nation was built at Fort Simcoe just after the fort was turned over to the Yakima Indian Agency as the new reservation headquarters. Methodist minister (and future Indian agent) James Wilbur, established the school in 1859, predating the first off-reservation boarding school, Carlisle School in Pennsylvania by twenty years. (Wilma P. B., 2005) (Meyers, It Happened Here: Fort Simcoe established near White Swan, 2018)

[37] Gossett, *Beyond the Bend*, p. 241.

John Emerick did finally find lasting companionship when he married another valley resident Mary Louise Stevens. He and Mary raised their children—and fruit—and lived the remainder of their lives on his homestead in the Naches River Valley. Emerick worked as a laborer on the Bumping dam and later on the road repair team which he said was a "difficult job" as the road was a "real dilly."

[38] Gossett, *Beyond the Bend*, p. 103.

[39] Ibid., p. 173.

[40] Ibid., p. 127.

[41] Fred. G. Plummer, *Forest Conditions in the Cascade Range, Washington* (Washington D.C.: Washington Government Printing Office, 1902), p. 37.

[42] Mike Hiler, interview by author, September 20, 2018.

[43] The **Coffin Brothers** (Arthur, Lester, and H. Stanley) ran one of the largest sheep operations in the Northwest and in 1894 moved their outfit from Oregon to Yakima. At times, Stanley pastured his herd of purebred Lincoln sheep in Goose Prairie on a land that he leased from homesteader Tom Fife. The payment for the summer's use was $300 dollars. Other sheepmen, Sam and Will Cameron favored the thick grass meadows near the Cascades crest between the headwaters of the Bumping and Cowlitz Rivers. Andy Wilson ranged his sheep there too, in addition to the entire Tumac Plateau (Twin Sisters Lakes) area which had forage enough to hold his flocks for a long season. (Gossett, 1979, pp. 118-119)

[44] Gossett, *Beyond the Bend*, p. 111.

[45] W. Gale Matthews, "Columbia Basin Reclamation Project," *History Link*, October 28, 2006, https://www.historylink.org/File/7963, retrieved September 10, 2021.

[46] Jedediah S. Rogers, "Chief Joseph Dam," (Washington D.C.: United States Bureau of Reclamation, 2008).

[47] Paula Becker, "Saint Joseph's Mission at Ahtanum Creek is founded in the Yakima Valley on April 3, 1852," *History Link*, February 23, 2003, www.historylink.org/File/5285, retrieved September 10, 2021.

[48] Within two decades, over **350,000 acres** would be under irrigation in the Yakima Valley. (Bumping Lake Dam Environmental Impact Statement, 1979)

[49] Lyman, *History of the Yakima Valley.*

[50] Timothy A. Dick, *Yakima Project*, U.S. Department of the Interior, Bureau of Reclamation, 1993, https://www.usbr.gov/projects/pdf.php?id=211, retrieved September 10, 2021.

[51] Rose. M. Boening, "The History of Irrigation in the State of Washington: The State Epoch of Canal Building," *The Washington Historical Quarterly, Vol 10, No. 1*, 1919, 21, https://www.jstor.org/stable/23908750?seq=1#metadata_info_tab_contents,   retrieved September 10, 2021.

[52] George O. Smith, *An Illustrated History of Klickitat, Yakima and Kittitas Counties* (Chicago: Interstate Publishing Company, 1904).
   It is thought that a **small sawmill** was set up on site at Bumping Lake that was powered by a water-driven Pelton wheel to cut the logs for the dam.

[53] Dick, *Yakima Project*, p. 5.
   Lyman, *History of the Yakima Valley*, p. 361.

[54] Ibid.

[55] Ibid.

[56] Smith, *An Illustrated History of Klickitat, Yakima and Kittitas Counties*, p. 316.

[57] Margaret Drennan, "Agricultural History of Yakima Valley," Washington State Department of Agriculture, no date.
   Dick, *Yakima Project*.

[58] In fact, of the **135 million dollars** spent by the Reclamation Service in the first twenty-five years, only ten million dollars were repaid, leading some to cast Reclamation projects as the largest welfare program ever created. So little repayment occurred that the Reclamation Service eventually restructured the terms with few incentives for the irrigators to repay construction costs or even pay for their subsidized water. Partly because of its fiscal crisis, the Service was reorganized in 1923 and renamed the Bureau of Reclamation with new terms and goals. (Rowley, 2006)
   As more federal money poured into the Bureau, it took on larger and more complex projects. During the Depression, huge multi-use WPA projects like the Grand Coulee Dam helped keep thousands of men employed. In Washington State, thirty-four Civilian Conservation Corps camps were run under the direction of the Bureau of Reclamation with men working to reline irrigation canals, clean ditches, and clear reservoir bottoms of debris and stumps. (Pfaff, The Bureau of Reclamation's Civilian Conservation Corps Legacy: 1933-1942, 2010)
   During WWII, several of the camps became internment facilities for Japanese Americans. In some cases, Reclamation work was continued by those interred at the camps.

[59] "About Us," *United States Bureau of Reclamation*, January 7, 2020, https://www.usbr.gov/main/about/, retrieved September 10, 2021.

[60] Christine E. Pfaff, *Harvest of plenty: A History of the Yakima Irrigation Project, Washington* (Denver, Colorado: United States Bureau of Reclamation Technical Service Center, 2001).

The partially completed **Sunnyside project** was purchased by the federal government. It would undergo some improvements under Reclamation and was one of the first projects to be scheduled for construction in the state.

[61] Christine E. Pfaff, *The Bureau of Reclamation's Civilian Conservation Corps Legacy: 1933-1942* (Denver, Colorado: United States Bureau of Reclamation Technical Service Center, 2010).

[62] "Establishment and Modification of National Forest Boundaries and National Grasslands," United States Department of Agriculture Forest Service, 2012, https://www.fs.fed.us/land/staff/Documents/Establishment%20and%20Modifications%20of%20National%20Forest%20Boundaries%20and%20National%20Grasslands%201891%20to%202012.pdf, retrieved September 10, 2021.

[63] Stephanie Whitey, "Dorthea Lange in the Yakima Valley," *University of Washington; The Great Depression in Washington*, 2010, https://depts.washington.edu/depress/dorothea_lange_FSA_yakima.shtml, retrieved September 10, 2021

[64] "A Very Brief History of the Bureau of Reclamation," United States Bureau of Reclamation, 1918, https://www.usbr.gov/history/borhist.html, retrieved September 10, 2021.

[65] Dick, *Yakima Project.*
The fact that **Congressman Wesley Jones**, who was an integral part of the drafting of the Reclamation Act and was instrumental to the restructuring of private irrigation in the Valley, represented Yakima, may also have had something to do with the decision to greenlight the project.

CHAPTER FOUR

[1] Betty Jean Ford Gallant, interview by author, August 2016.

[2] ***Devil's Elbow*** was a particularly difficult turn on the Bumping River Road that freighters had trouble negotiating. *Moon Shine Point* was supposedly named not for the libation, but for the way the little hill caught the moon's glow on still evenings. Tom Fife coined *Dead Horse Hill* after a pack horse he was leading slipped off the trail and rolled to the bottom of the slope splitting its abdominal wall in the fall. Fife sewed up its wound and the horse lived, but he always said by all rights, it should have died. Jack Nelson wrote at length about the origins of *Suicide Point* as the place where the body of a laborer on the Bumping Lake Dam was found after drowning himself in the Bumping River. But Nelson's details of a suitcase full of cash and the name Henry belong to another Reclamation worker who died by a falling tree. *Little* (and *Big*) *Slide* refer to spots on the Bumping Lake Road that were often blocked by snow slides. *Salt Pudding Camp* is a spot along Deep Creek Road on the way to Copper City where the cook for a road crew mistakenly added salt instead of sugar to the evening's dessert. *Lantern Point* was a turn a little further along where a light was

hung to mark the way. *The Pharmacy* is most likely the remains of the timber camp that was part of the dam construction infrastructure and dates from 1909. It seems as if there was a wagon road from the dam along the lakeshore to access the southern site. A sturdy bridge spanned a little creek to access the camp. Reportedly there was a horse barn and several buildings, and a small dam remains at the edge of the wet meadow to the south. Geographer Morris Uebelacker was told that the old timer's name, "The Pharmacy" may have been a coy insider's term since it seems at one point, a lot of drinking went on there. (Uebelacker, Professor of Geography Central Washington University, 2020)

[3] Theodore Winthrop, *The Canoe and the Saddle*, (Portland, Oregon: Franklin-Ward Company, 1913), p. 39.

[4] Christine E. Pfaff, *The Bureau of Reclamation's Civilian Conservation Corps Legacy: 1933-1942*, (Denver: Untited States Department of the Interior, Bureau of Reclamation, 2010.

[5] "Will Be Hard Road to Build," *Yakima Daily Republic*, July 13, 1906.

[6] Robert Danielson, *The Road with the Grandest View: Surveys and Construction of the Chinook Pass Highway 1892-1934* (Calgary, Alberta: self published, 2013).

[7] The **Fresno grader** revolutionized road and railroad construction soon after it was invented by Scottish immigrant James Porteous in 1883. The grader's blade was angled in such a way to move dirt conveniently off to one side. The relatively simple device was horse-drawn and easily operated and made land leveling and earth moving possible on a large scale. Porteous sold thousands of them from his wagon and implement shop in Fresno, California. Used in agricultural and civic contexts, the grader also played an important role in the construction of the Panama Canal and of infrastructure during World War I. (Bulls, 2010)

[8] Robert I. Ford, *The History of Goose Prairie and the Ira Ford Family*, self-published, 2003, p. 12.

[9] A **Chinook wind** is a relatively warm wind that blows from the southwest usually between late fall and early spring. The wind was named for the Indigenous people residing near the mouth of the Columbia River area from which the winds seem to come. Also called "snow eaters" by native peoples, these winds can cause very rapid snow melt.

[10] "Great Floods are Raging in the Valley," *Yakima Daily Republic*, November 14, 1906, p. 1.

[11] "State Road Ruined by Recent Floods," *Olympia Record*, December 4, 1906.

[12] "Naches and Yakima Rivers Almost Normal," *Yakima Daily Republic*, November 17, 1906.

[13] "The State Road #1 Damaged About $1800," *Yakima Daily Republic*, November 20, 1906.

[14] Gretta Gossett, *Beyond the Bend*, (Fairfield, Washington: Ye Galleon Press, 1979).

There are **no newspaper accounts of this work sequence** as it was related in Greta Gossett's book. Gossett's narrative was based on interviews of the people reportedly involved in the construction which commenced in the fall of 1908. (Gossett, 1979, pp. 276, 355) Reclamation Chief Clerk George Mair claimed to have no trouble hiring workers in September that year after hanging a sign at the corner of Yakima Avenue and Front Street in Yakima. The initial response was so great that he had to turn some men away and he subsequently sent out fifty-five workers within two days to work on the road to the dam. (Dam to be Built at Bumping Lake, 1908)

[15] "Bumping Lake Road Is Now Completed," *Yakima Daily Republic*, December 11, 1908.

Arthur P. Davis, *Reclamation Service 15th Annual Report* (Washington: Government Printing Office, 1916).

The **announcement of the road's completion** may have been premature. Horse crews were still at work grading in February of 1909 and probably well after. Even after improvement, most Reclamation officials admitted the road was dangerous. In multiple newspaper articles, officials warned the public that it was not a road to be used for pleasure driving due to its narrow width, high precipices overhanging deep canyons, and heavy freighting traffic. Sunday was suggested as the safest day as it was the freighters' day off. (Highway is Dangerous, 1909) In June, the State was preparing making plans to improve the length of the road in starting in 1910.

[16] "Reclamation Service May Build Dams, *Yakima Daily Republic*, December 3, 1906.

"Serious Are Difficulties on Government Project," *Yakima Morning Herald*, April 8, 1907.

Paul Dorpat and Genevieve McCoy, *Building Washington: A History of Washington State Public Works*. Seattle, WA: Tartu Publishers, 1998), pp. 237-238.

[17] Gossett, *Beyond the Bend*.

[18] A **sign on the storehouse at Camp 22** reading "46 miles-600 feet," specified the exact distance to the building from the warehouse in Naches which was needed when calling for bids on freight. The freighting charge was fifty cents per ton per mile which would equal twenty-three dollars per ton per trip. (Nelson, *We Never Got Away*)

The **meat contract** alone was worth $25,000, a huge sum in that day. It called for 100,000 pounds of beef (which was to be seventy percent steers), 20,000 pounds of pork, and 10,000 pounds of both veal and mutton with unspecified amount of beef livers, hearts, and tongues. It would be delivered over time as needed at the camp. The Yakima Meat Company received the contract having offered the lowest bid. ("Bids for Construction of Laterals on Tieton Project," *Yakima Herald*, March 3, 1909)

[19] Gossett, *Beyond the Bend*.

[20] "Bumping Lake Reservoir Being Rushed through Winter," *Yakima Herald*, January 6, 1909.

Jack Nelson, *We Never Got Away* (Yakima, Washington: Franklin Press, 1965).

[21] A Spokane Chronicle article indicates that **James Baillie retained a contract** for taking freight from Naches to Bumping Lake. There may have been multiple contracts to obtain enough teams for the huge job. In any case, in January Baillie traveled to Walla Walla to buy sixteen heavy horses for hauling. ("Buys Horses For Yakima," *Spokane Chronicle*, January 16, 1909)

[22] Gossett, *Beyond the Bend*.

[23] In his book, *The History of Goose Prairie and the Ira Ford Family*, Robert Ford wrote that **Devil's Elbow** was a tight bend on the Bumping River Road that was later removed when the road was straightened.

[24] Danielson, *The Road with the Grandest View*, p. 22.

[25] Nelson, *We Never Got Away*.

[26] Ibid., p. 26.

[27] "Passenger Contract for Government," *Yakima Herald*, February 23, 1910.

[28] Nelson, *We Never Got Away*, p. 27.

[29] "Fine Sanitation at Bumping Lake, *Yakima Morning Herald*, August 21, 1910.

[30] Nelson, *We Never Got Away*.

[31] **The light shop** almost certainly produced electricity for the arc lights that illuminated the worksite in later months when a third overnight shift was added to finish the dam by the end of the 1910 season. A water-driven wheel most likely would have created the power for the lights.

[32] Dorpat and McCoy, *Building Washington*.

[33] "Bunch of Figures on Bumping Dam," *Yakima Daily Republic*, November 14, 1910, p. 3.

[34] *Annual Report of the Reclamation Service, Volume 10*, (Washington: United States Government Printing Office, 1912).

[35] Although *Building Washington* by Dorpat and McCoy states there were as many as **506 laborers** at Bumping Lake, and newspaper articles announce the plans to have 500 men on site for the summer work season, the actual number of workers on site at all times was likely much lower. During the 1909 season, there were 152 men and 93 horses living and laboring at the lake. In 1910, a force of 250 men and 98 horses worked to finish the dam which seemed to be the largest number of workers at the site. (*Annual Report of the Reclamation Service, Volume 10*)

Jack Nelson was so appreciative of the hard work by the **hundreds of horses** that toiled so hard on the dam that he thought a statue of a horse, placed at the dam site to honor them was in order. (Nelson, *We Never Got Away*)

[36] Other **engineers or construction supervisors** were J.S. Conway, J.D. Fauntleroy, James Stuart and E.H. Baldwin. (Lyman, *History of the Yakima Valley, Washington, Vol. 1*, p. 369)

The **north rock quarry** was located near the bottom of a rockslide to the northwest the dam site. A wagon road was cut into the slope up to the rockslide where rocks could be collected. The road grade is still evident.

The **south rock quarry** was south of the old growth "Sanctuary" to the southeast of the dam site up against the slope of Nelson Ridge. The wagon road built to that site was more ambitious requiring several heavy bridges and sections of corduroy paving to get across wet areas in the Sanctuary. The loaded wagons coming out of the area were so heavy that the deep tracks can still be seen, discernible underneath layers of accumulating duff.

The **north water supply** was a pretty stream cascading straight down the mountain about a mile north of the end of the future dam. To convey water to the worksite, crews dammed the stream at base of a nearby waterfall and then redirected the water across the mountainside in a metal-lined sluiceway. The water was then conveyed via a short aqueduct and then into pipes to the dam site itself where it could be utilized for the hydraulic sluicing of fill material. After construction was completed, the system became the water source for the Nelson's in their house at the lakeshore and then later served their resort. The water system is still in place and in use more than a hundred and ten years later, providing fresh water (and green electricity) to Normandie.

The **south water supply** was Black Devon Creek located to the southeast of the dam site. Black Devon was originally named by Tom Fife in recognition of his Scottish homeland. It was later renamed Barton Creek after a supervisor at the CCC camp that was located there in the early 1940s. Locals thought Black Devon was the better name as it seems black due to dark algae on the bottom.

[37] The **clearing and subsequent sale of the valuable timber** covering dam sites and reservoir bottoms was an important issue that needed to be resolved prior to construction. It was estimated that a total of 64,000,000 board feet of marketable lumber stood on the sites of the six Yakima storage projects. A call for bids was made and while there is a record of lumber contractor's bids on all of the other projects, there are none for Bumping Lake. The costs of transport from this remote site were simply too high to interest lumber companies. The Reclamation Service made several calls for bids and finally gave up and did all of the falling and clearing work themselves by force account. (Annual Report United States Reclamation Service, Issue 7, 1908) (Lyman, *History of the Yakima Valley, Washington, Vol. 1*, p. 373)

[38] Nelson, *We Never Got Away*.

When sluiced with water, the **fine material** included in the glacial till from the borrow pit became almost as hard as cement. In modern times, Bill Garoutte used similar soil to create the roadbeds in the marina campground. The resulting surface became so durable that later when he needed to make repairs, he had to break through it with heavy machinery.

[39] "Yakima Police Hope to Locate Dead Man's Relatives by It," *Spokesman Review*, December 17, 1908.

"Ray Henry's Body is Finally Buried," Yakima Herald, March 17, 1909, p. 2.

Jack Nelson mixes the name of this reclamation worker with another fatality during the dam construction. In his book, Jack gives the name Mr. Henry to the man who committed suicide in Bumping River. That man's name was actually George Foster, and he died the following year. Foster had been acting strangely and after he went missing was found underneath a woodpile with his throat cut. His suicide attempt was not successful and after being sewed up by the camp doctor it was determined that he should be sent back to Yakima by the next stage. On the way out, he offered to walk for a section and disappeared. His lifeless body was found about ten days later in the river. ("Forster [sic] Dead; Wounds Found," *Spokesman Review*, April 25, 1909)

[40] Dorpat and McCoy, *Building Washington*.

[41] "Move 45-Ton Steam Shovel," *Spokesman Review*, February 28, 1909.

[42] "Bumping Dam is Delayed," *Yakima Herald*, July 21, 1909.

[43] Pfaff, *The Bureau of Reclamation's Civilian Conservation Corps Legacy*.

[44] **Small temporary dams** were built on Lakes Keechelus and Cle Elum in 1906. They were made of cribbed logs filled with rocks to provide interim storage until the Bumping Lake dam was finished. These low dams were built slightly upstream and were designed to be flooded when the permanent dams were constructed. ("Will be Completed for Next Summer," *Yakima Daily Republic*, October 25, 1906)

[45] Brad J. Buehler, *Engineering Geology of Washington, Volume I Bulletin 78*, (Olympia: Department of Natural Resources, 1989).

[46] Timothy A. Dick, *Yakima Project*, U.S. Department of the Interior, Bureau of Reclamation, 1993, https://www.usbr.gov/projects/pdf.php?id=211, retrieved September 10, 2021.

[47] Arthur Powell Davis, *Irrigation Works Constructed by the United States Government* (New York: John Wiley and Sons, Inc., 1917)

The **puddled core** was a difficult component to construct and is no longer used in modern dam building though it has proven to be stable at the Bumping Lake dam (and others). The sluicing, which was conducted by hand with cotton hoses topped by three-quarter inch nozzles, had to be thorough but carefully controlled. As the embankments rose on the upstream and downstream slopes, the center settling pond got narrower and became more difficult to maintain. When both of the banks got too narrow for the dump car trains, wheelbarrows were used, and men armed with shovels mixed the dumped material with the water in the pond. Finally, the puddle core was capped, and more fill was added on top. (Pfaff, The Bureau of Reclamation's Civilian Conservation Corps Legacy: 1933-1942, 2010)

[48] Gossett, *Beyond the Bend*.

[49] The **outlet channel**, which receives water at a high velocity after it exits the dam's conduit, was a troublesome part of the project. The stone paving that lined the channel was initially laid without mortar and washed out with the flow. It was repaired at the beginning of the 1910 season. That paving also washed out and was replaced by temporary timbers in July 1911 to protect the ditch until a permanent fix of poured concrete could be applied at the end of the working season in 1911. A series of metal baffles was also installed to slow the water exiting the conduit.

[50] If they were to be **hauling fill dirt from the borrow pit** that day, the animals would be taken along a shortcut road from the back of the tent corrals to the Borrow Pit. The road, and a newer (replacement) bridge over Barton Creek is still evident.

[51] The **fill dirt trains** consisted of six, 1.5 cubic yard capacity dump cars rolling on twenty-four-inch tracks. They were pulled by two horses or mules.

[52] Even though the **trestle's deck** at fourteen feet wide was sufficient for the width of two trains, the design did not take into account the psyche of the work animals. The tracks were close enough to the outside edges (which were not protected by any railings) so that as they walked onto the deck, the horses and mules tended to shy towards the center. It was quickly determined not to be practical to have two trains pass on the trestle at the same time. (Davis A. P., 1917)

[53] Davis, *Reclamation Service 15th Annual Report.*

[54] Thirty-four of the sixty-four **workers at the dam** construction site in May of 1910 were Bulgarian men between twenty and thirty years old and all but one of them spoke predominantly Bulgarian. Most of them were married (between three and thirty-three years) with their wives, at least for the time, back in the home country. These men were part of a large wave of immigrants who came to the United States from Bulgaria between 1903 and 1910. (Yu, 2020) How they came to work for the Reclamation Service in Washington State is unknown.

Interestingly, none of the non-Bulgarian foreigners, were married. The youngest laborer was sixteen years old and the oldest, at seventy-one, was M. Cunningham from England. The engineer in charge of the crew, Phillip Nolalan, was just twenty-two years old. (United States Census, Yakima County, 1910)

[55] **Communal bread ovens** were at the heart of traditional Bulgarian villages and bread making was and still is an important creative aspect of the culture. It is not surprising then, that traditional wood-fired ovens were built at Camp 22. The large ovens (ten to thirteen feet in diameter) have long since collapsed, but the perfectly dressed stones and careful jointing are still evident. They had well-designed air intakes and heavy iron doors and must have produced absolutely delicious bread.

[56] "Work at Bumping Lake Continued," *Yakima Daily Republic*, May 2, 1910.
"Study Bible in U.S. Camp," *Spokesman-Review*, May 4, 1910.

[57] "Fine Sanitation at Bumping Lake," *Yakima Morning Herald*, August 21, 1910.

[58] "Woods Burning at Bumping Lake," *Yakima Daily Republic*, August 10, 1910.

[59] "More Men Needed at Bumping Lake," *Spokane Chronicle*, June 17, 1909.
Dick, *Yakima Project*, p. 14.
Nelson, *We Never Got Away*.

[60] Davis, *Reclamation Service 15th Annual Report*.

[61] This **site has been the cause for a lot of speculation over the years.** Called "The Pharmacy" by old timers, the dam construction facility may have been used later by crews from Copper City to keep their horses. There is a large wet meadow adjacent that was partially dammed at some point perhaps to maintain forage for work animals.

[62] Nelson, *We Never Got Away*.

[63] "Progress of Reclamation," *Yakima Herald*, November 29, 1911.

[64] "Tieton Unit Work Ending," *Yakima Herald*, November 1, 1911.

[65] "Bumping Lake to be a Resort," *Yakima Herald*, May 22, 1912.
The **Nelson Lodge** complex and its successor the **Bumping Lake Resort** welcomed guests from 1912 until the resort was closed in 1972. It was the first recreational facility in the Wenatchee National Forest and one of the earlier in the state. At sixty years of continuous operation, the resort was also one of the longest operating recreational resorts in Washington State. The facility was relocated slightly (and renamed) when it moved from the south side of the Bumping Lake Road adjacent to the dam's spillway across the street to the north side of the road. Virtually all the original buildings have been replaced or removed.

The few buildings that remain at the Normandie lodge site are relics. Historically, in remote areas when a structure was no longer needed, it was either moved to be used in another location or the materials were recycled and made into another structure. Building supplies and especially milled lumber were precious so far from civilization. At the lakeshore, many of the resort buildings were relocated multiple times. The little icehouse initially was located at the original resort and the still-existing generator shed was constructed on site from two separate buildings.

The oldest and most mobile however, is a little structure that serves as a storage building now but was originally constructed as a workers' cottage during the dam's construction Camp 22. At some point it was moved to the Nelsons' first resort, then was relocated again up the hill where it stands today. Built in 1908-09, it is the oldest existing building in the Bumping River Valley. (Tom Fife's cabin in Goose Prairie was constructed around 1915 with the help of Jack Nelson and Dick Ball. It replaced his original cabin built earlier).

[66] Nelson, *We Never Got Away*.
For many subsequent years **Jack** delighted in taking summer visitors to that particular stand of lodgepole pines and having them guess what event caused all of the trees to be cut off a full twenty feet from the ground.

[67] "Pill Roller Seeking Open Spaces Spends 19 Years at Bumping Lake," *Yakima Morning Herald*, October 26, 1930.

CHAPTER FIVE

[1] X. was not **Tom Fife's** real middle initial. He had worked beside miner Frank X. Nagler, was intrigued by his initial and later adopted the "X" as his own.

[2] ""Uncle Tom" and his Happy Cabin in Shadow of Peaks," *Spokesman-Review*, April 9, 1922.

[3] Some old timers claim that the settlement was originally written as **Gooseprairie** and prefer that spelling, but it is now commonly written as two words: Goose Prairie. The earliest newspaper accounts dating from 1900 and the earliest inclusion on a map from 1902 all spell out the name as two words. Some accounts refer to a Canada goose sighting as the inspiration for the name rather than a snow goose. Another origin version refers to the shape of the prairie looking like the outline of a goose when viewed from the nearby ridges.

[4] **Fife's point of discovery** was not far from where the gold was first discovered in Washington State by Captain McClellan's geologist on the Naches River in 1853.

[5] Craig Holstine, *An Historical Overview of the Wenatchee National Forest Washington* (United States Department of Agriculture, 1994), 5.20.

[6] Gretta Gossett, *Beyond the Bend: A History of the Nile River Valley in Washington State* (Fairfield, Washington: Ye Galleon Press, 1979).

[7] Some of the other **miners who worked the Blue Bell** were Matt Laws, Joe Handy, Walter Lindsey, Charlie Lope, Ruben Root, and James Simmons. (Gossett, *Beyond the Bend*, p. 80)

[8] Gossett, *Beyond the Bend*, p. 81.

[9] Ibid., p. 73.
L. Hodges, "Mining in the Pacific Northwest," *Seattle Post Intelligencer*, 1897.

[10] Click Relander, "Chinook Pass Road Steeped in Early History," *Yakima Sunday Herald*, May 8, 1949.

[11] "Summit Mining District," *Buckley Banner*, September 18, 1896.

[12] "Gold Hill Development," *Yakima Herald*, January 25, 1900.
The **Summit Mining District** at the turn of the century might have been home to as many as 300 people living in three separate "towns." Fog City was up near the crest while Fidelity was the location of the post office. Jim Town (or Pickhandle Gap) to the west was named by Ed Collins after his neighboring miners Jim Forrest and Jim Farrell. ("Mines of

Summit," *Seattle Post-Intelligencer*, September 25, 1896) The moniker persisted long enough to be included on the 1902 Mines of Gold Hill map.

[13] William O. Douglas, *Of Men and Mountains* (New York, NY: Harper and Brothers, 1950), p. 222.

[14] "The Scatter Creek Road," *Enumclaw Herald*, April 24, 1909.
"Commissioners Join in Movement for Good Roads Here," *Yakima Herald*, June 3, 1908.

[15] Gossett, *Beyond the Bend*, p. 80.

[16] Ibid., p. 79.
Ralph Carmack and John Palmer hauled the main piece, a 500-pound hunk of metal, to the mouth of Union Creek where it was slung between two horses and packed straight up the mountainside by John Anderson's sturdy cayuses. John also packed in a steam boiler, cook stoves, and a machine drill to the settlement, creating a substantial mining complex.

[17] Relander, "Chinook Pass Road Steeped in Early History," *Yakima Sunday Herald*, May 8, 1949.

[18] "Mining Engineer Makes Good Report," *Yakima Morning Herald*, June 5, 1910.

[19] The **Elizabeth Gold Hill Mining Company**, consisting of nineteen claims, a ten-stamp mill, sawmill, rock crusher, blacksmith outfit, dining hall, bunkhouse and "other buildings," was auctioned and sold on March 10, 1918, for a sum of $2,000 dollars (only eight years after it was valued at 118 *million* dollars and was supposedly "a proven mountain of riches"). The Yakima Morning Herald reported on July 21, 1918 that Yakima County produced "little mining wealth" in 1917. Seven tons of ore were treated that year which gave 1.65 ounces of gold, 34 ounces of silver, and 1486 pounds of copper. For all that hard work, sweat, money, time, and lives, $468 dollars were gained.

[20] Nelson, *We Never Got Away*.

[21] Though the **Prairie was long referred to as Tom Fife's homestead**, he apparently did not get around to filing the requisite legal paperwork to receive the patent (ownership title) to his land until 1920, just two years before his death. Once he received title, he could legally sell parcels of the tract. ("Uncle Tom" and his Happy Cabin in Shadow of Peaks," *Spokesman-Review*, April 9, 1922, p. 7)

[22] Susan I. Anthon, "First Step Underway to Develop Tom Fife Museum," *Yakima Valley Mirror*, October 9, 1965.

[23] "Prosser Boy Scouts Show Zeal," *Spokesman-Review*, May 21, 1922.

[24] "Is Model Camp," *Spokesman-Review*, July 10, 1925, p. 4.

[25] Ibid.

[26] "Scouts Given Land," *Spokesman-Review*, December 25, 1929.

[27] *Yakima Herald*, July 16, 1935.

[28] "Land Given," *Spokesman-Review*, August 4, 1958.

[29] Janet Gallant, interview by author, July 21, 2020.

[30] In 2018, **Camp Fife** was in its ninety-fifth year of operation and continued to attract scouts and other groups from all over the state.

[31] Nelson, *We Never Got Away*.

[32] Ibid., p. 23

[33] "Eats 12 Eggs; suffers stroke," *Spokesman-Review*, July 27, 1922.

[34] ""Uncle Tom" Fife Shot Self When Teased by Boys," *Spokesman-Review*, November 14, 1922.

[35] "Pioneer Sleeps with Mountains," *Yakima Morning Herald*, November 15, 1922.

[36] "Aged Man Dies from His Wounds," *Spokesman-Review*, November 14, 1922.

[37] Patty Rose, "Remembering Yakima by Those Who Were There: Tom Fife...They Named the Boy Scout Camp After Him," n.d.

[38] **Dick Ball's** mine was located at or near the "Keystone" copper claim, owned by William Pemberton. Keystone was first staked by John W. Palmer in 1913.

[39] The Yakima Morning Herald reported that "**the donkey** would be rafted to the head of the lake where it would then pull itself to the mill site!" ("Mining Company Buys From Government," *Yakima Moring Herald*, July 20, 1916, p. 1)

[40] "Succumbs to Cold When Wagon Overturns on Mountain Road," *Yakima Daily Republic*, November 23, 1915.

[41] A **Palouser** was a homemade lantern consisting of a one pound can with one end removed and with a hole punched in one side through which a candle was pushed up. Held sideways by a wire handle, the candlelight shone out through the open end of the can. As the candle burned down, it could be pushed up from below. Jack Nelson reported that these were "not bright but they were effective" and withstood any amount of wind. (Nelson, *We Never Got Away*)

[42] Nelson, *We Never Got Away*, p. 141.

[43] The new city of **North Yakima** replaced the original Yakima City in 1885. The Northern Pacific Railroad had established their depot four miles north of Yakima City and offered free lots to all who would move to the new townsite. Some businesses stayed open as their buildings were slowly towed by teams of horses to their new locations. In the Guilland Hotel, boarders took their meals on the move. It is said that a farmer could tie up his rig at the hardware store, shop, and then load his wagon while his team slowly walked behind the building as it rolled down the street. In 1917, North Yakima officially became known as "Yakima" and what was left at Yakima City was renamed "Union Gap." (Lyman, 1919) (Oldham, "Northern Pacific reaches Yakima City, where it declines to build a station,")

[44] "Campers are Few along the Naches," *Yakima Morning Herald*, July 18, 1916.
   Snow in February broke records in a series of storms that shut down all Northwest trains, dumped twenty-nine inches on Seattle and fifty-four inches at Bumping Lake. All that stored snow melted quickly in the middle of June when temperatures in the mountains soared. By June 17, all tributaries of the Yakima were flooding and highway crews were scrambling to protect bridge abutments.

[45] Harold Stanislawsky, "Proof of Claim of Labor and Improvements on the Washington Tungsten Mine Company," Yakima, 1918.
   Gossett, *Beyond the Bend*, p. 86.

[46] "Organize Bumping Lake into Mining District," *Yakima Daily Republic*, August 12, 1913.

[47] **Zockseye** (also spelled Zokeseye) was an old Indian from the Cowiche area who gave some rich samples of silver ore to friends at the Indian agency at Fort Simcoe in 1862 but died before revealing the location of the deposit. Speculation swirled around his lost treasure which was already a local legend by 1918. One belief was that the ore came from the area around Bumping Lake but without any more concrete information, treasure hunters have been searching the surrounding area in vain for the past 150 years.

[48] Nelson, *We Never Got Away*, p. 38.

[49] A trapper by trade, **Billy Richmond** met another trapper, Nathaniel "Than" Galloway on the Green River in Utah when he was just twenty-three years old. The two started down the river on October 22, 1896 planning to trap and hunt along the passage through the Grand Canyon. They escaped pursuing Utes as they passed through the Indians' reservation and endured multiple portages for rapids. According to one account, when they wearied of portaging in Desolation Canyon, Richmond suggested a boat modification to keep their supplies dry. He cut up his heavy canvas bedroll and used it as decking on the bow and stern to create dry compartments. This effective modification influenced subsequent river boat design. (Aton, 2009) Near the end of their trip, they were prevailed upon to transport the bodies of two murdered prospectors down to Needles, California which they did by floating the men in their coffins behind the boats. They arrived in Needles on February 10, 1897. In addition to the dead men, they brought in seventy-nine beavers and other animals whose pelts netted them $600 dollars. As far as anyone knows, Billy never made another river passage. (Nelson, 1965, pp. 34-35) Galloway has since become known as the pioneer

of whitewater rafting with a revolutionary rowing style (the Galloway method) and boat design (the Galloway boat).

[50] Young **Victor Crosetti** volunteered and went to the front during WWI, serving in France in an artillery unit with another boy from the local forest, Ivan Brakovitch. Ivan, born in Austria, worked at Copper City until he enlisted at the commencement of US involvement. Ivan served with great valor and died a hero when he was hit by German shrapnel. Victor was badly injured in the war but survived, married, had three sons, and died in 1992 at age 99. ("Honor Roll," *Spokane Chronicle*, July 14, 1909)

[51] Gossett, *Beyond the Bend*, p. 85.

[52] Nelson, *We Never Got Away*, p. 36.

[53] Lyman, *The History of the Yakima Valley: Volume II*

[54] Nelson, *We Never Got Away*, 35-38.

[55] "Rich Deposits of Molybdenum," *Spokane Chronicle*, August 27, 1929.

[56] "$10,000 Plant in Offing," *Spokesman-Review*, September 12, 1929.

[57] C. Phillips Purdy, *Molybdenum Occurrences in Washington*, (Olympia: Olympic State Printing, 1954).

[58] Ray Foisy, interview by author, July 2016.

[59] Wayne S. Moen, *Preliminary Report on Mineral Resources of the Cougar Lake Limited Area*, (Olympia: Division of Mines and Geology Department of Conservation, 1962).

[60] **Cattle**, like all mammals, need salt to survive. When out on the range, ranchers need to supply salt—either loose or in blocks—to their animals.

[61] Gossett, *Beyond the Bend*.

[62] *Yakima Herald*, April 10, 1907.
   Other early **Copper City shareholders** were Mart Schichtol, Dan Sinclair, Josiah "Si" Fletcher, Allan Johnson, the brothers Morgan and Bruin Tuggle, P.J. Buwalda, Dr. John Nywening and Richard Strobach.

[63] Naches Ranger District, "Mother Lode of History," *Yakima Herald-Republic*, December 17, 1998.

[64] The **railroad never came to the Bumping River Valley**. The spur line was abandoned and the coal claims at Carleton Pass were never developed.

[65] Moen, *Preliminary Report on Mineral Resources of the Cougar Lake Limited Area*.

[66] The **Brick Saloon in Roslyn**, Washington could have been the inspiration for this contraption which one can see in the photograph showing a boxed water course running from the south side of building. Several of the Copper City miners were from the coal mines in Roslyn and might have built the spittoon as an ironic addition to their rough surroundings.

[67] Betty Jean Ford Gallant, interview by author, July 2015.

[68] Moen, *Preliminary Report on Mineral Resources of the Cougar Lake Limited Area.*

[69] Douglas Jenkins, Unpublished article, (Naches Ranger District, 1997).

[70] **Ira Ford's sled dogs** were from the Humane Society in Yakima. Betty Jean Ford remembers they had four in total, each with distinct personalities. Lady was the lead dog and was elegant and aloof. Mike was the strongest by far and was always in the wheel position. Pal was big and kind but did not like to pull and Boots was goofy and friendly.

[71] Much earlier, in 1916, **miners in the area asked for a post office at Bumping Lake**. Establishing a post office was a simple affair back then and permission was granted promptly with Jack Nelson as postmaster. (*Spokesman Review*, August 27, 1916) As a Fourth Class postmaster, he received the cancellations which did not amount to more than ten dollars a year. (Nelson, *We Never Got Away*, p. 69)

[72] Robert I. Ford, *The History of Goose Prairie and the Ira Ford Family,* (self published, 2003).

[73] Some of the **workers at Copper City** during the 30s and 40s were: Herb Teeter, Frank Crosetti (miners), Ray Dimmick (cook at Clara), Josiah "Si" Fletcher (sawmill), John Cossol (sold stock), Bud Simmons, Ralph Carmack, John Butler, Morgan Tuggle, Charlie Bedford, and two others named Art (maybe Hostellar or Grimes?) and "Egg".

The **first copper smelted** in 1913 (in Tacoma) from twelve hundred pounds of Copper City ore, came in at a respectable twelve percent. By the time transportation and smelting costs were subtracted from the returns, the profit left—and the first check cut for copper smelted from the east side of the mountains—was for a total of $3.47. (*Spokesman-Review*, October 22, 1913)

[74] S. W. Hobbs, *Report on the Copper Mining Company property, Bumping Lake Mining District, Yakima County, Washington,* 1942, https://pubs.usgs.gov/of/1943/0013/report.pdf, retrieved September 10, 2021.

CHAPTER SIX

[1] The historic **Yakima adjudication case** (Acquavella v Ecology) began in 1977 and issued its final decree on May 9, 2019. Superior Court Judge F. James Gavin has presided over the entire complicated process which sorted out water rights for nearly 2,500 individual users

and thirty major claimants on thirty-one tributary watersheds. Several appeals are pending as of 2021, so the case has still not completely concluded.

2 "Bumping News is Brought by Sloan," *Yakima Morning Herald*, August 17, 1915.

3 "Bumping Highway Funds Pinch Out," *Yakima Morning Herald*, June 11, 1922.
   Jack Nelson, *We Never Got Away*, (Yakima, Washington: Franklin Press, 1965).

4 *Bumping Lake Enlargement, Yakima Project: Environmental Impact Statement*, (United States Bureau of Reclamation, 1979).

5 Nelson, *We Never Got Away*.

6 There have been some suggestions that **Kitty Nelson sold bootleg liquor** at the Lodge during Prohibition. Not surprisingly, this claim has been hard to verify.
   State Senator Fred Redmon was one of those staples at the lodge at the Bumping Lake Resort. He along with his wife became lifetime friends of the Nelsons, writing letters to his friend until Jack died. (Ray Foisy, interview by Susan Summit Cyr, July 2016)
   One of several **judges** who left an impression upon Jack was State Supreme Court Chief Justice Steven Chadwick, who became a cherished acquaintance. Jack wrote, "Some of the finest hours in my life were spent listening, in front of the fireplace of our lodge, until late at night, to his philosophies of life and government." (Nelson, *We Never Got Away*)

7 Robert I. Ford, *The History of Goose Prairie and the Ira Ford Family*, (self published, 2003), p. 147.

8 Betty Jean Ford Gallant, interview by author, July 2015.
   The **restaurant china** *was* sturdy. The plates survived years of dishwashing at the Lodge and then were recycled to serve for many more years in another kitchen. When Kitty's old lodge was closed in 1946, she gave the entire collection to Kay Kershaw for use at her Double K Mountain Ranch, then being constructed. The thick chinaware was still being used in the early 1970s. (Franklin, interview, 2020)

9 Gretta Gossett, *Beyond the Bend, A History of the Nile Valley in Washington State*, (Fairfield, Washington: Ye Galleon Press, 1979), p. 408.

10 "Mountain Stream Summons Camper," *Yakima Morning Herald*, June 18, 1922.

11 *Yakima Daily Republic*, June 15, 1916.

12 "Bus Service to Bumping Likely," *Yakima Daily Republic*, June 23, 1926.

13 Ray Foisy, interview by author, July 2016.

14 Nelson, *We Never Got Away*.

[15] The **Fords in Goose Prairie kept a cow** that was named Kitty Belle. Betty Jean speculated that it was likely one of Lily's calves. (Gallant, interview, 2014)

[16] Nelson, *We Never Got Away*.

[17] Ibid.

[18] Ibid.

[19] "January Coldest Month of Record," *Yakima Morning Herald*, February 2, 1916.
"Now Expect to Open Road Through Cascades Tonight," *Yakima Daily Republic*, February 3, 1916.
"Bridge Goes Down on Bumping River," *Yakima Morning Herald*, February 6, 1916.

[20] "Open to Goose Prairie," *Yakima Morning Herald*, June 29, 1916.

[21] "Campers Are Few Along the Naches," *Yakima Morning Herald*, July 18, 1916.

[22] *Yakima Morning Herald*, January 16, 1918.

[23] Nelson, *We Never Got Away*, p. 139.

[24] "Road to Bumping Interests Public," *Yakima Morning Herald*, May 31, 1918, p. 5.

[25] "County Creeks Get Over Million Fish," *Yakima Daily Republic*, May 18, 1918, p. 1.
For decades, **trout** were transported into the backcountry on the backs of horses and mules. Fingerlings were placed in metal milk cans that were slung over pack animals' backs for the long journey into the mountains. The water needed to be changed regularly in the canisters for the baby fish to survive. Packers heading to the lakes above Bumping usually stopped at the Nelson's for the night, to rest themselves and allow the fish to refresh in the large horse trough at the resort. In the morning, they would be poured back into the cans to resume their journey up the mountain.

[26] "Pack Horse Used to Bumping Lake," *Yakima Daily Republic*, June 29, 1918.

[27] "Stone Raking is Next Sunday Job," *Yakima Morning Herald*, July 30, 1918.
Apparently, the **appeal for help** worked. More than a dozen cars carrying Yakima businessmen "armed with picks and shovels" were reported to be heading up to the trouble spots on the road. ("Will Work on Bumping Lake Road," *Spokesman-Review*, August 4, 1918.)

[28] "Refuses to Guard Reclamation Dam," *Yakima Morning Herald*, June 18, 1918, p. 1.

[29] Nelson, *We Never Got Away*.
All travel to and from the resort during the war years was along the backside of the dam over the old construction bridge on the outlet conduit or on the river gauge road just east of the resort that followed the river down to the main road near Bumping Crossing.

Fred G. Redmon became a Washington State senator in 1964 serving the 14th District in Yakima. He then served as a Yakima County commissioner and was the first chairman of the State Transportation Commission. The soaring Interstate 82 bridge at Selah Creek is named after Redmon.

In 2019, I came across a **copy of *We Never Got Away* inscribed to Mr. and Mrs. Fred Redmon** and signed by Jack Nelson. In the book was a typewritten note from Fred to Jack describing being run off the dam by him fifty years prior and celebrating the same number of years of shared friendship since that time.

[30] Nelson, *We Never Got Away*, p. 155-158.

[31] "Trip to Bumping is Thrilling One," *Yakima Daily Republic*, July 13, 1918.

[32] Clayne R. Jensen and Steven P. Guthrie, *Outdoor Recreation in America*, (Champaign: Human Kinetics, 2006)

[33] In 1899, **Mount Rainier National Park** was created out of the "Mount Rainier Forest Reserve" which was carved out from part of the earlier "Pacific Forest Reserve." It was the fifth National Park in the country.

[34] Gossett, *Beyond the Bend*, p. 221.

[35] "Agency Organization," *Forest History Society*, https://foresthistory.org/research-explore/us-forest-service-history/policy-and-law/agency-organization/, retrieved September 10, 2021.

[36] "Huckleberry Pickers are Still Busy at Gold Hill," *Yakima Daily Republic*, August 22, 1925.

[37] Gifford Pinchot, *Breaking New Ground*, (New York: Harcourt Brace, 1947).

[38] "Mt. Baker-Snoqualmie National Forest History," *USDA Forest Service*, https://www.fs.usda.gov/detail/mbs/learning/history-culture/?cid=FSBDEV7_001647, retrieved September 10, 2021.

[39] Gossett, *Beyond the Bend*, p. 233.

Other **early rangers** were Cap Simmons, Walter Reddon, Frank Dice, H. L. "Jim" Hurd, G. F. Allen, and Oliver Klingensmith. Henry Sedge was the first forest ranger for the Mount Rainier Forest Reserve, east of the crest. William Worrell was an early Forest Guard. (Gossett, *Beyond the Bend*, 233) Fred Hall was an early packer for the rangers, along with Harry Pruitt and Packey Howatt. (Nelson, *We Never Got Away*, p. 174)

[40] Gossett, *Beyond the Bend*, p. 231.

[41] "Crossed the Mountains on Foot in January," *Enumclaw Herald*, January 29, 1925.

[42] "Snow Jaunt in Mountains Not an Easy Trip," *Yakima Daily Republic*, February 3, 1925.

[43] "Local Men Hike Over Pass Route," *Enumclaw Herald*, March 25, 1926.

[44] A few of the earliest **Cascadian members** were Lex Maxwell who largely designed the American Ridge Ski Bowl, Louis Albrecht, and Dave Mahre, the father of Olympic champion skiers Phil and Steve and Mahre. (Ray Foisy, interview, July 2016)

[45] Edgar G. Coursen, "The Mount Adams Outing of the Cascadians," *Mazama: A Record of Mountaineering in the Pacific Northwest,* Volume 6, Issue 2, (1921): 46-47.

[46] Claude E. Rusk, *Tales of a Western Mountaineer,* (Seattle: The Mountaineers, 1978), p. 257.
"Ascent of Mount Adams is a Great Feat," *Seattle Post-Intelligencer*, August 28, 1921.

[47] Although these and other **wintertime Cascade crossings** seem impressive, it should be remembered that local Native Americans had long traveled over the passes and in wintertime, on snowshoes. One Cowlitz tribal member, **Mary Kiona**, regularly crisscrossed Cowlitz pass over the snow, to visit her relatives in the Tieton area. She carried her supplies in a large "burden basket" kept in place on her back by a wide strap across her forehead and wore snowshoes on her feet. (Bentley, 2018) The hikes must have been good for her. Kiona reportedly lived past the age of 117.

[48] "Yakima Snowshoe Hikers Go Across Snow Ridge and Get to Paradise in Five Days," *Yakima Daily Republic*, March 25, 1927.
"Girl Hiker Finds Cabins Under Snowbanks," *Spokesman-Review*, April 17, 1927.

[49] William O. Douglas, *Of Men and Mountains,* (New York: Harper and Brothers Publishers, 1950), p. 279.

[50] "Marathon of the Mountains," *Cascadian Annual*, 1980, 6, http://www.alpenglow.org/ski-history/notes/period/cascadian/cascadian-1980-89.html#cascadian-1980-p. 6, retrieved September 10, 2021.

[51] At 8,184 feet in elevation, **Gilbert Peak** is the tallest mountain in Yakima County. The full name, Mr. Curtis Gilbert Peak, honors the outdoorsman whose story follows in the text.

[52] Ibid.

[53] Douglas, *Of Men and Mountains.*

[54] **Truitt died of meningococcal meningitis** at just fifty-four years old while Gilbert died of a heart attack at fifty-three.

[55] Douglas, *Of Men and Mountains*, p. 292.

[56] "Ski Tourney Thrills Mountain Crowd," *Tacoma Tribune*, August 5, 1917.
"Girl on Skiis Jumps 36 Feet," *Tacoma Times*, July 30, 1917.

[57] "Ladies to Travel Trails on Rainier," *Yakima Morning Herald*, June 15, 1915, p. 4.

[58] "Answer Call of the Outdoors," *Spokane Chronicle*, August 7, 1926.

[59] "Spokane Woman Scales Shuksan's Icy Peak," *Spokesman-Review*, August 28, 1927. "Picture Exhibit Will Open Soon," *Spokesman-Review*, January 15, 1933.

[60] Chic Burge, "The Early Years of the Spokane Mountaineers," *Out There Outdoors*, March 13, 2015, https://outthereoutdoors.com/the-early-years-of-the-spokane-mountaineers-1915-1935/, retrieved September 10, 2021.

[61] "Spokane Mountaineers Proud of Twenty Year's Record of Club," *Spokesman-Review*, January 6, 1935.

[62] Nelson, *We Never Got Away*, p. 154.

CHAPTER SEVEN

[1] Betty Jean Ford Gallant, interview by author, August 2016.

It is clear that **Kitty constructed and managed the first boat facilities at Bumping Lake**. Very early on, she maintained at the least a floating dock on the northwest shoreline close to the resort. From that dock she rented boats to visitors and always kept a vessel for her own use as well. As early as 1915, there were reportedly twenty-five boats at the lake.

Later, more substantial structures were built further south at the **present marina site**. It is likely that the Nelsons contracted for and owned the facility. Though it is said that Hammond built all of the boats and in the beginning, Webb managed the facility, neither man were owners. Webb handled the boat rentals for the Nelsons and kept a small percentage of each rental as salary. Hammond took over the marina in the mid-30s perhaps buying it at that point.

In April of 1931, **Webb** was preparing for the summer season by testing his boat. When the balky motor died, he unscrewed the gas tank's lid and lit a match—presumably to be able to see inside for fuel. A fellow fisherman put out the resulting blaze with a bailing can and Webb put himself out by jumping overboard. Doctors later pronounced his burns not to be serious. ("Lights Match Over Tank," *Spokesman-Review*, April 28, 1931)

[2] Ray Foisy, interview by author, July 2016.

[3] Betty Jean Ford Gallant, interview by author, July 2016.

[4] "Concreting Big Ditch," *Spokesman-Review*, November 7, 1913, p. 10.

[5] "Bad Trip For Warden," *Spokesman-Review*, March 28, 1915.

[6] "Bridge Goes Down on Bumping River," *Yakima Morning Herald*, February 16, 1916.

[7] The new **County Game Warden E. C. Greenman** was enthusiastic about improving fishing all over the county and planted millions of young trout into local mountain streams and lakes. Bumping Lake received 500,000 Lake Mackinaw trout for the 1918 season. ("Millions of Trout for Fishing Holes," *Yakima Daily Republic*, May 18, 1918) 30,000 steelhead were planted in 1919 followed by one million Mackinaws in 1920. By the 1940s, kokanee salmon (or silvers) became popular, with Game Department stocking the lake with millions of young silvers in the first half of the decade alone. The bulk of stocking during the 1950s and to the present has been rainbow trout with some cutthroat as well. 4,000 rainbows were planted in Bumping Lake in 2020.

[8] **Indiscriminate stocking** of large numbers of fish often negatively affected the ecology of the waterways in which they were introduced. Invertebrate and amphibious populations suffered, and some native fish species were outcompeted by introduced species. Early on, the short-term human interests were valued above all other considerations. Present day fish and game departments are beginning to have a more holistic approach when managing waterways and their inhabitants—while still maximizing recreational opportunities.

[9] "Sportsmen Want Trap For Suckers at Lake," *Spokesman-Review*, July 13, 1939.

[10] "Wapato's Frank Bennett Retains Liars' Championship," *Spokesman-Review*, March 24, 1948, p. 16.

[11] "Article Describes Fish Eradication," *Spokane Chronicle*, December 17, 1951.
    The poison **rotenone** is derived from the roots of a variety of tropical plants in the legume family. Rotenone lethally interferes with fish's and other animal's ability to use oxygen. It is widely used as a natural insecticide in the garden as well as a pesticide for control of pests on pets. If ingested at a high concentration it can be toxic to humans and other animals as well. Rotenone is still being used in the United States to "rehabilitate" lakes and other bodies of water when a new balance of fishes is desired.

[12] "Bumping Reservoir Restored as Fighting Sport Fish Area," *Spokesman-Review*, December 15, 1951.

[13] Betty Jean Ford Gallant, interview by author, July 2015.

[14] "Bumping Reservoir Restored as Fighting Sport Fish Area," *Spokesman-Review*, December 15, 1951.

[15] **Betty Jean Ford Gallant** wishes that rotenone had never been used in the lake. Prior to that time, she maintains the "sucker trap" at Bumping Lake worked perfectly well and kept numbers of "trash fish" in check. Installed in the shallow area southeast of the dam, it was a one-way zigzag apparatus that caught chubs and suckers by the thousands. Those fish were regularly collected in burlap bags by lower valley residents to be consumed as a tasty—if bony—free protein source. (Betty Jean Ford Gallant, interview by author, August 2014)

[16] **Rogue campers** are not a new phenomenon. As far back as 1919, the Forest Service wrote:

"Where large numbers of people flock out on the forested highways…there is greatly increased danger [of fire]. The careless young folk and the inexperienced clerk with his family must all eat their lunch, enjoy the cool of the woods; and human nature away from the restraints of city police reverts to past barbaric instincts and revels in an abandonment of society's restrictions. A disregard of social demands is inherent in the city chap turned loose…Quickly enough, when brought into contact with the evidence of human handiwork in the improved campground he becomes respectable, appreciative and sympathetic." (Holstine, *An Historical Overview of the Wenatchee National Forest Washington*)

[17] In the **Yakima Valley**, migrant farm workers and seasonal pickers were hit especially hard. Living in rough hand-built shacks or outside in tents—sometimes for years—without running water or electricity, desperate families from the Midwest gathered together in squatter camps and "shacktowns." One hop picker photographed by Dorthea Lange said she "wanted to get out of this living like a dog." (Whitey, 2010)

[18] **Tom Fife's will** holds some interesting anomalies. In it, he specified arrangements for his funeral, asking to be buried on his land on Rattlesnake Creek in the Nile Valley. It is unknown why the change was made, but Tom's body surely rests not there but next to his father's in the tiny graveyard in Goose Prairie. The "neat and substantial iron fence" that Fife asked for was also not supplied; the boundary of his burial plot is simple wood pickets. And though Fife left substantial real estate holdings to his attorney James O. Cull and his children, to his half brothers and sister he left a tidy sum of just ten dollars apiece. Cull served as Fife's executor and was one of the most notable lawyers in Yakima, having held the office of city attorney in 1904. Fife's will was signed by witness George S. Rankin, an irrigation pioneer and one of the most prominent businessmen in Yakima at the time. He was Cull's business partner in the highly successful Selah and Moxee Canal Company.

[19] "Washington News," *San Juan Islander*, August 31, 1907.

[20] "Jack Nelson Will Build Big Hotel," *Spokesman-Review*, July 6, 1922.
    It is said that the **Goose Prairie sawmill** was moved down from Copper City, having outlived its usefulness there. (Gossett, *Beyond the Bend*) The mill operated only for a short time in the Prairie and shut down during the Depression. It may be that the machinery was then moved (back) up to Copper City since it appears it was operating there in the late 1930s.

[21] Betty Jean Ford Gallant, interview by author, August 2016.

[22] Jack Nelson, *A Brief History of Uncle Tom*, (unpublished, 1933).

[23] Robert I. Ford, *The History of Goose Prairie and the Ira Ford Family* (self published, 2003).

[24] Ibid., p. 37.

[25] "Will Provide School," *Spokane Chronicle*, June 26, 1931.

[26] "Nobody Will Claim this Yakima School," *Spokane Chronicle*, March 26, 1936.

[27] "School to Open," *Spokesman Review*, September 13, 1938.

Betty Jean Ford's recollection of the **teachers at the Goose Prairie school** is as follows: Margarita Bonjourm (1930-31), Dorothy Johnson (1931-32), Helen Welk (1932-1933), Mabel Keister (1933-34 and 1934-35), Sam Hansberger may have substituted near this time, Mr. Charles Thomas (Carlington) (1935-36), Miss Tressa Roskamp (1936-37), and Mrs. Jessie May Hornfield (1937-39). The school was permanently closed in 1940.

[28] Ford, *The History of Goose Prairie*, pp. 52-53.

[29] *The Klamath News*, April 22, 1924.

[30] Gallant, interview, 2016.

[31] Nelson, *We Never Got Away*.

[32] Christine E. Pfaff, *The Bureau of Reclamation's Civilian Conservation Corps Legacy: 1933-1942* (Denver: United States Department of the Interior, Bureau of Reclamation, 2010), p. 7.

[33] During the first quarter of the century, the **Forest Service did not have a budget for recreation** at all. The "Sanitation and Fire Prevention" fund was the only money allotted by Congress that could be used for recreational infrastructure. For the entire Northern Pacific Region that sum amounted to $7,500 dollars annually in the 1920s. Administrator Fred Cleator later wrote, "The division of this $7,500 per year among a thousand or more needy projects scattered here and there among some 25 million acres meant we had to be very canny and use the money to buy a few boards, nails, bridge bolts, a little water pipe, and cement. The Ranger and such of his helpers as could be spared cleared the brush, dug the garbage holes, toilet pits, ditches, fire breaks, and built the structures as time allowed." (Rosalie Ferri, 2006)

[34] Craig Holstine, *An Historical Overview of the Wenatchee National Forest Washington* (United States Department of Agriculture, 1994).

Although **Clinton C. Clarke** is often called the **father of the Pacific Crest Trail** for his advocacy of the 2,638-mile-long trace, two local sections of it were already built before his influence was felt. The idea was first articulated in 1926 by a school superintendent in Bellingham, Washington, **Catherine Montgomery**. She described to Mountaineer Joseph Hazard her vision of a trail that would run along the ridges of the Sierra Nevada and Cascade Mountain ranges from Canada to Mexico, similar to the Appalachian Trail in the East.

The first section of what would later become the Pacific Crest Trail was already begun in 1920 when ranger Fred Cleator surveyed the route for the Oregon Skyline Trail. Then, as Supervisor of Recreation for the region, he turned his attention to the Cascade Crest Trail in Washington, a 531-mile-long stretch which was surveyed in 1935. CCC crews completed most of that trail's construction, then added local connector trails to the main route. (Holstine, 1994) Large trail sections were later added in California, but it was not until 1993 that the last small section of trail was acquired to finally link an unbroken trail from border to border.

[35] Many of the buildings from **Camp Naches** still remain where they were built, clustered on both sides of Highway 410 near Cliffdell. The compound is now called Chinook Pass Work Center. It is used as needed as a fire camp serving as a command center and camp for wildfire crews.

[36] Edwin G. Hill, *In the Shadow of the Mountain: The Spirit of the CCC* (Pullman: Washington State University Press, 1990).

[37] Ibid.

[38] "Ranger on Naches Station Tightens Guard on Forests," *Yakima Morning Herald*, September 2, 1934.
The physical **legacy that the CCC left** is particularly strong in the Northwest which saw the full expression of the rustic style that was consciously developed during this era. Dubbed the Cascadian style, designers utilized local materials (especially native stone and timber) on a grand scale that reflected the scale of the surrounding natural environment.

[39] "Discover Quake Damaged Bridge," *Spokesman-Review*, December 11, 1939.

[40] "American River Guard Station," (U. S. Department of Agriculture Forest Service: 2020), https://www.fs.usda.gov/recarea/okawen/recarea/?recid=58105, retrieved September 10, 2021.

[41] Christine E. Pfaff, *The Bureau of Reclamation's Civilian Conservation Corps Legacy: 1933-1942* (Denver: U.S. Department of the Interior, Bureau of Reclamation, 2010).

[42] **Logging terms** are many and quite specific. *To fall* a tree is to cut it down. *To buck* one is to cut a felled and de-limbed tree into shorter lengths. *A spar tree* is a tall, strong tree to which rigging is attached for hauling felled trees with cables. *A bull block* is the main pulley (or encased pulleys) used to drag the trees.

[43] Nelson, *We Never Got Away.*

[44] Ibid., p. 162.

[45] **Jack Nelson served as LEM** for three summers with three CCC companies. They were in 1935: Company No. 297, 1936: Company No. 572, and 1937: Company No. 4752.

[46] Nelson, *We Never Got Away*, p. 164.

[47] The logging crew **water boy** was responsible for providing water to the working crews during their shifts as well as keeping the oil bottles full. Each sawyer would typically have a bottle filled with kerosene to lubricate his saw and remove sticky resin from the blade as he was cutting.

[48] Nelson, *We Never Got Away*, p. 165-168.

[49] Douglas, *Of Men and Mountains*, p. 16.

[50] Nelson, *We Never Got Away*, p. 160.

[51] Hill, *In the Shadow of the Mountains*, p. 157.

[52] Pfaff, *The Bureau of Reclamation's Civilian Conservation Corps Legacy.*

[53] America's involvement in **World War II marked the end of the CCC**. Men and money were needed for the war effort and the nation's finances were finally starting to stabilize. "With deep regret," the U.S. House and Senate terminated the CCC on July 30, 1942. (Hill, 138) Although expensive and initially politically controversial, the CCC was a resounding success with its participants from the beginning and quickly garnered enormous public support. In 1940, Rep. Clyde Ellis testified, *"I think that in all of the seven years of the New Deal nothing has been thought out and inaugurated that has more completely met the overwhelming approval of the American people than the CCC. Its benefits are both direct and indirect, are both immediate and remote and no doubt will be felt even in the next half of this century."* (Pfaff) The program cost over three billion dollars but performed over two billion dollars' worth of work while providing jobs and training to more than 2.5 million people. (Pfaff, p. 15)

[54] Holstine, *An Historical Overview of the Wenatchee National Forest Washington*, 9.13.

[55] "Gold Hill is to be Rushed," *Yakima Morning Herald*, August 17, 1910.

[56] Robert Danielson, *The Road with the Grandest View: Surveys and Construction of the Chinook Pass Highway 1892-1934* (Calgary: self published, 2013).

[57] Ibid.

[58] Ibid.

[59] Maurice Helland, *Our Valley, Too* (Yakima: self published, 1976).

[60] Danielson, *The Road with the Grandest View*, p. 107.
    At least **one road crew seems to have been a dream team for the contractor firm Meyers & Goulter**. The group of men regularly worked ten, and even twelve-hour days, though they were only being paid for eight. Despite the hard work, they were a spirited group. For evening entertainment, some had organized a band consisting of their cook, Mrs. John Stevens, on the comb and her husband and others on dishpans and other found instruments. They called themselves the "Wildcats from Hell's Crossing." (Hobbs V. , 1954)
    Workers were paid by daily voucher to be redeemed only when the job was completed. Since there was little money at the camp and one pastime was gambling, vouchers were used as gambling tokens, and it was said that the unlucky men came out at the end of the season as poor as when they started. (Helland, 1976)

[61] Ford, *The History of Goose Prairie*.

[62]   Ibid.

[63]   Danielson, *The Road with the Grandest View*, p. 110.

[64]   Ibid.

[65]   "Dedicate New Park Highway," *Tacoma Ledger*, September 14, 1931.

[66]   "Chinook Holds Beauty Crown," *Yakima Sunday Herald*, May 8, 1949.

[67]   There has been some speculation that these **cabins could have been moved over from the closed Bumping Lake CCC camp**, but it is unlikely. There were no structures in that camp that remotely match the little rental buildings. They seem to have been built as vacation rentals.

[68]   Ford Gallant, interview, 2015.

CHAPTER EIGHT

[1]   "Reclamation Men on Skees," *Spokesman-Review*, January 11, 1913.

[2]   Naches Ranger District, "American Ridge Ski Bowl," (Naches, Washington: 2018).

[3]   Betty Jean Ford Gallant, interview by author, August 2016.

[4]   E. John Allen, *From Skisport to Skiing: One hundred years of an American Sport, 1840-1940* (Amherst: University of Massachusettes Press, 1993).

[5]   C. Pratt, "The Gold Hill Experience," Alpenglow Ski History: Cascadian Annual, 1980-89, http://www.alpenglow.org/ski-history/notes/period/cascadian/cascadian-1980-89.html# cascadian-1985-p. 8, retrieved on September 10, 2021.

[6]   H. Bowlby, "Weekend at Scout Cabin," *Cascade Annual*, 3, 1939.

[7]   Roderick Peattie, *The Cascades, Mountains of the Pacific Northwest* (New York: Vanguard Press, 1949).
     Crystal Bowl, at the head of Silver Creek, was named by the Hesseys and was later developed as the Crystal Mountain Ski Area in 1962. The old prospector's cabin used by the Cascadians was finally replaced in 1960 by a new building designed by Otto Lagervall (who was the founder of Yakima Industries builders of the cartop equipment carriers we use and love). It was christened the C.F. Truitt Memorial Cabin. The Cascadians also owned a portable rope tow which they hauled all over the pass area depending on snow conditions and road access. They even obtained permission from the Forest Service to operate the tow at Lake Tipsoo in 1940 which may have led to the Forest Service considering putting in a trial ski resort there in 1949. The Forest Service, in conjunction with the State Highway

department, planned to build a ski area at Chinook Pass with four rope tows, a ranger and first aid station and parking for 350 to 400 hundred cars. (Peattie, 1949), (Hassell, 1940), ("Ski Area Previewed," *Tacoma News Tribune*, October 29, 1949)

[8]   The **American Ridge Ski Bowl** is sometimes erroneously referred to as American *River* Ski Bowl or even American River Lodge or Resort. The American River Lodge/Resort was a separate vacation facility once located nearby on the American River.

[9]   Carrie Covey and Mike Hiler, "Skiing American Ridge," *Signpost Magazine*, 1986.

[10]   J.W. Lundin, *Early Skiing in the Washington Cascades, Part 1: 1913-1937*, January 30, 2013, http://www.historylink.org/File/10312.
     "Jess Baird wins "B" Jump at Yakima Ski Tournament," *Wenatchee World*, January 18, 1937.

[11]   D. Zimmer, "The Ski Tournament." *Cascadian Annual*, 1940, p. 4.

[12]   Naches Ranger District, "American Ridge Ski Bowl," (Naches, Washington: 2018).
     Edwin G. Hill, *In the Shadow of the Mountain: The Spirit of the CCC* (Pullman: Washington State   University Press, 1990).

[13]   Covey and Hiler, "Skiing American Ridge."

[14]   Apparently, there was some sort of commercial structure at the site prior to the **American River Resort**. Gretta Gossett wrote that the American River *Hotel* was established by Alonzo Walters (Gossett, *Beyond the Bend*, p. 400) and there is a mention of an American River Hotel in the Enumclaw Courier on August 12, 1927. It was advertised as the American River Resort as early as July 1932 when it was managed by Sandy Sandberg. Signage indicates that it was known as the American River Lodge in the '40s and '50s. Fred Squires and his wife Crystal owned and operated the American River facility in the 1950s; other owners were the Ingrams and the Richards with the last owners before the property burned being Steve and Dee Kincaid. (Ford, interview, 2016)

[15]   Robert I. Ford, *The History of Goose Prairie and the Ira Ford Family*, (self published, 2003).

[16]   Covey and Hiler, "Skiing American Ridge."

[17]   Both the new lodges, **Whistlin' Jack and the American River Resort**, were graced by soaring stone fireplaces constructed from local stone and mortared together by the same master stonemason, Jimenez, who worked on Normandie.

[18]   The **Bumping Lake Summer Home tract** was initially administered through the Bureau of Reclamation. In 1950 the Bureau, seeking to get out of the summer home tract lease business, turned over the management of this tract (and many others bordering federal reservoirs) to the Forest Service who retains control to the present.

The road that serves the tract originally ended at the Bumping Lake Resort. At about the same time the marina was constructed and the summer homes started to be built, the road was extended south to the point where it ends today at the trailhead for the Bumping Lake Trail (#971). The road extension was originally called the Lake Homes Road.

The very **first vacation home built on the lake** was not part of the summer home tract. Sometime in the 1920s, the Nelsons' good friend Ross Dent built a rather extravagant cabin just past the couple's resort at what was then the end of the road. It had a fine view of the lake but was unfortunately located at the base of a steep slope on the northwest shore. In late January 1935, a massive snowslide slammed into the cabin and reduced the entire structure to kindling. ("Slide Crushes $4000 Home," *Spokesman-Review*, January 25, 1935) It was said that his pillows flew all the way to the dam. Ironically, though Dent was an insurance agent, he did not carry insurance on his $4000 dollar home.

[19] Naches Ranger Station, personal correspondence, August 2019.

[20] Nadine Nutley Maykut, interview by author, August 2018.

[21] "Travel Limited in Woods Area," *Spokesman-Review*, April 6, 1942.

[22] Horace Cooper, letter to Betty Jean Ford, July 6, 1943, Naches, Washington.

[23] Jack Nelson, Letter to J. S. Moore, March 14, 1944, Bumping Lake, Washington.

[24] Paul Taylor, Assistant Engineer, *Inspections Bumping Lake Dam*. (Yakima: Bureau of Reclamation, 1921-1947).

[25] **Pat Ford's contract** paid $2,400 dollars per year. Jack's salary had been substantially less.

[26] "Bureau to Lose Jovial Worker," *Spokesman-Review*, September 30, 1946, p. 1.

[27] **Pat Ford crafted two versions of a "snow machine"** in the forties. The first model looked like tractor with long treads and was difficult to steer. The second was much more nimble. Ed Bedford of Goose Prairie towed local kids behind a "snow mobile" of his own design and occasionally would drag them far enough up the Deep Creek road for them to ski back to Goose Prairie. (Ray Foisy, interview by Susan Summit Cyr, July 2016)

[28] Even though **elk were hunted** with enthusiasm in the fall, it seems as if residents generally took pity on errant elk in the wintertime. After a small band of elk was discovered stranded in deep snow in the winter of 1946, Jack appealed to the state game supervisor for help. Fred VanArsdol arranged for an airdrop of hay via a C-47 cargo plane from the Walla Walla army air base. Second Lieutenant W.A. Weid served as "hay bombardier" for the seventeen bales which Jack later reported fell exactly where they were needed for the hungry elk. ("Bumping Lake Elk Fed Well on Hay," *La Grande Observer*, February 14, 1946) ("Feed Dropped to Hungry Elk," *Spokesman-Review*, Septermber 15, 1946)

[29] "Dam Caretaker and Son Narrowly Escape Lake," *Spokesman-Review*, February 23, 1950.

[30] Robert Ford, *The History of Goose Prairie.*

[31] Ibid, p. 87.

[32] Stanley Rasmussen, "British War Bride," *Spokesman-Review*, March 21, 1948.

[33] It seems as if this **hydroelectric power plant** was not the Nelsons' first. The couple may have generated some electricity for their original resort from the energy of falling water. Though there is no documentation of the system or when it might have been installed, there are convenient clues to its existence. At exactly the same time that the Nelsons were removing the old lodge from Reclamation land and needing to clear all of their material, Jack was trying to sell a four-foot diameter Pelton wheel, with pulleys and control valve, intake pipe and even 300 feet of "used casing pipe." In other words, he had a surplus power plant he needed to get rid of. Even though it was advertised as "a bargain at $250 dollars," the equipment probably did not find a buyer since the remains of some of the system are still in place. (Classified Ads, *Spokesman-Review*, June 6, 1947)

The **little creek** that was apparently dammed to create a reservoir of water to ensure proper head pressure still holds, though the wooden barrier leaks like a sieve. The six inch penstock connected to it still carries water toward the river, though the rest of the system has been lost and the water spills back into Bumping River, unused.

[34] Jack Nelson, *We Never Got Away*, 155.

[35] In 1954 or 1956, **Pat Ford** jumped at chance to transfer to Lake Cle Elum which meant his family could be together year 'round. Pat put his trusty Weasel up for sale and packed his belongings. Tom Kern, with his wife Georgie, took over as the next dam tender at the Lake. Fred Schott and his wife Sue followed Kern as the fourth dam tender at Bumping Lake.

[36] Paul Taylor, Bureau of Reclamation Assistant Engineer, *Bumping Lake Dam Inspection*, November 23, 1945.

[37] Bob Hansen, "Yakima Reclamation Aid of 35 Years to Quit," *Seattle Post Intelligencer* September 21, 1946, p. 9.

[38] "Woman Catches Record Trout," *Spokesman-Review*, July 19, 1920.

[39] Nancy Cooke, interview by author, July 20, 2013.

[40] Nelson, *We Never Got Away*, p. 63.

[41] Sadly, **Frances and Emmett Higgins' union** was not long lasting. Emmett died just two years after they were married, at only forty-seven years old.

CHAPTER NINE

[1] *Yakima Daily Republic*, August 10, 1910.

[2] Gerald W. Williams, *The USDA Forest Service: The First Century* (Washington, DC: USDA Forest Service Office of Communication, 2005).

Interestingly, there are newspaper articles noting **fires burning near Bumping Lake** in 1908 and 1909 in addition to 1910. Were small fires much more common in the past and were they simply unnoted before there was significant development in the area or were they occurring as a result of that development? Or were these blazes intentionally set as part of the Yakama people's huckleberry field maintenance?

There are also records of a fire in the 1940s in the Red Rock Creek area in the Upper Bumping drainage and a few small fires made the papers through the years. But the Bumping River Valley as a whole has, for the most part, been spared catastrophic fire for at least the last century and a half.

[3] Gretta Gossett, *Beyond the Bend* (Fairfield, Washington: Ye Galleon Press, 1979), p. 307.

[4] Claude E. Rusk, *Tales of a Western Mountaineer* (Seattle: The Mountaineers, 1978).

[5] Fred G. Plummer, *Forest Conditions in the Cascade Range, Washington* (Washington DC, Government Printing Office, 1902).

[6] Williams, *The USDA Forest Service The First Century.*

[7] Robert I. Ford, *The History of Goose Prairie and the Ira Ford Family* (self published, 2003).

[8] In part because of the **high volume of timber being harvested** from the Naches Ranger District, protection of the forest from fire became a high priority. F.H. "Spike" Armstrong, District Ranger from 1958 to 1965, was particularly aggressive in preserving marketable timber. His fire suppression crews were poised to head into the mountains when lightening was still striking, assembling at the station before fires were even identified. Most were put out within the first few days of being spotted. (Phipps, 2021)

Notable fires in the Bumping River watershed at the time were the American Lake Fire in 1957, Old Baldy fires in 1963 and '64, and the Thunder Creek fire of 1968. Many fires were held to just a few acres, the Thunder Creek fire was larger at 70 plus acres. (Marcott, 2021)

[9] Gossett, *Beyond the Bend*, p. 321.

[10] Ibid., p. 327.

[11] The **Forest Service**, with considerable help from the **CCC**, built more than 8,000 **lookout structures** in the United States in the 1930s. Some 680 of those were in Washington State, of which approximately one hundred still stand. About thirty are still manned but the historic fire detection system has largely been replaced by planes, satellite imagery, live-

streaming cameras, and drones. (Garrison, no date)

[12] "Fire Tower History," USDA Forest Service Northern Region, https://www.fs.usda.gov/detail/r1/recreation/?cid=fsp5_030804, retrieved September 10, 2021.

[13] Gossett, *Beyond the Bend*, p. 313.

[14] Fred Beckey, *A Range of Glaciers: The Exploration and Survey of the Northern Cascade Range*, (Portland, Oregon: Oregon Historical Society Press, 2003), p. 409.

Bob and Pat Ford built one such access trail at the south end of Bumping Lake. A lightning-caused fire was threatening to blow up in the Red Rock Creek area. Forest Road 1800 had just been bulldozed into the Upper Bumping River area, but there was no path yet from the end of the road to the Bumping River trail. Ranger Cooper asked the boys to do the work. Over several days they worked with Pat blazing the trail, and Bob swamping it out. Their trail, Fish Lake #970, still serves hikers heading to the Bumping River Falls and into the back country. About a half a mile in, the trail leads up and over the roots of one of the largest Douglas firs in the entire county.

[15] The most common **design of fire lookouts** in the Northwest was the "L" Series built in the 1930s to 1950s. The buildings were available as pre-fabricated kits from a Vancouver, Washington company and were designed to be easily packed by mules to remote mountain tops where they would be assembled. (Duff, 2013)

The **first communication** between towers and stations was by means of "heliograph" which was a device that used two mirrors to reflect sunlight in order to send Morse code messages. Telephones replaced the heliographs which were in turn replaced by portable radios after WWII. (Fire Tower History, 2020)

[16] Ford, *The History of Goose Prairie*, p. 66.

[17] Timothy Egan, *The Big Burn: Teddy Roosevelt and the Fire that Saved America* (Boston: Houghton-Mifflin, 2009).

Jeff LaLande, "Forest Fires of 1910," *The Oregon Encyclopedia,* https://oregonencyclopedia.org/articles/forest_fires_of_1910/#.W1k74NJKg2x, retrieved September 10, 2021.

[18] Adam Sowards, "Wildfire Suppresion in Wilderness: A Decades old Conundrum," *High Country News*, August 29, 2018, https://www.hcn.org/articles/reckoning-with-history-wildfire-suppression-in-wilderness-a-decades-old-conundrum, retrieved September 10, 2021.

CHAPTER TEN

[1] **Yakima citizens raised $300** dollars and the Yakima Game Commission kicked in another $300 dollars to relocate the elk. The state of Wyoming charged just five dollars a head to round up and load the animals while the railroad made a token charge for freighting them. (Nelson, *We Never Got Away*, p. 58)

[2]   Maurice Helland, *Our Valley, Too* (Yakima: self-published, 1976).

[3]   John V. Ellis, "Notes from Bumping Lake, Yakima County, Washington," *The Murrelet*, January 17, 1927, p. 17.

[4]   **Elk** once roamed much of current Washington State, but populations had dwindled, and the native Roosevelt elk had largely disappeared from this part of the Northwest by the time white settlers arrived. Their decline was probably climate or habitat induced, rather than human caused, and linked to similar declines of bison and bighorn sheep. The suitable habitat for elk contributed at least in part, to their rapid expansion once the Rocky Mountain elk were transplanted to the area in the twenties.

[5]   We were lucky to have seen the magnificent **mountain goat**. Native to the Cascades, goat populations have been in a steady decline for the past fifty years. Washington State herds are down between seventy and ninety percent in the past few decades. There may be several factors in play, but several studies have shown that hunting, even at seemingly low levels is the leading cause. It may be that this unique North American mammal is especially sensitive to harvesting pressure and should no longer be allowed to be hunted at all. (Gay 2010) (Spring 1976)

[6]   Jack Nelson, *We Never Got Away*, (Yakima: Franklin Press, 1965).

[7]   Isabelle Lynn, "Year 'Round in the Mountains," *The Mountaineer Annual*: 1963, https://www.mountaineers.org/about/history/the-mountaineer-annuals/indexes-annuals-maos/the-mountaineer-1961.

[8]   Mort Cathro, "Spinsters Run Isolated Dude Ranch," *Oakland Tribune*, September 8, 1968.

[9]   **Kay Kershaw and Pat Kane** were business partners, best friends, and almost certainly lovers. In a time when homosexual couples were not recognized, much less celebrated, their relationship was likely not an open one.

[10]   **Douglas wrote** in the Double K guest book at the conclusion of his first visit: "Here's to the Double K—wonderfully hospitable and not too damn respectable."

[11]   Bruce A. Murphy, *Wild Bill The Legend and Life of William O. Douglas* (New York: Random House, 2003), 270.

[12]   William O. Douglas, "Justice Douglas Tells of Accident," *St. Louis Post-Dispatch*, November 25, 1949, p. 45.

[13]   *National Register of Historic Places Application: Goose Prairie Douglas Cabin*, (Olympia: United States Department of the Interior, 2018).

[14]   Murphy, *Wild Bill*, 504.

[15] William O. Douglas, *Of Men and Mountains* (New York: Harper and Brothers Publishers, 1950), p. xi.

[16] **Douglas' first book,** the best-seller *Of Men and Mountains,* contains a chapter devoted to Jack Nelson—along with Kitty. Upon its release, *Of Men and Mountains* received strong positive reviews. Many commented on the characters in the story including Jack Nelson. One reviewer singled him out this way: "*Douglas did not find full wisdom of the mountains by himself. There was Jack Nelson who lived in these same hills because he loved that noisy woodpecker who woke him up every morning, and all the conifers and the CCC camp where boys from Brooklyn and Chicago had their furtive instincts mellowed by the mountains.*" (Mountain Music 1950)

[17] Douglas, *Of Men and Mountains*, p. 18.

[18] Douglas contributed to an exhaustive **list of hundreds of wildflower species** for the Bumping River Valley that Jack Nelson along with Isabelle Lynn, Catherine and Cecil Clark, Anna Van Tobel and Tom Nielson compiled over the course of many years.

[19] Naydene Nutley Maykut, interview by author, August 4, 2018.

[20] William O. Douglas, *Go East, Young Man* (New York: Random House, Inc., 1974), p. 239.

[21] The **Double K Driftpin** was the Ranch's signature drink and one that was often served to Douglas. It was a vodka and gin martini with vermouth and a particular brand of bitters. The cocktail was served ice cold and garnished with an olive stufffed with a caper. (Franklin, 2019)

[22] Murphy, *Wild Bill,* p. 272.

[23] Ibid., pp. xv-xvii.

[24] Ibid., pp. 460-61.

[25] "Marshall Overrules Douglas' Bomb Halt," *Spokesman Review*, August 5, 1973, p. 1.

[26] Douglas, *Of Men and Mountains*, p. 27.

[27] **Blankenship Meadows** is a wide open expanse that seems to float on the edge of the mountain near the head of Nelson Ridge. It lies on the eastern edge of a subalpine plateau near Cowlitz Pass. The plateau—some twenty-five square miles—is a wet area, deep viridian all summer long that is dotted with nearly 250 lakes and ponds; so many that a map of the area looks more blue than green.

Tumac Peak, the first volcanic cinder cone to be identified in Washington State, rises 1,200 feet above the center of the plateau. The summit offers spectacular views of all of the major Cascade peaks from Oregon to Canada. Its name has an unusual derivation which the topographer Albert H. Sylvester describes: "Toward the summit of the Cascades in the

Carlton Pass area stands a fine example of a volcanic cinder cone rising some 1500 feet above the general level of the terrain. I asked a sheepherder its name. He said, "We call it the 'Two Macs Mountain.'" He then told of the two Scotch sheepherders, McDuff and McAdam, who used to race their bands to try to be first to get the pasturage on this mountain. I spelled two TU and added 'mac' for Tumac, which makes as fine a looking Indian name as I will ask you to find anywhere. My guess is that it takes humor as well as whimsy to name names." (Sylvester 1946)

[28] Douglas, *Of Men and Mountains*, p. 5.

[29] Jim Gosney, "Double K Combats "Progress," *Yakima Herald Republic*, September 18, 1987.

[30] In addition to pack trips and horseback rides, **the Double K** offered hiking, birdwatching, swimming in nearby Bumping Lake, and for some time, fishing there with the Ranch's two outboard boats. Evenings were taken up by slide shows featuring local flora and fauna, dancing, reading from the Ranch's library, or poker playing. Winters were quieter with cross country skiing, snow shoeing, and tobogganing advertised. Summer rates in 1947 were $85 dollars per week, including all meals. By 1963, that weekly rate had tripled to $285 dollars per week.

[31] Tom R. Hulst, *In the Footsteps of William O. Douglas: A Legacy of Place* (New York: iUniverse, Inc., 2004).

[32] **Kay and Isabelle had a staff of only two** to help them run the entire operation. Each summer they hired a "house girl" and a wrangler. The house girl was responsible for all cleaning, bedding changes, assisting Isabelle in the kitchen, serving the plated dishes at breakfast and dinner, and picking up the mail. She also made ice cream and squeezed oranges for fresh juice every morning). The wrangler was responsible for the care and feeding of all of the horses, leading daily rides and overnight pack trips, and maintaining the barn and fences. He had to chop and stack all of the firewood and lay four fires in the Ranch house daily (each with a different type of wood). The wrangler also conducted evening slideshows which introduced guests to the sights they would be seeing and to the flora and fauna of the area. He—or she—was also expected to entertain the guests—but not too much.

[33] Tim Franklin, interview by author, August 13, 2019.

[34] **Wranglers** were an important part of the Double K's educational mission. They were expected to share information about the natural history of the area to all guests on rides and outings. The first wrangler hired was Joe Blackburn, who disappeared before he even worked for the Ranch. A few others who followed were Eileen Ryan (one of the few female wranglers), Steve Chaffee, Kenny Clark, Marc Matson, John Ashbaugh, Arden Blackledge, Tim Franklin, and Michael McLean.

[35] Kathleen Tresham Anderson, *Birds, Bats, and Bailing Wire*, (self-published, 2009), p. 34.
Though Kay and Isabelle were **circumspect with the press** and much of the outside world, (sometimes passing themselves off as "spinsters"), with close friends they did not

hide their lesbian relationship. Author W.D. Frank posits that William O. Douglas' close friendship with the two women influenced a number of his judicial decisions that continue to affect legislation to this day.

[36] Ibid.

[37] A look at a **map of the Naches Ranger District** shows how heavily the District was—and continues to be—cut. Logging access roads crisscross the entire District stopping only on the western side at the very edges of the Norse Peak, William O. Douglas, and Goat Rocks Wilderness boundary lines. Logging roads snake up the valleys and across ridges to the north boundary with the Cle Elum Ranger District at Manastash Ridge and to the south at the edge of the Yakama Indian Nation. The roads peter out to the east onto private lands near the town of Naches. In this part of the Cascades, only the larger Cle Elum Ranger District has more miles of logging roads.

Historically, heavy cutting on local national forest lands supported primarily box companies (growing agricultural output required vast numbers of wooden fruit boxes for shipping) and railroad companies.

Chipmunk Creek is between Fifes Creek and Goat Creek on the Bumping River Road just north of age-old favorite Soda Springs Campground. The timber sale area is a notable void around which wraps the otherwise contiguous William O. Douglas Wilderness.

[38] Isabelle Lynn, "Year 'Round in the Mountains," *The Mountaineer Annual*, 1961, https://www.mountaineers.org/about/history/the-mountaineer-annuals/indexes-annuals-maos/the-mountaineer-1961.

[39] Part of the **Cougar Lakes area** had been considered for inclusion at the time of the founding of Mount Rainier National Park. In the 1940s the Forest service established the Cougar Lakes Limited Area which encompassed much of the land now in the William O. Douglas and Norse Peak Wildernesses. Limited Areas were a rare land-use designation used only in Oregon and Washington (Forest Region 6) and did not confer any specific protections on the land. Rather, they were areas recognized as exceptional and were set aside for future study to determine what level of protection they would merit. In the interim however, the Forest Service admitted that a limited area designation meant only that they "thought twice" about logging in them. (Lowry, "Report on Cougar Lakes")

[40] Kevin R. Marsh, *Drawing Lines in the Forest: Creating Wilderness Areas in the Pacific Northwest* (Seattle: University of Washington Press, 2007).

In the 1950s, the **timber harvest on Federal land** almost tripled going from about 3 billion board feet in 1950 to almost 9 billion board feet by the end of the decade. Much of that harvest occurred in the Pacific Northwest which was by then the major producer of softwood timber in the United States. (Williams, *The USDA Forest Service The First Century*)

In the **Naches Ranger District, timber harvest** was also heavy. Between 1960 and 1985 the two sections of the district (Tieton and Naches) harvested an average of 85 million board feet *per year*. Because of restrictions, shifting markets, and changing public sentiment that harvest now averages five to six million board feet a year out of the District. (Dale X. Phipps, interview, 2021)

[41] It is fortunate for wilderness protections that **Howard Zahniser** was a committed and persistent man. By the time the Wilderness Act was finally signed into law by President Lyndon Johnson, eight years had passed during which the author wrote sixty-six drafts of the bill and steered it through eighteen hearings. With the stroke of Johnson's pen, more than nine million acres of land in fifty-four areas was immediately preserved. (The Wilderness Act 2020)

[42] P. D. McCloskey, "Public Hearings on North Cascades," *The Wild Cascades*, October-November, 1963, pp. 3-6.

[43] Ralph Hodges of the Lumber Manufacturers Association nicely summed up the **federal land use policy**: *"The national parks were created by the government for play, preservation and aesthetic purposes. On the other hand, the national forests were created for the purpose of producing timber and water."* Brock Evans, a leading wilderness campaigner in the Northwest clarified that, *"The issues are not really wilderness purity and the legalism of the Wilderness Act or any of those things. The struggles always were over logging first."* (Marsh, *Drawing Lines in the Forest*)

[44] J. Michael McCloskey, "The Future of the Cougar Lakes Limited Area," *Wild Cascades*, October-November, 1964, p. 6.
Betty Lagergren, "The Cougar Lakes Wilderness Alliance," *Wild Cascades*, October-November 1972, p. 13.

[45] This large area to the north would become the separate **Norse Peak Wilderness** in 1984.

[46] Lynn, "Year 'Round in the Mountains."

[47] The chairman of the Study Team claimed he did not even know the **Cougar Lakes proposal** was included in their study despite evidence to the contrary. Nor did members of the study team visit the proposed wilderness area.

[48] "Cougar Lakes Should be Declassified," *Longview Daily News*, January 6, 1966.

[49] Adam M. Sowards, *The Environmental Justice: William O. Douglas and American Conservatism* (Corvallis, Oregon: Oregon State University Press, 2009).

[50] William O. Douglas, "Sierra Club v. Morton," *Findlaw,* https://caselaw.findlaw.com/us-supreme-court/405/727.html, retrieved September 10, 2021.

[51] Sowards, *The Environmental Justice*, p. 137.
Douglas would publish five environmental books between 1960 and 1967. T. H. Watkins points out that Douglas was "an environmental activist before Earth Day, before the word "ecology,"…before Environmental Studies became an academic discipline, [and] before any known president of the United States would be moved to describe himself deliberately and without shame as an environmentalist—and maybe even know what it meant." (Watkins 1990)

Douglas, unlike most of the other leading conservationists of the time could use his powerful public position to affect tremendous change on the growing national movement.

[52] Sowards, *The Environmental Justice.*

[53] The two stipulations, an impartial **review panel and public hearings**, were not legally required but were two changes that Douglas and others were pushing to be included in the new Wilderness Act.

[54] Though Lowry and others insisted that the **timber from the salvage sale** was nearly worthless since it had been on the ground or was infected with blister rust, Dale Phipps, who managed the sale for the Forest Service, is equally clear that the trees were a desirable mix of hard wood species in good condition that Boise Cascade paid top dollar for. (Phipps 2021)

[55] Carmelita Lowry, "Report on Cougar Lakes," *The Wild Cascades*, October 1961, pp. 6-7. Lynn, "Year 'Round in the Mountains."

[56] Lowry, "Report on Cougar Lakes."

[57] **Douglas' influence** was widely felt in Washington State in general, and the Naches Ranger District in particular. One local researcher recalls seeing a framed letter on the wall behind a ranger's desk in the old District office (in the Naches Valley). It read in part, *"If you cut one stick of timber in the Bumping River Valley, expect to be transferred to a forest with no trees."* The letter was on personal stationary signed William O. Douglas. (Uebelacker 2020)

[58] Forest Service engineers design the **logging roads** that private timber companies build on public lands in the National Forest to access timber. The logging companies are then credited for their costs to construct those roads against what they have bid and owe the agency for the purchased trees. The Forest Service incurs other costs having to do with logging activity including management of sales, replanting, and thinning operations. Historically, these combined costs often exceeded the amount the Service received for the timber.

[59] "Taxpayers Losing Money to Loggers on U.S. Land, Forest Service Admits," *Los Angeles Times*, November 22, 1997.

[60] William O. Douglas letter to Larry Barrett, September 7, 1961.
   Douglas sent a copy of this letter to Kay and Isabelle before mailing it to Barrett. His hand written note at the bottom asks Kay: "Is this too strong? Any suggestions? Love and kisses, Bill."

[61] Sowards, *The Environmental Justice.*

[62] Adam M. Sowards, "William O. Douglas' Wilderness Politics: Public Protest and Committees of Correspondence in the Pacific Northwest," *Western Historical Quarterly*, Spring 2006, pp. 21-42.

[63] William O. Douglas, "The Whims and Caprice of the Forest Service: Wallowas," *National Parks Magazine,* November 1960.

[64] **Carmelita Basin** near Bismark Peak is named after Carmelita "Lita" Lowry. The broad valley lies in the shadow of Mount Aix and was one of the highlights on the last trail ride that Lowry took in the area. Kay and Isabelle, Dagmar Hamilton and her two sons, William O. Douglas, and his wife Cathy were also on the weeklong pack trip. (Franklin, 2020)

Lowry, though "wraith-like" was a formidable and fierce fighter for the wilderness. Her background in science as a biochemist made her a quick study for environmental issues and she rapidly became an effective advocate for wilderness issues. She was involved in the fight for the Cougar Lakes Wilderness area from the very beginning, drawing the first map of the proposal and taking care of much of the earliest correspondence. (Lynn, "Carmelita Lowry")

Carmelita died of cancer in 1974 at just forty-nine years old.

[65] Sowards, *The Environmental Justice.*

[66] Carmelita Lowry, "Call to Action: Cougar Lakes in Congress," *Wild Cascades*, December 1970-January 1971, p. 2.

[67] Isabelle Lynn, "Review/Preview: The Cougar Lakes Wilderness," *Wild Cascades*, Spring 1977, pp. 27-28.

[68] Tim Franklin, interview by author, August 3, 2020.

[69] Ibid.

Michael McLean was the last wrangler hired by Kay who worked at the Ranch the summer of 1977. He too, met William O. Douglas as a young man and got to know him during his employment with the Forest Service working on trail and fire crews, and as a Forest Guard in the area. McLean describes the Justice in the same terms as Franklin. When they met for breakfast at the café in Goose Prairie, Douglas only wanted to talk about the mountains: the trail conditions, what birds McLean had seen, the weather. They swapped bear stories. Furthermore, Douglas shared with McLean the importance of "speaking up— no hollering up—for the preservation of natural resources," specifically for the forest that was gradually being logged and commercialized. (McLean, interview, 2021)

[70] Tim Franklin, interview by Susan Summit Cyr, August 13, 2019.

[71] This was not **Charles Reich**'s first visit to Goose Prairie. Through the 50s and 60s he stayed at the Double K Ranch at least four times starting in 1956. Reich wrote parts of his transformative book, *The Greening of America*, at the Ranch and while sitting in the middle of the grass fields of the Prairie itself. (Melissa Parsons, interview, July 2019)

Goose Prairie seemed to be conducive to writing, as Douglas wrote significant portions of his many books while summering there. The great mystery writer Rex Stout also spent time at Double K and reportedly wrote portions of his popular *Nero Wolfe* series while staying there.

[72] Murphy, *Wild Bill.*

[73] *Tributes to the Honorable William O. Douglas, Associate Justice of the Supreme Court to Commemorate the Occasion of His Retirement from the Supreme Court, November 12, 1975*, (Washington DC: US Government Printing Office, 1976), https://books.google.com/books?id=FwQIVwJLA6MC&printsec=frontcover&source=gbs_ViewAPI#v=onepage&q&f=false, retrieved September 10, 2021.

[74] Carmelita Lowry, Letter to Isabelle Lynn and Kay Kershaw, January 29, 1971.

[75] Craig Holstine, *An Historical Overview of the Wenatchee National Forest Washington* (United States Department of Agriculture, 1994).

[76] The **Wilderness Acts passed in 1984** were called by one wilderness advocate "release bills" since, while there had never been so much land protected in the Northwest at once, never before had Congress opened up so much land for resource extraction. Nationally, the Acts added 6.6 million acres into the wilderness system and at the same time it "released" 13.6 million acres for commercial logging. (Marsh, *Drawing Lines in the Forest*, p. 140)

[77] **Douglas did not live** to see the establishment of the Wilderness bearing his name. He died in 1980, still advocating for it until he was no longer able to speak. However, so much of his legacy lives on. His wish for public involvement in land use decisions was first articulated in the Wilderness Act of 1964 and then enshrined in adjustments to it. The National Environmental Protection Act (NEPA) focuses attention on environmental impacts of management decisions and the National Forest Management Act (NFMA) has led to a much more balanced multi-use approach of management of National Forest lands than in the past.

Douglas once confided to his wife Cathy he would like to be remembered simply "as one who helped make the earth a little greener." ("Douglas: A Big Legal Name," *Spokane Chronicle*, May 13, 1978, p. 9)

CHAPTER ELEVEN

[1] *Yakima River Basin Integrated Water Resource Management Plan: Final Programmatic Environmental Impact Statement*, 2012, United States Bureau of Reclamation: https://www.usbr.gov/pn/programs/yrbwep/reports/FPEIS/fpeis.pdf, retrieved September 10, 2021.

[2] **The Sierra Club** refused to compromise and continues to strongly oppose a new dam at Bumping Lake. They affirm that the project would destroy one of the finest examples of Eastern Washington old growth forests and the only one occurring in a level river valley. They also point out the irony of destroying endangered species habitat (bull trout spawning streams in the Bumping River Valley) to open up trout habitat elsewhere.

Friends of Bumping Lake is a grassroots group created to protect the environment of the Valley and continues to oppose a new dam both at the State and National levels through active participation in working groups, testimony, and education.

[3] **The Integrated Plan** does include money to improve efficiency including lining of some conveyance canals, but conservation measures for all users are voluntary. Until mandatory conservation is also in the plan, it is difficult to accept any justification to destroy the environment and build more dams if that additional water, which comes at such a high cost, will be wasted, too.

[4] "Water and Irrigation," City of Yakima, May 2012, https://www.yakimawa.gov/services/water-irrigation/files/2012/05/Irrigation-history.pdf, retrieved September 10, 2021.

[5] In general, the **cost of water** in our country reflects the price to transport it (and taxes) not the water itself, so the cost of water in the Great Lakes region for example, is quite low. Not so in the West where generally, the price of water is artificially low because of the federal government subsidy of the projects that continue to provide it. Since high price tends to discourage overuse and waste, cost is the biggest factor, along with the climate to the vast disparities in water use in the west and in Washington.

Water use in City of Yakima in 2017 was 233 gallons per day per person, *not* including irrigation water, one of the higher cities in the state. A particularly remarkable comparison is to Seattle/King County which was using 37 gallons per person per day at the same time. In 2019, the cost of water was $.71-4.71 per 100 cubic feet in Yakima verses $5.55-11.80 per 100 cubic feet in Seattle. (HDR Engineering Inc., City of Yakima 2017 Water Service Plan, Yakima County) (HDR Engineering Inc., *Yakima River Basin Study: Water Needs for Out-of-Stream Uses, Technical Memorandum,* (Olympia: United States Bureau of Reclamation, 2011).

[6] Samuel P. Hayes, *Conservation and the Gospel of Efficiency,* (Pittsburg: University of Pittsburg Press, 1959).pp. 22-23, https://digital.library.pitt.edu/islandora/object/pltt:31735002401192, retrieved September 10, 2021.

[7] T. E. Will, *Forestry and Irrigation and Conservation,* Vol XIII No, 1, January 1907, pp. 3-4.

[8] *Forestry and Irrigation and Conservation Vol. XIV, No. 2,* 1908, https://babel.hathitrust.org/cgi/pt?id=mdp.39015004583103&view=1up&seq=7&skin=2021, retrieved September 10, 2021.

[9] Chris Edwards and Peter J. Hill, "Cutting the Bureau of Reclaimation and Reforming Water Markets," February 1, 2012, *Downsizing the Federal Government,* https://www.downsizinggovernment.org/interior/cutting-bureau-reclamation, retrieved September 10, 2021.

[10] Ibid.

[11] Unfortunately, in spite of all of the **federal money spent** on all of the dams built in the United States, losses due to flooding are higher now than they ever have been, even in adjusted dollars. With a dam's destruction of flood-absorbing wetlands, siltation behind dams and elimination of flood plains, the promise of flood control benefits has not proved to be credible. (Hill C. E., Cutting the Bureau of Reclamation and Reforming Water Markets, 2012)

In the **Yakima River Basin** specifically, there have been thirteen major floods since 1862. Three of the four worst floods since recording began were *after* all the regions' dams were constructed. The four floods were in November 1909, December 1933, May 1948, and January 1974. (Reclamation, 1979)

[12] Only **four major rivers remain undammed** in the continental West: Yellowstone River, John Day River in Oregon, Salmon River in Idaho, and the Yampa River in Colorado. Many dammed rivers have multiple dams like the Snake River with four and the Columbia with fourteen major dams on the mainstem.

[13] "Bureau of Reclamation, United States," *Water Encyclopedia* 2019, http://www.waterencyclopedia.com/Bi-Ca/Bureau-of-Reclamation-U-S.html, retrieved September 10, 2021.

[14] Edwards and Hill, *Cutting the Bureau of Reclamation and Reforming the Water Markets.*
     At the time of **reorganization**, the Reclamation Service had spent $135 million dollars on its projects while repayments totaled less than $10 million.

[15] "Water in the West: Bureau of Reclamation Historic Dams and Water Projects," *National Park Service*, https://www.nps.gov/articles/2-water-in-the-west.htm, retrieved September 10, 2021.

[16] Edwards and Hill, *Cutting the Bureau of Reclamation and Reforming the Water Markets.*

[17] A retired official on the **Arizona's Central Arizona Project**, the same project that even the Bureau of Reclamation conceded was a "mad man's dream," admitted that he had to "fly all the way out to Denver and jerk around the benefit-cost numbers to make the [CAP] look sound." It was slipped into a larger bill and approved by Congress and completed in 1993 at a cost of nearly $5 billion. It came in at a net loss in resources by more than $1 billion. (Edwards and Hill, 2012)

[18] "Mission of the Bureau of Reclamation," *National Park Service*, January 13, 2017, https://www.nps.gov/articles/3-mission-of-the-bureau-of-reclamation.htm, retrieved September 10, 2021.

[19] Anna Leib, "Planet Earth: The Undamming of America," *Public Broadcasting Station*, August 12, 2015, https://www.pbs.org/wgbh/nova/article/dam-removals/, retrieved September 10, 2021.

[20] The **first recorded dam** was constructed in 1640 in what is now Scituate, Massachusetts. Historically, the first major structure to be built in a New World settlement was a church. After that, it was a dam. In the time before electricity, flowing water provided energy to power grist mills to grind corn, saw lumber, split shingles. Later, water wheels powered textile mills and ground wheat into flour for bread. Reservoir ponds provided block ice for food storage. The earliest white colonists could not eat or put a roof over their heads without a dam and a mill pond. (Lieb, 2015)

[21] Heather Hansman, "The Dam Problem in the West," *Nautilus,* April 4, 2019, http://nautil.us/issue/71/flow/the-dam-problem-in-the-west, retrieved September 10, 2021.

[22] Thousands of **dams** in this country have become obsolete, so-called "deadbeat dams," that are either so poorly maintained they no longer function or serve disconnected power sources (such as an old textile or lumber mill). Momentum has been building to remove these dams with over a thousand having been taken down as of 2011. The largest so far are the Elwha and Glines Canyon dams on the Olympic Peninsula where salmon and other fish runs have rebounded with astounding rapidity. Locally, the Condit Dam on the White Salmon River in southern Washington has seen a joyous rebirth of recreational activities and a similar return of salmon runs. The Nelson Dam on the Naches River just west of Yakima is one of the most recent to be slated for removal. At only eight feet high, this diversion dam nonetheless has been disrupting the passage of juvenile fish and sediments downstream for nearly one hundred years. The Yakama nation in conjunction with local, state, and federal agencies hope to have it removed by 2020.

[23] There have been nearly **continuous proposals to replace the dam at Bumping Lake** with a higher one since the original dam was installed over a hundred years ago. Interestingly, through the years, the justifications have varied, from safety and flood control, to better fish flows and wildlife habitat, to increased recreational opportunities and even pollution reduction. In reality, it has always been about more water storage. None of the players in the room really pretend otherwise anymore.

Countering an **enlargement proposal** in 1979, Isabelle Lynn pointed out that "They want to rip up a perfectly magnificent piece of country to build a dam that can't possibly do what it's purported to do. *You can't save the salmon by building more dams to make up for the dams you built earlier.*"

William O. Douglas was fighting the proposal too, though he was long retired and far from well. An aide to Senator Jackson allegedly quipped to Interior Department officials that "As long as Douglas is alive, this project will never be built." ("William O. Douglas Opposes New Dam," *The Californian,* March 1, 1979)

[24] Isabelle Lynn, "Bumping Boondoggle," *Wild Cascades,* 1967-1968.

[25] The latest plan for a **replacement dam in Bumping Valley** calls for a new barrier of 163 feet high (lower than the 223-foot-high dam proposed in 1979) that would impound 198,300 acre feet of water and flood approximately 1900 acres of land. (HDR Engineering I. , 2011) The proposal shows the same multiple problems that a new dam at Bumping Lake has always presented: 1. The substrate at the planned dam site is and always has been problematic. Bedrock is overlaid by nearly 250 feet of permeable glacial fill and there is lack of appropriate tie-in material on the right shoulder. A grout curtain has been proposed as an alternative to create a stable structure. Grout curtains are exorbitantly expensive to install and some dams with them have suffered catastrophic failures. 2. Almost all recreation at Bumping Lake will be eliminated. Under the current plan there is a single boat ramp, but the existing campgrounds and marina will be destroyed. They will be replaced by boat-in only campsites which will be inaccessible during all but the few months that the reservoir is full. All access to the high country via roads will be lost since there will be no vehicles permitted past the new dam. All current Forest Service trails around the lake will be destroyed. 3. The limited size of the watershed—sixty-eight square miles—is not large enough to fill a larger lake consistently. Current estimates show that it

will take from seven to seventeen years to fill a new larger reservoir at present precipitation levels. 4. The proposed dam does not include a fish ladder. Fish passage would involve trapping the returning fish below the dam and transporting them above the dam in tank trucks. This inefficient method of transit is costly and can be highly injurious to the fish.

Since the first thorough study in 1940, dozens of core drillings have been conducted at the proposed site at Bumping Crossing. The Bureau has continued to contract for core drillings over and over at this same spot and continue to obtain the same results. Not unsurprisingly, the underground geology has not changed. (HDR Engineering I. , 2011)

[26] Jonathan Yoder, et al, *Benefit Cost Analysis of the Yakima Basin Integrated Plan Projects*, (Pullman, Washington, State of Washington Water Research Center, 2014), 88, https://wrc.wsu. edu/documents/2014/12/ybip_bca_swwrc_dec2014.pdf/, retrieved September 10, 2021.

It should be noted that the **fish passage** proposed for a new dam at Bumping Lake would not be a fish ladder. Instead, returning fish would have to be trapped and transported by truck up and over the dam. This cumbersome and harmful method incurs significant ongoing expenses to operate.

[27] As an aside, the **State of Washington Water Research Center** did calculate the cost of the old growth forest at $1.85 billion which if added to the benefit-cost analysis (as it could and should be) would push the Bumping Lake Enlargement benefit down to an even more dismal range of two to five cents per dollar spent. (Yoder, 2014)

[28] Over the past decades and continuing to the present, the **Bureau of Reclamation** has spent uncounted millions of dollars on proposals, studies, site testing, and published reports (sometimes running into hundreds of pages) for a new dam and enlarged reservoir at Bumping Lake. Many studies replicate those undertaken before.

[29] **Water law in the west** guarantees a set amount of water to senior water rights holders which they must use or risk losing. Since they are "first in time, first in right" no one can order these users to switch from wasteful practices to more efficient water use methods such as drip irrigation and water metering which are used in dry climates around the world. Since rights holders cannot sell their water, the current system obviously sets up a huge disincentive to conserve. Irrigators holding junior water rights received theirs later in time and may lose a percentage of their allotment during water-short years.

[30] As far back as 1979, the **Bureau of Reclamation** concluded in its own **Environmental Impact Statement** for the Bumping Lake enlargement plan that water conservation alone could save 342,400 acre feet of water each year. 163,900 acre feet could be realized through increased irrigation efficiency of just sixty percent and 178,500 savings was possible through improved conveyance efficiencies (85-90% canal efficiency and no more than 5% operational waste or spill). (Bumping Lake Enlargement, Yakima Project: Environmental Impact Statement, 1979) More recently, the passage of the Dingell Act of March 2019 has set a goal to conserve 85,000 acre-feet of water in the Valley by 2029.

[31] HDR Engineering, Inc., *Yakima River Basin Study: Water Needs for Out-of-Stream Uses, Technical Memorandum*, (Olympia: United States Bureau of Reclamation, 2011), https://www. usbr.gov/pn/programs/yrbwep/reports/tm/2-1waterneeds.pdf, retrieved September 10, 2021.

[32] Total losses to **seepage and evaporation** in the Yakima irrigation districts average approximately 358,288 acre feet per year. In contrast, the new storage capacity at the proposed Bumping Lake is 190,000 acre feet. Total **conveyance** losses average 325,851 acre feet per year. Added together, the amount of water not utilized by crops is astounding. The rate of irrigation water wasted per year comes in at 38% of the diverted water. All figures are from are from the Bureau of Reclamation 2010 Yakima River Basin Study. (HDR Engineering Inc, *Yakima River Basin Study: Water Needs for Out-of-Stream Uses, Technical Memorandum*)

[33] "Freshwater: Supply Concerns Continue and Uncertainties Complicate Planning," United States Government Accountability Office, May 2014, https://www.gao.gov/assets/670/663343.pdf, retrieved September 10, 2021.
   Yoder, *Benefit Cost Analysis of the Yakima Basin Integrated Plan Projects*, pp. 37-44.

[34] Jim Gosney, "Double K Combats "Progress,"" *Yakima Herald Republic*, September 18, 1987.

CHAPTER TWELVE

[1] "Supersonic Flying Saucers Sighted by Idaho Pilot," *Chicago Sun*, June 26, 1947, p. 2.
   The **Kenneth Arnold sightings** have defied a good explanation for more than seventy years. While other incidents have been exposed as natural phenomena or hoaxes, Arnold's experience has been harder to discount. Even the Air Force report admitted that Arnold was rational, reasoned, and entirely credible. One more recent explanation has been that perhaps the man saw a series of lenticular clouds swept off of the summit of Mount Rainier, the most prolific producer of lens (or cap) clouds in the northwest. Photos of them bear a remarkable resemblance to flying objects from another worldly source. Due to all the ridicule and trouble that he received after making his report, Mr. Arnold stated that "If I ever saw (even) a ten-story building flying through the air, I wouldn't say a word about it." (Brown, 1947)

[2] "In 1946, He Rode Off Into Storm," *Des Moines Tribune*, December 20, 1965.

[3] Ibid.

[4] "150 Troops Will Search for Hunter," *Spokesman-Review*, November 19, 1965.

[5] L. Daily, "Still Missing," *Yakima Herald Republic*, October 20, 2002.

[6] "Missing Hunter Found Okay," *Spokesman Review*, October 19, 1985.

[7] "Lost Elk Hunters Rescued," *The Times News*, November 21, 1982.

[8] "Butte native's body found, death due to hypothermia," *The Montana Standard*, June 8, 1982.

9   "Bodies Recovered," *Spokesman-Review*, November 20, 1982.

10   Mort Cathro, "Spinsters Run Isolated Dude Ranch," *Oakland Tribune*, October 8, 1968.

11   Mike Hiler, interview by author, September 20, 2018.

12   Ibid.

13   Gretta Gossett, *Beyond the Bend* (Yakima, Washington: Ye Galleon Press, 1979).

14   Mike Hiler, "Hindoo John," *The Lookout*, 1997, p. 13.
   There are many **conflicting details of Hindoo John's story** in print. Some versions claim that a bear or an early snowstorm spooked the sheep. His death certificate is dated "about" August 10, 1896 and lists the cause of death as suffocation. The approximation of his date of death suggests that his body was discovered that year, not the following. Contemporary newspaper accounts relate that his death was investigated by Sheriff Lew Tucker and report that he was buried by sheep owner Sam Cameron who then notified the Yakima coroner. The two boys who supposedly found the bones of the man were Duncan McAllister and George Hinkle. Hindoo John's old gray mare was later found on the Nile Ridge trail wandering near the historic Clover Springs camp. (Gossett, *Beyond the Bend*)

15   "Skeleton of Pony Suggests Still Greater Tragedy," *The East Oregonian*, October 14, 1908.

16   Prospector **Jim Simmons** originally discovered the unusual spring and sent away a sample for analysis. The report indicated seventeen different salts in the water. He coined the little waterway "Skookum Limochene" which loosely means good lemonade in Chinook jargon. (Jack Nelson, *We Never Got Away*)

17   E. Guthman, "Prospector Hopeful Uranium Riches Beckon," *Seattle Times*, June 25, 1955.

18   Gossett, *Beyond the Bend*, p. 89.

CHAPTER THIRTEEN

1   **William O. Douglas** did not neglect to mention the water bird in his 1972 landmark dissent in Sierra Club v. Morton: "The river…is the living symbol of all the life it sustains or nourishes—fish, aquatic insects, **water ouzels**, otter, fisher, deer, elk, bear, and all other animals, including man, who are dependent on it or who enjoy it for its sight, its sound, or its life."

2   The **Columbia River watershed** equals 260,000 square miles, taking in parts of seven states and one province of Canada. Chinook salmon travel from their birth streams in North America thousands of miles to their feeding grounds in the Bering Sea off of Siberia, where they grow huge.

[3] The six **salmon species** were: Chinook or King, Sockeye or Red, Coho or Silver, Chum (or Dog), Pink (or Humpy), and Steelhead. In some literature, steelhead is listed as a trout (which is in the salmon family) and are almost identical to rainbow trout except that they migrate to the sea and unlike salmon, can return there after spawning in freshwater.

[4] Bureau of Reclamation, *Bumping Lake Enlargement, Yakima Project: Environmental Impact Statement* (Washington D.C.: United States, 1979).

[5] Farmer, "Bumpin Lake," *Northwest Magazine*, June 1886, p. 6.

[6] **Sockeye salmon** were also known as "Blue Backs" due to their indigo coloration while in the ocean. Breeding adults undergo a metamorphosis as they travel from the sea into fresh water and up to their spawning streams. Both sexes turn a deep scarlet color with olive green heads and a white lower jaw. Males develop a large hump on their backs and hooked upper and lower jaws which expose their prominent and rather frightening looking teeth.

Rather appropriately, one of the few remaining **wild sockeye runs** in the Pacific Northwest is to Redfish Lake, Idaho. Barely saved from complete extinction when just one wild fish returned to the lake in 1992, fisheries biologists have intervened and coaxed the run back from the brink. Several hundred sockeye now complete the 900-mile journey and 6,500 foot climb from the sea, navigating no less than eight major dams before they complete their life cycle.

[7] **Bumping Lake was heavily stocked with kokanee** over the years and most of the fish presumably are descendants of those plantings. The diminutive size of the present population results from there being too many fish for the food available in the lake. In an effort to reduce numbers, Washington State offers a "bonus" of sixteen kokanee per day to anglers willing to hook the tasty little fish.

[8] Bureau of Reclamation, *Bumping Lake Dam Environmental Impact Statement*, 1979.

[9] Theodore Winthrop, *The Canoe and The Saddle* (Portland, Oregon: Franklin-Ward Company, 1913).

Timothy Egan, *The Big Burn: Teddy Roosevelt and the Fire that Saved America* (Boston: Houghton-Mifflin, 2009).

[10] William A. Baillie-Grohman, *Fifteen Years' Sport and Life in the Hunting Grounds of Western America and British Columbia* (London: H. Cox, 1900).

[11] Timothy Egan, *The Good Rain* (New York: Knopf, 1990).

[12] Kit Oldham, "The first salmon cannery on the Columbia River opens at Eagle Cliff, Wahkiakum County, in 1866," *History Link website*, December 20, 2006, http://www.historylink.org/File/8036, retrieved September 10, 2021.

[13] Egan, *The Good Rain*, p.182.

[14] "Commercial Fishing," *Northwest Power and Conservation Council* website, 2019, https://www.nwcouncil.org/reports/columbia-river-history/commercialfishing, retrieved September 10, 2021.

[15] Finn J. D. John, "Fish wheels a legacy of when Columbia swarmed with salmon," *Offbeat Oregon* website, September 11, 2016, https://offbeatoregon.com/1609b.fish-wheels-and-gillnetters-408.html, retrieved September 10, 2021.

[16] "Dams: Impacts on Salmon and Steelhead," *Northwest Power and Conservation Council* website, 2019, https://www.nwcouncil.org/reports/columbia-river-history/damsimpacts, retrieved September 10, 2021.

[17] Ibid.

[18] "Hatcheries," *Northwest Power and Conservation Council* website, 2019, https://www.nwcouncil.org/reports/columbia-river-history/hatcheries, retrieved September 10, 2021.

[19] Ibid.

[20] In the **Yakima Integrated Plan**, there is consideration for construction of fish passage facilities on either the existing Bumping Lake Dam or its proposed replacement. Passage would be by "trap and haul" not a fish ladder. Returning salmon would swim into a holding pen below the dam and then be transported above the dam and released into the lake via a truck.

[21] "Yakima Basin Sockeye Reintroduction," *Yakama Nations Fisheries* website, 2019, http://yakamafish-nsn.gov/sites/default/files/projects/YNSockeye_CRITFC_Future_2011_poster.pdf, retrieved September 10, 2021.

[22] As a **keystone species**, anadromous (seagoing) salmon directly and indirectly benefit at last count, 137 other animals in both aquatic and terrestrial environments. Alive, they feed orcas, sealions, bears, humans. After their death, the fish carcasses feed otters, eagles, bears, coyotes, ravens. Scavengers drag their bodies into the forest where, as they decompose, they feed countless insects and microorganisms and contribute to the fertility of the soil. Carcasses that break down in the river contribute directly to the health and survival rates of hatchling salmon, other fish, and animals in the river. In this way, millions of tons of nutrients from the ocean are delivered to nutrient poor soil in the Pacific Northwest mountains. Like self-propelled bags of fertilizer, the cycle of returning salmon have been coined "a nutrient conveyer belt." It is no coincidence that the largest trees along the west coast grow huge alongside salmon-bearing streams. (Johnson, 2000)

[23] Jack Nelson, *We Never Got Away*, (Yakima, Washington: Franklin Press, 1965).
  Jack Nelson documented the occurrence of a **black oystercatcher** in Eastern Washington in the Murrelet Journal in 1947. Pat Ford had found a struggling bird on the Bumping Lake dam and delivered it to Jack. The disoriented shorebird was far from its regular habitat on the Pacific Ocean. Despite tender care, the bird died within a few days. Both Andrew Stepniewski in his book *Birds of Yakima County* and Dennis Paulson in his *Shorebirds of the*

Pacific Northwest note this extraordinary sighting for inland Washington State.

[24] "Yakima Lakes To Be Preserved," *Spokane Chronicle*, April 1, 1909.

[25] "To Visit Bird Reserves," *Spokesman-Review*, August 5, 1916.

[26] "Harding Kills Bird Sanctuary," *Spokane Chronicle*, July 21, 1921.

CHAPTER FOURTEEN

[1] "He Was His Friend," *Spokane Chronicle*, January 29, 1929.

[2] Ray Foisy, interview by author, July 2016.

[3] *Yakima Herald*, July 15, 1951.
Robert Ford, *The History of Goose Prairie and the Ira Ford Family*, self-published, 2003.

[4] Bob Hansen, "Yakima Reclamation Aid of 35 Years to Quit," *Seattle Post Intelligencer*, September 21, 1946, p. 8.

[5] When the **last dam tender** moved out in late sixties, the telephone wires were removed. All that remains of that vital connection are a few white insulators hanging by wires from the larger trees next to the road. The dam is now serviced by a tender who drives up from Naches several times a week to check conditions and adjust the gates.

[6] Betty Jean Ford Gallant, interview by author, August 2016.

[7] Peggy Post, "Ranch House Carved Out of Wilds by Two Girls," unknown newspaper, 1946.

[8] Dee Matson Petersen, interview by author, September 17, 2019.

[9] **Roth v United States** (1957) provided the basis for a test that the Supreme Court used to decide whether material was obscene or constitutionally protected. Douglas predicted at the time such efforts would backfire, and they did. The Court became increasingly fractured over the issue and got bogged over a backlog of pornographic material to review. The case Miller v California in 1973 effectively overturned the test and took the Supreme Court out of the business of determining the obscenity of given material. (Pacelle, no date)

[10] Melissa Parsons, interview by author, July, 2019.

[11] **Betty Jean Ford Gallant** died peacefully in Yakima on February 16, 2020. She was ninety-four years old.

[12] The **Andersons** sold the main buildings on two and a half acres to the Richardson family in 1995. The remaining acreage and horse barn was sold as several separate parcels. The Double K is now a private home and has been lovingly restored and maintained. The horse barn still stands silent in the trees, gathering dust. In the tack room, empty bridle holders bear the names of long-forgotten horses.

[13] Staff Report, Yakima County Planning Department, Yakima, July 23, 1982.

[14] At the time, the **zoning for Goose Prairie** was "Forest Watershed" which allowed one home per two acres along with specific protections of for water quality and watershed management.

[15] Kay Kershaw and Isabelle Lynn, Letter to Yakima County Commissioners, October 1, 1982.

[16] Joel Connelly, "Douglas' mountain home to be used for meeting center," *Seattle Post-Intelligencer*, August 11, 1989, p. A-1.

[17] C. Troianello, "Plans for Douglas cabin draw heated response," *Yakima Herald-Republic*, March 29, 1989, p. 6A.

[18] Ibid.

[19] Janet Gallant, interview by author, July 21, 2020.

[20] Brad Bond, interview by author, August 10, 2019.

[21] The **dam tender's cottage** and several storage sheds were moved in 1970 across the street to become another rental at the Bumping Lake Resort. When the resort was closed, Weldon McIntyre sold the cottage and a garage It is in Goose Prairie rebuilt as a vacation home.

The **single remaining building** on the Bureau's clearing is probably a relic from the CCC camp at Barton Creek. It was most likely constructed from two buildings in the summer of 1946 when the Bureau of Reclamation moved the last structures off of the old CCC site to the spillway clearing. (Taylor, 1946) The Bureau now uses it to store maintenance equipment for the lake and dam.

[22] Jack Nelson, *We Never Got Away*, (Yakima, Washington: Franklin Press, 1965).

[23] "Carry Relief by Ski," *Spokesman-Review*, January 11, 1930.

[24] Hansen, "Yakima Reclamation Aid of 35 Years to Quit."

[25] William O. Douglas, *Of Men and Mountains*, (New York: Harper and Brothers Publishers, 1950).

[26] Ibid.

[27] Jack Nelson, "Open letter of thanks," May 4, 1961.

[28] William Cyr, interview by author, September 21, 2019.

[29] Virginia Cyr, interview by author, March 27, 2005.

[30] **Forest Service Inspection reports** from this period are damning. Though some problems are kindly understated, the phrases, "safe wiring practices are virtually nonexistent," "sewer line does not reach septic tank," "pit toilet doesn't meet any kind of standards," and "references to specific code violations were kept to a minimum because of the number of them," paint a bleak picture. The district ranger at the time felt conflicted writing, "What really bothers us is that the resort is so run-down and worn out that short of replacing most of the buildings, it would be very difficult to bring this resort to a standard that the general public should be exposed to." The Snoqualmie Forest supervisor concluded in August of 1972 that the "…memo indicates this area to be beyond the point where upgrading to current standards is feasible."

[31] Large **budworm** outbreaks are not without precedent. A 1918 newspaper article describes a vast swarm of "butterflies" that descended into the Kittitas Valley in late September. The swarm was described as three to four *miles* wide and *fifteen* miles long. It was speculated that the adults were a product of caterpillars which had destroyed vegetation over a large area near Bumping Lake the previous summer. (Valley Visited by Vast Hordes of Butterflies, *Los Angeles Evening Express*, October 1, 1918)

[32] The **fungus** that infects the phloem (which transports sugars throughout a tree's trunk) turns it a distinctive blue color. This blue-streaked pine lumber has become popular lately as a decorative wood for everything from coffins to cell phone cases. (Oatman, 2015)

[33] Studies show that **mortality rates for trees** of all ages doubled in Northwest forests in the past seventeen years. Causes point to warmer temperatures which reduce snowpack, prolong drought, and increase susceptibility to insects and disease. (Hines, 2009)

[34] K. Wernex, "Mines in Cascades Date From 1880," *Yakima Sunday Herald,* September 16, 1962.

[35] Though her **death certificate** does not state it, Kitty's daughter Frances most likely died from the effects of alcoholism. She had suffered for years and was nearly incapacitated by the disease. Jean's son Stan Boyd said that late in life, Jack legally adopted Stan's parents, Ray and Jean as his children to avoid any problems with inheritance. He preferred that his modest estate be passed to his niece and her husband rather than his stepdaughter. Jack's funeral card lists Mr. and Mrs. Ray Boyd as his adopted children.

[36] Stan Boyd, interview by author, July 9, 2020.

BIBLIOGRAPHY

"A Very Brief History of the Bureau of Reclamation." United States Bureau of Reclamation. 1918. Accessed September 10, 2021, https://www.usbr.gov/history/borhist.html.

Abbott, Agatin. *The Geology of the Northwest Portion of the Mount Aix Quadrangle, Washington.* Ann Arbor: University Microfilms, 1953.

"About Us." *United States Bureau of Reclamation.* January 7, 2020, https://www.usbr.gov/main/about/.

"Agency Organization." *Forest History Society.* Accessed September 10, 2021, https://foresthistory.org/research-explore/us-forest-service-history/policy-and-law/agency-organization/.

Allen, E. John B. *From Skisport to Skiing: One hundred years of an American Sport, 1840-1940.* Amherst: University of Massachusetts Press, 1993.

"American Ridge Ski Bowl." Handout produced by the Naches Ranger District, Naches Washington, 2018.

"American River Guard Station." *United States Department of Agriculture Forest Service.* December 10, 2020, https://www.fs.usda.gov/recarea/okawen/recarea/?recid=58105.

Anderson, E.N. "Northwest Coastal Traditions: Indigenous Relationships with Plants and Animals." *Krazy Kioti.* March 10, 2019, http://www.krazykioti.com/articles/northwest-coast-traditional-indigenous-relationships-with-plants-and-animals/.

Anderson, Kathleen Tresham. *Birds, Bats and Baling Wire.* Self-published, 2009.

Annual Report of the Reclamation Service, Volume 10. Washington, DC: United States Government Printing Office, 1912.

Annual Report United States Reclamation Service, Issue 7. Washington, DC: United States Government Printing Office, 1908.

Aton, James M. *The River Knows Everything: Desolation Canyon and the Green.* Logan, Utah: Utah State University Press, 2009.

Baillie-Grohman, William A. *Fifteen Year's Sport and Life in the Hunting Grounds of Western America and British Columbia.* London: H. Cox, 1900.

Bartells, John H. "An analysis of reservoir storage contents for the proposed enlargement of Bumping Lake in Washington," 1981. Accessed July 8, 2018, https://pubs.er.usgs.gov/publication/ofr80440.

Becker, Paula. "Saint Joseph's Mission at Ahtanum Creek is founded in the Yakima Valley on April 3, 1852." *History Link*. February 23, 2003, www.historylink.org/File/5285.

Becker, Paula. "Yakima Indian War begins on October 5, 1855." *History Link*. February 26, 2006, https://www.historylink.org/File/5311.

Beckey, Fred. *A Range of Glaciers: The Exploration and Survey of the Northern Cascade Range.* Portland, Oregon: Oregon Historical Society Press, 2003.

Bentley, Judy. "Nine Thousand Years on the Yakama-Cowlitz Trail." *Washington State History*. Summer 2018, https://www.washingtonhistory.org/wp-content/uploads/2021/01/32-2-Summer-2018-CM_wCover_lo-rez.pdf.

Berger Knute. "Lessons for Goose Prairie." *Washington Law and Politics*. May 2, 2014, https://railingagainstsj.tistory.com/entry/Knute-Berger-Lessons-From-Goose-Prairie.

Boening, Rose M. "The History of Irrigation in the State of Washington: The State Epoch of Canal Building." *Jstor*. 1919, https://www.jstor.org/stable/23908750?seq=1#metadata_info_tab_contents.

"Boise Cascade Mill." *Washington State Department of Ecology*. Accessed September 10, 2021, https://apps.ecology.wa.gov/gsp/Sitepage.aspx?csid=12095.

Bond, Brad. Interview by author. Bumping Lake, Washington, August 10, 2019.

Bowlby, Hobert. "Weekend at Scout Cabin." *Cascade Annual*. 1939: 3.

Boyd, Stan. Phone interview by author. July 9, 2020.

Brown, Frank. "Air Force Memorandum for the Officer in Charge." *Project 1947*. Accessed September, 10, 2021, http://www.project1947.com/fig/kabrown.htm.

Buehler, J. Brad. *Engineering Geology of Washington, Volume I Bulletin 78.* Olympia, Washington: Department of Natural Resources, 1989.

Bulls, Diana. "The Fresno Scraper: A Mechanical Engineering Marvel." *Kings River Life Magazine*. August 14, 2010, http://kingsriverlife.com/08/14/the-fresno-scraper/.

Bumping Lake Enlargement, Yakima Project: Environmental Impact Statement. Washington DC: 1979.

"Bureau of Reclamation, United States." *Water Encyclopedia.* 2019. Accessed September 10, 2021, http://www.waterencyclopedia.com/Bi-Ca/Bureau-of-Reclamation-U-S.html.

Burge, Chic. "The Early Years of the Spokane Mountaineers: 1915-1935." *Out There Outdoors.* March 13, 2015, https://outthereoutdoors.com/the-early-years-of-the-spokane-mountaineers-1915-1935/.

Carroll, Cassandra. "They are like Children: Father Wilbur and Paternalism at Fort Simcoe: 1860-1890." *Central Washington University.* Summer 2020, https://digitalcommons.cwu.edu/cgi/viewcontent.cgi?article=2408&context=etd.

Casner, Nicholas. "Do It Now!" Yakima, Wash, and the Campaign Against Rural Typhoid." *American Journal of Public Health.* November 2001, https://www.ncbi.nlm.nih.gov/pmc/articles/PMC1446874/.

Cederholm, C. Jeff and David H. Johnson. *Pacific Salmon and Wildlife - Ecological Contexts, Relationships, and Implications for Management 2nd Edition.* Olympia, Washington: Washington Department of Fish and Wildlife and Department of Natural Resources, 2000.

Civilian Conservation Corps and the Forest Service. Washington DC: USDA Forest Service, 2016.

"Claude Ewing Rusk." *Wikipedia.* Accessed September 10, 2021, https://en.wikipedia.org/wiki/Claude_Ewing_Rusk.

"Commercial Fishing." *Northwest Power and Conservation Council.* 2019. Accessed September 10, 2021, https://www.nwcouncil.org/reports/columbia-river-history/commercialfishing.

Cooke, Nancy. Phone interview by author. July 20, 2013.

Cooper, Horace. Letter to Betty Jean Ford. July 6, 1943.

Cooper, Mary H. "National Forests: Should recreation take priority over logging?" *CQ Researcher.* October 16, 1998, https://library.cqpress.com/cqresearcher/document.php?id=cqresrre1998101600.

Coursen, Edgar G. "The Mount Adams Outing of the Cascadians." *Mazama: A Record of Mountaineering in the Pacific Northwest Volume 6 Issue 2,* 1921:46-47. Accessed September 10, 2021, https://archive.org/details/mazamarecordofmo06mazarich/page/n221/mode/2up

Croy, Robert. Phone interview by author. September 29, 2012.

Cyr, Virginia. Interview by author. Bumping Lake, March 27, 2005.

Cyr, William. Interview by author. Bumping Lake, September 21, 2019.

"Dams: Impacts on Salmon and Steelhead." *Northwest Power and Conservation Council.* 2019, https://www.nwcouncil.org/reports/columbia-river-history/damsimpacts.

Danielson, Robert. *The Road with the Grandest View: Surveys and Construction of the Chinook Pass Highway 1892-1934.* Calgary, Alberta: self-published, 2013.

Davis, Arthur Powell. *Reclamation Service 15th Annual Report.* Washington, DC: Government Printing Office, 1916.

Davis, Arthur Powell. *Irrigation Works Constructed by the United States Government.* New York: John Wiley and Sons Inc, 1917.

Dick, Timothy A. "U.S. Department of the Interior, Bureau of Reclamation: Yakima Project." *Bureau of Reclamation.* 1993, https://www.usbr.gov/projects/pdf.php?id=211.

Douglas, William O. *Of Men and Mountains.* New York: Harper and Brothers Publishers, 1950.

Douglas, William O. *Go East, Young Man.* New York: Random House, Inc., 1974.

Douglas, William O. Letter from W.O.D. to Larry Barrett, September 7, 1961. Double K Mountain Ranch Records, University of Washington: Special Collections, Accession # 2133-001, Box 1, Folder 42.

Douglas, William O. "Sierra Club v. Morton." *Findlaw.* Accessed September 10, 2021, https://caselaw.findlaw.com/us-supreme-court/405/727.html.

Douglas, William O. "The Whims and Caprice of the Forest Service: Wallowas." *National Parks Magazine.* November 1960.

Drennan, Margaret. *Agricultural History of Yakima Valley.* Washington State Department of Agriculture, no date.

Duff, Deanne. "Fire Lookouts: Their History in Washington." *Washington Trails Association,* September/October 2013: 18.

Edwards, Chris and Peter J. Hill. "Cutting the Bureau of Reclamation and Reforming the Water Markets." *Downsizing the Federal Government.* February 1, 2012, https://www.downsizinggovernment.org/interior/cutting-bureau-reclamation.

Egan, Timothy. *The Big Burn: Teddy Roosevelt and the Fire that Saved America.* Boston: Houghton-Mifflin, 2009.

Egan, Timothy. *The Good Rain.* New York: Knopf, 1990.

Ellis, John V. "Notes from Bumping Lake, Yakima County, Washington." *The Murrelet*, January 1927.

"Establishment and Modification of National Forest Boundaries and National Grasslands." *United States Department of Agriculture Forest Service*. 2012. Accessed September 10, 2021, https://www.fs.fed.us/land/staff/Documents/Establishment%20and%20Modifications%20of%20National%20Forest%20Boundaries%20and%20National%20Grasslands%201891%20to%202012.pdf.

Farmer. "Bumpin Lake." *Northwest Magazine*, June 1886.

Ferrari, Ronald L. "Bumping Lake 1990 Reservoir Survey." *United States Bureau of Reclamation*. January 1992, https://www.usbr.gov/tsc/techreferences/reservoir/Bumping%20Lake%20Reservoir%20Survey%201990.pdf.

Ferri, Rosalie M. "National Registry of Historic Places: Jack and Kitty's Nelson's Bumping Lake Resort." *National Park Service*. November 3, 2012, https://www.nps.gov/nr/feature/places/pdfs/13000211.pdf.

Ferri, Rosalie M. *National Register Eligibility Determination for Bumping Lake Summer Home Tract, Naches Ranger District, Wenatchee National Forest.* United States Department of Agriculture Forest Service: 2009.

"Fire Tower History." *United States Department of Agriculture Forest Service*. October 28, 2020, https://www.fs.usda.gov/detail/r1/recreation/?cid=fsp5_030804.

Foisy, Ray. Interview by author, Bumping Lake, July 2016.

Ford, Betty Jean from Jack Nelson. "A Brief History of Tom Fife." Essay, Goose Prairie, April 8, 1933.

Ford, Robert I. *The History of Goose Prairie and the Ira Ford Family.* Self published, 2003.

"Forest Service History." *United States History*. Accessed September 10, 2021, https://www.u-s-history.com/pages/h1602.html.

Forestry and Irrigation and Conservation Journal Vol XIV, No. 2 1908.

Franklin, Tim. Interviews by author. Bumping Lake, August 13, 2019 and August 3, 2020.

"Freshwater: Supply Concerns Continue and Uncertainties Complicate Planning." *United States Government Accountability Office*. May 2014, https://www.gao.gov/assets/670/663343.pdf.

Fuller, George W. *A History of the Pacific Northwest.* New York: Alfred A. Knopf, 1948.

Gallant, Betty Jean Ford. Interviews by author. Goose Prairie, Washington, August 2014, July 2015, and August 2016.

Gallant, Janet. Interview by author. Goose Prairie, Washington, July 21, 2020.

Galster, Richard W. *Engineering Geology in Washington: Volume I, Bulletin 78*. Olympia, Washington: The Division, 1989.

Garrison, Mary. "Fire Lookouts: From Hermit's Castles to Weekend Get-A-Ways." *Spokane Historical*. Accessed September 10, 2021, https://spokanehistorical.org/items/show/588.

Gay, Don and Clifford G. Rice. "Effects of Mountain Goat Harvest on Historic and Contemporary Populations." *Northwestern Naturalist Vol 91*, 2010.

"Goose Prairie Douglas Cabin." Application for the National Register of Historic Places: Washington State Department of Archaeology and Historic Preservation. Olympia, Washington: United States Department of the Interior, 2018.

Gossett, Greta. *Beyond the Bend: A History of the Nile Valley in Washington State*. Fairfield, Washington: Ye Galleon Press, 1979.

Guie, H. Dean. Letter to Jack Nelson, October 16, 1943.

Guie, H. Dean. *Tribal Days of the Yakimas*. Yakima, Washington: Republic Publishing Company, 1937.

Jensen, Clayne R. and Steven Guthrie. *Outdoor Recreation in America*. Champaign, Illinois: Human Kinetics, 2006.

Hansman, Heather. "The Dam Problem in the West." *Nautilus*. April 4, 2019, http://nautil.us/issue/71/flow/the-dam-problem-in-the-west.

Hassell, Bill. "Ski Trails for the Year." Excerpted from Cascadian Annual,1940: 8. *Alpenglow Ski History*. Accessed September 10, 2021, http://www.alpenglow.org/ski-history/notes/period/cascadian/cascadian-1940-49.html#cascadian-1940.

"Hatcheries." *Northwest Power and Conservation Council*. 2019, https://www.nwcouncil.org/reports/columbia-river-history/hatcheries.

Hayes, Samuel P. *Conservation and the Gospel of Efficiency*. Pittsburg: University of Pittsburg Press, 1959.

HDR Engineering Inc. *City of Yakima 2017 Water Service Plan*. Yakima, Washington: County of Yakima, 2017.

HDR Engineering Inc. *Yakima River Basin Study: Water Needs for Out-of-Stream Uses, Technical Memorandum.* Olympia, Washington: United States Bureau of Reclamation, 2011.

HDR Engineering Inc. *Yakima River Basin Study: Bumping Lake Enlargement Planning Design Summary Update.* Olympia, Washington: Bureau of Reclamation and State of Washington Department of Ecology, 2011.

Helland, Maurice. *Our Valley, Too.* Yakima, Washington: self-published, 1976.

Hiler, Mike. Interview by author. Bumping Lake, September 20, 2018.

Hiler, Mike. "Hindoo John." *The Lookout,* 1997:13.

Hiler, Mike and Carrie Covey. "Skiing American Ridge." *Signpost Magazine,* 1986.

Hill, Edwin G. *In the Shadow of the Mountain: The Spirit of the CCC.* Pullman, Washington: Washington State University Press, 1990.

Hill, Peter J. and Chris Edwards. "Cutting the Bureau of Reclamation and Reforming Water Markets." *Downsizing the Federal Government.* February 1, 2012, https://www.downsizinggovernment.org/interior/cutting-bureau-reclamation.

Hines, Sandra. "Tree death rate in Pacific Northwest doubled in seventeen years." *University of Washington News.* January 22, 2009, https://www.washington.edu/news/2009/01/22/tree-death-rate-in-pacific-northwest-doubled-in-17-years/.

"History and Culture: Mount Rainier National Park: Designing Mount Rainier: Rustic Architecture." *National Park Service.* Accessed September 10, 2021, https://www.nps.gov/mora/learn/historyculture/index.htm.

Hobbs, Samuel Warren. "Report on the Copper Mining Company property, Bumping Lake Mining District, Yakima County, Washington 1942." *United States Geological Survey.* July 8, 2018, https://pubs.usgs.gov/of/1943/0013/report.pdf.

Holstine, Craig (editor). *An Historical Overview of the Wenatchee National Forest Washington.* United States Department of Agriculture, 1994.

Hulst, Tom R. *In the Footsteps of William O. Douglas: A Legacy of Place.* New York: iUniverse, Inc, 2004.

Jenkins, Douglas. Unpublished article, Naches District Ranger Station, 1997.

Johansen, Dorothy O. and Charles M. Gates. *Empire of the Columbia: A History of the Pacific Northwest.* New York: Harper and Row, 1967.

John, Finn J.D. "Fish wheels a legacy of when Columbia swarmed with salmon." *Offbeat Oregon.* September 11, 2016, https://offbeatoregon.com/1609b.fish-wheels-and-gillnetters-408.html.

Kennedy, Clarence Hamilton. "Notes on the Odonata, or dragonflies, of Bumping Lake, Washington 1913." *Smithsonian Research Online.* July 8, 2018, https://repository.si.edu/handle/10088/14474.

Kershaw, Kay and Isabelle Lynn. Letter to Yakima County Commissioners. October 1, 1982.

Kilgannon, Anne. "Joel M. Pritchard: An Oral History." *Washington State Oral History Project.* 2000, https://apps.leg.wa.gov/oralhistory/pritchard/.

Lagergren, Betty. "The Cougar Lakes Wilderness Alliance." *Wild Cascades,* Oct-Nov 1972: 13.

LaLande, Jeff. "Forest Fires of 1910." *The Oregon Encyclopedia.* Accessed September 10, 2021, https://oregonencyclopedia.org/articles/forest_fires_of_1910/#.W1k74NJKg2x.

Leib, Anna. "Planet Earth: The Undamming of America." *Public Broadcasting Station: Nova.* August 12, 2015, https://www.pbs.org/wgbh/nova/article/dam-removals/.

"List of dams and reservoirs in the United States." *Wikipedia.* Accessed September 10, 2021. https://   https://en.wikipedia.org/wiki/List_of_dams_and_reservoirs_in_the_United_States.

Lloyd, Darryl. *Ever Wild: A Lifetime on Adams.* Portland, Oregon: Carpe Diem Books, 2018.

Lowry, Carmelita. "Call to Action: Cougar Lakes in Congress." *Wild Cascades,* December 1970-January 1971: 2.

Lowry, Carmelita. "Let's Not Take Conservation for Granted." *North Cascades Conservation Council News Vol III,* No 1, January 1959: 1-2.

Lowry, Carmelita. Letter to Isabelle Lynn and Kay Kershaw. St Louis, Missouri, January 29, 1971.

Lowry, Carmelita. "Report on Cougar Lakes." *The Wild Cascades.* October 1961: 6-7.

Lundin, Stephen J. and John W. "Early Skiing in the Washington Cascades, Part 1: 1913-1937." *History Link.* January 30, 2013, http://www.historylink.org/File/10312.

Lyman, William Denison. *History of the Yakima Valley, Washington, Vol. 1: Comprising Yakima, Kittitas and Benton Counties.* S. J. Clark Publishing Company, 1919.

Lyman, William Denison. *The History of the Yakima Valley: Volume II*. S.J. Clark Publishing Company, 1919.

Lynn, Isabelle. "Bumping Boondoggle." *Wild Cascades*. December-January 1967-1968.

Lynn, Isabelle. "Carmelita Lowry." *Wild Cascades*. June-July 1973: 28.

Lynn, Isabelle. "Review/Preview: The Cougar Lakes Wilderness." *Wild Cascades*. Spring 1977: 27-28.

Lynn, Isabelle. "Year 'Round in the Mountains." *The Mountaineer Annual 1962*. Accessed September 10, 2021, https://www.mountaineers.org/about/history/the-mountaineer-annuals/indexes-annuals-maos/the-mountaineer-1961.

Lynx, David and Yvonne Wilber. "Moxee Company, the (Yakima County)." *History Link*. November 30, 2009, http://www.historylink.org/File/9218.

Map: Bureau of Reclamation. June 1, 1935.

"Marathon of the Mountains." Excerpted from The Cascadian 1927: 6. *Alpenglow Ski History*. Accessed September 10, 2021, http://www.alpenglow.org/ski-history/notes/period/cascadian/cascadian-1980-89.html.

Marsh, Kevin R. *Drawing Lines in the Forest: Creating Wilderness Areas in the Pacific Northwest*. Seattle: University of Washington Press, 2007.

Matthews, W. Gale. "Columbia Basin Reclamation Project." *History Link*. October 28, 2006, https://www.historylink.org/File/7963.

Maykut, Naydene. Interview by author. Bumping Lake, August 4, 2018.

McCloskey, J. Michael. "The Future of the Cougar Lakes Limited Area." *The Wild Cascades*, October-November 1964: 6.

McCloskey, J. Michael and Patrick D. Goldsworthy. "Public Hearings on North Cascades." *The Wild Cascades*, October-November 1963: 3-6.

McClure, Richard H. and Cheryl A. Mack. "Vaccinium Processing in the Washington Cascades." *Journal of Ethnobiology Vol 22(1)*, Summer 2002: 35-60.

McCoy, Genevieve and Paul Dorpat. *Building Washington: A History of Washington State Public Works*. Seattle: Tartu Publishers, 1998.

McDonald, Lucile. "The First Crossing of Naches Pass from Seattle Times, November 1 and 8, 1953." *Naches Pass Trail*. Accessed September 10, 2021, https://www.nachestrail.org/media/pdf2/MCDONALD_1853_Roadbuilding.pdf.

McLean, Michael E. Phone interview by author. January 4, 2021.

Meany, Edmond S. *Origin of Washington Geographic Names.* Seattle: University of Washington Press, 1923.

Meyers, Donald W. "It Happened Here: Fort Simcoe established near White Swan." *Yakima Herald.* March 25, 2018, https://www.yakimaherald.com/news/local/it-happened-here-fort-simcoe-established-near-white-swan/article_8ed7a948-78af-11e7-8058-c70315431824.html.

Meyers, Donald W. "It Happened Here: Treaty of 1855 took land, created the Yakama Nation." *Yakima Herald.* June 4, 2017, https://www.yakimaherald.com/news/local/it-happened-here-treaty-of-1855-took-land-created-the-yakama-nation/article_99aed30c-49af-11e7-8f10-9f5f13ca79e6.html.

"Mission of the Bureau of Reclamation." *National Park Service.* January 13, 2017, https://www.nps.gov/articles/3-mission-of-the-bureau-of-reclamation.htm.

Moen, Wayne S. *Preliminary Report on Mineral Resources of the Cougar Lake Limited Area.* Olympia, Washington: Division of Mines and Geology Department of Conservation, 1962.

Molenaar, Dee. *The Challenge of Rainier: A Record of the Explorations and Ascents, Triumphs and Tragedies on One of North America's Greatest Mountains.* Seattle: The Mountaineers Books, 2011.

"Mount Baker-Snoqualmie National Forest." *United States Department of Agriculture Forest Service.* November 1, 2020, https://www.fs.usda.gov/detail/mbs/learning/history-culture/?cid=FSBDEV7_001647.

"Mount Rainier Wonderland: Administrative History." *National Park Service.* July 24, 2000, https://www.nps.gov/parkhistory/online_books/mora/adhi/chap5.htm.

Murphy, Bruce Allen. *Wild Bill: The Legend and Life of William O. Douglas.* New York: Random House, 2003.

Naches Ranger Station. Personal correspondence. August 2019.

Nelson, Jack. "A Brief History of Uncle Tom." Unpublished article, April 8, 1933.

Nelson, Jack H. Letter to John S. and Juanita Moore. Bumping Lake, March 14, 1942.

Nelson, Jack. Letter to Eileen Ryan. Yakima, January 28, c. 1963.

Nelson, Jack. Open letter of thanks. Bumping Lake, May 4, 1961.

Nelson, Jack. *We Never Got Away.* Yakima, Washington: Franklin Press, Inc, 1965.

Nisbet, Jack and Claire. "Hudson's Bay Company." *History Link.* July 24, 2011, http://historylink.org/File/9881.

"Nisqually Entrance Historic District." *Wikipedia.* August 4, 2019, https://en.wikipedia.org/wiki/Nisqually_Entrance_Historic_District.

Oatman, Maddie. "Bark Beetles Are Decimating Our Forests. That Might Actually Be a Good Thing." *Mother Jones.* May/June 2015, https://www.motherjones.com/environment/2015/03/bark-pine-beetles-climate-change-diana-six/.

Oldham, Kit. "First emigrant wagon train crosses Naches Pass through the Cascade Mountains in the fall of 1853." *History Link.* January 15, 2003, http://www.historylink.org/File/5053.

Oldham, Kit. "Northern Pacific reaches Yakima City, where it declines to build a station." *History Link.* February 18, 2003, https://historylink.org/File/5237.

Oldham, Kit. "The first salmon cannery on the Columbia River opens at Eagle Cliff, Wahkiakum County, in 1866." *History Link.* December 20, 2006, http://www.historylink.org/File/8036.

Oliver, Noah and Corrine Camuso. *Cultural Resource Evaluations of Howard Carlin Trailhead Park, City of Cle Elum.* Toppenish, Washington: Yakima Nations Cultural Resources Program, 2017. Accessed on September 10, 2021, https://cityofcleelum.com/wp-content/uploads/2018/09/Howard-Carlin-Project-Report-5.26.17.pdf

Olson D. "Klamath-Siskiyou." *World Wildlife Federation.* October 9, 2020, https://www.worldwildlife.org/ecoregions/na0516.

Ortman, David E. "Forestry and Irrigation History," personal letter. Seattle, August 2018.

Pacelle, Richard L. Jr. "Roth v United States 1957." *The First Amendment Encyclopedia.* Accessed September 10, 2021, https://mtsu.edu/first-amendment/article/414/roth-v-united-states.

Parsons, Melissa. Interview by author. Goose Prairie, July 2019.

Peattie, Roderick. *The Cascades, Mountains of the Pacific Northwest.* New York: Vanguard Press, 1949.

Peterson, Dee Matson. Interview by author. Goose Prairie, September 17, 2019.

Pfaff, Christine E. *Harvest of Plenty: A History of the Yakima Irrigation Project, Washington.* Denver, Colorado: United States Bureau of Reclamation, Technical Service Center, 2001.

Pfaff, Christine E. *The Bureau of Reclamation's Civilian Conservation Corps Legacy: 1933-1942*. Denver, Colorado: United States Department of the Interior, Bureau of Reclamation, 2010.

Phipps, Dale X. Phone interview by author. August 18, 2021.

Pinchot, Gifford. *Breaking New Ground*. New York: Harcourt Brace, 1947.

Plummer, Fred G. *Forest Conditions in the Cascade Range, Washington*. Washington DC: Washington Government Printing Office, 1902.

Pratt, Clar. "The Gold Hill Experience." Excerpted from Cascadian Annual, 1980-89. *Alpenglow Ski History*. Accessed September 10, 2021, http://www.alpenglow.org/ski-history/notes/period/cascadian/cascadian-1980-89.html#cascadian-1985-p8.

Pringle, Patrick T. *Roadside Geology of Mount Rainier National Park and Vicinity*. Olympia, Washington: Washington State Division of Geology and Earth Resources, 2008.

Purdy, C. Phillips. *Molybdenum Occurences of Washington*. Olympia, Washington: Olympic State Printing, 1954.

Rogers, Jedediah S. *Chief Joseph Dam*. Washington DC: United States Bureau of Reclamation, 2008.

Rowley, William D. *Reclamation: Managing Water in the West, Volume 1*. Denver, Colorado: United States Department of the Interior, 2006.

Rusk, Claude E. *Tales of a Western Mountaineer*. Seattle, Washington: The Mountaineers, 1978.

Skoog, Lowell. "Northwest Ski Club." *Alpenglow Ski Mountaineering History Project*. Accessed September 10, 2021, http://www.alpenglow.org/ski-history/subjects/N-info.html#nw-ski-club.

Smith, George Otis. *An Illustrated History of Klickitat, Yakima and Kittitas Counties*. Chicago: Interstate Publishing Company, 1904.

Sowards, Adam M. *The Environmental Justice: William O. Douglas and American Conservatism*. Corvallis, Oregon: Oregon State University Press, 2009.

Sowards, Adam M. "William O. Douglas' Wilderness Politics: Public Protest and Committees of Correspondence in the Pacific Northwest." *Western Historical Quarterly*. Spring 2006: 21-42.

Sowards, Adam M. "Should Nature Have Standing to Sue?" *High Country News*. January 19, 2015.

Sowards, Adam M. "Wildfire Suppression in Wilderness: A Decades old Conundrum." *High Country News.* August 29, 2018, https://www.hcn.org/articles/reckoning-with-history-wildfire-suppression-in-wilderness-a-decades-old-conundrum.

Splawn, A. J. *Ka-mi-akin Last Hero of the Yakimas.* Portland, Oregon: Kilham Stationary and Printing Co., 1917.

Spring, Ira. "It's Time to Prohibit Goat Hunting." *Seattle Times Magazine.* May 18, 1976.

Stanislawsky, H. *Proof of Claim of Labor and Improvements on the Washington Tungsten Mine Company.* Report by Yakima County, 1918.

Stewart, Christopher. "USDA Forest Service Burned Area Report Norse Peak Fire: Central Washington Fire Recovery." October 19, 2017, http://centralwashingtonfirerecovery.info/2017/wp-content/uploads/2017/11/Norse-Peak-Report.pdf.

Sylvester, Albert H. "Place Naming in the Pacific Northwest." from The Mountaineer Vol 39, No 1, *Alpental.* December 1946. Accessed September 10, 2021, http://alpental.com/m/1946.pdf.

"Tailed Frogs." *British Columbia Ministry of the Environment.* Accessed September 10 2021, http://www.env.gov.bc.ca/wld/frogwatch/publications/factsheets/frogs/tailed.htm#_1.

Tate, Cassandra. "Gold in the Pacific Northwest." *History Link.* December 6, 2004, https://www.historylink.org/File/7162.

Taylor, Paul. *Annual Inspection of Bumping Lake Dam.* Yakima, Washington: Bureau of Reclamation, 1946.

Taylor, Paul. *Inspections: Bumping Lake Dam.* Yakima, Washington: Bureau of Reclamation, 1921-1947.

Taylor, Paul. *Inspection of Bumping Lake Dam and Outlet Works.* Washington: Department of the Interior, November 23, 1945.

"The Wilderness Act." *The Wilderness Society.* July 25, 2020, https://www.wilderness.org/articles/article/wilderness-act.

Tributes to the Honorable William O. Douglas, Associate Justice of the Supreme Court to Commemorate the Occasion of His Retirement from the Supreme Court, November 12, 1975. Washington DC: United States Government Printing Office, 1976.

Uebelacker, Morris. *Land and Life in the Naches River Basin: A Cultural Resource Overview.*: United States Department of Agriculture Forest Service Region 6, 1980.

Uebelacker, Morris. Phone interviews. August 2, 2020 and December, 2020.

United States Census, Yakima County, 1910. Washington DC: Department of Commerce and Labor.

"Water and Irrigation." *City of Yakima.* May 2012. https://www.yakimawa.gov/services/water-irrigation/files/2012/05/Irrigation-history.pdf.

"Water in the West: Bureau of Reclamation Historic Dams and Water Projects." *National Park Service.* Accessed September 10, 2021, https://www.nps.gov/articles/2-water-in-the-west.htm.

Watkins, T.H. and Stephen L. Wasby (editor). *He Shall Not Pass This Way Again: The Legacy of William O. Douglas.* Pittsburg, Pennsylvania: University of Pittsburg Press, 1990.

Whitey, Stephanie. "Dorthea Lange in the Yakima Valley: Rural Poverty and Photography in the Depression." *The Great Depression in Washington State.* 2010. https://depts.washington.edu/depress/dorothea_lange_FSA_yakima.shtml.

Will, Thomas Elmer. Editorial in *Forestry and Conservation Vol XIII* No, 1. January 1907: 3-4.

Williams, Gerald W. *The USDA Forest Service: The First Century.* Washington, DC: USDA Forest Service Office of Communication, 2005.

Williams, J.H. *Notes in 1913 edition of Canoe and Saddle by Winthrop.* Tacoma, Washington: Franklin-Ward Press, 1913.

Wilma, David. "Yakima Tribesmen slay Indian Subagent." *History Link.* March 20, 2007, https://www.historylink.org/File/8118.

Wilma, Paula Becker and David. "United States Establishes Fort Simcoe at the foot of the Simcoe Mountains on August 8, 1856." *History Link.* February 24, 2005, https://www.historylink.org/File/5292.

Winthrop, Theodore. *The Canoe and The Saddle.* Portland, Oregon: Franklin-Ward Company, 1913.

"Yakima Basin Sockeye Reintroduction." *Yakama Nations Fisheries.* 2019, https://yakamafish-nsn.gov/restore/projects/yakima-basin-sockeye-reintroduction

Yakima County Planning Department Staff Report. Yakima, Washington, July 23, 1982.

"Yakima River Basin Integrated Water Resource Management Plan: Final Programmatic Environmental Impact Statement." *United States Bureau of Reclamation.* 2012, https://www.usbr.gov/pn/programs/yrbwep/reports/FPEIS/fpeis.pdf.

Yoder, Jonathan et. al. *Benefit-Cost Analysis of the Yakima Basin Integrated Plan Projects.* Pullman, Washington: State of Washington Water Research Center, Washington State University, 2014.

Yu, Eleanor. "Bulgarian Americans." *Countries and their Cultures.* October 21, 2020, https://www.everyculture.com/multi/Bu-Dr/Bulgarian-Americans.html.

Zimmer, Dick. "The Ski Tournament." Excerpted from Cascadian Annual, 1940: 4. *Alpenglow Ski History.* Accessed on September 10, 2021, http://www.alpenglow.org/ski-history/notes/period/cascadian/cascadian-1940-49.html#cascadian-1940.

ABOUT THE AUTHOR

Artist Susan Summit Cyr feels extremely fortunate to live half of the year with her husband Tom next to Bumping Lake in the historic Bumping Lake Resort lodge. An avid hiker, horsewoman, and bicyclist, she has traversed most of the trails and terrain of the magnificent William O. Douglas Wilderness. Drawing on her background in biology and training as an educator, she conducts field trips and presentations on both the living natural environment and the compelling human history of this unique pocket of Washington State. When not painting or writing, she is usually exploring somewhere in the mountains, looking closely and listening intently, trying to better understand the language of nature. *Tanum* is her first full length book.

INDEX

Printed in the USA
CPSIA information can be obtained
at www.ICGtesting.com
LVHW092035101024
793329LV00006B/126/J

9 780578 985305